Mirror On

1935

Cover photo: World land speed record racing driver Malcolm Campbell with his car 'Bluebird' at Brooklands in Surrey.

ISBN 978-1-9993652-4-0
© Newspaper Yearbook 2023
All Rights Reserved

INDEX

JAN		PAGE
1st	Death Of Cardinal Bourne	7
2nd	£100,000 Art Gems For Nation	8
10th	Humber Disaster: 12 Lost	9
18th	LL. G.'s Big Plan For Prosperity	10
19th	One-Hour Air Service To Paris	11
21st	Heroic Nurses Rescue 300	12
24th	Elephant In Ballroom Scene	13
28th	3-County Hunt For £22,000	14
30th	Kidnapped Boy Sensation	15
31st	Drama Of Ex-Wife's Cable	16

FEB		
2nd	Gracie Fields Will Get £100,000 By 2 Years' Work	17
5th	Petersen Title Hope Gone	18
6th	New Fokker 'Plane For Britain?	19
8th	Germany To Accept Air Pact	20
11th	Robber Gangs Swoop Again	21
13th	SOS From Biggest Airship	22
16th	Nine Dead In R.A.F. Disaster	23
18th	Airmen's Race With Death	24
21st	Police Net After £14,000 Jewel Haul	25
22nd	Mystery Motive Of Girls' Air Death	26

MAR		
2nd	The Prince's Own Jubilee Plan	27
7th	Duel Watched From Housetops	28
8th	Campbell's World Records	29
15th	All Germany In New Air Force	30
20th	Legless Body Found In Canal	31
22nd	Women Enlisted In Torso Hunt	32
26th	What Has Hitler Said?	33
27th	Lost Ships: Official Inquiry	34
29th	Litvinoff Toasts The King	35
30th	Abyssinia Breaks With Italy	36

INDEX - 2

APR

Date	Title	Page
1st	New Australia-England Record	37
4th	Air Raid Advice To Public	38
6th	Saw Himself Dying / Rich Woman Vanishes	39
10th	"Yard's" 4-In-A-Room Experts	40
15th	France's Warning To Europe	41
16th	The Little Man's Budget	42
18th	Germany Furious At Censure	43
25th	500-Seater Air-Liner Planned	44
27th	Ex-King's London Guard Riddle	45
30th	Sir Thomas Late For The Opera!	46

MAY

Date	Title	Page
4th	Amazing London Jubilee Scenes	47
6th	The King God Bless Him	48
10th	Britain's Two-Fold Air Drive	49
13th	Dockland Hails The King	50
17th	£120,000 For A London Hospital	51
21st	Bobsleigh's Derby Sensation	52
23rd	Air Force To Be Trebled	53
29th	Normandie's Record Bid To-Day	54
30th	Sea-And-Air Motoring Era	55
31st	Britain Looks To 1960	56

JUN

Date	Title	Page
4th	All Records For Normandie	57
5th	One, Two, Three For Aga Khan?	58
6th	The Queen At The Derby	59
11th	Where 44 R.A.F. Men Died	60
17th	Lightning Destroys Church	61
18th	15,000,000 Women Warned Of Threat To Rights	62
19th	Germany's New U-Boat Power	63
22nd	Armed Ulster Faces Crisis	64
24th	Britain Leading The World	65
26th	Twenty Storms Ring London	66

INDEX - 3

JUL		Page
1st	Thrilling Brooklands Rescue	67
2nd	Brothers' 27 Days In The Air	68
3rd	Night Attack On Three Girls	69
4th	"Evil Spirits" Peril Warning	70
6th	British Guns For Ireland	71
16th	1,000 Miles At 145 m.p.h.	72
18th	Every-Church-A-Cinema Plan	73
22nd	Greek Throne Drama In Hotel	74
25th	Britons In Secret Air Force	75
26th	Chorus Girl Replies To Bishops	76

AUG		
1st	200 People Flee From Flames	77
5th	Chose Death To Save Children	78
6th	Holiday Speed - And Slow Down	79
10th	Discovered Quiet - And Were Afraid	80
13th	Galli-Curci, 3,500 Miles Away, Sings For Us	81
14th	800 Perish In Dam Horror	82
21st	Leapt To Death While Wife Lay Dying	83
23rd	Skeleton Cabinet On Guard In London	84
24th	Mussolini Explains His Aims	85
28th	Cliff Race To Save Lovers	86

SEP		
2nd	Archbishop Justifies War	87
3rd	Italian Attack Launched?	88
4th	Abyssinian Midnight Sensation	89
11th	Armed Guard For An Inventor	90
14th	Smugglers In Car With The Royal Arms	91
16th	New 'Purge' In Germany - Drastic Jew Laws	92
18th	Threat To Stop Nation's Milk	93
21st	Royal Wedding Date	94
28th	112 m.p.h. Record By Streamline Train	95
30th	Two Women Prophesied Their Deaths	96

INDEX - 4

OCT   Page

Date	Title	Page
1st	8 Royal Bridesmaids Chosen	97
3rd	Abyssinia Fight	98
8th	Big 13 Vote For Sanctions	99
9th	A Boy For Marina	100
21st	2 British Ships Lost In Gale	101
22nd	'Divorce Rivals Air Peril'	102
23rd	Child Finds Drugs To Kill 2,000	103
24th	Italy's Peace Move	104
30th	Two Attacks On Women	105
31st	An Open-Air Royal Honeymoon	106

NOV

Date	Title	Page
1st	Frankenstein Test In Ravine Crime	107
4th	A King Hears His Fate	108
7th	The Duchess's Smile	109
14th	To-Day's Big Vote Riddle	110
15th	Socialists Are Held	111
16th	Govt.'s "Many Happy Returns"	112
18th	Floods Menace All Britain	113
19th	Sabre Charge On A Mob	114
22nd	Girls Who Incite Sex Talk	115
29th	Quads Born In Council House	116

DEC

Date	Title	Page
3rd	The King's Sister Dies At 3 a.m.	117
5th	Man-With-Past Saved By Girl	118
6th	Prisoners To Live Out!	119
7th	Britain Eats Dangerously	120
13th	Saved From Death By Prayer	121
16th	Downing-St. Mystery	122
17th	Film Star Dead In Car	123
21st	Britain's "If We Are Attacked…?"	124
24th	Prosperity Christmas!	125
30th	Nazis Starve Jews	126

THE DAILY MIRROR, Tuesday, January 1, 1935.

Broadcasting - Page 20

Daily Mirror

THE DAILY PICTURE NEWSPAPER WITH THE LARGEST NET SALE

THREE PEERS IN NEW YEAR HONOURS LIST
—Page 3

No. 9,701 Registered at the G.P.O. as a Newspaper. TUESDAY, JANUARY 1, 1935 One Penny

DEATH OF CARDINAL BOURNE

Life-Long Fight with Ill-Health

ENGLISH ROMAN CATHOLICS LOSE A GREAT LEADER

WE REGRET TO ANNOUNCE THAT CARDINAL BOURNE, ARCHBISHOP OF WESTMINSTER, DIED AT 12.25 THIS MORNING.

THE END CAME SUDDENLY, ONLY HIS NURSE BEING AT HIS BEDSIDE.

His death followed a recurrence of heart failure, with which he was stricken while on a visit to the Pope in 1932.

It was stated last night that the Cardinal's condition was critical, and the King and Queen caused inquiries to be made.

Cardinal Bourne will be mourned by non-Catholics, as well as Catholics. Apart from the great gifts he brought to his work, he was the most intensely English Cardinal since the Reformation.

He was a fervent patriot and a democrat.

Once he declared: "We can proudly say that England, even more perhaps than Rome, by its world-wide influence, makes for the general good of mankind."

His sympathy and love for the poor, whom he knew intimately as Bishop of Southwark, earned him the title, "The Poor Man's Archbishop."

His Rapid Rise

With these qualities went a tremendous organising ability which extended widespread the influence of his Church in this country.

The story of his rise is a remarkable one of conquest of early poverty and life-long delicate health.

He was born at Clapham in 1861, the son of a post office clerk and an Irish mother.

When eight years old his father died leaving the family practically penniless. A year before the boy Bourne had been sent to Ushaw, but his delicate health led to his transfer to St. Edmund's College, where in the course of five years he determined to enter the Church.

Beginning his training at St. Thomas's Seminary, Hammersmith, he continued it at St. Sulpice, Paris and afterwards at Louvain University.

He was ordained priest in 1884 and for five years assisted at Blackheath, Mortlake and West Grinstead. In 1889 he founded the Southwark Diocesan Seminary and became rector.

Thereafter his rise was rapid. Bishop of Southwark in 1897 at the age of thirty-five, Archbishop of Westminster at forty-two, Cardinal at fifty. When appointed Archbishop and head of the Roman Catholic Church in England, he was the youngest Bishop in the country.

"Black and Tan" Cardinal

In 1911, in solemn state at Rome, the Pope conferred the Cardinal's Red Hat on Archbishop Bourne. That hat has, according to custom, never been worn by him since. But it will rest on his coffin and above his sepulchre.

He was the fifth English Cardinal since the Reformation.

His lifelong work was the extension of his Church in England. In 1928 he raised a storm by suggesting that one day a future King of England would be a Roman Catholic.

During the Sinn Fein agitation he caused another sensation by denouncing Catholics who joined in secret agitation in the movement.

For this he was christened the "Black and Tan" Cardinal.

Cardinal Bourne will always be associated with the beautification of Westminster Cathedral, for which he collected thousands of pounds.

Cardinal Bourne.

1935—AND WE ARE WINNING THROUGH

THE Prime Minister, Mr. Ramsay MacDonald, in a message for 1935, says that despite manifold difficulties, we are winning through.

"The years we shall look back on have been historic, and during them the quality of our people has been tested severely. It has survived the tests alike of war and of economic disturbance and stress," says his message.

"Now I both hope and believe, despite the manifold difficulties which press upon us at home and abroad, that we are slowly but surely winning through.

"I would take this opportunity of appealing to the country to maintain its steadiness, its unity and its sturdy commonsense until the goal is reached.

"The year will be one of strenuous work by the Government in continuation of the efforts that it has made from the beginning to restore trade, find employment and create new opportunities for useful work for those who will not be absorbed by industry in its old form."

Kissing the ring of Cardinal Bourne at a garden-party which was held at Strawberry Hill, Middlesex.

Two Towns Rocked by Severe Earthquake

SHOCK CRACKS A CITY HALL

BIG earthquake shocks about 5,000 miles away were recorded last night on the seismograph of Mr. J. G. Shaw at West Bromwich and on that of a London store.

"The shocks must have been very severe," said Mr. Shaw. "They began at seven o'clock and lasted for two hours."

About the time when the first shock was registered on Mr. Shaw's instrument all the buildings in Anaheim (California) were rocked by an earthquake, says Reuter.

This was the third earthquake shock in California in two days.

Recorded in London

Three minutes earlier the earthquake alarm at the Carnegie Institute of the Washington Seismology Laboratory at Pasadena (California) sounded for two and a half minutes. At the same time slight tremors were felt in Los Angeles and Phoenix (Arizona).

At Brawley (California) a strong rolling earthquake shook the district known as Imperial Valley and cracked the City Hall.

At Messrs. Selfridge's Oxford-street store the first indications of a big earthquake were at 7.8 p.m. and the maximum was at 7.40. The tremors continued until 8.20.

35,000 Fewer Workless

There were 34,970 fewer workless in Britain on December 17 last compared with a month before. This was 138,261 fewer than a year ago.

THIS was revealed last night by the Ministry of Labour. Altogether 2,085,815 people are on the unemployed registers. Of these 1,717,005 are wholly out of work.

There was a further improvement in employment between November 26 and December 17 in coal mining, in the cotton and motor vehicle industries, and in the distributive trades.

THE DAILY MIRROR, Wednesday, January 2, 1935.

Daily Mirror

THE DAILY PICTURE NEWSPAPER WITH THE LARGEST NET SALE

Broadcasting - Page 20

LINDBERGH BABY TRIAL OPENS TO-DAY —Page 3

No. 9,702 Registered at the G.P.O. as a Newspaper.   WEDNESDAY, JANUARY 2, 1935   One Penny

£100,000 ART GEMS FOR NATION

"Aladdin's Cave" of Treasures Bought by Museums

ANONA WINN ILL

Miss Anona Winn, the well-known singer, has been lying ill at her London home for more than a week, and although her condition is improving, she was unable to take part in a "Songs From the Films" broadcast in the National wireless programme last night.

Her husband, Mr. Frederick Lamport, the theatrical agent, stated yesterday that her condition last week was so bad that she had to remain in bed throughout Christmas.

Anona Winn

"I hope that in a week or so she will be well again," he added.

'Gas Attack' in Streets

BRIGADES MOBILISED AFTER EXPLOSION

HALF choked by dense clouds of ammonia released following an explosion in a refrigerating plant, specially trained firemen who had been rushed from all parts of London fought desperately in relays last night to avert the spread of the fumes.

The explosion took place at the premises of Palmer's Cold Air Stores, Ltd., of Charterhouse-street, E.C.

Surrounding houses were shaken and people rushed from a nearby house in alarm.

Fumes drifted into the street and people 200yds. away were made to cry and sneeze. A police cordon kept spectators back.

Lucky Escape

William Desmond, the caretaker of the premises, who was taken to hospital, was the only person in the building at the time of the explosion. He had an extraordinary escape from death, being hurled through a heavy shutter door on to the pavement outside. He ran blindly for a few yards before being overcome by fumes.

Directly the first firemen arrived on the scene it was realised that the squads of firemen trained to deal with heavy smoke and fumes were needed.

The entire London strength of these men, who do no other work, was mobilised. They tumbled from their vans wearing gas masks. Two men journeyed from the East Greenwich Fire Station, a distance of seven miles.

Taken to Hospital

So difficult, however, was their task that a number of men lost consciousness.

About half a dozen of the worst cases were taken to St. Bartholomew's Hospital, where they were given restoratives. Some of the men returned and took their turn again at entering the building.

One of the men told the "Daily Mirror": "This is one of the worst jobs we have ever had to tackle. I have seldom known such dense fumes. Our task has been complicated by wreckage blocking the entrance to the lower basement, where the broken apparatus was."

The brigades stood by for two hours until the fumes had gone.

APPEAL TO PUBLIC

FOR £100,000 a world-famous collection of Chinese and Far Eastern works of art is to be bought for Britain.

The price is stated to be much below that which the collection would make if auctioned, and the public are to be invited to subscribe towards the cost.

Thirty years' work is represented in this wonderful collection, which belongs to Mr. George Eumorfopoulos, of Chelsea, who stated last night that "various circumstances" had forced him "with great grief" to part with his treasures, all of which were bought in London or Paris.

It was exactly a year ago that the Government asked for public money to purchase the Codex Sinaiticus for £100,000 from the Soviet Republic.

The Codex was primarily of importance to students of rare manuscripts. The Eumorfopoulos collection, however—a veritable Aladdin's cave of aesthetic treasures—will have a much more popular appeal.

The British Museum and the Victoria and Albert Museum are acquiring the collection jointly.

Back Thousands of Years

Sculptures, metal-work, jades, gold, silver, glass, ivories, lacquer, paintings and pottery and porcelain, many over thousands of years old, are all included; indeed, whole groups are represented, of which the national collections up till now have contained few specimens.

By the lowness of the price asked, Mr. Eumorfopoulos, it is stated, is in effect making a considerable gift to the nation.

Towards the initial payment contributions have been received from the National Art-Collections Fund. Sir Percival David and the Universities' China Committee, but to secure the remainder of the collection further payments will have to be made and it is towards these that members of the public are invited to contribute.

"What is the real value of the collection?" Mr. Eumorfopoulos was asked at his Chelsea home, a large house facing the river, last night.

"It would be several times the price at which it is being acquired," he said. "It would be difficult to put any value on some of the pieces."

Mr. Eumorfopoulos, who is a vice-president of the Greek firm of merchant bankers, Ralli Brothers, has made his home his museum. It is there that the collection has been housed.

Contributions may be sent to the director of either the British Museum or the Victoria and Albert Museum, or through the National Art-Collections Fund.

2,000 LETTERS FEARED DESTROYED

Fire in a Pillar Box

HOOLIGANS are believed to have set fire to a pillar box in Barking-road, Plaistow, E., last night, causing between 1,500 and 2,000 letters to be destroyed.

A policeman saw flames and smoke coming from the pillar-box, and when Post Office engineers arrived all they found was a smouldering mass of letters.

Anyone posting letters there should send duplicates, as they were all destroyed, a Post Office official told the Daily Mirror last night.

NEW "YARD" CHIEF

Colonel the Hon. Maurice Drummond.

Colonel the Hon. Maurice Drummond, C.M.G., D.S.O., Deputy Assistant Commissioner, has been appointed an Assistant Commissioner of Police of the metropolis. The appointment will take effect from January 7, 1935.

This announcement last night means that Colonel Drummond will succeed Sir Trevor Bigham, who has just retired after twenty-five years' police service. Colonel Drummond, who has been called aide-de-camp to Lord Trenchard, has had a meteoric career in the Metropolitan Police Force.

He was appointed to an entirely new post in the force in December, 1931, and took up his work as personal assistant to the Commissioner in the re-organisation department without definite rank as a police officer.

A year later he was made Chief Constable, and in July, 1933, became Deputy Assistant Commissioner.

* * *

For the first time in history two officers of the Royal Canadian Mounted Police are going to England to undergo a three months' special course with Scotland Yard, says a Reuter cable from Ottawa.

The officers selected are Assistant Commissioner T. Dann, of Manitoba, and Assistant Commissioner S. T. Wood, of Saskatchewan.

Miss Betty Williams, of Cardiff, and (left) Jack Petersen, the celebrated Cardiff boxer, whose engagement is announced. Miss Williams is eighteen years old.

PETERSEN'S ROMANCE

"Love at First Sight," Says Girl of 18

FROM OUR OWN CORRESPONDENT
CARDIFF, Tuesday.

JACK PETERSEN, the heavy-weight boxing champion of Great Britain, took on his biggest engagement to-day.

It was officially announced this afternoon that he had become engaged to Miss Betty Williams, daughter of Mr. and Mrs. T. B. Williams, of Ninian-road, Cardiff.

Miss Williams, the elder of two daughters, is a pretty girl of eighteen. She was born in Cardiff.

She told me she met Jack at a dance about eighteen months ago. "It was a case of love at first sight," she said.

Asked as to the date of the marriage, Miss Williams replied: "It will not be for some time yet."

Jack Petersen, who had just returned with Miss Williams from a New Year's Day shopping expedition, was as shy and secretive as ever.

He would not discuss his future plans, but said that when the wedding took place he hoped to have won a world's title. "We are both young yet," he added.

Pa Petersen, the boxer's father-manager-trainer, is delighted with the engagement.

"They are a very nice couple," he told me. "They became engaged on Christmas Day, but I cannot say if they will be married by next Christmas.

"Jack has several 'engagements' to fulfil before he is married."

THE DAILY MIRROR, Thursday, January 10, 1935.

Broadcasting - Page 20

Daily Mirror
THE DAILY PICTURE NEWSPAPER WITH THE LARGEST NET SALE

SHOT MAN'S DRAMATIC TALK TO FRIEND
— Page 3

No. 9,709 Registered at the G.P.O. as a Newspaper. THURSDAY, JANUARY 10, 1935 One Penny

HUMBER DISASTER: 12 LOST

Trawler Sinks Near Hull Harbour

MOTOR-BOATS RACE

IT is feared that twelve lives were lost when the steam trawler, Edgar Wallace, suddenly disappeared in the River Humber near Hull Harbour last night. Six other members of the crew are reported to have been rescued.

The disaster occurred at about eight o'clock, and, according to the Hessle police, the Edgar Wallace was in collision with a larger vessel.

As soon as the police heard of the accident, they telephoned to the Hull police, who sent fast motor-boats to the spot.

"Cries for help from the darkness over the water were the first intimation anybody had of the tragedy," said a Hessle resident to the "Daily Mirror" last night.

"The night was clear, but we could only see lights away in midstream.

"Soon after the shouting began we saw distress lights sent up from one of the ships. Then a ship's siren blared out a message for assistance.

"Terrible Moment"

"There was little we could do after informing the police but stand at the waterside and watch the ship's lights.

"After some time they disappeared. It was a terrible moment when they vanished."

According to Lloyd's, the Edgar Wallace is a steel-screw steam trawler of 336 tons. She was built in 1925 and is owned by the Newington Steam Trawling Co., Ltd., her port of registry being Hull.

Two survivors of the trawler were taken to Goole. One of them, Clarence Wilcox, was brought in on the steamer Goole. The other, whose name is Coleton, came on board the steamer William Cash.

John E. Sydes, the wanted thirty-year-old bank clerk.

FARMERS "LIVING IN TERROR"

Mr. H. Roseveare, chairman of the Kent and Sussex Tithepayers' Association, speaking yesterday said in the district of Ashford in Kent alone there were between 700 and 800 distraint orders out against farmers, who were keeping their doors locked and never speaking to strangers unless it was through a letter box or from an upstairs window.

"They are living in terror," he added.

Oxford Don Rides a Winner

WILL COMPETE IN GRAND NATIONAL

AN Oxford don rode his first successful mount at Worcester races yesterday, his horse beating the 1932 Grand National winner, Forbra.

"All being well, she is a certain starter for the Grand National, in which I shall ride her," he said afterwards. "She has twice proved her ability to jump the Aintree fences, and last November, I finished second on her in the Valentine Steeplechase at Liverpool."

Princess Mir's other experience of the Aintree fences was when she finished fifth to Noiseau in th Champion 'Chase last March.

New Search for Vanished Bank Clerk

ATTRACTIVE YOUNG WIDOWER

IT was revealed yesterday that a warrant has been issued for the arrest of a former clerk of Barclays Bank, Hoxton, N., who disappeared on June 1 last.

His name is John E. Sydes. He is described as thirty years old, tall and slim, about 5ft. 10in., with dark, wavy hair.

The warrant concerns an alleged theft of £950 from Barclays Bank.

Scotland Yard has been called in, and all the resources of the Yard are being employed to bring about the discovery of Sydes.

The wanted man is a widower, his wife having died two years ago, when Sydes' home was in Devonshire-way, West Wickham, Kent.

Following the death of his wife he lodged at an address in Woodford, Essex, where he took his two children.

When he disappeared in June his landlady, Mrs. Anderson, took the children to their grandparents' home in Broadstairs, where they have since been living.

Still in England?

When no trace of him could be found, it was at first thought that he might have gone abroad, but now the police think that he may still be in this country.

One of Sydes' relatives said last night:—

"John married very young. He was an attractive young man.

"After the funeral of Mrs. Sydes, her twin sister had charge of the children—the younger is now about ten years old.

"They stayed in Croydon for about a week, and then Sydes took them away to live in a house in Epping New-road, Woodford. Then he disappeared.

"None of John's relations has heard of or from him since his disappearance."

FOG AND SNOW ROAD PERILS

FOG caused many accidents and considerably delayed traffic over a large area of Britain yesterday.

Snow and frost added to the difficulties of transport and caused traffic to move at a walking pace even in places where there was little or no fog.

Flares were lighted at many important crossroads in Kent and Hertfordshire.

Some aeroplanes were unable to land at Croydon, the visibility being so poor, and shipping in the Thames was held up for hours.

Following the coldest night of the winter in London, yesterday was the coldest day for almost a year.

According to the experts, there is to be more fog in the south to-day, with frost early and late.

RADIO MAN MYSTERY

THE wireless operator of the London steamer Alnmoor, Mr. James Mahous, of York, was found dead on a lonely road near Portland, Oregon, yesterday (states Reuter).

The police are investigating the possibility that he was the victim of a "hit and run" driver; or that he was "slugged" and later thrown from a car.

The Alnmoor is owned by the Moor Line, Ltd.

BULL FIGHTING AT SEA was the novel experience of the crew of the German motorship, Cordillera, when two of the strongest of some bulls embarked in Spain broke loose during a gale. Above: Challenging all comers after a wave had smashed open his travelling box (in picture). Right: "What's all the fuss about anyway?" The bulls were en route for Venezuela.

9

Daily Mirror

THE DAILY PICTURE NEWSPAPER WITH THE LARGEST NET SALE

Broadcasting - Page 22

ZINOVIEFF SENTENCED —Page 3

No. 9,716 Registered at the G.P.O. as a Newspaper. FRIDAY, JANUARY 18, 1935. One Penny

LL. G.'s BIG PLAN FOR PROSPERITY
Huge Loan—Work, Not Dole

TWO BUDGETS EVERY YEAR— COUNCIL OF ACTION

Mr. Lloyd George emphasising a point in his New Deal during his speech at Bangor yesterday, his seventy-second birthday. He proposes reorganisation of the whole nation.

RECONSTRUCTION is the watchword of the big "New Deal" plan to bring back prosperity to Britain which Mr. Lloyd George, on his seventy-second birthday, put forward last night at Bangor.

"I confidently believe," said Mr. Lloyd George, "that if we act promptly on the lines I have sketched, then, by the spring of next year, the dark cloud of unemployment and consequent distress and despair will have disappeared from our skies." Chief among his proposals were:—

- **A Statutory Council to prepare schemes;**
- **A huge prosperity loan;**
- **Ruthless use of tariffs to fight obstacles to international trade;**
- **Two Budgets a year, one for ordinary expenditure and the other for capital expenditure;**
- **A Cabinet of five sitting continuously to deal with proposals.**

Land settlement figured largely in the plan, and big development schemes to provide work instead of doles. He visualised mobilising the resources of the State.

The functions of the Statutory Council he proposed would, he said, cover research into all fields of industrial activity and the putting forward of recommendations to enable any important branch of industry to reorganise itself.

Recommendations passed on to the Cabinet by the Council should be as definite plans of action.

The Cabinet of Five—on the principle of the old War Cabinet—would be free from departmental duties. It should consist of the ablest men available.

As security for loans to give Britain a safe road system he would use the revenue of the Road Fund.

Millions of money were lying idle. He believed a great Prosperity Loan would be oversubscribed.

A report of Mr. Lloyd George's speech is on page 4.

"W. M." writes on the proposals on page 11.

5,000 CHEER "WIZARD"

FIVE thousand people cheered madly when Mr. Lloyd George stepped on to the platform to launch his campaign.

He showed that he was still the "Wizard of Wales" as, with dramatic gestures and in a voice that was soft or ringing in tone, he sought to woo a Welsh audience who seemed to worship every word he uttered.

He was seventy-two yesterday—and the plan for prosperity seemed merely to serve as a background to a gigantic birthday party.

TERRORISED GIRL FOUND UNCONSCIOUS IN LANE

Schoolboy Brother Helps in Search

FROM OUR OWN CORRESPONDENT

TIVERTON (Devon), Thursday.

AFTER woods and roads had been scoured in vain, a girl who has received anonymous threatening letters and has been under police protection, was found just before midnight, unconscious, in a lane off the Uffculme, near Tiverton, main road.

She was not injured, but her condition from exposure was so serious that she was unable to throw any light on the mystery.

The girl, Miss Nancy Mildred Collier, twenty-one, a pretty brunette, the daughter of Mrs. F. Collier, a former actress, of Uffculme, left her employment at a Tiverton hairdresser's and returned to Tiverton Junction by the 8.30 train last night, and collected her bicycle at the Railway Hotel.

Menacing Notes

When she did not reach home a search, in which Miss Collier's brother, Jim, a pupil at Blundell's School, joined, was started.

Police-Constable Bedford, of Uffculme, found a bicycle against a hedge just off the main road. Further up the lane he found Miss Collier lying on her face, cold and unconscious. Miss Collier was rushed to her home by car, and two doctors were summoned.

The girl recovered slightly and called out: "Don't leave me," before lapsing into unconsciousness again.

Miss Collier began to receive threatening letters in August.

"I am going to do you in" was one of the passages in the letters, and when this was followed by other menacing notes she went to the police. Then came a message. It terrified her, for it read: "I see you have been to the police. I shall wear gloves, so there will be no finger prints."

Sea-Front Plunged Into Darkness

Part of the electric light supply at Dover failed last night and several streets and the seafront were in darkness for about six hours.

Hospitals and lighthouses were not affected, and trams continued running. Most of the shops had closed.

Rugby Star's Rescue Dive

SAVES THE LIFE OF DROWNING BOY

R. A. GERRARD, the Somerset and Bath Rugby captain, who is twenty-three to-day, rescued a boy from drowning yesterday at Bath Easton, near Bath.

Gerrard, who has been capped ten times for England, is on the staff of the Bath City Engineer and was surveying at the time.

"After setting up my surveying instruments," he told the *Daily Mirror*, "I walked along the river bank away from them to get an idea of the general layout.

"I heard my man say to two boys, 'Don't touch that instrument.' I turned my head, and noticed that one of the lads had got out on to a plank which jutted over the river and was washing his Wellington boots. Then he lost his balance and fell into the stream.

"The boy's companion shouted, 'Quick, he cannot swim.' I ran to the bank, threw off my coat and took a header. The boy was in deep water, and although I am a strong swimmer, I had a job, but I got him to the bank."

Gerrard went home for a bath and an hour later, was back in his office.

R. A. Gerrard.

Lady Caillard, formerly Mrs. Oakley Maund. She married the late Sir Vincent Caillard in 1927.

LADY CAILLARD'S WISH FULFILLED.—The cross on the gable of The Belfry, West Halkin-street, S.W., a former Presbyterian chapel and the home of Lady Caillard, the spiritualist, illuminated last night in accordance with her wish. Lady Caillard died on Wednesday night after foretelling her death in a book five months ago.

THE DAILY MIRROR, Saturday, January 19, 1935.

Daily Mirror

Broadcasting - Page 22

THE DAILY PICTURE NEWSPAPER WITH THE LARGEST NET SALE

BOY OF 17 HEAD OF TRAGIC HOME —Page 2

No. 9,717. Registered at the G.P.O. as a Newspaper. SATURDAY, JANUARY 19, 1935 One Penny

ONE-HOUR AIR SERVICE TO PARIS

British Plan to Use Fleet of 'Flying Hotels'

ROBOT PILOT

"DAILY MIRROR" SPECIAL NEWS

TO demonstrate the possibilities of a "Flying Hotel" Douglas air liner on an ultra-rapid passenger service between Gatwick and Le Bourget, Mr. Anthony Fokker, the Dutch aircraft designer, will land at Gravesend to-day in a machine of the same type as that which was second in the London-Melbourne air race.

He will demonstrate the machine to representatives of an English company which is contemplating using four Douglas 'planes if they reach a decision to establish the Gatwick-Le Bourget service.

If they do so decide, the service would be known as London-Continental Air Lines, and would commence operations in June with machines flying at hourly intervals.

Parmentier as Pilot

In a telephone talk with the *Daily Mirror* last night from Amsterdam, Mr. Fokker said that the Douglas air liner in which he would fly to England will be piloted by Parmentier, who flew in the Australia air race.

"The same mechanic, Prince, will also be with us," he added, "and there will be a number of guests who will bring the party up to about eight."

"I cannot say how long we shall stay in Gravesend, but while we are there we shall give a full demonstration of the performance of the air liner and also of an automatic pilot with which it is fitted.

"This is a feature which was not incorporated in the machine which flew to Australia. It is used on similar liners in America, but I believe it has not been shown in England before."

London-Continental Air Lines would seek to reduce the flying time between Gatwick and Le Bourget, the Paris airport, to one hour, the *Daily Mirror* was informed last night.

NOW HOW DID THAT HAPPEN?—S. Ingham looks round inquiringly at his mount, Moyanna, after their fall at the last jump in the Cardinal's Hurdle at Hurst Park yesterday. Ingham had a lucky escape from serious injury, being pinned beneath his horse which police and spectators had to drag away, but he stepped out of the ambulance calmly smoking a cigarette.

1,000 Men Mobilised for a Dockland Blaze

EXPLOSION PERIL—ROADS FLOODED

MORE than 500 firemen, 500 policemen, every available motor-pump of the London Brigade and three fire-floats were rushed last night to a blaze that raged through a Poplar oil warehouse, threatening to involve 2,000 tons of highly inflammable material and a petrol refinery.

A large section of London's dockland was isolated by police cordons and a number of families were ordered to leave their homes.

The powerful guns of the fire-floats, throwing out a jet of a thousand gallons a minute, and eight 60ft. water towers were brought into action. Firemen, working in relays because of the intense heat, mounted a wall to direct twenty-five hoses. Others climbed to a six-inch parapet twenty feet above the river.

Soon streets were flooded. Men had to work in two feet of water.

Tramcars, running a shuttle service, did a great trade in carrying sightseers attracted by the 50ft. flames and the "gun-fire" of exploding oil drums.

Rats Escape

When the fire was at its height hundreds of rats, squealing with fright, ran from the warehouse occupied by Messrs. Chetwin and Newark, grease and oil manufacturers, Ferguson's Wharf.

After about an hour and a half's work the blaze was got under control. Between 400 and 500 tons of grease and oil, the *Daily Mirror* was informed, were destroyed.

At one time the London Fire Brigade was in a serious position as other alarms would have compelled the withdrawal of machines.

In returning to her home after the fire Mrs. Marshall, aged sixty-seven, of Devonshire-terrace, Poplar, slipped on the flooded pavements and was carried into her house unconscious.

GOVERNMENT WILL CONSIDER Ll. G. PLAN

MR. Neville Chamberlain, Chancellor of the Exchequer, referred in a speech at Belfast yesterday to Mr. Lloyd George's "New Deal" campaign. Mr. Chamberlain said:

"The proposals, which at first sight seem rather disappointing and rather lacking in precision, will nevertheless be examined, when they are completed, with an open mind by his Majesty's Government."

Mr. Winston Churchill's comment last night was: "Mr. Lloyd George's proposals deserve the closest attention. They are at once virile and sober."

Fairy Queen Catches a Cold

Faith Bennett.

Drury Lane Fairy's ibana jailed her yesterday.

The Bow-street magistrate (what a villain!) fined her 20s. for "obstructing" the street with . . No, not her fairy coach; just a motor-car!

The Fairy pleaded: "I asked an attendant to move the car; I could not possibly get out myself —I was all dressed up in a gauzy fairy queen costume and was waiting the cue to go on the stage.

"I have already been severely punished," Fairy Queen urged, "because I caught a cold by having to go out scantily dressed.

"Then I got a bad scolding from the wardrobe mistress for soiling the nice white hem of my frock."

The Magistrate (who simply can't believe in fairies): I am afraid I cannot take these matters into consideration."

[P.S.—The fairy queen's other name is Faith Bennett.]

Nancy Mildred Collier.

TERROR ORDEAL —THEN BREAKDOWN?

Did Nancy Mildred Collier—the 21-year-old Uffculme (Devon) girl found unconscious in a lonely lane on Wednesday—break down under a terrifying mental ordeal?

THAT was the possibility being discussed yesterday while police were awaiting a statement from Miss Collier to help them in solving the double mystery of her ordeal and the anonymous threatening letters she had been receiving for six months.

Throughout the day Miss Collier's widowed mother kept watch at the bedside, but her daughter never recovered sufficiently to make a statement.

People who used the road from Tiverton to Uffculme on Wednesday have been interviewed. At least three persons saw a man's bicycle resting against Miss Collier's machine at the end of the lane, but the owner has not been traced.

11

THE DAILY MIRROR, Monday, January 21, 1935.

Daily Mirror

Broadcasting - Page 20

THE DAILY PICTURE NEWSPAPER WITH THE LARGEST NET SALE

SHOULD DIVORCE BE EASIER? Page 10

No. 9,718 Registered at the G.P.O. as a Newspaper. MONDAY, JANUARY 21, 1935 One Penny

HEROIC NURSES RESCUE 300
Peril of Panic Quelled by Calm Work in Fire

HOSPITAL ABLAZE

Three hundred patients—most of them aged and many bedridden—moved to safety within half an hour from wards threatened by fire... Plucky nurses carrying out the rescue work so calmly that any hint of panic was checked.

WHILE flames leaping from the roof of the City of London Institution for Chronic Cases, Bow, could be seen a mile away, and firemen were fighting to subdue them, this drama was taking place last night in the wards, men and women nurses working among their patients with remarkable courage.

The fire broke out in the roof of the west wing and the alarm was given by Nurse Seeby, who was on duty on "F" floor. She told the patients to keep calm and to try to dress themselves while she went for help. There were 130 women in the ward and another 170 patients on lower floors.

Double Staff on Duty

The whole staff—fortunately the duties were just being changed and day and night nurses were in the building—was ordered to the wing, and many patients who were unable to walk were carried down on stretchers.

Within a few minutes the unaffected wards looked like a field station during the war, as patients with blankets covering their nightdresses and nightshirts lay on the floor between the beds.

Some of the beds were taken into the hospital chapel.

Meanwhile an emergency call was circulated and twenty pumps, three water towers and a force of 150 firemen and men of the London Salvage Corps were ordered out.

Smoke masks were sent for and squads of men equipped with breathing apparatus forced their way into the building and prevented the lower floor becoming involved while thirty jets were played on to the fire.

Met by Sheet of Flame

In the wards the work of moving the patients went on without a hitch. One of the patients told the *Daily Mirror* of the nurses' bravery.

"I was just dozing off when I smelt burning on the floor above," he said. "I got out of bed and went to the door of our ward, and was met by a sheet of flame.

"The other patients had by this time started to get up, and it was wonderful how the nurses ran to us through the flames, and by their plucky behaviour avoided any panic."

Mr. E. T. Pinhey, the medical superintendent, said when he was called by a male nurse he went to the west wing, and found the staff performing rescue work with wonderful courage.

Mr. Pinhey was struck by a piece of burning wood, and his hair was singed.

A great crowd gathered in Bow-road to watch the blaze, and as there was a danger that they might hamper the firemen, who were working with over four miles of hose, a wireless message was sent to all patrolling police cars to proceed to the scene to help in controlling the people.

The fire was confined to the second and third floors of the south-west block.

More False Alarms

During the fire the brigade received seven false alarms—two from the Kensington district, and one each from Greenwich, Westminster, Islington, Kentish Town and Belsize Park.

They were also called last night to a house in Abbey-street, Bermondsey, where Eleanor Wilmott, nineteen, was badly cut about the legs in escaping, and to the Imperial Cinema Theatre, Edgware-road. This outbreak was quickly under control.

The glowing furnace inside the blazing building after part of the roof had fallen in. Firemen are seen playing a hose on the flames from an adjoining chimney stack.

Injured Doctor's Vain Bid to Save Woman in Air Crash

TRAGEDY ENDS A "JOY RIDE"

INJURED and dazed by a blow on the head, a young doctor made desperate, but vain, attempts to save the life of his woman passenger after the 'plane he had been piloting crashed in a field at Over Whitacre, ten miles from Birmingham, yesterday.

The woman passenger, Miss Dorothy Mills, aged twenty-eight, of Ascot Lodge, Ascot-road, Moseley, Birmingham, died in hospital last night—the third air crash death of the week-end.

After being lifted from the wrecked 'plane, the pilot, Dr. Talbot Dance, of Gravelly-hill, Erdington, made improvised splints for Miss Mills, using as bandages strips torn from his own clothing. When the ambulance arrived he collapsed.

After hospital treatment for a broken nose he was able to go home.

The machine belonged to the Midland Aero Club, Castle Bromwich, of which Dr. Dance is a member. Miss Mills, it is understood, was only enrolled as a day member.

"They were simply out for a short flight," a club representative said last night.

Picture on page three.

R.A.F. Deaths

Two R.A.F. men were killed during the week-end when their machine crashed in landing near Brackley (Northants) and "somersaulted," pinning them in the cabin.

They were:—

Sergeant Francis Hubert Land, the pilot, of Bicester, Oxfordshire, and

Sergeant Clifford Leonard Oliver Barker, of King's Lynn.

Chamberlain Wedding Postponed

OWING to the death yesterday of her fiancé's father, Brigadier-General Sir Arthur Maxwell, the wedding of Miss Diane Chamberlain, daughter of Sir Austen Chamberlain, to Mr. A. T. Maxwell has been postponed.

It was to have taken place at St. Margaret's, Westminster, next month.

Miss Chamberlain said yesterday:—"In view of Sir Arthur's death the wedding will be postponed."

Sir Arthur Maxwell, who was in his sixtieth year, died after an illness of several weeks at his London house in Cumberland-terrace, Regent's Park.

Lady Maxwell and their son and daughter were present when Sir Arthur died. Miss Chamberlain was also with the family.

Sir Arthur was managing partner of Glyn Mills and Co., the bankers. He had been hon. colonel of the London Regiment since 1923.

During the war, in which he served throughout, he was first a captain and then lieutenant-colonel commanding the 8th London Regiment.

Sir Arthur Maxwell.

12

THE DAILY MIRROR, Thursday, January 24, 1935.

Daily Mirror
THE DAILY PICTURE NEWSPAPER WITH THE LARGEST NET SALE

Broadcasting - Page 22

FIFTH GOSPEL DISCOVERY?

No. 9,721 Registered at the G.P.O. as a Newspaper.   THURSDAY, JANUARY 24, 1935   One Penny

ELEPHANT IN BALLROOM SCENE

Refused to Leave Balcony at West End Hotel

A 2-TON "SPOT OF BOTHER"

BY A SPECIAL CORRESPONDENT

"I AM afraid I have no time to talk to you. I have got a bit of trouble on." The manager of the Grosvenor House Hotel gave this explanation with a good reason to the *Daily Mirror* last night. He might well say that he "had a bit of trouble on."

His "bit of trouble" was Rosie, an elephant.

There she stood, an immovable mass on the balcony, obviously wondering what all the noise and turmoil was about.

Beneath her the gaily decorated ballroom was alive with dancers.

It was the Circus Ball in progress, and the elephant had been brought as an honoured guest from Bertram Mills' Circus.

Later, hearing the name "Rosie" bandied about with a familiarity not common to West End ballrooms, I inquired after the lady and found they were all talking about the elephant.

Then the admiration became too overpowering for modest Rosie.

She could stand so much and no more.

She Liked the Balcony

And the balcony was her hiding place! At first they tried to hand out favours and give her a ride up in the lift. But Rosie was by now in the mood to show her independence and preferred to go up in her own way. She chose the stairs, which she mounted with a grace so natural to her sex.

But once up aloft, and looking down upon the dancers in both ways, she "did her ballroom stuff" uninvited. Whether from joy or cussedness is immaterial. She did it, up and down the carpeted balcony, round and about the tables at which, to begin with, tired dancers were sitting out.

They did not need telling twice that when an elephant takes the floor of a balcony there could be no room for them. They melted into the crowd below, leaving Rosie in proud sole possession—as performer.

Once she buffeted into the cloakroom door, and it looked as if she was after the wrong hat and a quick exit. Nothing of the sort. She was just fooling them. She did not mean to go.

But the attendants considered it was high time she went home.

Then, horrors for a ballroom, someone turned up with chains! And the two-ton dancer found herself strung up by the legs by an iron girdle. Rosie gave in.

Mr. Bertram Mills arrived to soothe her wounded pride with a trayful of sugar, and finally Rosie permitted herself to be escorted to the lift, which took her off to the street level.

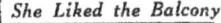
Maureen Edith Shea.

BOY AND GIRL DISAPPEAR

"Going to Make a Big Name for Herself"

SEEN IN LONDON

LEAVING a note that she was going away to make "a big name for herself," a thirteen-year-old St. Osyth (Clacton-on-Sea) schoolgirl disappeared from home on January 16—the day that a seventeen-year-old St. Osyth boy also went away.

The girl is Maureen Edith Shea, of Shamrock Villas, St. Osyth. She should have returned to school next day. The youth is Frederick Stanley Knight, of Victoria House, St. Osyth Main-road, Clacton.

It has been reported that the couple took a coach to London and alighted at King's Cross.

Boy's Worries

The girl's mother said Maureen told her she was going to the pictures, while the boy's father declared that his son had been worried because he had been out of work and had no money to bring home to his mother. He had expressed a desire to work in London.

The girl is within a month of her fourteenth birthday, but would pass as much older. She has a fresh complexion, hair permanently waved, grey eyes, and was wearing a brown tweed skirt, blue jumper and dark blue coat with red buttons.

The boy is 5ft. 6in. in height and of medium build. He has a fresh complexion and dark brown hair, and was wearing a blue suit with black overcoat.

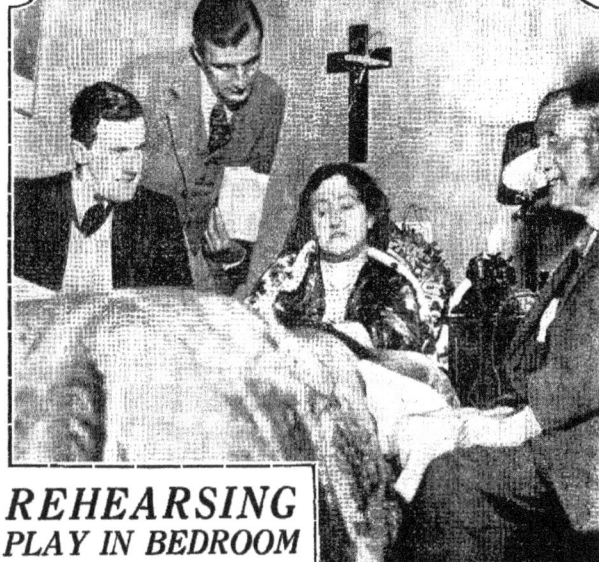

REHEARSING PLAY IN BEDROOM

Injured Actress Carries On as Producer

BY A SPECIAL REPRESENTATIVE

ALTHOUGH laid up with a severely sprained ankle, Miss Sara Allgood, the actress, is pluckily carrying on her duties as producer of a play in which she is to appear at the Kingsway Theatre on Sunday.

Round her bed in the small bedroom of her flat in Compton-street, W.C., yesterday, the other members of the cast stood as she rehearsed them in their parts in Synge's "Shadow of the Glen."

Fortunately, there are only four characters in this play, for the room was sufficiently full with Miss Allgood and Messrs. Jack Bland, G. V. Clarke and Charles Peters!

Miss Allgood met with the accident at the races last Saturday.

"The only compensation," she told me, "was that I backed two winners and three horses for a place, each of which came in second!

"I hope to be able to get up to-morrow without taking any risks, and I shall certainly be fit enough to appear on Sunday. Happily, I know the play quite well, so things are better than they might have been."

Miss Sara Allgood rehearsing for the play "Shadow of the Glen" in her bedroom.

Air Ambulance for Girl of 12

ST. MORITZ, Wednesday.

By road and then air ambulance, the twelve-year-old daughter of Lady Congleton will be taken the 500 miles to England—and home—to-morrow.

The little girl, the Hon. Jean Parnell, has for ten days been lying ill in an hotel at Sils, six miles from here, where Lady Congleton and her family have been spending a holiday.

Jean developed a severe cold and Lady Congleton left for London to arrange for an aeroplane to bring her daughter back home.

A 'plane, piloted by Captain W. Ledlie, left England to-day for the purpose; but had to land at Troie, in France, owing to fog.

The aeroplane will continue its journey to-morrow, and, if the weather is favourable, will then fly direct to Southampton with the little invalid.—Reuter.

The Hon. Jean Parnell (taller) with her younger sister, Sheila.

Explosion Kills Experimenter

WORKING ALONE ON NEW GAS

RETURNING to his work to see if an experiment on a new gas was going according to plan, a man was killed by an explosion at Barking last night. He was:

Frank Williams, aged forty-three, of Roman-road, Ilford, employed at the Fumigating Services, Limited, works, Hertford-road, Barking.

Early this morning detectives were investigating the explosion, which shook houses a quarter of a mile away.

Police who dashed to the works found all the windows smashed and a door wrenched from its hinges.

Braving the fume-laden atmosphere of the "experiments" shed, a policeman and another man dragged Williams out.

He had apparently been at work alone. A burst air cylinder was on the floor nearby.

"The firm fumigates places against rats and moths," Mrs. Williams said. "To-night my husband went back to the works to see if an experiment which they were carrying out to find a new gas for fumigation purposes was going on all right."

LADY WALEY COHEN

JERUSALEM, Thursday.

LADY Waley Cohen, wife of Sir Robert Waley Cohen, managing director of the Shell Transport and Trading Company, and chairman of the Palestine Corporation, Ltd., died in the Government Hospital here at 1.30 this morning, following injuries received in a motor accident on January 16.

Sir Robert received a broken rib, and is progressing satisfactorily.—Exchange.

13

THE DAILY MIRROR, Monday, January 28, 1935

Daily Mirror

THE DAILY PICTURE NEWSPAPER WITH THE LARGEST NET SALE

Broadcasting - Page 20

HAIL OF SHOTS AT A FIRE BRIGADE

Page 2

No. 9,724 Registered at the G.P.O. as a Newspaper. MONDAY, JANUARY 28, 1935 One Penny

3-COUNTY HUNT FOR £22,000

Gold That Dropped from Air Liner in Gale

FEARED LOST IN SEA

TO-DAY the police of three counties—Kent, Sussex and Essex—will resume their search for the £22,000 gold bars which fell from an air liner flying from Paris to Abridge (Essex).

They have already searched for twenty-four hours—and there is still no clue to the whereabouts of the treasure. But it is feared that it fell in the Channel.

The gold was missed when the 'plane landed at Abridge, after a stormy passage. The pilot found to his amazement that the door of the luggage compartment was open, having apparently been burst open by the gale.

First Thought To Be £6,000

At first the value of the missing bullion was stated to be £6,000, but Mr. F. G. Wadsworth, gold dealer for Messrs. Samuel Montagu, bankers, of Old Broad-street, E.C., to whom the gold was consigned, yesterday told the "Daily Mirror" that it was worth about £22,000.

Mr. E. L. Franklin, senior partner in the firm of Messrs. Samuel Montagu, also said the bullion might be worth £22,000.

He added that it would not be of much use to anybody except a broker or an expert thief.

It is understood that the bullion, which was packed in two wooden boxes, was fully covered by insurance.

Scotland Yard officials last evening, after the all-day police search, stated that no one had reported finding the bullion, and it is believed to have fallen into the Channel.

"Felt Weight Shift"

Mr. O. A. Hillman, managing director of Hillman Airways, Ltd., told the Daily Mirror yesterday that the pilot of the liner said that when nearing Dungeness he felt weight being shifted in the tail of the machine, but at the time he put it down to passengers moving about.

An official of Hillman Airways said: "The pilot signed for the package at the airport outside Paris. It was locked in the luggage compartment at the rear of the machine.

"When he set off it was blowing a gale, and the machine was badly buffeted.

"Landing in Essex, the pilot was amazed to find the door of the luggage compartment open. It was empty, having apparently been burst open by the gale and wind.

"Passengers' luggage had also been lost."

Scotland Yard were informed, and an immediate search was carried out.

Miss Mollie Sullivan, a 1935 debutante, realises the funny side of a fall on skis. See pages 14 and 15.

"Oh, this is grand!" exclaimed one future winter sports enthusiast, enjoying the snow on Hampstead Heath yesterday.

Car Lights Answer Bomber's "Shooting Star" Message

INGENUITY OF P.O. OFFICIAL WHO SAW MORSE COMING FROM SKY

MR. Norman Walls, a supervisor at Skegness (Lincs) post office, rubbed his eyes at 7 p.m. when, on his way home, he saw stars apparently shooting about in Morse. When they started asking "Name?" Mr. Walls began to believe in Martians. Until, behind the flashes, he saw the outline of a large 'plane. "Name?" the lights asked again. Mr. Walls replied.

[No, he did NOT dash off to the electricity works and use the town lights as a Morsesender. That's old stuff. Albany (Australia) did it during the Melbourne air race. And, anyway, Skegness is lit by gas and you can't mess about with that.]

He commandeered a motor-car and had the headlights switched on. Running into a chemist's shop he borrowed a hand-mirror and requested the chemist to hold it in front of the headlights at an angle that reflected a ray of light into the sky.

Then, using a book as shutter, Mr. Walls sent out:—

. . . — . — — . . .

Which interpreted is "Skegness."

The 'plane, believed to be an R.A.F. bomber, signalled "O.K." and turned off south-west.

And Mr. Walls, a man of ingenuity, continued his way home.

£70,000 JEWEL THEFT

Jewels insured for $350,000 (£70,000) were stolen when two masked bandits invaded an exclusive hotel at Miami (Florida), states a Reuter message.

The jewels belonged to Mrs. J. E. Bell who, with another resident, was held up by the gangsters and left bound and gagged in her suite.

Mrs. Bell said that the bandits warned her that if she uttered a word they would return and shoot her dead.

CROWD MOBS KREISLER

Fireman Checks Rush for Platform

KEPT at bay for a time by a fireman, the audience stormed the stage of the Albert Hall yesterday and mobbed their idol—Kreisler.

As the last note from the violin faded and Kreisler was going below stage, there was a rush for one of the entrances to the platform. The fireman kept the people back.

Kreisler had to return. His music once more held the vast audience spellbound. There were three encores.

The applause went on. Kreisler again bowed and left the stage. The lights were turned down and the fireman, thinking all was over, left his post.

He was wrong. The applause grew. Once more Kreisler had to appear.

Surrounded by a big crowd, he stood bowing and smiling.

Kreisler, the violinist, acknowledging the triumphant reception given to him

HE DANCES TO SOME TUNE!

At fifty-four years of age, Mr. W. H. Heath, a Putney builder, can tread the Light Fantastic Toe better than any young man.

At Nice, on the Riviera, yesterday in the international dancing championships he won the amateur championship with his partner, Miss Nellie Wood.

It is the sixth year in succession that he has won the event.

And until he was forty-three he had never danced a step.

Lost-Memory Man Mystery

WELL-DRESSED AND SOLDIERLY

POLICE are trying to discover the identity of a well-dressed man, of military appearance, who is in Kingston and District Hospital, Kingston, suffering from loss of memory.

The man was found wandering in Ewell-road, Surbiton, on Saturday. He has been unable to give any account of himself.

He is about forty-five, 6ft. 1in. in height, pale complexion, dark brown hair well brushed back, dark moustache, brown eyes and of slim build.

14

THE DAILY MIRROR, Wednesday, January 30, 1935.

Daily Mirror

THE DAILY PICTURE NEWSPAPER WITH THE LARGEST NET SALE

Broadcasting - Page 20

FIVE YEARS FOR DESERT LOVE FEUD MURDERER —Page 3

No. 9,726 Registered at the G.P.O. as a Newspaper. WEDNESDAY, JANUARY 30, 1935 One Penny

KIDNAPPED BOY SENSATION

Court Sequel 31 Years After He Vanished

FOUND IN AMERICA

SPECIAL "DAILY MIRROR" NEWS

SENSATIONAL details of a kidnapping drama—details which will touch both sides of the Atlantic and bridge a gap of thirty-one years—will be revealed in Sheffield police court to-morrow.

It was on Tuesday, October 18, 1904, that the first act of the drama was played, for on that day Johnny Whitnear, aged five, of Woodbourn-road, Sheffield, vanished.

Johnny's mother is now Mrs. Woodward, and lives in Cobble-street, Sheffield. She has received a subpoena to attend the police court.

She understands that her appearance is in connection with Johnny's disappearance as a boy. Other people, it is stated, have also been called to attend the court.

Johnny Whitnear—thirty-six years old now—is believed to be in Sheffield, but his address is not revealed. He has been served with a court notice.

On the day the child vanished, a man aged about thirty-five had asked the permission of his mother to take him fishing at Keveton, seven miles away.

He did not come back. For weeks the anxious parents searched in vain. Months passed into years. They had nearly given up hope of ever seeing him again. Then they got news.

At the beginning of March, 1909, the Sheffield police were informed by a man, who did not wish his identity disclosed, that the alleged kidnapper was living under an assumed name in Newark, New Jersey, with a boy who was almost certainly Johnny Whitnear.

But the American police insisted that a member of the family must identify the child before he could be given up.

All Their Money Gone

The boy's father, an artisan in a Sheffield steel works, was not well enough to make the journey to America, so the eldest son, William, aged twenty-one, was chosen to go in his stead.

All the resources of the family went to pay for that journey, but it brought their boy back

(Continued on page 3)

Johnny Whitnear in his mother's arms when he was restored to her in 1909.

AIR LINER'S LOST GOLD FOUND

Digging by Night to Recover £22,000

3 FEET DOWN

BURIED three feet beneath the frozen ground in a field near Oisement, two and a half miles from the main Paris-Treport road, the missing consignment of £22,000 worth of gold, lost from a Hillman aeroplane flying from Le Bourget to London on Saturday, was found last night (states Reuter).

A woman walking across a field in the Department of the Somme noticed the debris of a wooden box. There was no sign of any gold, but the woman immediately informed the police.

Gendarmes at once organised a digging party with the help of a few local inhabitants.

The ground was frozen hard and darkness had already set in. Torches and flares cast a yellow flickering light on the diggers working silently in the deserted countryside.

In spite of the cold great beads of sweat stood out on their foreheads as they dug into the iron ground.

Eleven bars of gold have already been retrieved and it is believed that all will be recovered.

According to French law, adds the Exchange, the woman who noticed the broken boxes will receive ten per cent. of the total value of the gold recovered.

FOUR MILES UP

PARIS, Tuesday.

The French airwoman, Madeleine Charnoux, with another woman flyer on board, Miss Edith Clark, to-day reached an altitude of 20,100ft.—nearly four miles—the highest altitude ever attained by a woman piloting a small aeroplane. The previous record was 15,000ft.—Exchange.

OXFORD COLLEGE FIRE

Firemen from Oxford and Abingdon fighting the flames yesterday when fire destroyed the west wing of Ripon Hall, the famous Oxford theological college at Boar's Hill. They were severely handicapped by shortage of water. The library reading room was involved in the blaze but thousands of valuable books were saved as well as furniture. See page 2.

Oxford Boat Race Crews May Desert the Isis

"RIVER IS NOT FIT FOR TRAINING"

IF Oxford wins the Boat Race this year, the Varsity Eight will never again be seen in home waters until the Isis is improved. "We have been going to Henley," the Oxford President, Mr. Michael Mosley, told the *Daily Mirror* last night, "because the river there is fit for training, and at Oxford it is not.

"We used to sneer at Cambridge's little ditch, but the Cam is far superior to the river at Oxford.

"The journey to Henley every day does not take so much longer than it used to take us to negotiate one of the locks.

"We have had no illness this year, while in previous years there has been nothing but illness in the crew.

"The crew has improved tremendously."

Mr. Mosley suggests the dredging of the river at Oxford, the building of a tow-path all the way to Abingdon and the removal of Iffley lock.

An appeal for some of these improvements to be made is likely if Oxford win.

BOHEMIA "LET LOOSE" AT TRIAL

FONTAINEBLEAU, Tuesday.

SCENES reminiscent of a Bloomsbury highbrow party were seen in court here to-day when Jean Charles Millet, grandson of the famous French landscape painter, was charged with selling forgeries of the master's works.

Along with him was charged M. Paul Cazot, a professional picture copier.

The public benches, crowded with eccentrically-dressed Bohemians, were a sea of gesticulating hands and raised eyebrows.

"Amazing sense of perspective"—"What a skyline"—"An obvious forgery"—"A mediocre copy"—were among the expressions heard on all sides.

The verdict was postponed for a week.—Reuter.

Mr. M. H. Mosley

THE DAILY MIRROR, Thursday, January 31, 1935.

Daily Mirror

Broadcasting - Page 20

THE DAILY PICTURE NEWSPAPER WITH THE LARGEST NET SALE

WIFE'S FIGHT FOR HAUPTMANN
—Page 3

No. 9,727 Registered at the G.P.O. as a Newspaper.   THURSDAY, JANUARY 31, 1935   One Penny

GRAIN FIRM'S FAILURE
DRAMA OF EX-WIFE'S CABLE

Friendship Went On—Till Death

LAST 'GOOD LUCK'

BEHIND the cablegram signed "Marjorie" read at the inquest in Bombay on Mr. H. C. Whitehouse, the manager in India of Messrs. Strauss and Co., Limited, the grain firm whose affairs have created a sensation in the commercial world, is a story of friendship that a marriage failure did not end.

For the "Marjorie" who signed the cable, "Try not worry; good luck and love," is Mr. Whitehouse's former wife, now the wife of Mr. J. G. Nicholson, of Aldingham House, Shoppenhangers, Maidenhead.

By the first marriage there are two children—a boy aged nineteen and a girl a little younger, also at college.

It was for their sakes that Mrs. Nicholson, with the full knowledge of her present husband, maintained since the divorce a pact of friendship with Mr. Whitehouse.

Whenever Mr. Whitehouse came to England he stayed at Aldingham House.

"Cannot Face It"

Feeling anxious about Mr. Whitehouse because of his ill-health and business worries, it was decided by Mr. and Mrs. Nicholson, as a gesture of real friendship, to send him a cablegram, and it was dispatched by Mr. Nicholson.

"It was a gesture of encouragement and friendship in his trouble," Mr. Nicholson said last night, "and it is a great pity that it was ever disclosed at the inquest."

The cable, it was stated at the inquest yesterday, was received by Mr. Whitehouse only a few minutes before he threw himself to death from the fourth floor of the Taj Mahal Hotel on Tuesday.

It was revealed, says Reuter, that Mr. Whitehouse's suicide had followed worry about the financial affairs of the firm. A verdict of Suicide while temporarily insane was returned. A letter written by Mr. Whitehouse shortly before his death read:

"I can't face the tangle. Had they let me know a month ago I should have been fit enough to clear up their affairs."

Picture of Mr. Whitehouse and City Editor's comments on the affairs of Messrs. Strauss—page 3.

NOW YOU KNOW WHAT HAPPENS

Remember when that nice big snowball burst smack on the side of your head? Here is the slow-motion camera's record of exactly what happened from the moment it struck you until it burst.

Hospital Patients Watch 'Plane Crash in Grounds

PILOT INJURED IN AVOIDING LANDING IN STREETS—PASSENGER ESCAPES

PATIENTS in Springfield Mental Hospital, Tooting, last night saw an aeroplane, brilliantly lit by advertising signs, circle round and then nose-dive into the hospital grounds. The pilot, Percival Phillips, of the Aerodrome Hotel, Croydon, who was dragged from the wrecked cockpit by nurses and porters, had a broken leg and head injuries. He is in St. James's Hospital, Balham.

His passenger, James Edward Fry, of Gloucester-terrace, W., was unhurt.

The noise of the crash was heard throughout the hospital and several of the 1,500 patients suffered from shock.

Engine Trouble

The 'plane, owned by Air Services, of Croydon, was on a flight round London when, it is believed, it developed engine trouble.

Faced with the alternative of crashing into streets of houses which he could see outlined by the street lamps or diving into a patch of blackness, the pilot chose the unknown.

The "patch of blackness" turned out to be the hospital sports ground.

A similar crash occurred at the same spot five years ago.

THEIR BLOOD FOR CHIEF SCOUT

During Lord Baden-Powell's serious illness last year, a Ranger and a Rover Scout helped to save the life of their chief by giving transfusions of their blood.

This was revealed in the Red Cross Society's blood transfusion service quarterly circular, issued last night:

It is not the practice to report names, but an exception has been made in this case.

TRAIN SAVED —BY 3 YARDS

How One-Armed Hero Averted Disaster

DASH ALONG LINE

WITH a lorry which had crashed through level-crossing gates blocking the railway, a one-armed L.N.E.R. gateman yesterday dashed along the line with detonators and a red flag—just in time to bring a crowded train to a halt three yards from the crossing.

In its crash through the gates the lorry had hurled wreckage against a perambulator. the baby inside was flung on to the road, but was unhurt.

Train Stopped

The gateman, Mr. Hugh Ager, ex-Serviceman, member of the Stowmarket Urban Council and secretary of the local branch of the National Union of Railwaymen, was on duty at Stowmarket.

As soon as he found that the lorry, which was blocking both lines, could not be moved, he began his dash along the line to stop the Bury St. Edmunds-Ipswich train then due and carrying 100 passengers.

He had just time to place the detonators on the line and wave his flag.

A train from Ipswich to Norwich was also due, but this was stopped in Stowmarket Station.

There was no serious delay to traffic.

HOW THE CONSTABLE GOT IN

Delicate Work, but Solicitor Said It Was "Crushing"

IT was a delicate task for a constable, fishing with a piece of wire, to get a key from the inside of a door.

So no doubt he was shocked when, at Morpeth (Northumberland) police court yesterday a solicitor called it—

"The most crushing bit of police work I have encountered in twenty-five years' experience."

The constable, giving evidence against a lorry driver he had followed to his house but was unable to rouse, said that on a sergeant's instruction he got a piece of wire, pushed the key, which was inside the door, out of the lock on to the floor, and then pulled it under the door with the wire.

The constable denied that he had used an iron crowbar—one was produced in court—to force the door, and a sergeant declared he had not exceeded his duties.

He said that under the circumstances he was justified in entering the house as he did.

But the defending solicitor protested. He said there were marks on the door of the house which showed that it had been forcibly opened.

"It does seem to me wrong in this enlightened age that the police have the right to break into a house and pull people out of bed at that time of the morning," he added.

The Bench found the lorry driver not guilty of driving under the influence of drink, reduced a charge of dangerous driving to careless driving, and fined him £3, and for failing to stop imposed a fine of £1.

Nurses beside the wrecked 'plane in the grounds of Springfield Mental Hospital, Tooting.

THE DAILY MIRROR, Saturday, February 2, 1935.

Broadcasting - Page 21

Daily Mirror

THE DAILY PICTURE NEWSPAPER WITH THE LARGEST NET SALE

VITAL ISSUES AT LONDON CONFERENCE —Page 3

No. 9,729 Registered at the G.P.O as a Newspaper. SATURDAY, FEBRUARY 2, 1935 One Penny

GRACIE FIELDS WILL GET £100,000 BY 2 YEARS' WORK

High-Speed Earnings Rival Those of Greta Garbo

SAYS SHE IS "TERRIFIED"

BY A SPECIAL CORRESPONDENT

BY a £100,000 film contract, which she signed yesterday, Miss Gracie Fields will receive a salary during the next two years equal to Greta Garbo's. It commits her to act in at least three films in the next two years for Associated Talking Pictures.

It is far and away the biggest sum ever paid to a film star in this country for a minimum of three pictures.

Yet after she had put her name to the contract Gracie said she was "terrified," and soon afterwards she hurried away by taxi, back to the solace of her knitting.

"I'm frightened to death," said Gracie, and when I asked with envious unbelief: "Is that true?" she said: "As true as I stand here."

We were in the London office of Mr. Bert Azar, who is her brother-in-law and her manager, and on the table was the contract she had just signed.

"What is there to be afraid of?" I asked.

"I'm Scared Stiff"

"The responsibility," she replied promptly. "I'm not joking. Honestly, I'm scared stiff. It makes me feel that such a lot depends upon me. See all the lines on my face? They've come through sleepless nights wondering what I can do to meet this responsibility."

"Well, and what is the first thing you're going to do?"

"Get back to my knitting."

It was no use; not even the responsibility of a £100,000 contract could overwhelm Gracie's sense of the absurd.

Then she said: "I don't really like it. Give me a cottage and 10s."

Above her signature on the contract appears that of Mr. Basil Dean, chairman of the company, and Mr R. P. Baker, joint managing director.

Mr. Baker told me this was the first long-term contract offered her. "Since 1931 she has been playing for us on a picture-to-picture basis, and has often rejected tempting offers from other companies.

"This is a two-year contract which secures her services to us for films throughout 1935 and 1936.

"Miss Fields will start on the first of her three pictures on March 4 at our Ealing Studios. Mr. J. B. Priestley is now writing the scenario. It will be directed by Mr. Basil Dean."

SLANTING KERBS FOR PRAMS

Mothers and nursemaids may live to bless Friern Barnet (Middlesex) Council. An experiment is to be tried by the Council of lowering the kerb on both sides of a street intersection for the quicker and easier passage of perambulators. The kerbs will be relaid in a slanting position to make the footpaths more continuous.

The Sartorial Burglars—

WHO WERE TURNED OUT PERFECTLY

Now WHY did two young men in Southampton want, in a hurry, two perfectly-tailored, best quality and complete outfits of evening clothes?

When the manager of a tailor's shop in Above Bar, Southampton, arrived yesterday morning he found the place had been burgled.

Two dinner-jacket suits were missing, also two evening overcoats, an evening muffler and dress shoes.

Other suits of assorted sizes and half-sizes were lying on the floor; they had obviously lacked something in measurements.

The occasion must have been a pretty urgent one for the Men Who Wanted Dress-clothes, because to reach the shop they had to:—

Climb a 10ft. wall and a 20ft. stack-pipe;
Walk along a narrow ledge 60ft. above the ground; and
Climb through a window.

Incidentally, they entered four other premises in the same block, and purloined 5s. 8d. from a post's cash-box.

Which, with such elegant persons, will hardly cover the cloakroom fees and tips!

WOMAN HURT HUNTING

Remarkable Mishap After Her Horse's Missed Step

WHILE hunting with the Quorn yesterday Mrs. Reginald Farquhar, formerly the Hon. Mrs. Gilbert Greenall, met with a remarkable mishap.

Her horse missed its footing while descending the steep Burrough Hills, near Melton Mowbray.

Mrs. Farquhar was thrown over the animal's head, the horse stumbled then rose completely over its rider, who lay unconscious for several minutes.

Mrs. Farquhar recovered later.

Gracie Fields signing her £100,000 contract. Beside her is Mr. R. P. Baker.

DOCTOR'S 2-STORIED CARAVAN

Iris Adrian, the film actress, and Miss Margaret Crane (bareheaded) with the portable auto-camp invented by Dr. E. H. Crane, of California.

"Yard" Hunt for Blonde

BELIEVED TO HAVE STOLEN £20,000 GEMS

SCOTLAND Yard chiefs want to meet a beautiful blonde, well dressed and cultured—purely on official business. They believe her to be responsible for the disappearance of nearly £20,000 worth of jewellery; and know her to have stolen clothing worth a small fortune.

The Yard yesterday issued a second appeal to police forces of the seaports for special investigation into the activities of the woman, described as being aged about thirty, a natural blonde, and exceedingly well spoken.

Her Hat Boxes

The Yard explains:—

This cultured young woman arrives armed with the knowledge of the arrival of a vessel from overseas.

She explains at the reception offices of the best hotels that her husband is arriving by an expected boat—sometimes New York and again Yokohama and Shanghai.

With her, she carries two hat boxes, used now by many women as week-end bags, and these, it is alleged, she packs with evening gowns, travelling suits, afternoon tea dresses and sets of lingerie of the most expensive character stolen from the bedrooms.

Scotland Yard point out also that this blonde may be responsible for the theft of jewellery worth nearly £20,000 stolen in the past five months from hotels in Hull, Liverpool, Southampton, Plymouth and elsewhere.

ARSENAL SIGN NEW SCOTTISH STAR

Robert Davidson, Inside Forward —Big Transfer Fee a Secret

ROBERT Davidson, the St. Johnstone "star" footballer, was last night transferred to the Arsenal.

Mr. Muirhead, the St Johnstone manager, declined to reveal the transfer fee.

It is hinted that the fee is about £7,000.

Mr. Allison told the Daily Mirror last night that Davidson was a player of remarkable ability—"the prototype of Alex James, with a quick-thinking mind and feet that respond to it."

"He will join the Highbury team Tuesday," said Mr. Allison. "When we will play I cannot say. I regard him as a player with a great future." Davidson stands 5ft. 7in. and weighs 11st. He is twenty-one.

R. Davidson.

17

THE DAILY MIRROR, Tuesday, February 5, 1935.

Broadcasting - Page 20

Daily Mirror
THE DAILY PICTURE NEWSPAPER WITH THE LARGEST NET SALE

BIGGER OLD-AGE PENSIONS —Page 2

No. 9,731 Registered at the G.P.O. as a Newspaper TUESDAY, FEBRUARY 5, 1935 One Penny

PETERSEN TITLE HOPE GONE

'Pa's' Surrender Signal in Great Fight

NEUSEL'S VICTORY THRILLS 11,000

By STANLEY LONGSTAFF

Jack Petersen's hopes of capturing the world's heavy-weight championship were exploded violently at Wembley last night when Walter Neusel, the blond German, battered him into submission in eleven rounds.

THE end was pitiable from a British standpoint.

We had the regrettable sight of our Empire champion, with the blood streaming from his left eye, being unmercifully punched from pillar to post, reeling from one side of the ring to the other before a battery of terrific hitting.

His vision impaired by the wound which Neusel had opened in the course of a savage assault in the tenth round, Petersen strove gallantly to ward off defeat.

But defeat was certain, and it was a relief to 11,000 spectators in the arena when Pa Petersen, in what must have been the bitterest moment of his life, tossed in the towel.

No fighter breathing could have overcome the handicap which mastered Petersen.

Nevertheless, I detected a moment near the end of the ninth round when I thought Petersen's chances of victory were destroyed.

It was when Neusel, the battle-light in his eyes, his chin tucked in between his massive shoulders, swept in to do-or-die and sent in a pile-driving right-hand punch.

A grunt escaped Petersen as he crumpled up nearly double on the ropes, and the bell.

(Continued on page 26)

SHE HID HERSELF AFTER THE FIGHT

Petersen's Fiancee Does Not Like Boxing

FROM OUR OWN CORRESPONDENT
CARDIFF, Monday night.

South Wales, where Jack Petersen is idolised, received the result of his fight philosophically.

But there was one young woman to whom the result must have been a great disappointment.

She was Miss Betty Williams, Petersen's eighteen-year-old fiancee.

Miss Williams does not like boxing and was not at the ringside at Wembley. Instead, she remained at her home and refused to discuss the fight after the result had become known.

To-night she hid herself even from her friends, and all visitors to her Cardiff home were politely but firmly told she could not be seen.

Miss Betty Williams.

At Cardiff crowds waited in the rain for the result of the fight, and the general opinion seemed to be—"It will do Jack good."

Petersen half through the ropes, with Neusel waiting for him to rise.

Mr. C. B. Thomas, the referee, holding the towel thrown in at the eleventh round by Pa Petersen, who is helping the defeated British champion back to his corner.

Cut Out the "Amen"

DR. TEMPLE DEPLORES AN "EVIL HABIT"

DEPLORING the "evil habit" of singing "Amen" at the end of hymns, the Archbishop of York (Dr. Temple), at the annual banquet of the Incorporated Guild of Church Musicians at the Holborn Restaurant, last night, said that if a tune was a good tune it came to an end by itself.

Speaking of "vestry prayers," he wished them to be said quietly, and not intoned, and that the "Amen" should be said and not "bellowed."

It was all wrong for a man who had been talking like a perfectly rational being suddenly to sound a note with his lips closed, and say, "M-m-m, let us pray."

Canon Bullard, rector of Melsonby, said: "Why cannot we have church tunes so beautiful that the butcher's boy as he goes down the street, or the maid-servant, as she dusts the dining-room, will hum or whistle church music?"

CRASH AVERTED AS MAN DROPS DEAD AT CAR WHEEL

Woman Passenger Jams on Hand-Brake

WHEN the driver dropped dead over the steering wheel of a car, his passenger, Mrs. Gladys Francis, saved herself and the lives of others on the road by jamming on the brake. She was able to stop the car by the side of the road, giving a clear passage to other traffic.

This drama was played out on the main Rushden-Wellingborough road yesterday, near Tunnel's Hill.

The driver was Ernest Pack, fifty-eight, an engineer, of Rushden, Northants.

Mrs. Francis, who is a boot operative living in Wellingborough, was being given a lift home.

It was not long after she had entered the car that she noticed Mr. Pack was showing signs of illness.

He appeared to be breathing with difficulty and was leaning over the wheel. Suddenly the car began to move towards the grass on the roadside.

Mrs. Francis screamed for help and at the same time pulled on the hand brake.

Two motorists who were near the spot stopped in answer to her calls for help; one went for the police and the other for a doctor.

Mr. Pack, however, was dead. He had suffered for some time from heart trouble, but recently had been much better in health. He leaves a widow and two children.

POWDER—AND SHOCK— IN A BUS

When Oxford City Council met yesterday, Councillor H. C. King objected to what he described as women "dressing" in city buses.

He explained that what he meant was that some of them did not hesitate to paint their lips red and powder their faces white, regardless of how other passengers might view the proceeding.

"I suggest," he said, "that each bus should have a dressing-room."

The council took no action in the matter.

Night Dash for Reprieve

CONDEMNED MAN'S SISTER ACTS

WHILE David Maskill Blake sat with his wife and baby in Armley Gaol, Leeds, yesterday—three days before the date fixed for his execution—his sister, Mrs. Bousfield, was setting out on an all-night dash to London in a last effort to obtain a reprieve.

Mrs. Bousfield has with her a petition with 10,000 signatures.

She will be met this morning at the House of Commons by Major J. Milner, Socialist M.P. for South-East Leeds, who will introduce her to the Home Secretary.

Travelling to London last night, too, by express post was an affidavit sworn by a woman which, it is claimed, throws new light on the crime—the murder of Emily Yeomans, a waitress.

It is understood that a conversation between the woman and Emily Yeomans a fortnight before the murder, in which Miss Yeomans is said to have discussed her friendship and arrangements with a man other than Blake, is set out.

It is urged by Blake's solicitor that the statement at least demands further inquiry.

THE DAILY MIRROR, Wednesday, February 6, 1935.

Daily Mirror

THE DAILY PICTURE NEWSPAPER WITH THE LARGEST NET SALE

Broadcasting - Page 20

DOLE CUTS TO BE RESTORED —Page 3

No. 9,732 Registered at the G.P.O as a Newspaper. WEDNESDAY, FEBRUARY 6, 1935 One Penny

NEW FOKKER 'PLANE FOR BRITAIN?

ONE FALSE STEP AND—

A remarkable Alpine picture which illustrates the perils faced by mountaineers when negotiating the jagged edge of a deep chasm made doubly dangerous by snow and ice.

Airspeed Company's Plan to Build Fresh Type

£20,000 FOR DESIGNER

FOLLOWING the announcement of the sums which Airspeed (1934), Ltd., are paying to Mr. Anthony Fokker, the Dutch expert, the "Daily Mirror" is now able to reveal that

The company's agreement with Mr. Fokker is expected to lead to the planning and building of an entirely new type of aircraft.

Airspeed (1934), Ltd., who have obtained the concession for the British Empire to build all Fokker aircraft, including the famous Douglas machines, will, it is understood, pay Mr. Fokker £20,000 and a royalty of £600 for each of the first twenty machines.

If the sales of these machines exceed a gross revenue of £150,000 Mr. Fokker will receive a further £20,000.

He will act as special consultant to Airspeed for a period of seven years and will receive one per cent. of the profits for his services.

"The agreement with Mr. Fokker will make an enormous difference to our company," Mr. A. H. Tiltman, joint managing director of Airspeed (1934), Ltd., told the *Daily Mirror* last night

Famous Liners

"We have at present made no plans for production. Nothing is settled as yet, but we are going to consider the types of aeroplane we shall build.

"It is unlikely that we shall build Douglas machines at first. It is most likely that we shall build a new type of aeroplane altogether from the new designs that are now available to us through this concession."

Mr Fokker holds the licence for the manufacture in Europe of the American Douglas air liners, one of which was second in the England-Australia air race.

It is probable that one result of the new arrangement will be the expansion of Airspeed's Portsmouth works.

Miss Margaret Gregson, a Leicester girl, gave a lucky horseshoe to Walter Neusel, who beat Jack Petersen in their fight at Wembley. Neusel yesterday denied rumours of romance.

James Maurice Brown, of Stainshaw, Portsmouth, boy, first class, in H.M.S. Hood, whose father has been notified of his death by drowning in Arosa Bay. No one saw him go overboard

FILM STAR ADOPTS BABY

Jessie Matthews Finds New Happiness

JESSIE Matthews, the famous stage and screen star, has adopted a three weeks old baby girl.

Last December Miss Matthews gave birth to a son. He lived only a few hours.

Miss Matthews and her husband, Sonnie Hale, were heartbroken. They had made great plans for their child. A new wing had been built to their house at Hampton, Middlesex.

It contained a day and night nursery. Together they had planned and arranged everything for their child.

Ever since December the nursery wing, spick and span with new paint, has stood empty. It was a building of sadness.

Then Miss Matthews decided to adopt a baby. A little girl was chosen from the National Adoption Society and for the past week she has slept in the little boy's cot.

The nursery wing is a building of happiness now.

BURNING VESSEL RACES FOR HELP

Fire Engines Sent on Luggage Boat to Meet Her

WHEN the Newcastle steamer Bretwalda (5,293 tons), inland bound from Brazil, was twenty miles off Liverpool last night she sent out an SOS for a serious fire had broken out in one of her holds.

The vessel raced for the Mersey, where salvage vessels were waiting, together with two fire engines sent by Liverpool brigade on a chartered luggage ferry.

The salvage vessels, with the assistance of the brigade, went alongside the steamer and endeavoured to get the outbreak under control. But the fire was burning furiously, and early this morning it was feared that the steamer would have to be beached owing to the tremendous amount of water pumped into her.

The Bretwalda is loaded with nuts and rice and other highly inflammable material.

THIS DOG LOST —AS HE WON!

In the 8.30 hurdle race at Catford last night Spent Money fell immediately in front of the winning line. His tail was actually across the line and his body in front.

While he was getting to his feet again two other dogs passed him and the race was awarded to Double Deed.

Mother Flings Baby to Safety

CHILD CAUGHT BY MAN AS BALE WRECKS PRAM

A FEW seconds after a mother had thrown her six-week-old baby into the arms of a man, the perambulator in which the child had been sitting was smashed by bales of wool which crashed from a lorry at Stepney, E., yesterday.

The mother, Mrs. J. Standing, of St. George's-street, Stepney, was struck by one of the bales, but was not hurt seriously.

Dragged to Safety

Her four-year-old son, Frank, who was by his mother's side, was dragged to safety by the man who caught the baby.

Eight bales of wool, each weighing about 3cwt., fell from the lorry as it was turning from Christian-street into Cable-street.

Mrs. Standing and her two children were taken to St. George's-in-the-East Hospital, where they were detained until they had recovered from the shock.

Nude Cabaret Dancer Defies Ban

PARIS ALLOWS HER "TURN" ON STAGE

FROM OUR OWN CORRESPONDENT
PARIS, Tuesday.

DANCING in the nude as a cabaret "turn" has been banned by the Paris Prefect of Police—though the same performance on the stage has brought no objection.

But the ban is to be defied.

The dancer, Joan Warner, of Chicago, will, it was announced to-night, appear "as usual" in the cabaret at a restaurant where she is dancing after the theatre closes.

The dance taken from the theatre show, "La Revue Nue," is performed in a "moonlight" setting.

It is argued by some that the performance is not a dance in the nude as Miss Warner carries either a scarf or a fan.

Joan Warner, of Chicago, who has been dancing in the nude in Paris

19

THE DAILY MIRROR, Friday, February 8, 1935.

Broadcasting - Page 22

Daily Mirror

THE DAILY PICTURE NEWSPAPER WITH THE LARGEST NET SALE

PEPPER GAMBLE DEVELOPMENTS —Page 2

No. 9,734 Registered at the G.P.O as a Newspaper FRIDAY, FEBRUARY 8, 1935 One Penny

GERMANY TO ACCEPT AIR PACT

Ready Also to Return to League of Nations

EUROPEAN PEACE IN SIGHT

FROM OUR SPECIAL CORRESPONDENT ("Daily Mirror" Exclusive)

BERLIN, Thursday Night.

I AM able to announce that there is the greatest likelihood of Germany's accepting the Franco-British invitation to join in the London Air Pact.

There is also a reasonable possibility of her return to the League of Nations.

In a special interview this evening, the Press Secretary at the German Ministry of Propaganda said to me:
"Germany's presence in the Air Convention is absolutely necessary; without Germany, it would lead nowhere.
"A thorough working agreement between France, Germany, Italy and Great Britain would present the greatest possible security for Europe.

"Russia's co-operation is not necessary, and a united front in Western Europe would render any possible attack by air from Russia out of the question.

"Russia is too distant from the principal centres in Europe for an unsupported attack to succeed."

I asked him if the Rome and Eastern Pacts stood in the way of a solution.

"Not at all," he replied, "an Air Pact can be formed without reference to them, and, in fact, would help to solve the question of the Eastern frontiers of Europe."

League Return Too

Then I asked the Secretary whether there was any possibility of Germany's return to the League of Nations, and whether or not the present situation offered any obstacles to the London Air Pact.

"Germany's return to the League can follow the Air Pact," he replied. "But now Germany has no mandate; every nation represented on the League has a mandate, and the League's methods are still too bureaucratic.

"When Germany's freedom is recognised and she can take her place with the rest of Europe, then there is not the slightest reason why she should not return. But we must have equality in armaments.

"The Air Pact is a good, new effort for peace," he concluded, "and when it is ratified and Germany is back on the Council of the League, peace will be assured for Europe."

LOSS TO SCIENCE

Death has robbed Science of two eminent people.

Professor Arthur Thomson, one of the most eminent of British anatomists, professor of anatomy at the Royal Academy for thirty-four years died at Oxford yesterday

Mr. Herbert Weld, of Lulworth Castle, Dorset, who explored and mapped the unknown course of the Blue Nile below Tsana to the Sudan, and whose discoveries enrich many British and foreign museums, has died at the age of eighty-three.

Alice Delysia.

"I HAVE NO FILM FACE"
Says Delysia

DELYSIA arrived in London last night —the same vivacious, light-hearted Delysia.

Impending divorce proceedings in Paris have brought her back from Australia, "the land deliciously in love with the Mother Country," as she put it.

When I met her in her suite at the Savoy Hotel (writes a *Daily Mirror* representative) she discussed her prospective divorce quite freely. With considerable emphasis, she declared: "I have done nothing wrong."

The probability of an early reappearance on the London stage made her clap her hands.

Last night she was discussing parts with Leslie Henson. To-morrow she will be meeting "one of the finest and best managers in the world," Mr. Cochran.

"I have been asked about films, but oh, my face," she said. "They told me the film was good but I thought my face was too, too terrible. Still, I may play in a film; I don't know.

"All I do know is that I am going to have the first holiday I have ever had in England. It has always been work and work only before.

"Now I am going to play, and in between times make arrangements for the future."

Delysia was married in the Roman Catholic Church in Leicester-square, in November, 1928, to M. Georges Denis, a Paris newspaper manager and well-known Rugby player.

Mr. Herbert Weld.

Prof. Arthur Thomson.

MOSCOW'S PARACHUTE TOWER.—To give the youth of the Soviets calm and presence of mind, they are being exercised in parachute jumping from special towers constructed in all the principal towns of the U.S.S.R. Here is a young comrade making a descent at Moscow. Parachute-jumping is becoming the favourite sport, not only of men, but also of the girls.

Actress's Home in Danger

FIRE FIGHT AT BUNGALOW TOWN

FIRE which damaged the parish hall at Shoreham Bungalow Town (Sussex) last night endangered the church and the home of Miss Florrie Forde, the actress.

Chief Officer A. C. Turrell left his sick bed to fight the flames, and the brigade were assisted by people who were at the hall to take part in a rehearsal.

Shoreham Council recently issued fire warnings to the occupants of the many wooden bungalows on the beach.

FLYING SQUAD CHASE

After a five-mile chase which started at Woodside Park Garden Suburb, North Finchley, yesterday, a Flying Squad patrol car overtook another car in Naylor's-lane, Finchley.

Later a man and a woman were taken to Finchley Police Station

JUBILEE "FLY-PAST"

Saturday, July 6, is the provisional date fixed for the Jubilee review by the King and Queen of the Royal Air Force.

The grand "fly past" will take place at Mildenhall Aerodrome, Suffolk, from which the Melbourne air race started.

More Jubilee plans—see page nine.

NO CAILLARD WILL SUIT

Opposition Withdrawn by Her Son

Opposition to the will of Lady Caillard, who died recently, has been withdrawn.

This was announced last night by Lord Molesworth.

"No law suit is now likely," he said, "and the will is expected to be admitted to probate within the next few weeks."

Lord Molesworth, who is one of the executors of the will described it as a very complicated one.

A caveat against the admission of the will to probate was entered by Commander Guy Maund, Lady Caillard's son by her first marriage He withdrew his opposition after seeing a copy of the will.

Lord Molesworth said that Commander Guy Maund had his own estate provided out of the will of his father

He described to a reporter a recent seance held at the belfry, West Halkin-street, S.W., where Lady Caillard died.

"Lady Caillard came through," he said, "and reminded us that we had not carried out her instructions before she died that champagne was to be drunk at her funeral."

"She wanted to impress upon us the fact that there was no need to grieve for her.

"Throughout the seance the casket containing Lady Caillard's ashes stood on a chair in the room."

THE DAILY MIRROR, Monday, February 11, 1935.

Daily Mirror

Broadcasting - Page 20

THE DAILY PICTURE NEWSPAPER WITH THE LARGEST NET SALE

No. 9,736 Registered at the G.P.O. as a Newspaper. MONDAY, FEBRUARY 11, 1935 One Penny

YARD MOVES IN ISLAND RIDDLE
—Page 2

ROBBER GANGS SWOOP AGAIN

FLYING ON SKIS—THE NEW THRILL

New Outbreak of Raids During the Week-End

£2,000 JEWEL HAUL

JEWEL-thieves and safe raiders made a number of sensational swoops in various parts of London during the week-end—but they kept away from the northern side, where, after a series of raids, the residents are asking for stronger police patrols.

The most serious robbery of the week-end was at South Croydon, where police were informed that jewellery value £2,000 had been stolen from a house in Croham Valley-road.

The occupant, Mrs. Gladys Barton, was away on holiday, and the house was temporarily unoccupied.

The thieves got in at the back of the house, which adjoins Croham Hurst golf links, and after searching room after room walked out by the front door.

Yesterday morning a milkman named Charles Smith, of Waddon, saw the door open and told a neighbour, Mr. C. E. Boast, the Croydon borough engineer, who informed the police.

This is the latest of a series of robberies in the district.

A fortnight ago eight houses were burgled in ten days at Shirley, Croydon, and on Saturday night a house was robbed in East Croydon.

The burglaries are believed to be the work of the same gang.

Watched for Chance

Another robbery this week-end was at the house of Mr. V. Gennaro in Gwendyr-street, West Kensington. A deed box and jewels worth about £100 were taken.

Mr. Gennaro, his family and the maid were all out at the time.

"Evidently the burglars had been watching the house," said Mr. Gennaro.

A heavy iron safe containing £60 in cash and £15 worth of insurance stamps was stolen from the premises of Messrs. Spaight and Partners, Ltd., sewerage contractors, of Charlton-road, Shepperton, Middlesex.

It is believed that two or three men must have been concerned, and that they used a car.

(Continued on page 2)

Looking like a giant bat: Krupa, a Viennese ski-ing expert, combining the arts of ski-ing and gliding in the Tyrol. He has flown 225ft. at a height of 35ft.

Radio SOS Solves Injured Girl Rider Mystery

IDENTIFIED BY BROTHER | UNCONSCIOUS IN ROAD | CRASH THAT NO ONE SAW

A RADIO SOS broadcast last night solved the mystery of the identity of a young woman rider who was found unconscious on the Cockfosters-road, near Hadley Woods.

She is Miss Winifred Martin, twenty-six, of Green-lanes, Clissold Park.

A brother who heard the wireless appeal went to the North Middlesex Hospital, Edmonton, and saw his sister, who is dangerously ill.

Miss Martin had hired a horse earlier in the day from a riding school in Southgate, and when she was found unconscious the animal was standing uninjured a short distance up the road.

Mr. William Bramley, the proprietor of the riding school, told the Daily Mirror that the circumstances of the accident were a mystery.

"Miss Martin," he said, "hired the horse from us and went out with a party under one of my men through Hadley Woods.

"They were returning from the ride, when she went on ahead of the others and my man knew nothing of the accident until he was told some time later.

"Neither he nor I can explain it in any way.

"It was the second occasion on which she had come to the school. Though she gave her name as Miss Martin I did not know where she came from.

"When she came to-day she asked for the same horse as she had been given a fortnight ago, a big docile animal we know well.

"When the accident occurred no one was near enough to see exactly what happened."

Hoax on the Duke's Ship?

BELIEF THAT SOS WAS JUST A "JOKE"

WAS the British cruiser Australia with the Duke of Gloucester aboard hoaxed when she raced all night to the rescue of a small American pleasure schooner?

An SOS call for help was sent out by the schooner Seth Parker that she was in danger of capsizing in a Pacific gale 700 miles east of Samoa.

When the Australia overhauled her at 3.50 a.m. yesterday, says Reuter's special correspondent on board the cruiser, there was no sign of damage.

It had been rumoured that the Seth Parker was a broadcasting ship, and this was confirmed by a message from her.

"We are shortly going to broadcast over the network of the National Broadcasting Company of America. Please give us the captain's name so that we give him the credit for his kind assistance."

The Australia then signalled: "Please report when satisfied that you no longer need me. The Duke of Gloucester is aboard."

The Seth Parker replied:—

"We wish to pay homage to the Duke of Gloucester and also to express our sincere thanks to the captain, officers and crew of the Australia for their kindness and assistance.

"We are all right now and your assistance is no longer needed. Your arrival has been like that of a doctor before whom trouble always disappears just before he arrives."

Searchlight and grille fitted to one of the windows of a house in Bishop's-avenue, East Finchley.

THE DAILY MIRROR, Wednesday February 13, 1935.

Daily Mirror

THE DAILY PICTURE NEWSPAPER WITH THE LARGEST NET SALE

Broadcasting - Page 22

ISLAND DRAMA: SIR B. SPILSBURY GOING BACK —PAGE 3

No. 9,738 Registered at the G.P.O. as a Newspaper. WEDNESDAY, FEBRUARY 13, 1935 One Penny

SOS FROM BIGGEST AIRSHIP
'We Are Falling' Message from Macon

FEARS OF AN EXPLOSION

"S O S ... S O S ... HAVE HAD BAD CASUALTY ... SHIP FALLING ... WAIT ..."

THESE were the dramatic messages flashed out early this morning by the world's biggest airship, the U.S. Navy's Flying Fortress, Macon, which was battling with a Pacific gale about 110 miles south of San Francisco.

The last message stated that the crew of ninety-nine intended to abandon the airship on descending. Then silence.

Coastguard cutters and destroyers dashed to the rescue of the crippled dirigible.

Meanwhile a wireless station at San Diego picked up an unconfirmed report that the airship had come down in the Pacific.

While no details of the trouble are available, states Reuter, wireless officers in San Francisco surmise that there may have been an explosion on board the Macon.

Akron's Sister-Ship

She was last seen from land by observers at Santa Barbara and Santa Monica, who report that the Macon was forced by a gale eight miles to the south.

The Macon is sister ship to the Akron, which crashed in the Atlantic with the loss of seventy-three men in 1933.

She made her maiden flight on April 21, 1933, only a few weeks after the disaster to the Akron.

The Macon is 785ft. long, carries 6,500,000 cubic feet of helium non-inflammable gas in her cells, weighs 215,000 pounds with a full load and has a cruising range of about 11,000 miles without refuelling.

She carries a nest of five aeroplanes.

Her captain is Lieutenant-Commander Herbert T. Wiley.

He was the only officer to escape from the Akron when it fell into the sea off New Jersey.

During a flight from California to Miami, Florida, in April, 1934, the Macon broke two of her girders, weakening her framework.

In the following month she successfully took part in manoeuvres and launched all her aeroplanes.

"FLYING FORTRESS" MACON, the biggest airship in the world, in a flight over San Diego.

Woman Who Was Stavisky's Secret Love Shoots Herself in Flat

HER MONEY MADE HIS FORTUNE, BUT SHE DIED PENNILESS AND ALONE

FROM OUR OWN CORRESPONDENT

PARIS, Tuesday night.

SECRET lover of Stavisky, founder of his fortune and known throughout France as "the woman of the diamonds," Viviane Lamarre is dead.

She shot herself in her flat with her revolver, penniless and alone.

Stavisky first met her in 1916. He was then a poor man known as Monsieur Sacha. In the early days of the war he had been the manager of a small theatre, but this had failed, and he was almost without means.

Viviane was wealthy. She had as her lover one of the richest men in France, who made her an allowance of £2,000 a month.

She fell in love with Stavisky, lent him money and introduced him to influential people.

In 1926, when Stavisky was at the height of his prosperity, he heard that Viviane had been deserted by her protector, that she had had to sell her famous diamonds, and was in dire straits.

Remembering her kindness to him, he established her in a flat in Paris, and repaid her generosity to him with gifts of money and diamonds, which she loved so much.

When Stavisky crashed Viviane was again left to face the world alone—a middle-aged woman of faded beauty and with no resources, except the gems the dead financier had given her.

By selling these she managed to live for a few months until this week, when, unable to face the future, she took her life.

LINDBERGH "CONFESSION"

MINISTER'S OUTBURST STAGGERS COURT

TRIAL CLIMAX

The voice of a clergyman, shouting that a man other than Hauptmann had confessed to him that he kidnapped the Lindbergh baby, provided a dramatic climax to the end of yesterday's hearing in the Hauptmann trial.

MR. WILENTZ, chief prosecuting counsel, had just ended his final plea, in which he demanded the death of Hauptmann, when the clergyman was heard crying: "A man confessed to the crime to me in my church."

Instantly the court-room was in an uproar. A deputy sheriff leaped forward and hustled the clergyman from the court. He would not go without a struggle. He floored one of the court assistants.

The court was cleared, but people attempted to rush the doors. Police drove them back.

Outside it was learned that the clergyman was a Congregational minister, the Rev. Vincent Burns, a brother of the author of the best-seller, "I'm a Fugitive from a Georgia Chain-Gang," which was adapted into a very successful film.

He declared, states Reuter, that a man resembling Hauptmann, "but not Hauptmann," virtually confessed to the kidnapping "in my church on Palm Sunday, 1932."

"World Enemy No. 1"

Mr. Burns said that he told the man to tell his story to the defence and the prosecution but he was not called as a witness.

After being questioned and warned, Mr. Burns was released.

Almost the whole of yesterday's hearing had been occupied by the last impassioned appeal to the jury by Mr. Wilentz, Public Prosecutor.

These were some of the things Mr. Wilentz had to say about Hauptmann:

"He's cold, yes he's cold; but he will be thawed out when he hears the switch of the electric chair turned on.

"A fellow with ice water in his veins.

"This animal—Public Enemy No. 1 of the world."

Judge Trenchard will sum up to-day.

CARS LOST IN FIRE

Several cars were lost in a fire which early this morning destroyed Fitch's Garage, at the junction of the London and Reading roads at Hook, near Basingstoke.

Lieutenant-Commander H. T. Wiley.

THE DAILY MIRROR, Saturday, February 16, 1935.

Daily Mirror

Broadcasting - Page 22

THE DAILY PICTURE NEWSPAPER WITH THE LARGEST NET SALE

GERMANY'S AIR PACT REPLY —Page 3

No. 9,741 Registered at the G.P.O. as a Newspaper. SATURDAY, FEBRUARY 16, 1935 One Penny

NINE DEAD IN R.A.F. DISASTER
Flying Boat Hits Mountain and Bursts Into Flames

PEASANT TELLS OF CRASH IN DENSE FOG

Relative of Lord Beatty a Victim

AIR SEARCH FAILS

Nine Britons were killed when a giant R.A.F. flying boat crashed into the fog-wreathed side of a mountain not far from Messina, Sicily, yesterday.

The machine crashed at high speed and burst into flames. When a rescue party reached it there was nothing but a tangled mass of wreckage from which the nine bodies have been recovered. One of the victims was a step-brother of Lord Beatty.

NEWS of the disaster—one of the most terrible in the whole history of the R.A.F., reached San Filippo, a village about twenty-five miles from Messina, yesterday afternoon when a carter handed a piece of burned wreckage to the police.

He said he had seen the 'plane, a burnt-out wreck, on the side of the Mandrazzi, in the Peloritina mountains, and at once a rescue party set off.

After travelling for hours through fog and rain over mountain paths, they reached the 'plane.

From the lips of a peasant named Cardile, the only man who saw the crash, they heard the full story of the tragedy. Cardile had been working on the mountain side before the carter who carried the news to San Filippo passed by.

"I was digging one of the terraces on the mountain side at about 9.30 this morning," Cardile told Reuter's correspondent, "when I

Flt.-Lieut. Beatty.

Mr. R. J. Penn.

heard the roar of an aeroplane. It burst out suddenly from the clouds nearby which hung over the mountain top.

"It was on a tremendous slant, one wing right down and the other up in the air. It

THE DEAD

Flight-Lieutenant Henry Longfield Beatty, Co. Wexford (step-brother of Lord Beatty).
Flying-Officer John Alexander Charles Forbes, South Africa and Bedford.
560464 Sergeant Herbert James Willis, Co. Fermanagh.
365652 L/A.C. William Patrick Wallis, Limerick.
363239 L/A.C. Roland Dennis James Rees, Pembroke.
562415 L/A.C. Cyril Norton Allen, Glamorgan.
359103 Corporal Stephen Thomas Bailey, Frome.
564901 Aircraftman (First Class) Leslie Wogan, Glamorgan.
Mr. Reginald John Penn (passenger), from the Royal Aircraft Establishment, Farnborough, Hants.

seemed to sweep the side of the mountain with the lower wing.

"Suddenly I saw a big puff of smoke which was followed by a tremendous explosion and the machine burst into flames before it hit the mountain side.

"After that it seemed to break into pieces and fell down the hill side.

"I rushed down after it and came up to it when the flames were burning high in the air. It was impossible to approach.

"I saw two men half burned in the front part of the machine. I could do nothing.

"I could not take my eyes off their chests, where their medal ribbons seemed to reflect the light of the flames and remained after the rest of the bodies seemed to have disintegrated.

"I then rushed down the hill as quickly as I could to the Carabinieri at San Filippo. It is about four miles over difficult ground and I did not arrive there until about 10.30."

Firemen in the rescue party poured water on the still-burning wreckage. As night fell the work went on by torchlight.

At last, when the nine bodies had been recovered, they were wrapped in flags and borne reverently down the mountain to Messina, where to-day they will be placed on board

(Continued on page 3)

Fated never to reach her destination—the flying boat taking off from Pembroke on January 15. Right: Flying-Officer Forbes, who is among the nine men who lost their lives.

SCRAPS OF PAPER MEAN FORTUNE TO HER

£10,000 for a Song—Never Had a Lesson

BY A SPECIAL REPRESENTATIVE

A GIRL who, without ever having had a music lesson, wrote a song which earned her £10,000, arrived in London yesterday. The song was "Lullaby of the Leaves." The girl is Bernice Petkere, who has come to England with her husband for a holiday.

Three years ago she knew nothing about song-writing; now it has made her rich. Dark, shy and pretty, she seems dazed by the whole business.

Not knowing how music is written, she writes all her songs in a kind of musical shorthand which she has evolved. Others then translate it into conventional score.

She writes anywhere. Her home, she told me, is covered with scraps of paper on which ideas and inspirations are jotted down.

"And I've just one superstition," she added. "The piece of paper, or back of a box, or whatever it is, on which I write my first version of each new song, is religiously stored away. If I lost one of those scraps of paper I don't know what I'd do."

She also composes her own words. She has no hours, no routine. She just writes when the inspiration comes along. Her first song was written on the back of a menu during dinner in a restaurant.

"Close Your Eyes" is another of her compositions. It is still bringing her money. So are other "hits," and she still goes on writing on scraps of paper.

Picture on page 16.

Royal Jubilee Secret

THE Prince of Wales is to inaugurate a scheme for a national thank-offering to celebrate the King's Silver Jubilee.

An official statement issued from St. James's Palace last night said:

"The Prince of Wales is holding a meeting on March 1 at St. James's Palace to which Lords Lieutenant, Lord Mayors, Lord Provosts, Mayors and Provosts have been invited.

"At this meeting his Royal Highness will make proposals for a national thank-offering in celebration of the twenty-fifth anniversary of his Majesty's reign."

The meeting will be one of the Prince's first engagements after his return from his winter sports holiday in the Tyrol. He is expected back in London at the end of the month.

Details of the Prince's scheme are being kept a close secret. They will be revealed for the first time at the meeting when the Prince addresses his guests.

Daily Mirror

THE DAILY PICTURE NEWSPAPER WITH THE LARGEST NET SALE

Broadcasting - Page 20

MOTHER SEEKS BABES LOST 37 YEARS AGO

No. 9,742 Registered at the G.P.O as a Newspaper. MONDAY, FEBRUARY 18, 1935. One Penny

AIRMEN'S RACE WITH DEATH

Engine Stalls Over Sea

500-MILE DASH BACK TO LAND

BY A SPECIAL CORRESPONDENT
PORTE PRAIA (C. Verde Isles),
Sunday.

TWO airmen raced with Death for 500 miles across the South Atlantic to-day, to land on these islands.

They were M. Codos and M. Rossi, the French holders of the world's long-distance flight record.

They had left Marseilles to fly 5,543 miles non-stop to Rio de Janeiro (South America), and further if they could, in order to beat their previous "hop" record of 5,690 miles.

At 4.30 a.m. to-day they flew wide of Cape Verde Islands—all going well.

Then, three and a half hours later there came out of the blue that feared signal of the sea and air—SOS.

Five hundred miles over the ocean, away from the commercial routes, and with no ship at hand, the oil pressure of the engine had failed.

Five hundred miles ahead of them lay the lonely and desolate Rocky Isles; 500 miles behind, Verde Islands.

But the wind, also, was ahead—and the airmen dare not gamble. They turned back.

Safe—at Last

With the oil pressure failing more and more and the engine becoming hotter and hotter, they fought mile by mile to land.

As they flew their S O S went out unceasingly to ships and to land.

Luck was with them; at 1 p.m. they sighted the islands.

Even then they were not altogether safe. "We shall empty petrol before landing," they wirelessed; obviously in view of the chances of a crash (with their now badly working engine) and fire.

They landed safely at 1.30 p.m. completely exhausted.

But they had been unlucky in this respect—two-thirds of what would have been a record flight had been accomplished when Fate turned them back—into the face of death.

Here is the airmen's own story of their flight for life, an epic of the ether.

It begins about three and a half hours after they had left Cape Verde Islands on their left, and were about 500 miles between there and St. Paul's Rocks:—

8 a.m.—SOS—SOS: Eight latitude north; 27 longitude west (a position midway between Cape Verde Islands and the Rocks Islands).

8.30 : Oil pressure is weakening. We are turning back towards Cape Verde Islands. We may have to come down on the sea.

(Continued on page 3)

Maurice Rossi and Paul Codos (with cigarette), the famous French airmen.

No reply, and no wonder—flood water from the River Wharfe pouring in a raging torrent down a road at Otley (Yorks) and marooning a telephone kiosk, which was soon afterwards overturned and swept away. Other gale and flood pictures on page 14.

Sir Malcolm Campbell Robbed of Chance to Do 300 m.p.h.

CONDITION OF BEACH THE "WORST EVER" | **MUST BE SATISFIED WITH NEW RECORD**

BY TRANSATLANTIC TELEPHONE

JUST back from an inspection of Daytona Beach where he hopes to break his own world's land speed record of 271 m.p.h., Sir Malcolm Campbell talked to the *Daily Mirror* last night by transatlantic telephone of his chances of success.

To-night and to-morrow night will be the critical times for the attempt, for then the moon will be at the full and the tides should leave the beach clear.

Owing to bad weather the condition of the beach is very bad. "It is worse than I remember it ever being before," said Sir Malcolm.

His inspection of the beach, he confessed, had not encouraged him.

"It looks as though the attempt may not be possible for a few days.

When Sir Malcolm was asked whether, if conditions suddenly improved, he would take the risk of letting Bluebird "all out" without a second trial run, he said, "It all depends; I might."

"It certainly will not be possible to do as I hoped and go for 300 miles an hour. All I can expect is to put up the record substantially."

He explained that not only is the beach in bad condition but its effective length is shorter than previously.

"WHOOPEE" SEED AS PIGEON TRAP

Wood pigeons are the bete noir of East Riding farmers.

A big shoot was organised, and for six weeks hundreds of guns tried to wipe out the pest, but—

Either the farmers were poor shots or the pigeons took the pellets as bird seed, for the birds seemed to thrive!

Then came the big idea—in a letter from the Irish Free State. It was read at a Farmers' Union council of war at Bridlington :—

"Soak seeds in whisky. Place seeds around trees. Next morning collect inebriated pigeons and dispose at leisure."

Betty Gow Back to Lindberghs

NURSE TO BROTHER OF MURDERED BOY

Coming Home First

BETTY GOW, the Scottish nurse to the murdered Lindbergh baby, is expected to return to America in a few weeks to become the nurse of Colonel and Mrs. Lindbergh's son, Jon.

Before Betty left on the Berengaria for England after the trial of Bruno Hauptmann, she was given a farewell party, and it was at this party (states Reuter) that the host, Mr. J. Donald Grant, said that Miss Gow had told him that she had been definitely invited to work for the Lindberghs and had made up her mind to accept.

"She did not say just when she was coming back, but I gathered that she was returning in about a couple of months," Mr. Grant added.

Jon Lindbergh is now about eighteen months old.

Miss Betty Gow.

Betty Gow was one of the most important witnesses for the prosecution at the trial of Hauptmann, who was sentenced to death, but is appealing. Her home is in Glasgow, and she is going there after reaching England.

THE DAILY MIRROR, Thursday, February 21, 1935.

Daily Mirror
THE DAILY PICTURE NEWSPAPER WITH THE LARGEST NET SALE

Broadcasting - Page 20

PERFECT MAID GIVES NOTICE
—Page 2

No. 9,745 Registered at the G.P.O as a Newspaper.   THURSDAY, FEBRUARY 21, 1935   One Penny

POLICE NET AFTER £14,000 JEWEL HAUL

Motor Bandits Take Cases from Barrow

DAYLIGHT RAID

FROM OUR SPECIAL CORRESPONDENT
NORTHAMPTON, Wednesday Night.

SCOTLAND Yard and police forces throughout the country were searching to-night for motor bandits who stole jewels worth between £14,000 and £20,000 from a traveller's barrow in Northampton yesterday.

A gang who have carried out many large-scale robberies is believed to have been responsible.

With only five minutes' start on their pursuers when the robbery was discovered they had, up to a late hour, succeeded in evading the police net.

Three Number Plates

As the hunt went on elaborate preparations were revealed.

Three different registration numbers used on the motor-van in the raid were each found to be false.

The jewels, which belonged to Messrs. S. Blancknesse and Sons, of Birmingham, had been taken to Northampton by their traveller Mr. C. Hurden.

After a morning tour of shops with a porter and barrow, which he had engaged, Mr. Hurden went to an hotel for lunch. It was while there that the two cases of jewels were taken from the barrow.

Midnight Death Riddle in Park

Following the discovery in Whitworth Park, Manchester, of the body of an eleven-year-old boy shortly before midnight, detectives were making inquiries early to-day.

The boy was Stanhope Haig, of Crofton-street, Moss Side, Manchester.

Haig left his home shortly after five o'clock last night and it is understood that he had been seen playing in the park. As he did not return home at a reasonable time his family became alarmed, and one of his brothers got into touch with a park keeper and together they searched the park.

Alfred Sharman.

GALE PARALYSES THE MAJESTIC.—One of eight tugs that tried to help the Majestic when she sought to leave her berth at Southampton yesterday in the teeth of the south-wester. It was eventually decided not to risk towing the giant liner, which presents an area of three acres to the wind, out into deep water. Her departure is now fixed for eleven o'clock this morning.

Boy Missing 18 Months Is Safe

WALKED INTO POLICE STATION

EIGHTEEN months ago Alfred Sharman, a fifteen-year-old schoolboy, waved good-bye to his mother at their home in Pier-terrace, Kingston-by-Sea, Shoreham, rode off on his bicycle—and vanished.

Last night, the months of searching, the months of anxiety, ended. The boy walked into the police station at Brixton.

The boy's parents were at once informed. A policeman knocked at the door of their home. "Will you fetch your son from Brixton?" he said.

Reunion

Mr. Sharman left immediately for London and there was a dramatic meeting between father and son in the waiting room at the police station.

His mother's joy when she heard that her boy was coming back to her again was almost too great for her to bear. Tears came into her eyes. For a long time she was unable to express her happiness. Then she said, "I have always felt he was alive."

The boy stated last night that shortly after arriving in London he obtained a position in a shop in Peckham, where he had been working ever since.

It was on September 19, 1933, that the boy vanished. Everything possible was done to trace

MOTHER'S PREMONITION FULFILLED

him. His father spent all his savings trying to find him. Scotland Yard men gave their help, appeals were broadcast by the B.B.C. and by Continental stations.

The Salvation Army and the Seamen's Mission co-operated. Clairvoyants were consulted. It was all in vain. The months went by but no news came.

Then, a few days ago, his parents received two notes, stating that their boy was dead and had "been given a proper burial."

But even these messages could not shake the faith of Mrs. Sharman.

DAY OFF FOR THE JUBILEE

HERE'S good news for schoolchildren. They will get a day's holiday as part of the celebration of the King's Silver Jubilee.

"In many cases it will probably be found that the most convenient way of associating the schools with the celebrations would be by the grant of some extra holiday," announced the Board of Education last night.

"In the case of day schools, Monday, May 6, will generally be found the most suitable date; in the case of boarding schools arrangements will no doubt be made to suit each particular case."

£1,000,000 IN GALE HOLD-UP

Liner Could Not Dock to Fetch Bullion

BECAUSE a sixty mile an hour gale made it impossible for the French liner Ile de France to dock at Southampton last night, £1,000,000 in gold bullion had to be left in trucks on the quayside.

It had been arranged for the Ile de France to take the ninety boxes of gold to America.

These plans had to be suddenly altered on account of the weather, and instead of coming up to port the liner anchored in Cowes Roads to embark passengers there by tender before continuing her journey.

The ninety boxes of gold bullion remained in trucks on the quayside and it is anticipated that these will be shipped in the Cunard-White Star liner Majestic, which will sail this morning after being delayed twenty-four hours in port by the gale.

Hurricanes at sea and incessant rain in various parts of Britain have disorganised shipping and caused widespread flooding.

Liners due at Plymouth yesterday and to-day to land hundreds of passengers and mail have wirelessed that they are delayed by their battles with the storm.

If the gale persists, the 400 officers and men of the Essex Regiment, the first British troops to leave the Saar to-day, will have a rough crossing from Calais where they will embark.

60 ft. Cliff Moving

In Yorkshire the flooding of an aqueduct is believed to be the cause of a landslide which blocked the main London Midland and Scottish Railway line from the Midlands to Scotland with 500 tons of earth.

The landslide was between Dent and Ribblehead stations, and expresses were delayed.

Flood water from the moors has swamped a 60-ft. cliff and the entire mass is moving forward towards the railway. This section of the line may not be put into service for a few days.

(Continued on back page)

THE DAILY MIRROR, Friday, February 22, 1935

Daily Mirror

THE DAILY PICTURE NEWSPAPER WITH THE LARGEST NET SALE

Broadcasting · Page 16

SCHUSCHNIGG: AMAZING PARIS PRECAUTIONS —Page 3

No. 9,746 Registered at the G.P.O. as a Newspaper. FRIDAY, FEBRUARY 22, 1935. One Penny

MYSTERY MOTIVE OF GIRLS' AIR DEATH
Why Did Sisters Leap 6,000 ft. from 'Plane?

Flying-Officer Forbes and (right) Flight-Lieutenant Beatty killed in the recent British flying-boat disaster in Sicily, who were friends of the dead girls.

STORY OF ROMANCE WITH VICTIMS OF R.A.F. TRAGEDY DENIED

THE two sisters were friends of the Crown Princess of Italy, Princess Marie Jose, and once Elizabeth told the Princess's fortune by cards.

At the time the Princess was worried because her marriage had been childless, but Elizabeth told her she would have a girl and then a boy. In 1934 a daughter was born.

Strange Secret of Two Letters

What secret lies behind the deaths of two beautiful young sisters who, hand-in-hand, leapt to death from a British air liner 6,000ft. over Upminster (Essex) yesterday?

THE SISTERS WERE JANE DU BOIS, AGED TWENTY, AND ELIZABETH DU BOIS, AGED TWENTY-THREE, DAUGHTERS OF THE U.S. CONSUL-GENERAL IN NAPLES.

It was reported in Paris newspapers yesterday that they were engaged to Flying-Officer Forbes and Flight-Lieutenant H. L. Beatty, step-brother of Earl Beatty, who were among the nine victims of the R.A.F. flying-boat disaster in Messina.

This, however, could not have been true in the case of Flying-Officer Forbes, who at the time of his death was engaged to Miss Kathleen Blakely, of Bedford, while inquiries among relatives of Flight-Lieutenant Beatty last night failed to disclose any such engagement. His mother stated, however, that in his last letter home Flight-Lieutenant Beatty mentioned that he had met the two girls.

Two letters found in the plane addressed to the girls' parents will be read at the inquest on Monday.

"TWO HAPPY, VIVACIOUS GIRLS"

BY A SPECIAL CORRESPONDENT

"They were both young, vivacious girls, happy in their home. I cannot understand why they should do it, a friend of the dead girls told me last night.

"There seems no doubt that it was suicide and yet they were the last people you would expect to do such a thing."

Why did they do it, these two beautiful, accomplished society girls?

They came to England on Tuesday from Paris. Friends in the French capital say that they seemed happy when they left.

In London they occupied a costly suite in the Ritz Hotel. They went about on pleasure seemingly normal. On Wednesday night they dined together and went to a theatre.

Mystified Friends

They said a smiling good-bye to the hotel door porter yesterday morning.

Yet they had even then deliberately booked all the seats in a six-seater 'plane in order to be alone in the air.

Had planned how they would draw the curtains across the cockpit window so that the pilot could not watch them.

Had written farewell letters to their parents to leave in the 'plane before they jumped to death.

WHY? In Naples, in Paris, and in London people who knew and met them can find no satisfactory answer.

Before they had left Naples for a holiday they had become friends with Flying-Officer J. Forbes and Flight-Lieutenant H. C. Beatty, two of the crew of the R.A.F. flying-boat which crashed at Messina.

Their parents had entertained the officers; the girls had been in their company nearly every day during the flying-boat's enforced stay.

The night before the Messina crash the officers and the dead girls had had a farewell dinner. It was stated in Naples that they had become engaged... Then next day the two officers were dead.

I am able to state that in the case of Flying-Officer Forbes, at any rate, no such romance has existed. The officer was engaged to Miss Kathleen Blakely, whose parents live in Park-avenue, Bedford. Mr. Blakely told me last night: "My daughter and Mr. Forbes intended to get married on his return from Singapore some time in April or May next."

(Continued on page 3)

Sacha Guitry with his bride, Mlle. Jacqueline Delubac.

SACHA GUITRY'S BIRTHDAY WEDDING

Married Actress Who Has Appeared in His Plays

FROM OUR OWN CORRESPONDENT
PARIS, Thursday.

THE famous French comedy-writer, M. Sacha Guitry, whose marriage with the beautiful actress Mlle. Yvonne Printemps was dissolved last November, gave himself a birthday present to celebrate his fiftieth birthday to-day.

He married Mlle. Jacqueline Delubac, who has played in a number of his pieces. The wedding was performed here. It is understood that the bride is only twenty-five years of age.

M. Guitry's previous wife was well known on the London stage, where they had played together.

MANY EAGER TO ENGAGE 'MODEL MAID'

Dozens of Housewives Ring Up "Daily Mirror"

MISS Edith Saville, "model" housemaid and central figure in the "enticement" action, was the most sought-after young woman in the country yesterday.

Dozens of eager housewives telephoned to the "Daily Mirror" office during the day, offering substantial wages and a good home to this domestic paragon.

Mr. Henry Pinder-Brown, the solicitor who acted for Mr. H. M. Stretch, of Cookham Dean, the successful plaintiff in the action, said to the Daily Mirror:—

"It is hoped to arrange for Miss Saville to go to the seaside. She is in need of a complete rest and change of surroundings before she undertakes another job.

"Actually, she has already received a number of good offers, and doubtless she will accept one of these after her holiday."

On inquiry at the house of Mr. A. F. Sim, defendant in the case, whither Miss Saville returned on Wednesday night after the verdict, it was stated that no information concerning her whereabouts could be given.

Miss Kathleen Blakely.

26

Daily Mirror

THE DAILY PICTURE NEWSPAPER WITH THE LARGEST NET SALE

LL. G.'s NEW DEAL: CABINET INVITATION —Page 3

No. 9,753 — SATURDAY, MARCH 2, 1935 — One Penny

THE PRINCE'S OWN JUBILEE PLAN

National Campaign to Give Youth New Opportunities

THANKS FUND OPENED

THE Prince of Wales has planned a "permanent living memorial and national thank-offering" for the Royal Jubilee.

It will be the King George's Jubilee Trust, a nation-wide fund launched in the cause of Youth, a cause, as the Prince said yesterday, in which the King and all his subjects are alike interested.

The trust will not inaugurate any new juvenile organisations. It will extend the work of the existing and approved voluntary movements, increasing their facilities for physical recreation and the training of their leaders, providing for the cultivation of abilities, for the extension of camping and other health-giving holidays.

Those were some suggestions made by the Prince yesterday, when he revealed his plan at a meeting summoned by him at St. James's Palace and attended by the Lord-Lieutenants, Lord Mayors and Lord Provosts, Mayors and Provosts of England, Scotland, Wales and Northern Ireland.

"For," said the Prince, "every hope that we have for the future of our people must be bound up with our ambition for the next generation and its successors."

The Three Gifts

At present it would be impossible to decide in detail how the fund should be used, and the Prince said he proposed later on to form a committee.

"But," said the Prince, "youth, as I see it, needs three things to fit it for life. It needs discipline; it needs friends; and it needs opportunity.

"These three gifts are in our power. They will help youth itself to master the means of making life worth while."

"Millions of people in this country," said the Prince, "wish to express to the King their deep thankfulness for his reign over us during the past twenty-five years.

"But a year—even a Jubilee year—is soon gone and very many people, I am sure, feel that 1935 should not be allowed to pass without leaving some living and permanent memorial among us.

"I have ascertained that nothing else would give the King and Queen such pleasure as the devotion of a national thank-offering to the welfare of the younger generation," he said.

The Prince said he would invite subscriptions to be sent to him at St. James's, but he wanted to make it easy for all who wished to do so to contribute—pennies as well as pounds.

(Continued on page 3)

The Queen of the Belgians.

ROYAL VISIT SECRECY

King and Queen of the Belgians Here

THE King and Queen of the Belgians arrived at Dover last night by Channel boat from Ostend.

After coming ashore with other passengers they entered, with their personal attendants, two waiting motor-cars and drove away to an undisclosed destination.

It is understood that the King and Queen went to London to stay with friends, but late last night the names of their hosts were not known.

Their arrival was a complete surprise Belgian Embassy officials had no knowledge of the visit. Not even the Belgian Consul at Dover had been informed.

First Visit as King

This is the first visit to England of the King of the Belgians since his coronation at Brussels on February 23 last year.

It was learned, however, at Compton Place, Eastbourne, where the King and Queen are staying, that nothing was known of the visit.

Hotel proprietors at Eastbourne also stated that they knew nothing of the visit.

THE HUMAN BIRD WITH HIS WINGS

Dædalus up to date, but, unlike the Athenian bird-man, Clem Sohn, of Michigan, is no myth. With these home-made wings and "tail" of balloon fabric, he dropped from an aeroplane 12,000ft. over Daytona Beach on Thursday, and not only flew, but thrice looped the loop before finally coming down by parachute.

What Now, Lawrence of Arabia?

AIRCRAFTMAN SHAW HAS GONE TOO | SAYS HE HAS DONE WITH THE R.A.F.

BY A SPECIAL CORRESPONDENT

Here's a new mystery of Lawrence of Arabia. Or is it a riddle of Aircraftman Shaw? Who knows? Only Lawrence of Arabia and Aircraftman Shaw—and neither will tell.

THESE facts, as the police say, are known.

A few years ago the romantic Lawrence of Arabia vanished. And there in his place, in oily overalls, stood Aircraftman Shaw.

The aircraftman did special duty for the R.A.F. He was posted to Bridlington, working on bombing targets.

A couple of days ago Aircraftman Shaw put on his "civvies," told his landlady he was leaving the R.A.F., got on his motor-cycle, and set off in the direction of Dorset. And near Moreton, in Dorset, is his home.

Last night a man rode up to the cottage on a motor-cycle. He looked like Aircraftman Shaw, and he looked like Lawrence of Arabia.

He denied being either. Indeed, he refused to give his name.

He did admit coming from Bridlington, but to all other questions his simple reply was: "Nothing to say."

He hid his face when a flash lamp was shone on him.

"It is 10.45," he said. "You're late for an interview." But the time, I told him, was 9.30 p.m. "Then I must be fast," he said. "I can't tell . . . My future? I cannot tell you."

Mr. Shaw is referred to in the village as the Uncrowned King of the Arabs

Lovers Leap to Death from 'Plane

WOMAN LEADS IN "JOY RIDE" TRAGEDY

FROM OUR OWN CORRESPONDENT
BASLE, Switzerland.

TWO lovers jumped to death out of an aeroplane near Basle late this afternoon. The circumstances are similar to those in the case of the sisters who fell to death from an aeroplane flying over England a few days ago.

The victims were a woman and a man teacher. They took an aeroplane at Basle for a "joy ride" over the city.

Suddenly the woman opened the door of the cabin and jumped out. The teacher followed her immediately.

Money Troubles

Everything happened so quickly that the pilot was unable to prevent them falling. The teacher was named Grieder and the woman was Miss Jory They fell in the village of Lausen.

Before going up in the aeroplane both were seen in the restaurant adjoining the aerodrome. They seemed to be in good spirits.

It is understood that the teacher was in financial difficulties.

THE DAILY MIRROR, Thursday, March 7, 1935.

Daily Mirror

THE DAILY PICTURE NEWSPAPER WITH THE LARGEST NET SALE

Broadcasting - Page 20

BLOW TO BUDGET HOPES —Page 4

No. 9,757 Registered at the G.P.O. as a Newspaper.   THURSDAY, MARCH 7, 1935   One Penny

DUEL WATCHED FROM HOUSETOPS

Hundreds See Famous Paris Lawyer Wounded

POLICE STEP IN—TOO LATE

FROM OUR SPECIAL CORRESPONDENT

PARIS, Wednesday.

WHILE hundreds watched from the windows and roofs of houses near, two men stood in the middle of a Paris football ground to-day with pistols in their hands ready to fight a duel.

A signal. Two shots that sounded like one, and the right arm of one of the duellists fell limp against his side.

He was taken to hospital. And a few minutes later the Police Commissioner dashed up in a car to forbid the fight that was over. The duellists, who stood 35ft. apart, were:—

| M. Cesar Campinchi, a famous French lawyer and a Corsican deputy in the Chamber. | M. Horace de Carbuccia, director of the weekly "Gringoire." Also a Corsican deputy. |

The Corsican blood of M. Campinchi boiled when he read in "Gringoire" some comments written by M. de Carbuccia.

He challenged him to fight, but the witnesses decided that the affair was not serious enough to necessitate a duel.

But you can't stop two Corsicans when their vendetta spirit is roused.

So rather than have them taking pot-shots at each other it was decided to stage the duel at the Parc des Princes, a large football stadium in Paris.

Witnesses Took No Chances

The two men were on the scene early, both clad in black, as is the custom for affairs of honour.

They walked to the pitch. Their witnesses took charge, did a lot of talking and ground measuring.

Two walking-sticks were stuck into the ground and the duellists took up their positions.

While the pistols were being loaded they took off their overcoats and pulled up the lapels of their jackets to make the target less visible.

The pistols were then handed to M. Campinchi and M. de Carbuccia—and the witnesses took care to get well out of the line of fire.

The umpire gave his signal. In a split second the duel was over.

The doctor came running on to the pitch to aid M. Campinchi. The triumphant M. de Carbuccia waited unperturbed.

The wound was rather a bad one, and before Campinchi was taken to hospital the witnesses tried to get the two duellists to shake hands. They refused and walked off—enemies still.

ANOTHER STRING TO HIS BOW

Heifetz May Give Up Violin for Ping-Pong!

MR. Jascha Heifetz, the violinist of the wizard fingering, arrived in London last evening with another string to his bow.

A reputation for ping-pong.

"In fact," he said, "I may give up violin playing for ping-pong. I have just had two new rackets given to me and I love the game. My training is running from the violin to ping-pong."

PRODIGY OF THE SCREEN.—Freddie Bartholomew, the ten-year-old London boy, as David Copperfield, with W. C. Fields as Mr. Micawber, in a scene from the new Dickens film in which the boy reveals himself as a prodigy of the screen. See page 2.

OUR BOY SOLDIERS

ETON is making quite sure that the battle-winning reputation of its playing fields will not be damaged—according to the *Angriff*, official Nazi paper.

The newspaper presents to its readers (says Reuter) this picture of British life:—

Cinema audiences are always seeing war-like parades of boys;
Generals review big march past of troops at Eton;
Government subsidises University chairs for "Brass-Hat" lecturers (lectures "illustrated" by tanks, machine-guns and aeroplanes).

Germany, the writer bewails, is different. It has not the means for such training.

FOUR DIE IN SMASH

BORDEAUX, Wednesday.

Four people were killed and twelve injured to-night when the Bordeaux express to Libourne was derailed between Ambarès and St. Loubès.—Exchange.

WHAT FUN TO MAKE THEM ALL POP!

A strong temptation seems to have seized this otherwise innocent child, to judge by the sly impishness of its smile. Ah, dear me! If only it had a pin!

HE'S AS STRONG AS SIXTEEN MEN

Training on a diet of electric light bulbs. Samuel Bessford, an unemployed miner, demonstrated his strength in Sunderland yesterday. He:

Held on his head a brick while it was smashed with a 4lb. hammer;
Made paper chains of an iron bar 15in. long and 1¼in. thick;
Bent a thinner bar between his teeth and another over his head; and
With a rope noosed round his neck defied the efforts of sixteen men (eight aside) to throttle him!

Aged 75—and Lost in London

COULD NOT SPEAK WORD OF ENGLISH | **FOUND SAFE—BUT WITHOUT BOOTS**

LONDON, it seemed, had swallowed up seventy-five-year-old Rowland Humphreys, a Welsh farmer, who came to the City to attend the wedding of his landlord, Sir Michael Duff-Assheton-Smith.

One minute he was with his friends in the Strand. The next he had "vanished." Scotland Yard were informed.

Then late last night a police-constable saw him in Charlotte-place, Tottenham Court-road, his attention being attracted to the old man because he was not wearing boots.

Went Sightseeing

And Humphreys was handed over to the care of friends of the party who had remained behind in London to look for him.

The rest of the party travelled back to Wales early yesterday.

Before he left his village home his wife, who is seventy-three, warned Humphreys to "mind the traffic," and stitched his name and address in his overcoat and hat.

This old farmer speaks only Welsh, so could not ask his way, and he has never been in London before. When he disappeared he had only a few shillings in his possession.

Mr. Humphreys is a tenant farmer on Sir Michael Duff-Assheton-Smith's estate at Bangor. He was one of the twenty-five tenants and employees invited by Sir Michael to the wedding.

"He arrived in London on Monday evening, and before the wedding on Tuesday morning set out with two friends on a sight-seeing tour," Mr. Hardy, Sir Michael's agent, told the *Daily Mirror* last night.

"After several hours they returned to the Strand, where their hotel is. They were then standing outside Africa House.

"The two others crossed the road to the hotel and, reaching the other side, saw Humphreys still on the opposite pavement.

"One of them re-crossed the road, but by the time he had done so, Humphreys had disappeared."

NEW EPSTEIN STORM

Yesterday the "Daily Mirror" stated its intention not to reproduce a photograph of Mr. Jacob Epstein's new statue "Behold the Man."

Mr. Epstein, we declared, had made an error in associating such a grotesque symbol with Christ.

Yesterday brought a large volume of support for the "Daily Mirror's" attitude. Messages are on page 5.

28

THE DAILY MIRROR, Friday, March 8, 1935.

Broadcasting - Page 22

Daily Mirror
THE DAILY PICTURE NEWSPAPER WITH THE LARGEST NET SALE

FIRE CONSPIRACY SENTENCES —Page 5

No. 9,758 Registered at the G.P.O. as a Newspaper.   FRIDAY, MARCH 8, 1935   One Penny

CAMPBELL'S WORLD RECORDS
276 Miles an Hour—Then Played Golf

Sir Malcolm Campbell's Bluebird hurtling over the sands at Daytona Beach with Sir Malcolm (also portrait inset) at the wheel.

M.P. and Epstein Statue

DEMAND FOR REMOVAL —"BLASPHEMOUS"

Mr. Jacob Epstein's statue, "Behold the Man," is to be the subject of a question in Parliament.

Sir Cooper Rawson, Conservative M.P. for Brighton, is to ask the Home Secretary on Monday:—

"Whether in view of the resentment aroused among people of different religious denominations by the present exhibition in London of a statue which offends against the public decency he will, in exercise of his powers to prevent blasphemous or obscene exhibitions, instruct the police to remove or confiscate the statue in question, or what other steps he will take to guard against any breach of the peace which might be provoked by this spectacle."

"A Grave Affront"

"I consider that this statue is too utterly repulsive for words," said Sir Cooper Rawson to the Daily Mirror last night. "That is why I have put down my question.

"It is bound to be a grave affront to thousands of decent Christian people throughout the country, and it will do nothing to increase Britain's prestige in art.

"The photographs which have been published are a sufficient indication of the unpleasantness of this subject.

"And in this connection I should like to congratulate the Daily Mirror most heartily for its courageous refusal to inflict this monstrosity on its readers."

When a reporter informed Mr. Epstein of Sir Cooper Rawson's pending question, the sculptor said: "What about Hitler and Goering? When are they to be asked for their views on the statue? That is all I want to say."

(See page 6 for letters of protest against the sculpture.)

£ IS "UNSHAKEN"

"THE internal value of the pound is unshaken," Mr. Neville Chamberlain told the House of Commons last night. "There is absolutely nothing in the position which need give us in this country a moment's uneasiness."

Referring to the fluctuating character of gold, he said: "It is clearly impossible for us in such circumstances to attempt to stabilise our currency on gold again.

"While ultimately I see no better international standard than gold, and while some day I think that we and other countries may go back to that standard, I am not prepared to take any steps to put this country back until I can see conditions so favourable that, having once gone back to gold, we can be pretty certain we can remain there."

WOMEN SCOOP UP SAND FROM TRACK AS SOUVENIR

Sir Malcolm Campbell smashed his world land speed record of 272.108 m.p.h. (set up in February, 1933) by establishing an average speed of 276.816 m.p.h. over the measured mile at Daytona yesterday. Then, disappointed that he hadn't gone even faster, he went off to play golf!

NEW world records for the flying start kilometre, five kilometres and five miles were set up in the giant Bluebird.

THE MAN

Sir Malcolm Campbell, fifty, born Chistlehurst, Kent, educated at Uppingham.

Worked in City but found time to build his own 'plane in 1909. It flew a few feet.

Joined Royal Flying Corps. After the war started gambling with death on record breaking car runs.

Set up records at Fanoe, Pendine and Daytona. Knighted in 1931.

Once fined for riding a bicycle furiously.

These were Sir Malcolm's times and speeds over the measured mile yesterday:

	Time.	Speed.
Southward	13.20s.	272.727 m.p.h.
Northward	12.81s.	281.030 m.p.h.

His speeds over the other distances were:—

Flying kilometre	276.160 m.p.h.
Five kilometres	268.474 m.p.h.
Five miles	251.396 m.p.h.

Before he set out on his record-breaking run, Sir Malcolm told officials, "This is just a test," but the officials have got to know what he means by "test," and there was a general feeling that he would go for the record.

Fifty thousand people gathered on the beach. For miles around the roads were blocked with cars.

Below, Lady Campbell in a special interview with the Daily Mirror over the transatlantic telephone, tells how women collected sand from the beach over which the Bluebird had thundered.

THE CAR

The Bluebird was transformed after Sir Malcolm's record in 1933. Has twelve-cylinder Rolls-Royce Schneider Trophy engine, developing 2,500 brake horse power. Squat and wide in appearance at first glance, but perfectly streamlined. Overall length of body, 28½ feet. Petrol consumption is 2.9 gallons a minute.

Top gear is not engaged until the car has reached a speed of 200 m.p.h.

"I FELT ALL WOULD BE WELL"

By LADY CAMPBELL

THE excitement is bewildering: thousands of people are still cheering madly; the beach is packed with them. I can't get anywhere near my husband.

Women are collecting handfuls of the sand the Bluebird passed over. They say it is a miracle. That is all they seem capable of saying. "It's a miracle; it's a miracle!" And when they stop saying that it is only to join in the roaring cheers.

I've never seen such excitement. And yet, somehow, I am not feeling a little bit like that. I am glad it is over, but I don't feel it strongly enough to say I don't want another experience like it.

He may go out again. I don't know. But it is quite possible, and I am not frightened. As soon as he gets rid of those photographers he is going off to play nine holes of golf.

He decided to do that before the run, and he's just told me he means to get those nine holes in. He looks fit for eighteen.

(Continued on page 3)

HE WAS MAGNIFICENT!

This is what Jean Campbell, Sir Malcolm's eleven-year-old daughter who accompanied her father and mother to Daytona, told the "Daily Mirror" about her biggest thrill.

"Oh, I can't tell you how much I was thrilled. It was beautiful and I wasn't a bit frightened. I saw Daddy all the time and he was grand; he was magnificent. I am as proud as proud can be of Daddy, but they won't let me go to him yet. I want to ever so much. I want to kiss him and tell him I am proud of him."

VISIT OF NAZI MYSTERY MAN

With Tidings of Hitler's Cold?

HERR von Ribbentrop, Hitler's personal representative and Nazi Mystery Man, is coming to London (says an Exchange message from Berlin).

The Daily Mirror understands that he will doubtless:—

Clear up any misunderstandings aroused by Mr MacDonald's arms warning;

Smooth the way for Sir John Simon's postponed visit to Berlin;

Bring tidings of Hitler's cold—the official reason for the delay in the Anglo-German talks.

No definite meetings have yet been fixed, but Herr von Ribbentrop is expected to seek an early opportunity of calling at the Foreign Office and possibly at 10, Downing-street.

Meanwhile, it was announced in the House of Commons yesterday that Mr. Anthony Eden, Lord Privy Seal, is to pay official visits to Moscow and Poland. He will be the first British Minister to visit Moscow since 1917.

POPE REFUSES PRINCESS'S PLEA

Paris, Thursday.

Princess Charlotte of Monaco will be unable to re-marry as the Pope has declined to grant the annulment of her marriage with Prince Pierre de Polignac, from whom she obtained a divorce about two years ago.

Prince Louis of Monaco, her father, was so anxious to obtain her freedom that he made a special journey to Rome about a month ago, but in vain, for the Papal authority was not forthcoming.

It will be recalled that Princess Charlotte renounced all her rights to the throne of Monaco in favour of her children at the time that her divorce was granted.—Reuter.

THE DAILY MIRROR, Friday, March 15, 1935.

Broadcasting - Page 22

Daily Mirror
THE DAILY PICTURE NEWSPAPER WITH THE LARGEST NET SALE

IF I WERE DICTATOR:
By MAUDE ROYDEN
—Page 12

No. 9,764 Registered at the G.P.O. as a Newspaper.   FRIDAY, MARCH 15, 1935   One Penny

ALL GERMANY IN NEW AIR FORCE
Men and Women to Drill by Law

NATION'S RING OF AERODROMES

Every man and woman in Germany is to be rigorously drilled in air raid defence next month.

THIS is part of Herr Hitler's gigantic plan to make Germany impregnable to air attack.

Behind it there is already starting into being the greatest peace-time operation in history to guard a nation.

Only a few days ago General Goering, the Prussian Premier and German Minister of Air, announced the establishment, from April 1 of a vast air force. Yesterday Reuter telegrams from Berlin described in detail plans of how the force will be founded and worked. They include:—

(1) The provision of an adequately trained Air Defence Force;

(2) The protection of the civil population (more than 66,000,000) by rigorously drilling every member of the public in air defence.

Great Aerodromes

Already, great new barracks and aerodromes are springing from the ground near the largest towns to accommodate the newly-formed squadrons of the flying corps.

More than a dozen such bases are being built round Berlin alone, at a distance of about sixty miles from the city, forming a formidable ring of defences for the heart of the nation.

In the north (on the Baltic coast) seaplane bases are also being built. An important one is near Rostock, which is also near the Heinkel Works, at present the centre of great activity

Adequate provision for the storage of ammunition and huge quantities of petrol is made by the building of underground cellars made of concrete and invisible from above.

The Junker aircraft works at Dessau are working at full pressure.

Meanwhile, measures for the protection of civilians are being hurried forward. A new "air protection" law is now being prepared by the Air Ministry by which it will be possible to order citizens to take part in the exercises which are being arranged for their benefit.

Detailed air-protection instructions to all citizens are being given in the newspapers.

"Talkie" lectures are compulsory features of cinema programmes.

Mrs. Ursula Eileen Lloyd, described as a £100,000 heiress, who sued Mr. Reginald Dixon Weatherell (left), a speedboat expert, in the King's Bench Division yesterday claiming a declaration that a letter in the form of an agreement was not binding upon her. It is alleged that the letter was obtained from her by fraud. See story on page 5.

SIR J. SIMON HAD STAGE AMBITION

"I have always had a hankering wish to be an actor," declared Sir John Simon, the Foreign Secretary, when he paid a tribute yesterday to Sir Nigel Playfair at the memorial exhibition of Sir Nigel's work in London.

Gust of Flame in Man's Face

TWO BURNED BY GAS EXPLOSION

TWO men were badly burned last night by a gas explosion in the third floor of Wren House, Tatchbrook Estate, Lupus-street, S.W.

They were Arthur Ware, thirty-two, a gasfitter, and John Mahoney, twenty-nine, a furniture remover. Both are in Westminster Hospital.

The caretaker of the flats told the Daily Mirror last night that a gas-meter was being adjusted outside the flat when there was a terrific explosion.

Vivid flames shot into Ware's face, while Mahoney, who was carrying furniture into the flat, was also caught by the flame. Both were burned about the head and neck.

No damage was done to the flat.

"QUINS" GUARDIANS

TORONTO, Thursday.

THE guardianship of Toronto's quintuplets is to be placed in the hands of three men—their father, Mr. Oliva Dionne, Dr. Dafoe, their doctor, and the Ontario Minister of Public Welfare as special guardian.

This pronouncement was made in the Legislature to-day by the Minister of Welfare in connection with the Government's Bill to make the babies "Wards of the King."—Reuter.

DICK AND THE MERMAID at the "adventure in fairyland" children's party held at Claridge's yesterday, in aid of the Clapham-road Home for Mothers and Babies.

DEFENDING BRITAIN AGAINST ATTACK

No more effective defence for Britain could be devised against an attack from Germany than a strong force of aircraft carriers under the protection of a dominant Navy, said Mr. Amery, speaking in the Commons last night on the naval estimates.

Pleading for greater development of the Naval Air Arm, he said air power would enable the Navy to fight hundreds of miles inland instead of being confined to bombardments of coastlines.

Sir Bolton Eyres-Monsell's speech—page 9.

NO CHANGE AT NORWOOD

Only Fifty-Three per Cent. of the Electorate Poll

THE result of the Norwood by-election was announced early this morning:—

Mr. Duncan Sandys (Nat. Con.) .. 16,147
Mrs. Barbara Ayrton Gould (Soc.) 12,799
Mr. Richard Findlay (Ind. Con.) .. 2,698
    Majority 3,348.   No change.

Mr. Findlay loses his deposit.

Fifty-three per cent. of an electorate of 59,390 voted.

Mr. Sandys, interviewed after the result, said:—"I am glad that in view of the great issues which were at stake, between the National Government, on the one hand, and Socialism, on the other, that this fight has proved, after all, a straight fight between myself and the Socialist candidate."

He has received the following telegram from the Prime Minister: Heartiest congratulations on your success against such heavy odds.

A cordon of police escorted Mr. Sandys from the counting hall to his car. A crowd greeted him with a mixture of booing and cheers.

The figures at the General Election in 1931 were:—

Sir Walter Greaves-Lord (Con.) 30,851; Mrs. A. J. Anstey (Soc.) 7,217. Majority 23,634.

TELLING ITS OWN STORY.—The outstretched arm of this dummy Berlin policeman dressed in a gas-proof mask and suit, indicates one of the bureaus of the Reich's Air Protection Association, where information can be obtained regarding the darkening of Berlin for two hours on Tuesday night for air raid drill.

AIR AID FOR WOMAN IN WILDS

Taken Ill on Lone Exploration

AN R.A.F. 'plane with a doctor aboard left Aden yesterday on a 300-mile dash to take aid to Freya Madelaine Stark, one of the world's most daring young women explorers, who (states Reuter) is lying seriously ill at Shibam, Hadramaut, Arabia.

Miss Stark, who was educated in London, has had adventure after adventure.

Last year she received the Burton Memorial Medal for her exploration work in Persia.

She was the first woman ever to win this award.

In Luristan she discovered the last stronghold of the Assassins, a Mahomedan sect whose rulers killed by dagger and poison centuries before the Crusades.

Yet into all her adventures she goes unarmed.

She said once, "I felt safer among the tribesmen of Luristan than I do in the streets of London.

"I used to walk ahead of my miserable guide, because even a bandit would stop to ask questions before shooting when he saw a European woman strolling on alone, hatless."

Miss Freya Stark

THE DAILY MIRROR, Wednesday, March 20, 1935.

Daily Mirror

THE DAILY PICTURE NEWSPAPER WITH THE LARGEST NET SALE

Broadcasting - Page 20

"THE BORGIA RING" —Page 19

No. 9,768 Registered at the G.P.O. as a Newspaper. WEDNESDAY, MARCH 20, 1935 One Penny

LEGLESS BODY FOUND IN CANAL

'Yard's' Midnight Conference

SPILSBURY CALLED IN—'LEGS' MYSTERY LINK?

FROM OUR SPECIAL CORRESPONDENT

BRENTFORD (Middlesex), Wednesday morning.

THE legless and headless body of a man was recovered from the Grand Junction Canal, near the Great Western Dock, here, late last night.

Detectives were rushed to the spot to try to ascertain if this latest find is associated with the "legs-in-the-train" riddle which has puzzled them for three weeks.

They had to bear in mind that Brentford lies three miles from Hounslow, the starting point of the train in which the severed legs were found. It was that train's second stopping place.

For several hours after the discovery the torso lay as it was found—in a grey flannel shirt and enclosed in a sack—on the towpath. By the light of a torch and a hurricane lamp Chief-Inspector Donaldson, responsible for the "legs" investigations, made an examination.

Then the body was taken to Brentford Mortuary while police conferences went on until early to-day.

Sir Bernard Spilsbury.

Sir Bernard Spilsbury is to make an examination.

People who saw the discovery declare that there were several wounds on the left breast. The body had been in the water for some time.

It was now possible that Scotland Yard, reluctant to make a public appeal for information in the absence of definite clues to the "legs" mystery, may now decide to "come into the open."

Children playing on the towpath made the discovery.

One of them, twelve-year-old Fred Smitherman, of Glenhurst-road, Brentford, said to me: "We stopped to watch an animal—it was a rat or mole—which was swimming in the water.

"Just then a barge passed. It stirred up the water, and we saw something floating.

"It came near to the side, and we saw that it was a sack. We were able to hook it out with sticks and lift it to the side of the canal. Then we found a body was inside.

"I was frightened, and ran for a policeman."

Mr. Frank Heath, of West End-road, Southall, who was working on the railway, took up the story.

"I heard shouts," he said, "and on looking over the embankment saw a policeman climbing the slope leading to the towing-path.

"There were four boys on the towing path and half in the water was a large sack with one end open.

"I hurried down and joined the policeman and saw that inside the sack was the trunk of a man.

"I could see that the head had been severed. The arms had been cut off at the elbow.

"From the shape of the body the legs must have been severed at the thigh."

The body suggests a powerfully-built man of small stature.

(Continued on Back Page)

GRACIE ALSO WISHES TO MEET LORD HEWART

THE wish of Lord Hewart, Lord Chief Justice, to meet Miss Gracie Fields may be granted. The comedienne yesterday invited him and Lady Hewart to watch her at work on her latest film.

She wrote to Lord Hewart, following his disclosure at a London concert the previous night that he had "twice been lured to London by the representation that I should meet Miss Fields."

The sack lying on the towpath beside the hurricane lamp by the light of which Chief-Inspector Donaldson made a quick examination.

The three boys who found in the canal the sack containing the body: Ronald Newman (tallest) between John Deane (cap) and Fred Smitherman.

MAN ATTACKED IN THE STREET

Found by Constable—Story of Robbery

DETECTIVES were inquiring early to-day into an alleged assault and robbery of a man in Braithwaite-place, Paddington, last night.

A police officer found Benjamin Fisher, of Walford-road, Stoke Newington, lying injured on the ground.

Fisher said that five people had been concerned in an affray and he was left injured in the road. He complained that he had been robbed of £6.

He was taken to St. Mary's Hospital, but was allowed to go home after treatment

FOR SUNDAY GOLF

ALL-DAY golf on Sundays on their courses was approved by 67 votes to 21 by the L.C.C. last night.

Beacon the King Will Light

HYDE PARK "SIGNAL"

THE King, it was learned last night, will light a huge wooden beacon, built by Boy Scouts in Hyde Park on Jubilee night at 9.55, Monday, May 6.

The beacon, 20ft. high, will act as a signal fire for the lighting of the Boy Scouts' chain of about 700 beacons all over the country at ten o'clock.

"It has been arranged that the King should press a button at Buckingham Palace and by means of an electric circuit set the beacon afire," said Admiral E. M. Phillpotts, County Commissioner for London of the Boy Scouts' Association.

While the King and Queen were walking on the front at Eastbourne yesterday they were caught in a dense sea mist which suddenly enveloped the town. They immediately returned to their car.

4-POWER TALKS AT WHITEHALL

Ambassadors of 3 Nations Visit Foreign Office

Ambassadors of three foreign Powers—France, Italy and Russia—had important conferences with Sir John Simon and Mr. Anthony Eden at Whitehall yesterday.

It was an indication that the statesmen of Europe are anxious to woo Britain's support and to know what proposals will be made by Sir John and Mr. Eden when they visit Hitler in Berlin.

These were the moves at the British Foreign Office yesterday:—

M. Corbin, French Ambassador in London, had two talks with Sir John.

SIBERIA FOR 41 PRINCES

Among 1,074 Accused by the Soviet

SCORES of members of the old Russian aristocracy have been arrested by the Soviet in Leningrad — some of them charged with counter-revolutionary activities on behalf of foreign Powers.

The list of 1,074 arrested includes:
- 41 Princes
- 33 Counts.
- 76 Barons.
- 142 Former Tsarist statesmen.
- 122 Former capitalists.
- 457 Ex-generals and high officers of the old Imperial Army.
- 113 Ex-gendarmes and secret service officials.

Some of those arrested, states the Exchange, are accused of violation of the passport system. Those charged as counter-revolutionaries will be handed over for trial, and the entire group of 1,074 will be exiled to Siberia.

Signor Grandi, Italian Ambassador, interviewed Sir John, and the Soviet Ambassador, M. Maisky, visited Mr. Eden.

Effects of the German announcement of the introduction of conscription were discussed by the Lord Privy Seal and M. Maisky, as well as the prospects of Mr. Eden's visit to Moscow, following the Berlin conversations.

France is annoyed that the British Government has decided to go on with the Berlin conversations.

London has dropped a bombshell which, while not creating such dismay as Germany's conscription move, nevertheless has led to real confusion, states Reuter from Paris.

Mr. A. Duff Cooper, Financial Secretary to the Treasury, speaking at Maidstone yesterday, said that the European situation was more dangerous and more threatening than at any time since 1914. But that was no reason for despair.

THE DAILY MIRROR, Friday, March 22, 1935

Daily Mirror

Broadcasting - Page 22

THE DAILY PICTURE NEWSPAPER WITH THE LARGEST NET SALE

"CLOTHES AND THE MAN" SHORT STORY —Page 21

No. 9,770 Registered at the G.P.O as a Newspaper. FRIDAY, MARCH 22, 1935 One Penny

WOMEN ENLISTED IN TORSO HUNT
Police Theory of "Passion Crime"

SKULL DISCOVERY GIVES 'YARD' MEN ANOTHER PROBLEM

SPECIAL "DAILY MIRROR" NEWS

FOR the first time in the history of crime in this country, Scotland Yard has enlisted specially-trained women detectives to help to solve a murder mystery. That was the sensational development in the Brentford torso mystery late last night.

The women are employed by a private inquiry firm.

Their help has been sought as a result of the belief that this is a crime of passion, and that information may be obtained from individuals more easily by a woman than by a man.

Meanwhile, as the evidence that the crime was committed locally is strengthened, the concentration of inquiries round London grows.

The police have asked local authorities to search refuse dumps, and it was revealed last night that a skull found at the Ealing destructor is now in the hands of the police. It was discovered a few days ago.

Hopes that a new clue had been discovered were dashed when it was found that the skull was probably about twenty years old.

The skull, the *Daily Mirror* learns, was fractured. Its finding therefore brought to light yet another mystery for the police to tackle.

12 Missing Men

In their efforts to establish the identity of the torso victim the police have searched registers of men reported missing during the past six weeks within a radius of four or five miles of Brentford.

They have found there are more than a dozen whose description corresponds roughly with that of the torso crime victim. Efforts are being made to trace these men.

Support for the theory that the body was dismembered in the district was given yesterday by Mrs. Curtis, wife of Mr. Harry C. Curtis, manager of the Brentford Football Club.

Mrs. Curtis, whose home is in Boston-gardens, Brentford, and back, on some fields leading to the canal, informed the police that about 9 o'clock one morning between three and five weeks ago she saw a man carrying a sack on his shoulder among the undergrowth and bushes on White Horse Island.

This island is nearly half a mile above the place where the body was found.

IULIKA SINGS, TOO.—Gitta Alpar, the famous Viennese coloratura, with her nine-months-old daughter, Iulika. Miss Alpar came to London yesterday to discuss her part in a forthcoming West End production, but is flying back to Paris to be with her baby again. See page 14.

THE PRINCE IN A SOFT EVENING SHIRT

The Prince of Wales wore an evening shirt with a soft front and soft cuffs—a fashion which he set while on holiday in Austria—at last night's London dinner of the British Iron and Steel Federation.
[Huge Order Won by the Prince—page 2.]

SIX DIE AS 'PLANE FALLS IN FLAMES

Victims' Identity Secret

RENNES (Brittany), Thursday.

ALL six occupants of a big French naval seaplane were killed when the machine crashed in flames to-night close to Brest Harbour.

The seaplane was flying from Lanlnon air base, near Brest, the famous French naval station at the western tip of the Brittany Peninsula.

Up to a late hour the identity of the victims has not been announced by the naval authorities.—Reuter.

LEVEL CROSSING CRASH.—The wreck of the car in which Colonel J. S. Hobbs, of Warden House, West End, Southampton, was injured yesterday, when it was in collision with a train at a level crossing at Haunsdown, near Southampton. The engine of the train was put out of action.

KNEW THE KING'S "MUM AND DAD"

DUSTY Matthews, well-known character on Eastbourne front, was presented to the King while out walking.

"Pleased to meet you, captain," said the eighty-six-year-old boatman. "I knew your mum and dad."

Dusty and eighty-three-year-old wife live with son at Warnock-road, Eastbourne. For years Dusty fished off Plymouth. It was there he saw King Edward unveil memorial.

Dusty Matthews.

TO SURPRISE YOU

EVERYDAY words, these. They are in to-day's news. Behind each lies a story to surprise you.

Tea Parties: Do you like them? Four hundred women showed yesterday that they didn't. Find out why on page 7.

Champagne: It was poured over a girl's head yesterday. By whom? What for? Answers on page 2.

Telegrams: Do you feel anxious when one comes to your door? Sir Kingsley Wood explains why you should not on page 8.

Pay-Packets: Your "boss" is better paid than you are. But on page 9 you'll read of "bosses" who get less than their subordinates.

JUDGE AIDS FAINTING WITNESS

WHEN a man giving evidence in a civil action at Manchester Assizes yesterday collapsed in the witness-box, Mr. Justice Singleton immediately left his seat and went to his aid.

The Judge had asked the man a question. After a moment's hesitation he fell back in the witness-box, striking his head.

ONE DEAD, FIVE HURT IN PIT ACCIDENT

A BOY was killed and five men injured when a runaway tub dashed down a steep slope at the Nunnery Colliery, Sheffield, late last night. The dead boy was George Parker, fifteen, of Manor Estate, Sheffield.

A doctor accompanied rescue brigades to the pit bottom and relieved the sufferings of the injured by injecting morphia.

6,000-Mile Talk to Mother of 80

BY A SPECIAL REPRESENTATIVE

WHEN you are nearly eighty years of age, it is very thrilling to talk to a son, whom you have not seen for four years, over 6,000 miles of land and sea telephone line.

Small wonder that Mrs. L. Cooper, of Genesta-road, Plumstead, S.E., was excited when she reached home last night after this experience.

Seated in a little room in the General Post Office, St. Martin's le Grand, E.C., this handsome old lady, with her crown of soft white hair and blue eyes proudly heard her son, Mr. H. C. Cooper, chief lighthouse engineer to the Union of South Africa, tell the world how he built the Cape Point lighthouse.

The broadcast was in connection with the Imperial Press Conference.

But the great surprise for Mrs. Cooper came when she was told that she could carry on a two-way conversation with her son at the lighthouse.

"Just Magic"

"Hullo, Claude, my dear, isn't this wonderful?" she said, hesitantly.

But reassurance came when her boy replied: "Very well, my dear old mother. This is a great day for us both."

"You are quite famous now; soon you will be in Hollywood."

And so the happy exchange went on, to be ended with a mutually affectionate farewell.

"It was just magic," this very happy mother told me. "I could hear every word, and I recognised every intonation of Claude's voice.

"I couldn't sleep last night, I was so excited. And when they told me I was to talk to him—"

Mrs. Cooper is intensely proud of her son's rise to success. "He was only nineteen when he built his first lighthouse in Australia," she confided.

THE DAILY MIRROR, Tuesday, March 26, 1935.

Daily Mirror

THE DAILY PICTURE NEWSPAPER WITH THE LARGEST NET SALE

Broadcasting - Page 22

CELL DRAMA MAY ALTER LAW—P. 5

No. 9,773 Registered at the G.P.O. as a Newspaper. TUESDAY, MARCH 26, 1935 One Penny

Woman Chief of Varsity to Wed Taxi-man

"I SHALL CONTINUE TO DRIVE MY CAB"

BY A SPECIAL CORRESPONDENT

ONE of the most brilliant woman scholars in England, an M.A. of Cambridge, and Director of Studies of Tutorial Classes at the University of London, Mrs. Barbara Frances Wootton, is to be married shortly to a Fulham taxi driver, Mr. George Wright.

Mr. Wright told me last night: I shall go on driving my cab as usual after we are married—that is, until something better comes along, and Mrs. Wootton will continue her career, of course.

It is a romance of the Halls of Learning.

Mrs. Wootton is the scholarly daughter o scholarly parents. Her father was Dr. James Adam, Senior Tutor of Emmanuel Cambridge; her mother was a Fellow of Girton, where Mrs. Wootton herself was educated.

Mr. Wright told me last night how he met his future bride.

"I had gone to the London School of Economics to study economic history, and political theory, because I felt that it was right that I should know something more of the problems of to-day than I do," he said.

Brilliant Scholar

"Mrs. Wootton was a great help to me in my studies, clarifying many points which might otherwise have proved intricate. Since then we have seen a great deal of each other, and we have been engaged for some time.

Mr. Wright, a good-looking, fair-haired young man, lives at his parents' house in Protheroroad, and has been driving cabs for nearly ten years, using the rank opposite Brompton Oratory as his headquarters.

He has ambitions, but what they are he refuses to say. A rumour is going round his cab rank that he will stand as a Socialist candidate at the next General Election. But he laughed at this.

Mrs. Wootton, after serving for two years as Director of Studies and Lecturer in Economics at Girton, became Research Officer to the Trades Union Congress and Labour Party Joint Research Department. In 1926 she became Principal of Morley College for Working Men and Women.

In 1924 she was appointed, together with financial leaders and the heads of great industries, to serve on the Government Committee to investigate the question of the National Debt. She was then only twenty six!

Her husband, a fellow-student at Cambridge was killed within four days of getting into the line during the war.

Mrs. Barbara Wootton

WHAT HAS HITLER SAID?

The Fuhrer is clearly expecting an answer, but both Sir John Simon and Mr. Anthony Eden are looking grave and seem doubtful about their reply—a dramatic picture during yesterday's conversations—fateful for the peace of Europe—at the Berlin Chancellery.

Problem of European Peace —World Watches Talks

While Sir John Simon and Mr. Anthony Eden were discussing yesterday with Hitler, the German Dictator, momentous questions on which the peace of Europe depends—and in which the whole world is interested—Switzerland was protesting to Berlin about the alleged kidnapping on Swiss territory of an anti-Nazi German journalist, who is now under arrest in Berlin.

FOR seven hours yesterday, while crowds waited in the street, Sir John Simon and Mr. Anthony Eden probed the problems that threaten European peace.

And at night the dominant note everywhere was: Hitler has spoken. What has he said?

When Sir John Simon left the Chancellery he looked very tired. An hour afterwards waiting journalists at his hotel were told that he was too tired to appear.

A brief statement said: Some of the points in the Anglo-French communiqué of last month had been discussed, and that the questions would be resumed to-day.

It is believed, says Reuter's Berlin correspondent, that Hitler gave Sir John Simon a very full elucidation of points in German foreign policy, and that on the menace of Bolshevism he took up a very firm attitude.

No Pact with Russia

The latter, according to the Central News, was the point he stressed most strongly. His attitude is thought to have pronounced the doom of the Eastern Pact which France has stressed strenuously.

Germany will not enter a mutual pact of defence which includes Russia.

One of the points Hitler urged for Germany's need of adequate means of defence was that she should act as a buffer State against the Bolshevist menace.

The French appeal to the League of Nations on Germany's reintroduction of conscription is a hampering factor in the negotiations.

Concerning Austria, the German attitude is that the position cannot be satisfactorily cleared up until the Austrian people have had an opportunity of expressing their own views in a General Election.

Such an election is regarded as likely to pave the way for union between Austria and Germany.

It is probable that Hitler offered that Germany would return to the League of Nations

HOW GERMANY STANDS

ARMAMENTS. — No discrimination; limitation if the others do.
EASTERN PACT. — A "source of danger." She will not risk being involved in other people's quarrels.
DANUBE PACT. — Must not prevent natural relations developing between Germany and Austria or lead to other nations intervening in Austrian internal affairs.
AIR PACT—Agreed.
LEAGUE OF NATIONS—No decision until security and equality are accorded.

if her full sovereignty was recognised by the Powers and Russia excluded from any possible pacts.

Meanwhile, the organisation of "passive defence against attacks from the air" will become obligatory for French citizens throughout the country by the new "Passive Defence" Bill, which was adopted by the Chamber of Deputies last night

"Take Cover" Orders

"Take Cover" exercises will be carried out simultaneously with air defence manœuvres, and anyone refusing to take part in these exercises will be liable to a fine of nearly £3 for a first offence and from six days to a month's imprisonment for a second offence.

Berthold Jacob, the German anti-Nazi journalist, concerning whose alleged kidnapping Switzerland has protested to Germany, was announced yesterday at the meeting of the Swiss Federal Council by M. Mocca, chief of the political service, to be in Germany.

From other sources it is learned that Jacob will be accused of high treason and that he will be brought very soon before a special court.

INVALID-CHAIR DRIVING BAN

Then Cripple Found Burned

A FEW hours after he had been disqualified for three months from driving a motor-driven invalid chair, a forty-seven-year-old cripple, Daniel Ashman Gulliford, of Peasedown St. John, was admitted to Bath Royal United Hospital last night suffering from extensive burns.

Relatives heard screams coming from the outhouse of his home where he kept his chair and found him in flames. It is believed that he was cleaning the machine when it caught fire.

Earlier in the day, at Radstock, Gulliford was convicted of driving the chair without due care and attention. He was fined 10s. and 24s. costs, disqualified from driving for three months, and his licence was endorsed

BARONET M.P. KNOCKED DOWN BY CAR

SIR Nairne Sandeman, M.P., was knocked down by a car as he was leaving the Houses of Parliament last night, but although he received head injuries he called a taxi and drove to his home in Tufton-street, S.W.

A doctor and nurse were in attendance last night as Sir Nairne was suffering from shock and slight concussion, but his condition was not serious

ENGLAND RUGBY CAPTAIN ENGAGED

D. A. Kendrew, who captained the England Rugby team in their first two matches this season, is to marry.

His engagement was announced last night to Miss Nora Elizabeth Harvey, youngest daughter of Mr. John Harvey, of Malin Hall, Malin, Co Donegal.

TWIG PULLED TRIGGER

A TWIG is believed to have fired the shot which killed Joseph Butcher, seventy, of Paultow-avenue St. John's-lane, Bedminster, Bristol.

Butcher was shooting rabbits near Bristol and shot one in a hedge. It is thought that in retrieving it Butcher caught his gun against a twig and that the second barrel went off.

THE DAILY MIRROR, Wednesday, March 27, 1935

Broadcasting - Page 20

Daily Mirror

THE DAILY PICTURE NEWSPAPER WITH THE LARGEST NET SALE

SOLVING THE LINCOLN PROBLEM —Page 25

No. 9,774 Registered at the G.P.O as a Newspaper. WEDNESDAY, MARCH 27, 1935 One Penny

LOST SHIPS: OFFICIAL INQUIRY

BOLTS DRAMA IN COMMONS

··· ––– ···
S O S

THIS tragic call of the sea sounded over the Atlantic yesterday. It echoed through the House of Commons last night.

M.P.s, stirred by that echo, welcomed the announcement by Mr. Walter Runciman, President of the Board of Trade, that official inquiry is to be made into the recent losses of British ships.

They heard Mr. Runciman promise that the inquiry would cover the cases of the Usworth, Blairgowrie, Millpool and La Crescenta.

And 1,500 miles away the Jean Jadot, one of the gallant ships which answered the Usworth's last call, was drifting helplessly. A new rescue race was on. It is described on page 3.

The chairman of the new inquiry which is to cover the "widest possible ground" will be Lord Merrivale, ex-Divorce Court president, and one of the counsel in the appeal arising out of the Titanic disaster.

Commenting last night on the Government's decision, Captain W. H. Coombs, general manager of the Officers' (Merchant Navy) Federation, told the Daily Mirror: "Merchant officers and seamen and their relatives will be greatly relieved. It is to be hoped that the inquiry will hear evidence from officers in ships which successfully combated the gales. ... If the lessons to be learned are applied it may be that the seamen did not die in vain."

"A Crime"

The question of an inquiry was raised in the Commons by Mr. Arthur Greenwood (Soc., Wakefield).

In 1933 the tonnage lost, he said, was 59,000, but there were lives lost which were even more valuable than British capital. The loss of those lives was a "crime against the nation."

He quoted a resolution by the Imperial Merchant Service Guild suggesting a searching inquiry and added a touch of drama by holding up to view several bolts.

These bolts, he said, were taken from a liner when repairs had to be done. They had never been inspected, he was told, for twenty years.

After Brigadier-General Nation (Con., Hull) had taken the opportunity to point out that 40,000 British seamen are out of work, Mr. Runciman replied.

Sails Suggestion

He held up our manning scale and method as a model to the world. He said that the Board of Trade had been raising the standard year by year.

He realised that every loss meant the disappearance of the breadwinners of many families, but he warned the House against running away with the idea that the losses of the British Mercantile Marine had got out of hand or were more serious than usual.

Commander Marsden (Con., North Battersea) suggested that all tramp steamers under a certain tonnage should be fitted with a certain amount of canvas.

If ships lost had had sails they might have been hove to and have weathered the gales.

BIG CITY BLAZE

FIRE broke out last night in an office on the top floor of premises in Whitefriars-street, London, centre of newspaperland.

The blaze, which at one time threatened adjoining property, including newspaper offices, was got under control after strenuous efforts.

HOW ARE THE MIGHTY FALLEN!

Old aeroplanes, like old soldiers, never die. This once giant bombing seaplane serves as an admirable roof and advertising sign for a "hot dog stand," or wayside refreshment counter, between Bradentown and Sarasota, Florida.

Bandits' Attack on Woman

STARS' DIVORCE

Virginia Cherrill, the screen star, and Cary Grant, the British actor, from whom she was granted an interlocutory decree of divorce at Los Angeles yesterday. They were married in London in February, 1934.

CASHIER BOUND AND GAGGED IN RAID

IN a daring daylight swoop on an office yesterday two bandits attacked an Ilford woman cashier, trussed her up and gagged her—*while twenty of her father's employees were working only a few yards away unaware of the raid.*

The cashier, Mrs. L. Pryke, of Morden-road, Seven Kings, was in her father's office at the Newbury Park Sand and Ballast Company, Hornes-road, Barkingside, waiting for him to return from Rainham so that she could pay £38 into the bank.

A man engaged her in conversation while another man entered at the back door and struck her to the ground.

When she recovered and attempted to run out the bandits tripped her up and bound and gagged her.

"My daughter was talking to the first man through a small window," said Mrs. Charles Thomson, "when the wind blew some papers to the ground.

"As she bent down to pick them up she was struck on the head with a heavy instrument.

"Later she recovered and attempted to run out, but the men tightly bound her and then covered her with one of the firm's sandbags. She is now in bed suffering from shock."

Besides taking the money from the safe, the bandits took Mrs. Pryke's handbag.

Dog's Picnic in a Shop

SHOP assistants and policemen were kept at bay for two and a half hours last night by an Alsatian dog that dashed behind the counter of a shop in Arthur-road, Wimbledon Park, S.W.

It sprang on the counter and helped itself to bacon. The manager of the shop tried the ruse of bringing it a large bone, a pound of liver and some biscuits. It ate them all, licked its lips and still refused to let anyone approach it.

A police van with two more policemen wearing leather gloves and carrying ropes and chains arrived.

Then the dog was lassoed and taken away in the van.

Died an Hour Before His Wedding

COLLAPSE AS FRIENDS TOASTED HIM

BY A SPECIAL REPRESENTATIVE

ONE hour before he was to have been married yesterday Mr. Everard Bert Knight, a fifty-seven-year-old telephone operator, collapsed and died.

He had been chatting with friends of his bride-to-be, Mrs. Emily Williamson, a thirty-six-year-old widow, in a room in her mother's house at Penwith-road, Earlsfield, S.W.

Someone suggested that they should drink a toast to the couple before they set out for Wandsworth Register Office.

Glasses were filled. But as the friends raised their glasses they noticed that Mr. Knight was still sitting motionless in a chair.

While they had been filling their glasses he had collapsed and died.

Visit to Home

Mrs. Charles Kemble, Mrs. Williamson's mother, told me to-night that her daughter gave up a position in domestic service at East Grinstead (Sussex) a fortnight ago to marry Mr. Knight.

Yesterday morning they paid a last visit to the bungalow in Vernon-road, Bexley Heath, where they were to live after their marriage.

"As Mr. Knight sat down to lunch," she went on, "he turned to me and said: 'Well, mother, the glorious day has come.' He seemed perfectly happy and in the best of health."

"He had had an attack of flu about three weeks ago, but we thought he had recovered."

Mr. Knight was a widower with a son and married daughter living at Coulsdon (Surrey).

VILLAGE STILL IN GRIP OF DROUGHT!

THERE is in Warwickshire a small village still dependent for its water supply upon a water-cart, which travels to the village daily from a nearby town.

It is Bearley, near Stratford-on-Avon, which has yet to recover from the effects of the drought of last summer.

Many other villages in the Midlands are also suffering from this water shortage, and unless the rainfall shows a substantial increase they are likely to be in a desperate plight before the summer.

'Spanish Scholar No. 1'

Senor de Ayala.

"THE Prince of Wales is the first, in every respect, of the Spanish scholars in Great Britain," declared the Spanish Ambassador, Senor Don Perez de Ayala, at Cardiff yesterday.

The Ambassador was beginning a two-day tour of South Wales.

He referred to the work being done by the Ibero-American Institute of which the Prince is president. It was, he said, becoming more vital and more influential in the future destiny not only of Great Britain but also of the whole civilised world.

English and Spanish, he said, were the only two Imperial languages of modern times, as was Latin in the old world. The time would come when the greater part of Western civilisation would be represented by peoples speaking in these two tongues.

"As Spain's representative I have great pleasure in expressing once more the gratitude of all my fellow-countrymen towards the Prince, to whose love for our language is due the increasing spread of Spanish in this country," he added.

Daily Mirror

THE DAILY PICTURE NEWSPAPER WITH THE LARGEST NET SALE

Broadcasting - Page 22

HEALTH EDUCATION FOR ALL —Page 3

No. 9,776 Registered at the G.P.O. as a Newspaper.   FRIDAY, MARCH 29, 1935   One Penny

LITVINOFF TOASTS THE KING

First Royal Honour by Soviet

UNION JACKS FLY IN MOSCOW

"I raise my glass to the health of his Majesty the King of England, to the prosperity and happiness of the British people, and to your very good health, Sir."

THUS M. Litvinoff, Foreign Secretary of Communist Russia, last night to Mr. Anthony Eden, first British Minister to visit Moscow since the revolution.

It was the first occasion on which a Royal toast has been honoured in Soviet Russia since the Tsarist regime went down in a welter of bloodshed eighteen years ago.

Mr. Eden, Lord Privy Seal, coming direct from the Berlin talks with Hitler, Dictator of Germany, to talk with Stalin, Dictator of Russia, was welcomed with high honour.

Union Jacks lavishly decorated the station at which he arrived.

Glittering Splendour

A crack Soviet regiment lined the platform, says Reuter. He had travelled in a super-luxury train from the frontier.

The reception to Mr. Eden in the evening, at which M. Litvinoff toasted King George, was one of glittering splendour.

It was one of the most distinguished receptions the Soviet Republic has seen. There was dancing in the glistening white ballroom of the palace where the function was held to the strains of a modern rumba.

After welcoming Mr. Eden, M. Litvinoff said:

"The visit of Mr. Eden to Moscow is the more significant in that the time selected for it is one in which serious and alarming impediments to the preservation of normal peaceful international order have arisen.

"Never since the World War has there been such misgivings about peace as now. These misgivings are shared by all the friends of peace and by the principal masses in all countries.

"Prevention Is Better—"

"Circumstances then make every State anxious to take all possible measures for averting the danger. As we all know, the wise English proverb has it, 'Prevention is better than cure.'

"It is now universally realised that the danger of war hanging over Europe, and consequently over the whole world, can only be averted, or its risk reduced to the utmost possible extent, by the collective efforts of all States, especially of the Great Powers.

"The British Government by the agreement with France on February 3 has already taken a step towards the collective preservation of peace."

Sir John Simon's statement on Germany—page 3.

The Duke of Gloucester coming ashore at Portsmouth from H.M.A.S. Australia, and (above) acknowledging cheers as he drove from Victoria Station to Buckingham Palace in a State landau. Further pictures of the Duke's arrival are on pages 16 and 17.

CLUE TO TRUNK CRIME No. 1

WHILE making inquiries into robberies at Walthamstow, C.I.D. officers have discovered a clue which may reveal within a few days the identity of the man responsible for Brighton Trunk crime No. 1.

The nature of the clue is being kept a strict secret, but it is believed to be connected with a man who lived in the neighbourhood about the time the crime was committed.

The trunk was made by a Leyton firm, and the police have been unable to trace a Spitalfields woman who has been missing.

Following a midnight conference at Scotland Yard, all officers were sworn to secrecy, and so important is the clue considered that two detective-inspectors have been released from their duties at Brentford to work with Divisional Detective-Inspector Salisbury at Walthamstow.

SILENT HEIRESS

Guard at Door of Princess Alexis Mdivani's Cabin

NEW YORK, Thursday.

Barricaded in her suite, with a bodyguard at the cabin doors, Princess Alexis Mdivani, formerly Miss Barbara Hutton, the Woolworth heiress, arrived at New York this afternoon in the Bremen.

The Princess announced in London ten days ago that she would apply for a Reno divorce, but when a large number of American journalists boarded the Bremen, hoping for further details, the Princess refused to receive them.—Reuter.

HOMECOMING HONOUR FOR ROYAL DUKE

A G.C.M.G.: Members of Staff Knighted

ON his return from his seven-month tour of Australia and New Zealand, the Duke of Gloucester has been invested by the King with the insignia of a Knight Grand Cross of the Most Distinguished Order of St. Michael and St. George.

Honours for three members of the Duke's staff were also announced in last night's *Court Circular*.

On Major-General Richard Howard-Vyse, the Duke's Chief of Staff, the King conferred a knighthood and invested him with the insignia of a K.C.M.G.

Captain Arthur Curtis, private secretary to the Duke on his tour, receives a knighthood with the insignia of a K.C.V.O.

Bronzed Duke

Captain Howard Kerr, the Duke's Equerry, was invested with the insignia of a Companion of the Most Distinguished Order of St. Michael and St. George.

Knighthoods have also been conferred on Mr Holman Gregory, the new Recorder of London, and on Mr. Peter Bark, who is managing director of the Anglo-International Bank Limited. He was formerly vice-governor of the Imperial Bank of Russia, managing director of the Volga-Kama Bank, Under-Secretary of State of the Ministry of Commerce (1911), and Russian Finance Minister from 1914 to 1917.

When the Duke of Gloucester, sun-tanned and looking very fit, reached London yesterday, he was greeted at Victoria Station by the King and Queen, the Princess Royal and the Duchess of York.

The Prince of Wales and the Duke of York had met him at Portsmouth and travelled to London with him.

ARRIVED AFTER 85 YEARS

OKEHAMPTON, Devon, have discovered a treasured document—a letter posted to their Mayor eighty-five years ago, which has just been delivered.

The letter was found without an envelope on a railway station at Tidworth by Mr. Singleton, an employee of the G.W.R., who dispatched it by registered post to the present Mayor, Mr. W. B. Chamings.

No one can give any account as to how the letter was lost, but it is believed that it has been kept as a curio by some person, who mislaid it last week.

Addressed to Mr. Henry Robson Colling, who eighty-five years ago was Mayor of Okehampton, the letter is dated May 3, and the signature is that of Mr. W. W. Rundell, of Waterloo-street, Stoke, Devonport.

It requests the Mayor to convene a public meeting in connection with the great exhibition of works and industry of all nations held in 1851.

THE DAILY MIRROR, Saturday March 30, 1935.

Daily Mirror

Broadcasting - Page 22

THE DAILY PICTURE NEWSPAPER WITH THE LARGEST NET SALE

No. 9,777 — Registered at the G.P.O as a Newspaper. — SATURDAY, MARCH 30, 1935 — One Penny

WHAT SOVIET DICTATOR TOLD MR. EDEN —Page 3

ABYSSINIA BREAKS WITH ITALY

Grave Warning in Rome of Nearness of War

DANZIG 'INSULT' DENIED

Last Night

Feeling so strained between Italy and Abyssinia that General Baistrocchi, Under-Secretary for War in Italian Senate, said: "No one can tell when war may break out. It may happen unexpectedly within a few days following a period of political tension." He urged that each citizen must be organised in the "military culture" of the nation.

German Cabinet passed law authorising acquisition of land for training her new Army of 500,000.

Report from Danzig that League Commissioner had been threatened that he might be driven from the city. This he denied.

GENERAL Baistrocchi's warning coincided with the announcement in Rome that the Ethiopian Government had abandoned direct communication with Italy, says the Exchange.

It is understood that officers' wives and children have been told to leave Eritrea and Italian Somaliland.

General Baistrocchi stressed, adds Reuter, that each citizen must be organised in the military culture of the nation so that Italy may be as effective as possible.

War material was being manufactured as quickly as possible. "In this feverish armaments race Italy insisted on having arms in keeping with her right as a great nation.

"By next spring," he went on, "we shall have about 600,000 men perfectly armed and organised besides a whole class in reserve, namely, the 1912 class (which means another 300,000 men)."

It is understood that, with the breakdown of direct negotiations, the Abyssinian Government are demanding arbitration, and it is considered in unofficial quarters in Rome that a Commission of Arbitration would have to be set up under the auspices of the League of Nations but it is believed there may be some difficulty in the constitution of a Commission whose judgment both countries would accept as binding.

"Tissue of Lies"

What is the mystery behind the sensational reports that Mr. Sean Lester "Ruler" under the League of Nations of the Free City of Danzig, has been threatened that he may be driven out of the city, publicly insulted by Herr Greiser, President of the Senate, and that crowds threw mud at his car?

Mr. Lester, speaking from his home at Danzig last night, said the report was nothing but a tissue of lies.

"I want the 'Daily Mirror,'" he said "publicly to deny them. I have not been insulted by the President of the Senate, nor have I been threatened that I shall be driven out of the city.

"No crowd has assembled or thrown mud at my car. It is perfectly true that I have

---

THE shadow of a possible war looms over the world. There is a race in armaments. Japan is spending half her national revenue in war material. Germany is arming at feverish haste.
Sir Herbert Samuel, at Plymouth.

I WANT to say most emphatically that I do not believe that war is either imminent or inevitable.
Mr. Arthur Henderson, at Clay Cross.

---

had discussions with Herr Greiser, but they have been friendly ones about the constitution of Danzig."

Working as League High Commissioner it is Mr. Lester's difficult task to hold the balance fairly between the rival parties fighting for power in Danzig Diet at the elections which take place next month.

Mr. Eden's talk with Stalin and Scotland Yard's part in Nazi "kidnapping" inquiry—Page 3.

THE PRINCE SUMS UP THE FIELD

The Prince of Wales taking stock of the horses from the paddock rails before the Grand National won by Reynoldstown at Aintree yesterday. The other picture shows Princess Mir coming to grief. Uncle Batt is ahead and Lazy Boots, who finished fourth, has just come over. See also pages 14 and 15.

Boy Chauffeur Accused of Murdering His Employer

THERE was a sensational development at Bournemouth yesterday to the death of Mr. Francis Mawson Rattenbury, a retired architect, aged sixty-seven, who lived with his thirty-one-year-old wife in Madeira Villa, Manor-road, Bournemouth.

Mr. Rattenbury was found with severe head injuries in his home on Sunday night.

His wife, Alma Victoria Rattenbury, was later arrested, and subsequently was remanded on a charge of wounding with attempt to murder him.

On Thursday Mr. Rattenbury died.

Yesterday, George Percy Stoner, a nineteen-year-old chauffeur, whose address was given as the Rattenburys' villa, was charged with the murder of Mr. Rattenbury.

Police-Inspector Carter told the magistrates that he saw Stoner alight from a London train at Bournemouth Central Station.

He went to him and said: "You know me for a police officer?" Stoner replied, "Yes." The inspector said he was then cautioned.

On this evidence Superintendent Deacon asked for a remand until Tuesday.

BROTHER FINDS BOY OF 16 HANGED

POLICE officers and ambulance men worked in relays for nearly an hour trying to revive Eric Oakey, sixteen, of Bruce-grove, Tottenham, who was found by his brother hanged in his bedroom last night. Their efforts were in vain.

It is understood that the dead boy recently had a slight operation.

Health of the Princess Royal

THE Princess Royal has cancelled a visit to the National Union of Teachers' Conference at Scarborough on April 25.

A lady-in-waiting conveying the decision, writes:—

"The Princess Royal is advised on medical grounds not to undertake any other public duties in view of the numerous celebrations in connection with the Silver Jubilee which Her Royal Highness has to attend."

City's welcome to the Duke of Gloucester; the Duke of Kent's Jubilee Thanksgiving Plans—page seventeen.

NUNS ARRESTED ON SMUGGLING CHARGE

BERLIN, Friday.

A number of Catholic priests, monks and nuns, have been arrested in Germany on suspicion of violating the currency regulations.

It is officially stated that an investigation revealed that at least two and half million marks had been illegally smuggled out of the country. —Reuter.

THE DAILY MIRROR, Monday, April 1, 1935.

Broadcasting - Page 22

Daily Mirror
THE DAILY PICTURE NEWSPAPER WITH THE LARGEST NET SALE

TOO MUCH NOISE —Page 12

No. 9,778 — Registered at the G.P.O. as a Newspaper. — MONDAY, APRIL 1, 1935 — One Penny

NEW AUSTRALIA-ENGLAND RECORD

Brook's 7 days 20 hours Solo

CHEERS THAT HE NEVER HEARD

FROM OUR OWN CORRESPONDENT
FOLKESTONE, Sunday.

MR. H. L. Brook, thirty-nine-year-old Harrogate airman-accountant with eighteen months' flying experience, landed at Lympne, near here, to-day, having flown from Australia in 7 days 19 hours 15 minutes.

He had beaten by more than thirteen hours the unofficial solo flight record set up by James Melrose, the Australian, last September and by more than a day Mr. J. A. Mollison's official record made in 1931.

A crowd of 200 saw his red aeroplane glide to earth. Brook, looking as though he had been on a short pleasure trip stepped from the cockpit.

Cheering rang across the field. But Brook never heard it. Listening to the roar of his brave little engine for seven days had robbed him of his hearing.

Arrangements had been made by his fellow members of the Yorkshire Aviation Club to give him an aerial escort across the country to Harrogate to-night, but Mr. Brook decided to stay with friends at Sutton, Surrey, and his welcome back to Yorkshire has been postponed until Tuesday.

Mr. Brook's father, a seventy-eight-year-old retired woollen machinist of Lancaster Park-road, Harrogate, was unable to make the journey to Lympne as he is recuperating from a serious illness, but he motored to Plompton in anticipation that this son would fly on to Harrogate.

50-m.p.h. Gale

These were Brook's first words about his achievement: "Really, there is not much I can say to you."

"Everything has gone off well," he went on. "I have been flying for the best part of eighteen to twenty hours a day, getting about five or six hours' sleep every night, but it really has not been a hard flight.

"My machine and I had a rough time over the Timor Sea. I was buffeted about pretty badly, and to make matters worse visibility was nil at times. Then I had to land on a delta near the mouth of the Ganges one night.

"From Athens to Rome, on the later stage of the flight, I ran into a strong head-wind of 50 m.p.h.

"The longest hop I had was from Jodhpur to Basra, a distance of 1,700 miles."

The engine that carried him from Mildenhall to Melbourne in the great air race in 26 days 20 hours had battled back—and won. Castrol was used throughout.

He was officially welcomed by Captain J. P. Morkam, on behalf of the Air Ministry.

MR. BUCHAN DENIES PEERAGE RUMOUR

Mr. John Buchan, M.P., Governor-General-Elect of Canada, stated yesterday that a rumour that he had "chosen a title" was "quite absurd."

"The grant of a peerage is entirely at the discretion of his Majesty," said Mr. Buchan. "The matter has not yet been raised, and therefore I have not given a thought to the question of a title."

Congratulations for Mr. H. L. Brook as he stepped out of his aeroplane at Lympne

Man of 80 Charged with the Murder of His Wife

STRANGE DRAMA OF "DEVOTED COUPLE" AFTER 40 YEARS' HAPPINESS

BY A SPECIAL REPRESENTATIVE

AN eighty-year-old man, Mr. Harry Hans Edwards, will be charged at Streatham Police Court to-day with the murder of his seventy-three-year-old wife. The wife was found shot with an automatic pistol at their home in Canterbury-grove, West Norwood, yesterday.

Mr. Edwards, an official in a shipping company, had been married to Mrs. Elizabeth Edwards for forty years. Most of that time they lived in the house in Canterbury-grove.

Yesterday morning Miss Dorothy Edwards, a daughter, went to her parents' bedroom. She found her mother lying on the bed shot twice through the chest.

She ran through the streets to call Dr. Barrett, of Norwood-road. He returned with her, but could only say that Mrs. Edwards had been killed instantly.

Intended to Retire

Later, Mr. Edwards was arrested and charged with the murder of his wife. Neighbours speak of the couple as devoted.

Despite his age, Mr. Edwards still went to his office every morning, accompanied by his daughter, who was also employed there.

Mr. Avory, who lives in the adjoining house, told the *Daily Mirror* last night: "I have lived here twenty-one years and know Mr. Edwards most of the time, but he was not a talkative man.

"He told me last December that he intended to retire, but he has carried on since. About the time he was going to retire a large notice announced that his house was for sale.

"I understood he could not get what he considered a reasonable figure for the house.

"Mrs. Edwards did not like the idea of leaving the home they had occupied so long, and often wept over the prospect. She said she could not bear to settle in a poky flat."

WOULDN'T TAKE £1,000 A WEEK!

MISS Sheila MacDonald, the Prime Minister's daughter, told reporters at Hollywood nothing would induce her to submit to a screen test, "not even £1,000 a week."

OPERATION ON M.C.C. CAPTAIN?

That his jaw was believed to be broken in three places was revealed by R. E. S. Wyatt, captain of the M.C.C., when the team arrived back in England yesterday from their tour of the West Indies.

Wyatt was injured in the last Test match by a fast ball from Martindale. When he reached Avonmouth yesterday he had his chin bandaged, and explained that he was going to have his jaw X-rayed. He thought an operation might be necessary.

21 YEARS AFTER

Sore throat prevented the Bishop of London, Dr. Winnington Ingram, from preaching yesterday at the twenty-first anniversary of St. Barnabus Church, North Finchley.

By a strange coincidence he was unable to consecrate the church twenty-one years ago on account of a severe attack of influenza on the day of the ceremony.

JEWESS PREACHES TO ANGLICANS

Former Non-Stop Variety Dancer in Pulpit

MISS Olga Levertoff, a former non-stop variety dancer, preached the sermon at St. Bartholomew's Church, East Ham, last night.

It is believed that she is the first Jewess to preach in an Anglican church. Her ambition is to achieve a union between the Christian and Jewish people.

Miss Levertoff was invited by the vicar, the Rev. M. O. Hodson, to preach, and she received the permission of the Bishop of Chelmsford and the parochial church council.

A section of the congregation which objected to the new departure were not present last night, but the church was almost full.

It was Miss Levertoff's first sermon. She is a Christian Jewess, her father, Dr. P. P. Levertoff, having been converted to the Church of England before she was born.

Since 1924 he has been curate-in-charge of Holy Trinity Church, Shoreditch.

Miss Levertoff acts as her father's secretary in his mission work among Jews in the East End.

THE DUKE OF GLOUCESTER 35

The Duke of Gloucester, who was thirty-five yesterday, spent the day quietly at Buckingham Palace.

During the morning hundreds of messages of congratulation reached him from friends all over England and abroad. In the afternoon the Duke went for a drive alone.

THE DAILY MIRROR, Thursday, April 4, 1935.

Broadcasting - Page 22

Daily Mirror

THE DAILY PICTURE NEWSPAPER WITH THE LARGEST NET SALE

RECIPE FOR HAPPINESS —Page 12

No. 9,781 Registered at the G.P.O as a Newspaper   THURSDAY, APRIL 4, 1935   One Penny

AIR RAID ADVICE TO PUBLIC

ESSAY IN NEGRO ART

Three-year-old Robert Gray, of Pasadena, California, feeling an artistic urge, used his seventeen-month-old brother as a canvas and motor-car enamel as his medium. Doctors had to finish the picture.

HIS HOPES ARE IN A CRYSTAL

In an effort to trace his missing wife and daughter, a heartbroken London man intends to spend to-day consulting crystal-gazers and fortune-tellers.

He is Mr. H. Phypher, of Tooting, S.W. A fortnight ago his wife and daughter vanished from their home in Moring-road, Upper Tooting.

The only clue Mr. Phypher has is a note posted in Tooting saying " My nerves are so bad that I am going away."

Yesterday he collected the names and addresses of crystal gazers and fortune tellers.

"GAS MASK" RESCUE

HEARING a cry of agony as a cylinder containing sulphur dioxide burst, a man, using a handkerchief as a gasmask, dragged the unconscious victim to safety, last night.

The injured man, whose face was splashed by acid, was J. Moreton, of Clapham, S.W. He was overhauling the refrigerating plant at the premises of E. A. Gunn and Son, provision merchants, New-street, Kennington. His rescuer was Mr. Gunn, junr.

Home Will Be Safest Spot

HOW TO SHUT GAS OUT

Air raid dangers and how to meet them figured in the news last night simultaneously with the disclosure in a Berlin cable that Germany is turning out five aeroplanes every day.

"THE British Red Cross Society is training a large body of voluntary workers to protect and aid the civil population in the event of war from the air."

This announcement was made at a London lecture last night to the medical profession by Major H. S. Blackmore, R.A.M.C., an expert on poison gas.

" The safest shelter in the event of an air raid is an ordinary room rendered gas-proof on or about the first floor," he said.

" People who rush into tubes or dug-outs will not be so safe as those who go quietly upstairs to the anti-gas sitting-room, where they should remain until all danger is past. Gas is so heavy that it sinks rapidly."

" Most rooms can be made gas-proof by sticking brown paper around the cracks of doors

M.P.s CALL FOR DEBATE

Arrangements are expected to be made after Easter for another defence debate in Parliament in view of Sir John Simon's statement yesterday. (See page 2.)

This estimate of the German air strength differs considerably from the information placed before the House of Commons by Mr. Baldwin last November, when he contradicted Mr. Churchill's assertion that Germany was rapidly approaching equality in the air with Great Britain.

and windows and over the entrance to chimneys.

" Two wet blankets should be hung over the entrance door—one on the inside and one on the outside with the door between.

" To enter such a room a person should pass behind the outer blanket and then open and pass through the door. Care should be taken not to disturb the inner blanket until the door has been closed behind one.

" Thus a ready and convenient 'air-lock' is formed which prevents the gas getting into the room.

" Paper glued over window-panes would prevent flying glass splinters in the event of high explosive being dropped.

" In the last war people ran into the streets immediately after a bomb dropped. Nowadays this would be to court instant peril. Some gases are invisible and odourless, and days may elapse before an area could be scheduled as free from gas.

" Anti-gas drill would probably be divided into three parts. Firstly there will be workers in the streets who will be trained to control crowds and who will deal with street casualties.

" Then there would be the Red Cross first-aid stations and hospitals, and thirdly de-contamination brigades, whose job it would be to clear away the gas from danger areas and to de-contaminate the clothes of casualties.

(Germany's new 'planes—see page 2.)

The Luckiest Motorist

TRAPPED IN CANAL— AND ESCAPED

WHEN his car plunged into the canal at Newhow Bridge, near Addlestone, Surrey, yesterday, Mr. R. Poole, of Oxford, was trapped beneath the water.

The car turned over on its side, but Mr. Poole managed to force a door open and swim to safety.

The bridge, which is wooden, is on a bend, and is one of the most dangerous in Surrey.

Mr. Poole was driving a sports saloon from Byfleet when he crashed into some wooden posts and dropped several feet into the canal. At this point the water is about 10ft. deep.

He was taken uninjured to a nearby cottage.

Three People

THE WIDOW who couldn't forget: she died in her honeymoon hotel with a note to " Dear Wilfred " by her side (Page Three).

THE WIFE who thought life for her and her family was going to be much happier; she died as chance brought £2 a week to end her struggles (Page Three).

THE FATHER whose hopes and dreams have all been shattered; he lived to tell this story . . .

DIED STRIVING TO BE FIT

Father's Remorse—"I Pressed Him"

" I feel . . . I feel . . . feel that I must have been pressing him too hard, pressing him too much, because I wanted him to get fit for the Royal Air Force, my old corps. I wanted him fit and was pressing . . . pressing. . . . Oh, God."

WING-Commander Alfred Steele-Perkins, R.A.F., of Fanling, West End, Chobham (Surrey), broke down after he had said this at an inquest yesterday on his eighteen-year-old son, John Horace, who collapsed and died when training on Chobham Common, on Sunday.

Just previously, the father had told how the boy brought him a cup of tea on Sunday morning and then dressed in shorts for his usual morning run.

Failed at Examination

The mother said her son had failed at Guy's Hospital in his Christmas medical examination. " He and his father took his failure too seriously," she added. " He was the type of lad who never told anyone how he felt."

Dr. Eric Gardner, of Weybridge, said that death was due to asphyxiation of the lungs and acute dilation of the heart, following sudden exertion.

Death from natural causes was the verdict.

A GOOD STORY, it may confidently be supposed, is being told by Mr. J. H. Thomas to the Duke of Gloucester at the Royal Empire Societies' dinner last night.

Daily Mirror

THE DAILY PICTURE NEWSPAPER WITH THE LARGEST NET SALE

Broadcasting - Page 24

SATURDAY IN THE GARDEN —Page 26

No. 9,783. Registered at the G.P.O. as a Newspaper. SATURDAY, APRIL 6, 1935. One Penny

SAW HIMSELF DYING

Doctor Tells of His Struggle

'ASTRAL HELL'

How he died and came to life again, and his experiences while in a state of "suspended animation" were described by a doctor last night.

DR. G. B. Kirkland, who was formerly a Government medical officer in Southern Rhodesia, made these dramatic disclosures in a lecture to the International Institute for Psychical Research.

"This is what happened to me. In September, 1913, after a long series of desperate operations, grave-faced doctors stood by my bed and pronounced that I could not possibly live through the night.

"At one o'clock in the morning I officially died, and remained in suspended animation for some time.

"Suddenly, to my intense surprise, I saw myself lying on my back. The thought flashed through me that I did not think much of me—in fact, I did not approve of me at all.

"Almost before the thought had time to materialise, I found myself and others very faintly discernible in a tunnel like a railway tunnel, with a little speck of light at the end."

Long Struggle

"They were all hurrying along as fast as they could, and I did not seem to make much headway. I was terribly cold, and I kept pulling round myself some grey garments which proved of no use in keeping out the cold.

"After a long struggle, I managed to get into a fairly good stride, and the cold was not so bad. I was beginning to enjoy myself, and the light was gradually getting visibly brighter.

"Suddenly someone, or something, flashed up in front of me and blotted out the light. Instantly the intense cold returned. I was furious, and fought violently with this something or somebody. In the middle of the struggle everything went black again, and the next thing I knew was that I was alive again—though only just."

Certain psychic investigators, Dr. Kirkland added, had told him quite definitely that he would never repeat that experience, because it was a very clear description of astral hell. (Laughter.)

To save his face, he must disagree, but even if it were so, he had not decided whether to consider it as a warning or a prophecy. (Laughter.)

PRISON GATES REUNION DRAMA

BY A SPECIAL REPRESENTATIVE

THERE was a dramatic reunion between a mother and her fifteen-year-old daughter outside the gates of Holloway Prison yesterday.

The mother is Mrs. Adelaide Squilloni, who was released after serving a month's sentence for failing to disclose an additional income of 12s. in her wages as a charwoman while applying for relief.

Outside the prison the two hugged each other tightly, with tears of joy streaming down their cheeks.

Mrs. Squilloni's former employers are to take her back to do cleaning at nights.

TEMPLE OF THE WINDS FOR R.A.F.

Broadcasting - Page 24

MAN FREED FROM DEATH SENTENCE

Reginald Woolmington (taller), with his solicitor yesterday afternoon, when he had become once again a free man, the House of Lords having allowed his appeal against the death sentence passed on him on December 10. See page 2.

M.P. HIS OWN "CHUCKER-OUT"

MR. H. G. Williams, M.P. for South Croydon, likes to be his own "chucker-out."

When stewards at his meeting in North End Hall, Croydon, last night, were about to eject an interrupter he stopped them.

"I demand the right to speak against the murderous raids by the Air Force upon the North-West Frontier of India," shouted the interrupter.

Mr. Williams: "The only rights you have in a public meeting are the rights to behave in a peaceful manner.

"If there is any chucking out to be done..."

The interrupter: "You'll do it."

Mr. Williams: "I will.

"It is an accepted fact that when anyone misbehaves himself at any meeting which I address in Croydon if there is any chucking out to be done I do it."

...y, Secretary for Air, opening at South Farnborough, Hants, a new aeroplane testing tunnel for the R.A.F. which he referred to as a temple of the winds. It will, he hoped, result in a reduction of the R.A.F.'s annual petrol bill.

£976,000,000 to Make Work

"STOP-THE-DOLE" BILL PASSED IN U.S.A.

WASHINGTON, Friday.

AMERICA'S most determined effort to provide work for many thousands of her unemployed was given a step forward to-night when the £976,000,000 Relief Bill, sponsored by President Roosevelt as one of the planks of his "New Deal" programme, was passed.

Fund for Relief

Now all ready for signature at the White House, the Bill is intended to supersede the dole system of relief.

It provides a huge fund for relief work "at the discretion and under the direction of the President."

The highway funds will be taken from this amount and apportioned under the existing procedure, but, apart from this, the President has wide powers as to the disposal of the money.—Exchange.

PEER IN BREACH ACTION

Baronet Also Sued—Jewels Claim

BREACH of promise actions against a baron and a baronet will be heard in the King's Bench Division next week.

Miss Angela Joyce, the film actress, is claiming damages against Lord Revelstoke, who is twenty-four.

RICH WOMAN VANISHES

Lived in House of Mystery

NIGHT CRIES

BY A SPECIAL REPRESENTATIVE

DAGENHAM police are investigating the mysterious disappearance of a well-educated woman, believed to be either French or Spanish, from her home in Surrey-road, Dagenham.

Her name is thought to be Mrs. Saunders, and on Thursday workmen, who had been instructed by her to heighten the wall in front of her house, discovered a pane of glass broken in the french window at the back.

Inside, it was discovered, a trail of blood led from the room, along the banisters to an upstairs room.

Massive bolts are fitted to all the doors, and windows have been covered with whitewash.

Only two rooms are furnished. In the living room a hundredweight of coal was found stacked in a corner. There were no chairs.

In the bedroom there were an old chest, wicker chair and a bed. No electric light or gas has been installed, although the house is a modern one.

Last night the house was guarded by a policeman.

Neighbours told me that the missing woman was of an eccentric character.

Woman's Scream

She had a specially high fence put round her garden and rarely spoke to anyone, but always appeared to have plenty of money.

Mr. J. Lines, a night watchman who is on duty while the road is being made up, told an amazing story.

"On Wednesday at about midnight," he said, "I was sitting in my box when I heard two people arguing. A little later I heard a scream and a woman's voice shouting, 'You are murdering me.' Then I saw a tall woman running across the road. Before I could do anything she had disappeared."

Another neighbour said that the woman never opened the front door gate, but just hopped over the wall, which was quite low.

She was always well dressed. She wore good shoes and silk stockings, and her hands were always gloved expensively.

The police describe her as about 5ft. 6in. tall, aged about thirty-five, slim build, smartly dressed and of dignified carriage.

TWO MOTHERS

THEY ran, as all mothers must do, at some time, the gamut of agony and joy.

JOY Mrs. Woolmington, of Oborne (Dorset), is waiting to see, to-day, her son, twice tried for murder and sentenced to death. The House of Lords, for the first time in history, yesterday quashed the sentence—and sent him back to her. (Story on page two.)

AGONY In Guernsey, Mrs. le Page stumbled, blinded with tears, to a witness-box there, in halting tones, to give evidence against her daughter, charged with murder. Across the court their eyes met. (Story on page three.)

Lord Revelstoke was married last March to Miss Flora Fermor-Hesketh, a daughter of Sir Thomas and Lady Fermor-Hesketh, of Easton Neston, near Towcester.

In the other breach action, Miss Emily Fender, formerly a registered nurse, claims damages against Sir Anthony St. John Mildmay. She is also claiming the return of certain jewellery.

Sir Anthony, who served with distinction in the war, was married last May to Mrs. Beatrice May Dickeson.

Daily Mirror

THE DAILY PICTURE NEWSPAPER WITH THE LARGEST NET SALE

Broadcasting - Page 22

FASHION WEEK: FREE PATTERNS DAILY

No. 9,786. Registered at the G.P.O. as a Newspaper.   WEDNESDAY, APRIL 10, 1935   One Penny

"YARD'S" 4-IN-A-ROOM EXPERTS

Overcrowding Is Rife Again

EXPANSION—OR A NEW SITE

SCOTLAND YARD IS BEING HAMPERED IN THE WAR IT IS WAGING ON CRIME BY INADEQUATE ACCOMMODATION.

Senior officers, guardians of the secrets of crime detection, are working three or four in a room.

Interviews go on in corners because there are not enough waiting-rooms.

In the finger-print branch the staff are crowded together like warehouse clerks in a Christmas rush. Many work in a corridor by artificial light.

Criminal records, frequently in demand, are piled to the ceiling in a passage.

Extensions have been added from time to time. But Scotland Yard has outgrown them.

"Urgent Necessity"

Lord Trenchard, in his third annual report issued last night, declares that the expansion of Scotland Yard is again an urgent necessity.

"Unless this can be provided for in the immediate vicinity of the present building," he adds, "a complete removal to a new site will have to be contemplated."

And while the heart of the law is being constricted the arm of the law is lengthening—and radio has done the lengthening.

As a direct result of Metropolitan Police wireless organisation, 821 arrests were made in the last six months of 1934.

Lord Trenchard reports: "In a number of cases the time that has elapsed between the crime and the arrest has been a matter of minutes only, and there is no doubt that this speed of action has often come as a surprise, as well as something of a shock, to the offenders."

"Muckin' Up Crime"

If the loss of a car is observed and reported to the Information Room within a few minutes of its disappearance, it becomes almost an impossibility for that car to circulate in the Metropolitan Police district without being "picked up" by one of the many police patrols that are watching for it.

And if the police recognise radio's importance, so do criminals.

An "old lag" (says Lord Trenchard) was unexpectedly arrested.

"Look 'ere," he said, "your blinkin' squadrons are fair muckin' up crime."

DEATH CRASH FROM HOSPITAL WINDOW

A WOMAN patient, whose identity is being kept secret, crashed to her death from a window at the Metropolitan Hospital, Kingsland-road, Dalston, E., late last night.

She was seen to fall on to the pavement in St. Peter's-road, which adjoins the hospital.

"POISON GAS" ATTACK

An English town suffered an intensive "poison gas" attack yesterday. See the back page

JUST TO SHOW HIM HOW

"Now Watch Me," but Mrs. Margesson's Littlejohn was far too disgusted at his own misfortune to admire the spirited leap of Mr. Lindsay's Jane Grey over the water in the novices' class at the Grafton Hunt hunter trials near Towcester, Northants.

Woman World Forgot

SHE CHERISHED A MEMORY 30 YEARS

FOR twenty years the world had forgotten seventy-nine-year-old Mary Ann Woodford. No one ever wrote to her. No one ever called.

But through all that time Mary Ann Woodford had not forgotten a broken romance.

It happened thirty years ago.

Since then she had used the name of Tripp —the name of the man she loved.

Alone in her room in Rodney-street, Walworth, she read countless romantic novels.

It was there that she was found dead yesterday.

BROKE HIS £300 LEG IN COURT

IN a motor accident, Joseph Crowley, sixty-four, of Evergreen-street, Cork, had his left leg broken.

He was awarded £300 damages against the motorist at Cork yesterday.

As he was leaving the court he fell down two steps and broke his leg again.

His wife fainted.

SAUSAGE-AND-BEER TOASTS

Gen. Goering's Eve-of-Wedding Reception

HITLER "BEST MAN"

BERLIN, Tuesday.

WITH beer and champagne, huge sandwiches and sausages, Nazi leaders to-night toasted General Goering and the opera singer who will to-morrow be his bride—Fraulein Emmy Sonnemann.

They were attending a reception held by General Goering in the foyer of the State Opera House.

After the opera guests watched from special stands a great torchlight procession and tattoo carried out by Adolf Hitler's guard of honour.

Later seventy-five military aeroplanes flew through the whole repertory of aerobatics over the city.

It was all a prelude to what will be Germany's most spectacular wedding since the war.

Thirty-three thousand people have been given a day's holiday so that they may form a guard of honour outside the Cathedral, where the wedding will take place. They include 18,000 Storm Troopers, Hitler Girls, Black Guards and Hitler Youths.

Adolf Hitler will be one of the two witnesses or "best men" at the civil ceremony in the Town Hall, which will precede the service in the Cathedral.—Reuter

Picture on page 2.

"THE ABERRATIONS OF GENIUS"

SOME of Epstein's works were criticised by Sir Herbert Samuel at the Royal Society of British Sculptors' annual dinner in London last night.

"While to many of us the portrait busts of Epstein have upon them the authentic marks of genius, some of his monumental works, such as 'Genesis,' the one on exhibition now, 'Behold the Man,' and the Hudson Memorial, seem rather to be the aberrations of genius," Sir Herbert declared.

THE DAILY MIRROR, Monday, April 15, 1935.

Daily Mirror

THE DAILY PICTURE NEWSPAPER WITH THE LARGEST NET SALE

Broadcasting - Page 22

HOW TO HELP THE CHILDREN —PAGE 12

No. 9,790 Registered at the G.P.O as a Newspaper. MONDAY, APRIL 15, 1935 One Penny

FRANCE'S WARNING TO EUROPE

NON-STOP PEACE PRAYERS

HUNDREDS of special trains are to carry ex-Servicemen from Britain, France and Italy to Lourdes in ten days' time.

There, says Reuter, they will join in three days and nights of uninterrupted prayers for world peace.

Force Alternative to Treaty-Scrapping

STRESA AGREEMENT

By OUR DIPLOMATIC CORRESPONDENT

AS the Stresa Conference was breaking up last night, with the delegates smiling and Mr. MacDonald talking of a "lasting contribution to peace," the text of France's Note denouncing Germany to the League of Nations became known.

It is a stern document. It will make to-day's meeting of the League—when the protest will be considered—momentous. This is one warning it gives:—

"If the method of unilateral denunciation of international engagements becomes general, then there would soon be no room for any other policy than that of force."

Then creeps in a bitter note.

"Is it worth while," asks France, "continuing international efforts to conclude pacts of non-aggression and mutual assistance if they are to be repudiated and if international contracts are treated as void with no consequences other than moral reprobation?"

Eight-Point Accord

On this protest the official report on the Stresa Conference says that the Powers agreed on "a common line of conduct."

It was one of eight things on which they agreed.

These were the other points:—
Eastern Pact negotiations to be continued.
Consolidation of Austrian independence to be worked out by a conference at an early date.
Further study of western air pact.
Germany's conscription law is "regretted," but the Powers pledge themselves still to work for international agreement on disarmament.
Measures to be taken for a settlement of armaments for Hungary, Austria and Bulgaria.
Italy and Great Britain re-affirm obligations under Locarno Treaty as guarantors.
Three Powers agree to oppose one-sided infringement of treaties by all practicable means.
France is well satisfied with these results, though it still looks on Britain's policy as the embodiment of weakness.

Germany's Reminder

Germany, on hearing of the French Note, declared: "A clever speech for the defence in the form of a prosecution indictment," and reminded France of the obligation she assumed in the final Locarno Protocol to proceed immediately with her own disarmament.

Mr. MacDonald is now on his way home. The curtain is down at Stresa. It goes up again this morning at Geneva.

PLEASED

Mussolini shows that he can smile when he waves to admirers on the Isola Bella at the end of the Stresa Conference, a contrast with (inset) his usual sternness.

Jill Green, seven, of Bromley, Kent, and her brother Michael, nine, seated at Croydon in an aeroplane bound for Hounslow

They Fly to School

SEASON TICKETS OF MICHAEL (9) AND JILL (7)

BY A SPECIAL CORRESPONDENT
CROYDON, Sunday.

MICHAEL stood on the tarmac at Croydon air port.

"That's the prop," he said technically, pointing to the propeller. Sister Jill coo-ed with excitement.

Michael is only nine, his sister seven.

They live at Bromley, Kent, and are the only two schoolchildren—at any rate in that part of London—who will regularly travel to and from school by aeroplane.

Michael showed me his season ticket—a piece of green cardboard. Already he knows the value of it.

He said, "After to-morrow's flight the pilot has promised to autograph it for me. When I'm a man it may be valuable."

They travel on a new service opened officially to-day and known as the Inner Air Service, travelling from Croydon to Heston hourly.

These two children attend school at Hounslow, and leave the Croydon air port at 9 a.m., arriving at Heston at 9.10.

The service is being run by the Commercial Air Hire Ltd. After a month's experiment with the Inner Air Service, an outer circle service will be run on similar lines from Croydon to various air ports outside the London area.

WOMAN OF 82 DIES IN FIRE

Gallant Rescue Attempts

FAMILIES' ESCAPE

A woman of eighty-two burned to death—gallant rescue attempts by another woman—three children saved by firemen—man and wife slide down sheets to street.

THIS was the drama enacted when fire raged through a house in Albion-place, Clerkenwell, E.C., last night.

The dead woman was Mrs. Mary Ann Ryan, known in the district as Granny Banks. She lived alone in a room on the ground floor of the three-storied building.

Three Brothers Saved

Neighbours rushed to her aid when they saw flames and smoke coming from the windows. Among them was Mrs. Ada Pastson.

Time after time she ran into the doorway of the room with buckets of water, trying to fight her way through the flames. Her head was burned. Eventually she was beaten back.

Meanwhile Mr. and Mrs. Blakeman, who were on the first floor, had managed to reach safety by sliding down sheets lowered from the window.

At the top of the house three brothers, Johnny Bassett (aged seven), Teddy (aged five) and Ronnie (aged three), were in bed asleep.

After being rescued by firemen they were sent to St. Bartholomew's Hospital suffering from shock.

Escape Bid?

Mrs. Ryan was last seen alive by her granddaughter. She was then sitting in front of the fire with an oil lamp.

Her body was found near the window as if she had died trying to get out of the blazing room.

FIGHT WITH OCTOPUS

SAN FRANCISCO, Sunday.

HELPLESS in the grasp of an enormous octopus, whose tentacles had imprisoned both his legs and his left arm, a San Jose resident, Frank Coltrin, was saved from death here by a friend, who stabbed the sea giant with a knife.—Reuter.

HER UNKNOWN LOVER

BEAUTIFUL Liane Haid, Viennese film star, stopped her car on the Novisad Bridge, in Belgrade, and threw a wreath of snowdrops and violets into the water—in memory of a young man who died for love of her.

Night after night (states Reuter) he went to see her on the screen. Again and again he wrote passionate letters to her. She sent him a signed photograph. But Liane never saw him.

Distracted, the youth threw himself over the Novisad Bridge into the Danube—to death.

HOW SLIMMING IS MADE SIMPLE

HOW to keep slim, as recommended by film actress Rosemary Ames:—

Get a large box of matches, and scatter the matches all over the floor. Then pick them up—one at a time.

That is all. But—the knees must be kept straight when stooping down to pick up all those matches.

Daily Mirror

THE DAILY PICTURE NEWSPAPER WITH THE LARGEST NET SALE

Broadcasting - Page 22

THE SPENDTHRIFT SEX —Page 12

No. 9,791 — Registered at the G.P.O as a Newspaper. — TUESDAY, APRIL 16, 1935 — One Penny

THE LITTLE MAN'S BUDGET

Chancellor's Share-Out Pleases the Country

TAXPAYERS' £10,000,000 | WAGE CUTS RESTORED | THE FAMILY ALLOWANCE

REVENUE	£734,470,000
EXPENDITURE	£733,970,000
SURPLUS	£500,000

THE "Little Man's" Budget. That was the general opinion last night on Mr. Neville Chamberlain's fourth Budget.

Most of the Chancellor's concessions—including £10,000,000 for income tax—are aimed at helping the man with an income up to £500, the man who was thanked by Mr. Chamberlain in his broadcast last night for so promptly paying his taxes.

"It may be called a poor man's Budget, for it contains no relief for the wealthy," he said in this speech.

By M.P.s the Budget was given a cheerful reception. There was general praise for the Chancellor on the distribution of his concessions.

And even though he has raided the Road Fund of £4,470,000, M.P.s were more disposed to smile than to reprove, feeling that the end justifies the means.

Here are the main points of the Budget that has lightened Britain's load of taxation and provided her with more spending power

First £135 of taxable income to be charged at 1s. 6d. in the £ instead of 2s. 3d. Between £135 and £175 of taxable income, the rate to be 4s. 6d. instead of 2s. 3d.

For 2,250,000 taxpayers—70 per cent of the whole—this means a tax cut of 9d. in the £.

Personal allowance raised from £150 to £170 for a married man, and the allowance for each child after the first raised from £40 to £50. "I think if we can give this little help to those who are carrying on the race the money would not be mis-spent," said the Chancellor.

The exemption limit is to be fixed at £125 for all types of income, whether wholly or partly derived from investments. For income between £125 and £140 there is to be an over-riding provision that the tax shall not exceed one-fifth of the excess over £125.

These concessions will cost £10,000,000 in a full year.

Entertainment seats up to 6d. are relieved from all duty. This will cost £2,300,000. There is to be a reduction of duty on seats over 6d. in which living performances are given. This will cost £400,000, and last night, Mr. A. M. Wall, secretary of Equity, said he hoped this would restore touring companies to something like their former place and provide employment for 500 or 600 actors.

Mr Chamberlain

WALKING THE CHANNEL

This Man Will Try It on Monday

A man walked across Dover Harbour last night.

ENCOURAGED by his success, he now hopes to walk across the Channel next Monday.

The water-walker is Friedrich Walther, a German who has been living in Canada recently.

His water shoes consist of canoe-shaped pieces of metal weighing 55lb. each, six feet long, eight inches deep and ten inches wide, to each of which one of his feet is strapped.

Standing upright on these he holds in each hand a six foot bamboo stick, to the end of which is attached a metal cylinder. As the cylinders are forced upon the water the shoes are pushed forward.

Walther said that travelling at five miles an hour he hoped to walk the Channel in five hours.

ROAD FUND RAID

A full restoration of the economy pay cuts in the public services is to be made from July 1. This will cost £4,000,000 in the current year.

There is to be transferred from the Road Fund to the Exchequer £4,470,000 from a balance which had accrued owing to the curtailment of work under the economy policy.

The "raid" on the Road Fund, an official of the A.A. told the "Daily Mirror," "would be bitterly resented by motorists."

Any surplus available from the Fund should have been used to eliminate dangerous conditions, he declared.

The duty on heavy oil used by road vehicles is to be raised in August to 8d. per gallon. This is expected to produce £800,000.

Mr. Chamberlain's speech (writes our City Editor) is likely to be received with considerable satisfaction in the City, for it shows that the level-headed policy which has brought with it industrial recovery and rising share prices is to continue.

Mr. Chamberlain's speech and Income-Tax table on Page Five. Editorial Comment—Page Thirteen.

YES, THEY HAVE MET AT LAST

Lord Hewart, the Lord Chief Justice, handing sandwiches to Gracie Fields when he and Lady Hewart (holding teaspoon) took tea with her yesterday. Below: Lord Hewart with Gracie as a Girl Guide.

TRAPPED IN LIFT— HE APOLOGISED

Boy Released by Firemen After 40 Minutes

FOR forty minutes Howard Edwards, fifteen, of Old Gloucester-street, W.C., was trapped between the lift and the lift walls of Oakley House, Bloomsbury-street, W., last night.

But while he waited in pain to be freed, the boy apologised to business men for having made them walk down from their offices.

The boy was trapped by his ankle while going to deliver a message.

He called for assistance and firemen who were called had to cut away part of the lift.

Edwards was taken to hospital and detained for observation

Gracie Meets Lord Hewart

HE HAS SUCH A SIDE-SPLITTING TIME

LORD Hewart, the Lord Chief Justice, who expressed his desire several times to meet Miss Gracie Fields, had his wish fulfilled yesterday. He saw her acting for a film and he took tea with her.

The two famous Lancastrians were introduced to each other at one of the studios of the Associated Talking Pictures at Ealing, W., where Gracie is making her new film.

They took one long look at each other, and immediately became friends.

Lord Hewart's car glided in at the studio gates yesterday, and Lady Hewart and he were taken immediately to the set where Gracie was working. It represented the interior of a multiple store.

A minute later a young woman dressed as a gawkish Girl Guide, wearing steel-rimmed spectacles and a huge hat two sizes too small for her, strode up to Lord Hewart, and Gracie presented herself.

Suddenly she took Lord Hewart's arm, remarking, "Come on, we have got to be talking."

"Coom This Way, Lad"

"Well," asked the Lord Chief Justice, "what shall we say? You had better begin."

"All right," said Gracie, "shall I say something funny?"

"What is gormless?" "Sort of 'oop the pole," replied Gracie.

Lord and Lady Hewart watched a shot being taken, during which Gracie had to lead a party of raw Boy Scouts across the store to the lift. Then Gracie led Lord and Lady Hewart to tea

Arriving at the tea room she exclaimed in broad accent, "Coom this way for the buns and cake, lad," to which Lord Hewart replied, "That is the most homely remark I have heard."

Before Gracie went back to her work Lord Hewart invited her to pay him a return visit at his "local police court," which she readily accepted

THE DAILY MIRROR, Thursday, April 18, 1935.

Daily Mirror

Broadcasting - Page 22

THE DAILY PICTURE • NEWSPAPER WITH THE LARGEST NET SALE

WHAT NOT TO DO AT EASTER —Page 25

No. 9,793 Registered at the G.P.O. as a Newspaper. THURSDAY, APRIL 18, 1935 One Penny

GERMANY FURIOUS AT CENSURE

THE VAMPIRE OF THE TOWER

Mr. Gregory Dye, the twenty-four-year-old garage proprietor of Earl's Court, S.W., rehearsing the leap from a turret at the Tower which he will make as Colonel Blood in the forthcoming Tower of London Pageant. Colonel Blood makes the leap after stealing the Crown jewels. Mr. Dye was selected from 600 to 700 applicants.

'Saddled with New War Lie'

BITTER TALK

Germany is furiously angry.

THIS is a statement from Berlin last night after the Council of the League of Nations at Geneva had condemned the re-armament of the Reich.

Berlin, says Reuter, regards the Geneva action as a spanner thrown into the cogwheels of European diplomacy which threatens to break up the whole machine just at a moment when there seemed a possibility of making it run smoothly.

There is bitter resentment that Germany should have been "saddled with a new war threat guilt lie."

The possibility of Germany's return to the League is now regarded as remote.

One possibility spoken of in Berlin last night was a new plebiscite to demonstrate to the outside world German unity on the question of armaments.

The isolation of Germany, resulting from Hitler's policy, is explained to the German public as due to "French pressure on the Powers."

There are allegations of "incredible intrigue behind the scenes," and especially is anger

"Stresa was good, Geneva was better," was Sir John Simon's summing up of the diplomatic situation just before leaving Geneva last night for England, says Reuter.

directed against "the speech of hatred" delivered by Litvinoff, the Soviet delegate at Geneva, who accused Germany of re-arming with the intention of attacking her neighbours.

That Litvinoff should bear ill-will to Germany can be understood, it is stated, but it is less understandable that the European Powers, who "cannot expect anything good from Bolshevism, should be blind enough to serve these lies."

Condemnation of Germany's re-armament was passed by the Council of the League with only one State—Denmark—abstaining from voting.

Litvinoff, in his attack, hinted at Germany as "the State ruled by people who have announced to the whole world a programme of revenge."

Mr. Ramsay MacDonald, in a statement in Parliament yesterday on the Stresa conference and in a broadcast speech last night, emphasised that Britain had undertaken no new commitments.

TUNNEL NOT A BUILT-UP AREA

Is the new Queensway Tunnel, Liverpool, a built-up area?

This was the poser put to the Liverpool stipendiary yesterday, when a man was accused of having driven through the tunnel at more than thirty miles an hour.

The police contended that the tunnel was a built-up area.

The magistrate decided that it was not, because there was no system of street lighting within the meaning of the Act.

DUCHESS AT THE BALL

Dancing Debut with Duke of Kent

THE Duchess of Kent will make her first public ballroom appearance with the Duke at the Empire Ball in aid of St. George's Hospital at Grosvenor House, Park-lane, on May 8.

A feature of the ball will be one of the prizes for ladies, which consists of a choice between a magnificent pair of diamond clips worth £835 and a diamond bracelet of similar value.

These jewels, which have been presented by a donor who wishes to remain anonymous at present, will be on view at Grosvenor House after the Easter holiday.

THE EGG PORTRAIT

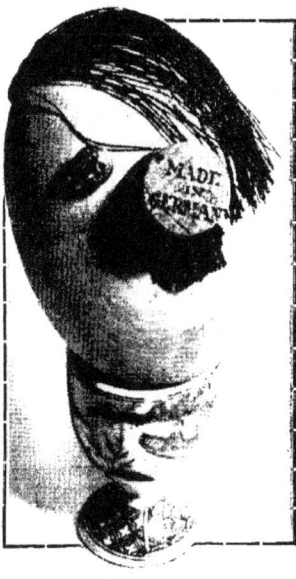

Let us praise famous men in Easter eggs, says "W. B.," the designer of this novel caricature. The recipe is: Take a wooden Easter egg and garnish with oddments—corks, a silk tassel, and so on. You've guessed who this one is!—Herr Hitler.

Bandits Fire on Sleeping English Girls

ONE WOUNDED IN ESCAPE DASH

FIVE Spanish bandits fired on two English girls near Santiago last night and wounded one of them.

When they were attacked the girls, Miss Emily Reilly and Miss Dorothy Dowman, were sleeping in their car.

In an attempt to escape, Miss Reilly braved a hail of bullets by racing into the open and trying to start the car. She was wounded in the shoulder.

What happened afterwards is not yet clear (says Reuter).

Gunmen Vanished

After the gunmen had vanished the Civic Guards found the girls and took them to the village of Ordenes, where they were detained pending inquiry.

They were later released following representations by the British Vice-Consul at Corunna, Mr Henry Guyatt.

The girls spent the night at Santiago, and intend to motor to Lisbon to-day and embark for England.

Last Pilgrimage to Wife's Grave

SINCE the death of his wife, seventy-year-old Charles Ely, a retired business man, of Lincewood Park-drive, Langdon Hills (Essex), regularly visited her grave to place there flowers to her memory.

Yesterday he plucked some flowers and set out on his pilgrimage of love. Soon afterwards he collapsed in the street.

He died still clutching his bouquet.

Three-County Hunt for Woman

FROM OUR OWN CORRESPONDENT

ALDERSHOT, Wednesday night.

POLICE of three counties are to-night searching for Mrs. Lucy Rose Townsend, aged thirty-nine, of Winton, Winchester - street, South Farnborough (Hants), who mysteriously disappeared three days ago from her home.

Contents of a letter left have prompted the search, and long stretches of the Basingstoke Canal and also Cove Reservoir, on the fringe of Farnborough Aerodrome, have been dragged.

Before her disappearance Mrs. Townsend said she might visit relatives at Guildford, but inquiries there revealed that she had not been in that district.

Mrs. Townsend and her husband are well known in Farnborough.

THE DAILY MIRROR, Thursday, April 25, 1935.

Daily Mirror

Broadcasting - Page 22

THE DAILY PICTURE NEWSPAPER WITH THE LARGEST NET SALE

A TALK TO UNTIDY PEOPLE —PAGE 26

No. 9,798 Registered at the G.P.O. as a Newspaper. THURSDAY, APRIL 25, 1935 One Penny

500-SEATER AIR-LINER PLANNED

German Faith in Steam-Planes

GIVING HER THE LION'S SHARE

Shock for guests at a Paris hotel.—Herr Kemmerich, famous German swimmer, breakfasting with his lioness, so tame that she can be fed with a teaspoon. He bought her when she was a few months old.

VALUE AS TROOP CARRIERS

BY A "DAILY MIRROR" SPECIAL CORRESPONDENT

Giant aeroplanes, capable of carrying 500 passengers, fitted with steam-turbine engines, and easily convertible into troop-carriers in time of war, are likely to be the next development in flying.

IN Germany air leviathans of this type have already been designed. Construction, according to Mr. Claude Grahame-White, the flying pioneer, who has seen the designs, might start any time if the necessary capital was put up.

Mr. Grahame-White has just returned from Germany. Yesterday, the twenty-fifth anniversary of his glorious failure to win Britain's first air race from London to Manchester, he told me of his faith in the future of the giant steam-driven 'plane.

"Such machines," he said, "will undoubtedly be the big development of the future. In Germany I saw a marvellous turbine, which can develop 5,000 horsepower, at 27,000 revolutions per minute, without any vibration."

Stainless steel, he believes, is the principal factor in the use of turbines.

"When, in pre-war days, they made experiments with steam-driven machines, the turbines had to be made of mild steel, which would not stand up to the strain," he said. "And when will the first of these steam-planes take the air?"

Britain Lagging Behind?

"This year, next year . . ." says Mr. Grahame-White, for "the trouble with pioneer efforts is always lack of capital." But he added:—

"It is impossible to say that Germany may not start to build at once. But, as to this country, well, heaven knows when."

Some months ago it was revealed that engineers were working in Berlin on a "Flying

(Continued on back page)

Twenty-five years ago Mr. Claude Grahame-White landed at Rugby in this 'plane, one of the pioneer heavier-than-air machines which have grown into—

—such aerial giants as the Do. X., and now, according to Mr. Grahame-White, look like developing into steam-driven clippers of the clouds carrying 500 people.

Steel Magnate Sees Tragedy

TWO MEN KILLED IN A COLLISION

TWO motor-cyclists were killed and their pillion passengers injured in a road smash in which Sir William Firth, the steel magnate, and Lady Firth were involved at Malden (Surrey) late last night.

The dead were:—

Albert Sidney Malcolm, aged twenty-five, of Kilburn-lane, W., and

Frank Walter Barnes, aged twenty-two, of Marlow-drive, North Cheam.

The injured pillion passengers are:—

Miss Rita Kelly, of Charrington-street, St. Pancras, and

Harold Arthur Barnes, aged twenty-one, of Marlow-drive, North Cheam, brother of one of the dead men.

Head-on Crash

Sir William Firth's car was being driven by his chauffeur along the Kingston by-pass towards Tolworth.

Shortly after passing the roundabout at Malden cross-roads the car was in a head-on collision with a motor-cycle. The car swerved and crashed into a fence.

Another motor-cyclist, following closely behind the other vehicle became involved.

Sir William and his wife escaped unhurt, though Lady Firth suffered from shock.

Acrobat's Crash on to Stage

SCREAMING WOMEN IN AUDIENCE

WHILE the drums were rolling for the big moment in an acrobatic act at the Broadway Cinema, Stratford, E., last night, a man balancing on top of a 15ft. pole held by his partner crashed to the stage and was seriously injured.

Margie Clifton was holding the pole while Franchon Janssens was balancing on his hands on the top. The act would have concluded with the girl placing the pole on her shoulder and letting go with her hands.

Then Janssens seemed to collapse. He fell, turning a somersault before he hit the stage.

Women screamed and became hysterical and the curtain was lowered, but when Janssens had been taken to hospital the programme was resumed.

"We have done the turn hundreds of times," Margie Clifton told the Daily Mirror. "All I can think is that he fainted. If he could have held on to the pole I could have thrown him on to his feet."

Janssens has a fractured hip and arm.

MISSING WOMAN DEAD ON COMMON

FOR days search has been made for Mrs. Louise Rose Townsend, thirty-nine, of Winton, Winchester - street, Farnborough (Hants). Last night she was found—dead in some bushes on Farnborough Common.

The discovery was made by a Farnborough motor engineer.

Since the woman's disappearance ten days ago the Basingstoke Canal and the Cove Reservoir have been dragged by the police, and inquiries had been made in several counties.

Beauty may be only skin deep, but it is found among dark skins just as much as white. This particular example is Miss Tripoli 1935, winner of a beauty contest in the North African province.

15,000 GIRLS ARE SAYING THIS!

They All Want To Be Miss Golden Voice

BY OUR EXPERT TELEPHONIST

CAN you say this?

"On the third stroke it will be three thirty-three precisely."

Mind you trroll your R's prrroperrrly. Then try these:—

"She has a fan in her hand."

"The new rule will prove a boon"

Or this: Have you had Hatch End 866?

These are some of the tests that are being put to 15,000 telephone girls who are competing in the Post Office's search for the Girl with the Golden Voice.

Tests to find her are now in full swing. All exchanges are entering, and in the opinion of those who have already completed the tests are very difficult.

This Is the Test

Here is what the girls have to do.

They are handed a piece of paper on which are the test sentences and told to speak into an ordinary telephone instrument of the new type—with the earpiece and transmitter in one.

First they have to speak their number. Every girl on an exchange has a number and they enter on that number. No girl entering is known by her name.

Then they have to count from one to twelve —afterwards "five, ten, fifteen, twenty," and so on up to "fifty-five".

Then come the test sentences.

The winning girl's voice will be heard by subscribers telling the time on the newly-invented "talking clock".

THE DAILY MIRROR, Saturday, April 27, 1935.

Broadcasting - Page 23

Daily Mirror

THE DAILY PICTURE NEWSPAPER WITH THE LARGEST NET SALE

JOHN BUCHAN'S BOOK ON MONDAY

No. 9,800 Registered at the G.P.O. as a Newspaper. SATURDAY, APRIL 27, 1935. One Penny

EX-KING'S LONDON GUARD RIDDLE

Bigger Than for British Royalty

HIS ASTONISHMENT

By A SPECIAL REPRESENTATIVE

WHAT is the mystery behind the amazing police precautions at Victoria Station last night when the ex-King of Greece arrived in London from Paris?

More detectives and policemen were on guard about the station and on the platform than are present when one of our own Royal Family travels.

It is rumoured that ex-King George has come to London to consult with Greek royalists here about his chances of regaining the throne.

Did the police fear an attempt at a demonstration or something worse by anti-royalists? There was no indication that anything of the sort was intended.

Many of the people meeting the boat-train were asking in surprise what all the policemen were doing. They did not even know an ex-King was arriving.

Double Lines of Police

Half an hour before the boat-train arrived, with Special Branch officers travelling on it, detectives from Scotland Yard and uniformed policemen were on the platform, and subjected those meeting the train to careful scrutiny.

Just before the train steamed in a posse of constables paraded under superintendents and grouped themselves at the point where ex-King George would alight from his Pullman coach.

A large saloon car was drawn up at the side of the platform at this point, and when the train drew up a double line of policemen, detectives and railway officials formed a passage-way for the visitor from train to car.

Short, plainly dressed in a brown travelling coat and brown pork-pie hat, and wearing a rimless monocle, the ex-King himself looked rather astonished at the array of uniforms to greet him.

Hurried to His Car

Before he could do more than glance round he was hurried to his car.

At the door of the car I leant forward to speak to him, intending to ask him if the rumours of his return to Greece were correct, but he anticipated my question, and, as he entered the car, said hurriedly:—
"Quite untrue, quite untrue!"

At the same moment a photographer who was on the platform lifted his camera and was instantly seized by two policemen.

Holding both his arms, they marched him down the platform protesting.

At the same time other policemen told photographers standing in the station yard to put away their cameras.

Orders had been given, it was stated, that no photographs of the ex-King were to be taken—not even of his car leaving the station.

DUKE OF KENT A KNIGHT OF THE THISTLE

THE Duke of Kent has been appointed a Knight of the Thistle. His three brothers are already members of the Order

THE "FINAL"

SUNSHINE is promised for to-day, so there is every chance of the King taking his place with the great cheering crowd of enthusiasts at the Cup Final.

By dawn this morning thousands had arrived in London from the provinces. On Page 5 they will find suggestions for places to visit. On Page 12 a Welsh miner tells of weeks of "scraping" to get the money for the trip. The teams' chances are discussed on Page 30, and on the back page are pictures of the "star" players.

ST. PAUL'S GAINS A NEW BEAUTY

The lofty gilt cross towering in a pool of light above the vast dome last night, when for the first time the roof and turrets of St. Paul's Cathedral were floodlit—a rehearsal for the Jubilee celebrations. Nearly 100 lamps have been installed and when another thirty have been placed in position St. Paul's will be completely illuminated.

Mr. Antony Tudor.

Week-End Trip to Cape Town

CAMPBELL BLACK OUT FOR RECORDS

DURING the summer Campbell Black, who, with C. W. A. Scott, won the great air race to Australia, will attempt four record-breaking week-end trips.

The first trip will be made in July to Cape-town and back, the second to Canada and back, the third to the Far East and the fourth to a destination unknown.

The flights are being financed by a Sheffield man, and it is understood that the cost will be about £40,000. They will start from the newly-formed £100,000 Firbeck Country Club, near Sheffield.

This announcement was made last night at the opening of the club.

Mr. Black is having constructed a Super-Comet machine, which, it is stated, will be the fastest and biggest long-distance machine in the world.

There's Romance Still—Even at Smithfield

THIS MARKET CLERK DANCED TO FAME

BY A SPECIAL REPRESENTATIVE

A YOUNG Englishman, who once worked as a clerk in Smithfield meat market, is one of the important people behind the Covent Garden Opera Season which opens on Monday.

He is Mr. Antony Tudor. At the age of twenty-four he has composed the entirely new choreography and dances for the ballets in "La Cenerentola" and "Schwanda the Bagpiper."

And he is going to dance in his own ballets.

Mr. Tudor was a discovery of Marie Rambert, whose ballet is taking part in both operas.

Some years ago he went to her and said that he wanted to study dancing, but could not attend classes until four o'clock in the afternoon. Asked the reason for that, he explained that he was working.

Later, he confessed that he was a clerk in Smithfield meat market and that he had to start work early in the morning and did not finish before three in the afternoon.

And so Mr. Tudor started to study dancing. He got up at 4.30 every morning and went to Smithfield. When he had finished he went on to ballet classes.

His Smithfield days are now over, and he is now one of the leading British choreographers. His ballet, "The Planets," is well known.

HOLLYWOOD SHOOTINGS

SEARCH FOR MYSTERY COUNTESS

"Too Important To Be Named"

HOLLYWOOD, Friday.

A MYSTERY Countess, described by the police as "too important and well-known to be named," is now being sought for questioning in connection with the shooting of Paul Wharton and Professor Bolte.

The quest follows the finding of a telegram to the Countess in the flat tenanted by Howard, Wharton's chauffeur, who committed suicide.

Two men and two women have already been questioned.—Reuter.

Story of the shootings—page seven.

"QUINS" WORTH £30,000

IT pays to be a quintuplet! Already an estate valued at 151,000 dollars (about £30,000) has accumulated for the famous Dionne "quins"—£6,000 each.

THE DAILY MIRROR, Tuesday, April 30, 1935.

Daily Mirror

THE DAILY PICTURE NEWSPAPER WITH THE LARGEST NET SALE

Broadcasting - Page 22

SPLENDOUR AT ARCHBISHOP'S ENTHRONEMENT —Page 4

No. 9,802 — Registered at the G.P.O. as a Newspaper. — TUESDAY, APRIL 30, 1935 — One Penny

SIR THOMAS LATE FOR THE OPERA!

Audience's Ironic Clapping— They Had Obeyed His 'Be Early' Instruction

The only man who held up the start of the Opera last night.

WINGS DRAMA OF SINGER'S BAD LUCK

By DONALD MALLETT

OPERA - GOERS, warned by Sir Thomas Beecham that the doors would be locked against late-comers, had filled every seat a minute before 7 o'clock at the opening of Covent Garden last night. But there was one late-comer—SIR THOMAS BEECHAM!

At six o'clock, an hour before the opera was due to begin, the fashionable society audience began to arrive at the Opera House and stand about in the foyer. All had taken immense care not to be late.

At one minute to seven every seat was taken. Everyone was in place.

Seven o'clock came ... one minute ... two minutes past ... three minutes past, but still Sir Thomas did not appear at the conductor's desk.

At four minutes past seven the house began gently to barrack. Faint, derisive bursts of clapping came from different parts of the house.

In another minute the whole house had taken this up, and was clapping loudly, ironically.

Another Surprise

Then five-and-a-half minutes past seven Sir Thomas arrived. He was greeted with a tremendous burst of applause.

Imperturbable and unsmiling, he faced the audience, and bowed several times gravely. Then, without a gesture he turned round and began to conduct the National Anthem.

Then came another surprise, for at the close of the National Anthem Mr. Geoffrey Toye appeared on the stage, and announced that Max Hirzel, who was to have sung the name role of Lohengrin, had a serious cold.

Melchior, a great Covent Garden favourite, was to take his place, but he was singing without any rehearsal at all. "He asks for your indulgence," said Mr. Toye.

(Continued on back page)

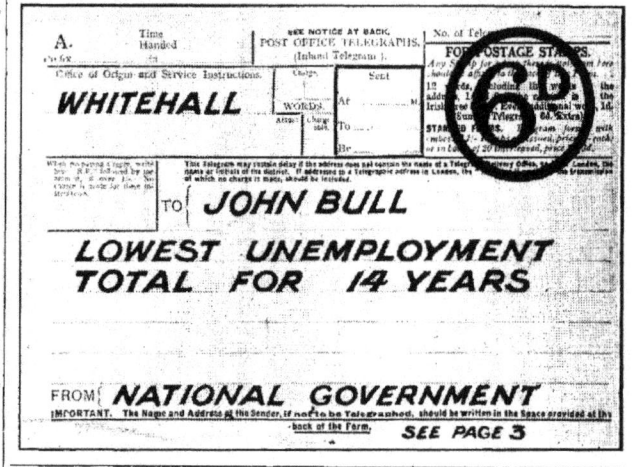

As promised, the exclusion notice was put up as soon as the conductor appeared.

Banbury Cross, in Fact Very Cross!

2,000 SPECTATORS CHASE FOOTBALL REFEREE

THERE were "doings" at Banbury Cross last night.

But instead of the nursery rhyme "fine lady on a white horse" there were 2,500 people riding the "high horse"; and the "music wherever one goes" was a deuce of a discord.

Banbury Spencer football eleven were playing Kings Sutton in the semi-final of the Banbury Cross Gold Cup.

A penalty was awarded to Spencer during extra time. The other side disagreed—and the whole team walked off the field!

Two thousand jeering spectators chased the referee (Mr. O. Wilson). He got away in his shorts, with his everyday trousers tucked under an arm!

But first of all he awarded the match to Spencers.

CONSTABLE ASSAULTED

While on plain clothes duty in Penton-street, Kings Cross, last night, a police constable was assaulted by three men.

Three men will appear at Clerkenwell Police Court this morning in connection with the affair.

WHITEHALL

TO **JOHN BULL**

LOWEST UNEMPLOYMENT TOTAL FOR 14 YEARS

FROM **NATIONAL GOVERNMENT**

SEE PAGE 3

AUGUSTUS JOHN FIGHTS FIRE

Art Treasures Destroyed at Artist's Home

MR. AUGUSTUS JOHN, the artist, and his son, Robin, wearing pyjamas and dressing-gowns, helped other members of the family to fight a fire which broke out at their home at Fordingbridge (Hants) yesterday.

With extinguishers and buckets of water, they put out the flames before the fire brigade, stationed seven miles away, arrived.

The room was badly damaged and antique furniture and a number of paintings, including some by Mr. John himself, were destroyed.

Mrs. John stated last night that the pictures were rather valuable.

DEARER PETROL?

Rumours of an increase in the price of petrol were again current in London yesterday, but no definite information could be obtained.

It was suggested that an increase—possibly 1d. a gallon—would come into force in two or three days.

Opera-goers passing through Covent Garden market on their way to "Lohengrin."

POLICE PAY £1,089 THAT A P.-C. STOLE

Some months ago a police officer embezzled £1,089—money he had collected after serving summonses against rate defaulters in Croydon.

He was sentenced for the crime.

Yesterday the Finance Committee of the Croydon Borough Council reported that the Metropolitan Police had paid them the £1,089, and had paid it "cheerfully, willingly and without quibbling"

12-YEAR-OLD GIRL "PAGANS"

Never Heard of The Lord's Prayer

THE headmistress of a secondary school was telling a class of twelve-year-old girls the story of Holy Week, of the trial of Christ and the Crucifixion.

She intended to divide the lesson into series, but when she stopped on the first day, with the scene of Christ before Pilate, the children cried in chorus:

"Oh! Do go on. We want to know what happened. Did He get off?"

This incident actually happened. The headmistress herself related it to the Dean of Canterbury, Dr. Hewlett Johnson, who told it again last night to a Queen's Hall audience which included the Duchess of York.

The girls came from well-known families, said Dr. Johnson. They had never heard of the Lord's Prayer or the Ten Commandments.

He deplored the fact that there was growing up in some of the better-class suburbs a "sheer paganism."

DOCTOR'S SEA DEATH

Dr. Alpin McGregor, medical officer on the British steamer Baronessa, is reported to have fallen overboard while the vessel was on a voyage from London to Buenos Aires.

Dr. McGregor was thirty-eight. He played Rugby for Bart's and for the Barbarians, and was a brother of Mr. Duncan McGregor, a Scottish international player.

Another brother, Dr. Hector McGregor, is in practice at Birmingham.

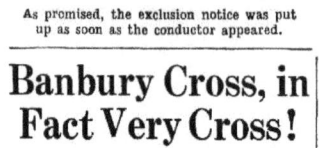

THE DAILY MIRROR, Saturday, May 4, 1935.

Broadcasting - Page 23

Daily Mirror

THE DAILY PICTURE NEWSPAPER WITH THE LARGEST NET SALE

SHORT STORY —Page 25

No. 9,806. Registered at the G.P.O as a Newspaper.   SATURDAY, MAY 4, 1935   One Penny

AMAZING LONDON JUBILEE SCENES

Crowds in Scramble to See the Palace— Horseback Sightseers

One street in which the pavements were packed, and also at times the traffic had to crawl. The scene in Ludgate-hill looking towards St. Paul's, showing the dense throng out to view the gay wealth of garlands and bunting.

TAXI - DRIVERS' RICH HARVEST IN TRAFFIC CHAOS

BY A SPECIAL REPRESENTATIVE

On Monday the Royal coach, travelling with ceremonial dignity, will cover the Jubilee procession route in fifty-six minutes.

Late last night a London taxi-driver, dodging in and out of the "jams," took two hours.

THAT gives an idea of the press of people and traffic in the West End last night. Pavements were a seething mass of sightseers.

Robot lights flashed red and green —but traffic could not move.

Buckingham Palace seemed to cast a spell over the swaying crowds. Battery after battery of the giant floodlights was brought into play until the whole front of the building seemed ablaze.

The Queen Victoria Memorial in front of the Palace was also floodlit. Scores of people scrambled over the chains flanking the base of the statue to get a better view of the Palace. They were quickly stopped by the police.

At Piccadilly Circus and in Oxford Circus it was, at times, impossible to move more than a few yards in half an hour.

It was a great night for taxi-drivers. Never have they had such a harvest. Every cab in London seemed to be engaged, and most of them were open, so that their occupants could see the decorations.

One unusual sight was about a dozen sightseers, men and women, riding horseback along the Embankment and up Northumberland-avenue.

It was all like a Continental fiesta, but without the noise. That was the strange thing about the crowds—everyone seemed silent and awe-struck to think that London, usually so solemn and staid, could ever become such a bower of colour.

FOREIGNERS BEWILDERED

And the crowds, as they stood, allowed themselves a sly chuckle....

The joke was at the expense of a host of very mystified visitors from Paris, Berlin and Vienna and all those other cities whose glamour is quoted in contrast to London's drabness.

For you could have searched to the ends of the earth without finding a rival to the jollity and high jinks of the night.

(Continued on back page)

Other Jubilee news on pages 4 and 5. London theatre guide on page 9. Special trains, buses and trams, page 20. Pictures on pages 14, 17, 19 and 26.

BIG OIL BLAZE AFTER EXPLOSION

AN auxiliary transformer blew up and 200 gallons of oil burst into flame at the Central Electricity Board's works at Creeks Mouth, Barking, last night.

Employees ran into the transformer room and tried to put out the fire with extinguishers, but the flames were too fierce. Barking fire brigade was called and had the blaze under control in forty minutes.

Extra workers were sent from their homes in cars so that the electricity service would not be interrupted.

Nazi Official 'Plane Lost

SECRET KEPT FOR THREE DAYS—3 ON BOARD

BERLIN, Friday.

A GERMAN Government passenger aeroplane has been missing for three days, it is revealed in an official announcement to-day. Beyond saying that an officer, his wife and child were on board, the authorities do not give further particulars.

The aeroplane, a six-seater Junker W. 34, was one of several used exclusively for transport of official personages. It set out on April 30 from Boeblingen, near Stuttgart, for Breslau. Normally it should have reached Breslau in five hours.

Since its departure nothing has been heard of the machine.

News of the disappearance was presumably withheld till now in accordance with Nazi official practice, whereby air accidents are either not allowed to be mentioned in the Press at all or only in short official bulletins.

SAID WITH FLOWERS

Real flowers are being used to decorate the offices of the Ministry of Health in Whitehall—though the job of the man on the plank doesn't look any too healthy!

Empire Congress to Plead for Right to Marry Young

BAR AGAINST IT IS PERIL TO SOCIETY

REGULATIONS against early marriage which are imposed by public bodies and other employers are to be discussed by delegates to the Imperial Social Hygiene Congress, which meets in London on July 9 next.

A committee has been appointed "to analyse the present position regarding artificial barriers to early marriage and the social effects of these barriers."

Discussing the denial of the right to marry early, Mrs. Neville Rolfe, secretary-general of the British Social Hygiene Council, said last night that the Council believed that once young people had decided on marriage partnership they should marry with a minimum of delay.

"Long engagements are highly undesirable," she said. "If the couple are separated during a long engagement they tend to develop along individual lines—away from each other—thus jeopardising their future marriage relationship.

"If they are together during a long engagement an undesirable emotional and physical strain is imposed on both.

"The public toleration of this practice tends to force young people into a philandering attitude towards sex," added Mrs. Rolfe. "Few things do more to upset the stability of future marriage and increase the risk of infection with its dangers for the future children of the nation."

EARTH TREMORS IN NOTTINGHAM

People Alarmed by Terrific Report at 2.30 a.m.

EARTH tremors alarmed residents in Aspley, a suburb of Nottingham, early yesterday. They are attributed to subsidences in the ground.

The first minor 'quake occurred at about 2.30 a.m. It was followed by another about twenty minutes later.

Mr. F. G. H. Harris, a local cycle dealer, said that he was awakened by a terrific bang and thought that all the cycles in his shop had fallen over.

THE DAILY MIRROR, Monday, May 6, 1935.

Daily Mirror

THE DAILY PICTURE NEWSPAPER THE LARGEST NET SALE

No. 9,807 — Registered at the G.P.O. as a Newspaper. — MONDAY — One Penny

THE KING
GOD BLESS HIM

Your Majesty:—

YOU and we have watched together a whole world turn and destroy itself—a world that never came back.

You and we together have built a new one—where men are fed and women are sheltered, and each one of us can walk free from the fear of death once more about his own occasions

And now, to-day, with full hearts, we turn and thank you.

We thank you for your labours as a man who has borne with us the bitter freight of those years when the only pay was blood—borne it side by side with us and earned a handclasp from us all. It was your bearing then that kept our shoulders straight

We thank you for the destiny of your birth as our King. It is the greatest of all fates that can befall a man, and you have borne it greatly.

But most of all to-day we thank you—you who had the chance of choosing to be so great a King of heralds and of battles—for stepping down out of the centuries into the market-place of life, and being instead a King of hearths, of firesides, and of handclasps.

May God defend you and yours.

THE DAILY MIRROR, Friday, May 10, 1935.

Broadcasting - Page 24

Daily Mirror
THE DAILY PICTURE NEWSPAPER WITH THE LARGEST NET SALE

No. 9,811. Registered at the G.P.O. as a Newspaper. FRIDAY, MAY 10, 1935 One Penny

PARLIAMENT'S HOMAGE TO THE KING
—Page 7

BRITAIN'S TWO-FOLD AIR DRIVE
"Get Ready" Order to 'Plane Firms

FAMOUS BOTH: QUEEN AND ADMIRAL AT M.P.'s TEA-PARTY

COMPULSORY DRILL FOR ALL PLANNED

MOVES TO STRENGTHEN BRITAIN'S AIR POWER IN BOTH ATTACK AND DEFENCE BECAME KNOWN LAST NIGHT.

The Air Ministry has asked aircraft contractors to accelerate deliveries, be ready for R.A.F. expansion and inform them of any foreign or civil orders before committing themselves.

Whitehall officials and municipal representatives have been discussing compulsory air raid drill for civilians.

Air power will, it is expected, figure largely in the Defence Debate in the House of Commons the week after next.

Its postponement for a week, to give the Government a chance to hear—and be guided by—Hitler's foreign-affairs pronouncement in the Reichstag, brings the debate to within three days of Empire Air Day May 25 which is aimed at making Britain air-minded.

An immense increase in general interest in this second Air Day has been predicted by Lord Wakefield. The co-operation of local authorities with Whitehall following the Government's first announcement on air-raid drill has been an index of that interest.

The talks have been the means of preparing scheme to "educate" the public in air perils without unduly alarming them.

Raids Rehearsed

The authorities feel that this education should be in the German manner, with air raids specially staged. This is because the dangers of an air attack may largely lie in psychological effect.

Camouflage measures, the obscuring of lights and the adjustment of gas-masks will all come into the scheme of education.

Great importance is attached to the contribution which a well-informed and well-disciplined civilian population can make in hiding targets both by day and by night.

Meanwhile, a committee of eminent scientific men appointed by the Air Ministry and a special committee of the Committee of Imperial Defence are inquiring into means of countering air attacks and night bombers.

Two-Year Plan

The Air Ministry's letter to aircraft firms advising them of the possibility of considerable demands as a result of R.A.F. expansion brought this explanation from an official of a leading British firm:—

"The letter asks what maximum output could be secured, and infers that for a considerable period ahead sufficient orders will be available to keep the works at full pressure.

"I understand that this applies to military aircraft, and refers to a period of at least two years."

In America and in Europe yesterday important air developments took place.

With warlike secrecy forty-eight U.S. 'planes, manned by 200 men, left Honolulu yesterday on a mass flight of 1,200 miles to Midway Island, an important base on the route from the United States to the Far East, says Reuter.

Rome the stage is set for Franco-Italian air discussions.

General Denain, the French Air Minister will arrive there to-day, says Central News.

One of his aims will be to ensure close technical collaboration between the two air services. This will involve the sharing of technical secrets between the air staffs of France and Italy under the general supervision of General Denain.

Queen Marie of Rumania talking with a fellow guest at the tea party given by Commander Locker-Lampson, M.P., at the Savoy Hotel, while Admiral of the Fleet Earl Jellicoe gets on with his tea. Queen Marie was the guest of honour.

MAX BAER SHOT DURING
RADIO ACT REHEARSAL
Operation for Mystery Injury—Doctor's Vigil

FROM OUR SPECIAL CORRESPONDENT
NEW YORK, Thursday.

MAX Baer, world heavy-weight boxing champion, was wounded over the heart to-night by a shot from a pistol supposed to contain only blank cartridges.

He was rehearsing for a radio act in New York when the accident occurred. He was rushed to hospital at Long Branch (New Jersey). An operation was performed and an anti-tetanus injection was given.

Baer—still unconscious—was later taken back to his training quarters. A doctor remained with him all night, and it is stated that his fight with James Braddock, due to take place on June 13, will probably have to be cancelled.

When the news spread that the Romeo of the ring had been injured, his manager, Mr. Ancil Hoffman, told me to-night, the wires began to burn.

The Human Bulletin!

"All I have done for the last four hours," Mr. Hoffman said, "is act like a bulletin and a paper knife, clipping open telegrams from women!"

I asked Mr. Hoffman about Max's new romance; the rumour that he is to marry a Middle West girl and settle down to earn big money with his entertaining ability.

"I just can't tell you, son. Max is a strange fella. Every time I see him he raves.... either she's a blonde, brunette or redhead. Believe me, they are just boy flirtations."

"You should see his file. First one reigns supreme. Then I never hear any more about her."

Shoal of Telegrams

"Just look at the pile of telegrams I have here now. All worrying about Max. But in a couple of days he will be up and training again. Still, you can't take risks with a champion. No, sir.

"You can tell England that Max may soon be over there—but it is for film work in London. And now I must open more telegrams."

Max Baer.

£20,000 WRECK CLAIM

Damages of £20,000 are claimed against Captain W. F. Wake-Walker, of the British cruiser Dragon, in an action which began yesterday in the Admiralty Court at Montreal over the sinking of a ship, says Reuter.

The Man Who Must Not Know
BITS OF PAPER HE THINKS ARE RARE STAMPS

An aged blind man gets out each day the stamp albums he spent years, and a fortune, in filling, and handles with loving care—pieces of worthless paper.

Seldom has a more moving story been told than this Story of the Man Who Doesn't Know, related yesterday by Mr. Robson Lowe, a London philatelist.

HERE it is in Mr. Lowe's own words as he told it yesterday to a Southampton gathering of collectors.

"While on a visit to America in quest of stamps I heard of an old man who was reputed to possess one of the world's finest collections, and went to visit him. He was living with his two daughters, and was quite blind.

"His stamps were his most precious possession. He refused to part with them at any price, but he said he would be proud and happy to allow me to inspect them.

"The old man brought out his albums. To my amazement I found on opening them that they contained nothing but pieces of paper of a similar size to stamps.

"Realising that something was wrong, I made no comment, but pretended to admire the collection.

"Later one of the old man's daughters told me the secret. After the world war, she explained, her father experienced considerable capital losses, and the family were hard put to make ends meet.

"One by one all their valuables were sold. The father, unaware of his family's poverty, stoutly refused to part with his precious stamps.

"One day the second daughter hit upon the plan of taking out a few stamps and replacing them with pieces of paper of similar size.

"The family managed to live on the proceeds of the sale of the stamps.

"This went on for years, and at the time I arrived the entire collection had been sold. The old collector," Mr. Lowe concluded, "was left proudly and contentedly handling pieces of worthless paper."

THE DAILY MIRROR, Monday, May 13, 1935

Broadcasting - Page 22

Daily Mirror

THE DAILY PICTURE NEWSPAPER WITH THE LARGEST NET SALE

ANOTHER MEMORABLE WEEK —Page 4

No. 9,813 Registered at the G.P.O. as a Newspaper.   MONDAY, MAY 13, 1935   One Penny

DOCKLAND HAILS THE KING

Among London's Poorest

JUBILEE'S MOST AMAZING SCENES

Boys running beside the royal car and dwellers in the street cheering enthusiastically when the King and Queen were passing through Pigott-street, Limehouse—a typical scene during their Majesties' surprise drive to the East-End yesterday. Other pictures on page 32.

Will There Be a Reconciliation?

EX-KING GEORGE OF GREECE AND WIFE

THE possibility of a reconciliation between ex-King George and ex-Queen Elizabeth of Greece is stated to have been discussed in Bukarest between the Greek Foreign Minister, M. Maximos, and the ex-Queen herself.

M. Maximos, who is in Bukarest in connection with the meeting of the Balkan Entente, visited ex-Queen Elizabeth (states Reuter).

A reconciliation, it is stated, would be a preliminary to an eventual restoration of the monarchy in Greece.

[Exiled from his country eleven years ago, ex-King George and his wife have lived apart for a number of years.]

"BASTILLE" STORMED— BY SUFFRAGETTES

WITH chains round their necks, wrists and ankles, Parisian suffragettes yesterday marched to the Place de la Bastille.

There, says Reuter, they cast off their fetters, threw them on a bonfire, and listened to a speech.

Then 10,000 pamphlets urging "votes for women" fluttered down on the crowd.

HAPPY AIR RETURNS

Lord Londonderry, the Air Minister, who is fifty-seven to-day, will receive from his wife an unusual birthday present—an aeroplane hangar erected on his estate at Mount Stewart, Northern Ireland.

The Minister, a qualified pilot, owns two private aeroplanes.

CHILDREN CLAMBER ON THE ROYAL CAR

INTO those streets where the children play barefoot in the gutter, where strange Eastern names are over many of the shops—into the streets of London's East End, went the King and Queen yesterday afternoon to "return the compliment" which Dockland's thousands in their loyalty have paid to their Majesties during Jubilee week.

For the East End may be poor, but it has decorated its streets with the best, and nightly has sent its crowds to Buckingham Palace.

For nearly two hours the royal car, in which the Princess Royal and Princess Elizabeth accompanied their Majesties, crawled along—5 m.p.h. was the limit of its pace.

"I KNEW nothing of the visit to my division until a constable reported to me that the King and Queen had passed through.

"In no other country in the world, could a sovereign make a surprise visit to any part of his capital with no more police than were necessary to clear a way for his car."—An East End police inspector.

The police had not been told of their coming. Point duty men were taken by surprise. Parked vehicles held up the royal car. Traffic lights flashed red and stopped it.

And on to the running boards of that shining limousine jumped the barefoot children of Dockland. Jumped on and stayed on. Fathers and mothers ran out into the streets. Solid crowds blocked the narrow roadways, waving wildly, shouting their greeting and their joy.

No escort of Life Guards this time; but an escort no less loyal—of cyclists. They rode in front and behind their Majesties' car.

One house at which the car stopped was in Grenade-street, Limehouse.

Neighbours call it "the Red, White and Blue House," for it has been painted in the national colours.

Sixty-seven-year-old Mrs. Emily Bee lives there. "The King and Queen, bless them, seemed delighted with it," she said.

(Full story on page 3)

Masked Bandits Raid a Train

SIGNAL PUT AT "STOP"

THREE armed and masked bandits who held up an express in Silesia got away with boxes from the mail van containing 48,000 marks (about £3,840) in cash.

The raiders first attacked a signal-box near Rothwasser, says Reuter.

They overpowered the signalman. Then they set the signals to danger.

The driver of the train pulled up in answer to the signal, and the raiders climbed into the mail van.

Princess Mdivani May Be Countess To-day

Princess Mdivani.

IF Princess Mdivani, formerly Miss Barbara Hutton, the Woolworth heiress, succeeds in obtaining a Reno divorce to-day, it is likely that she will be married before sundown to Count Hangwitz Reventlow, a young Danish nobleman.

Princess Mdivani, says the Exchange, will bring her suit in the Reno courts this morning against Prince Alexis Mdivani.

It is believed that the racing pilot, Colonel Roscoe Turner, will fly Count Reventlow to Reno (adds Reuter).

THE DAILY MIRROR, Friday, May 17, 1935

Daily Mirror
THE DAILY PICTURE NEWSPAPER WITH THE LARGEST NET SALE

Broadcasting - Page 22

BETTER DOCTORS PLAN —Page 9

No 9,817 Registered at the G.P.O as a Newspaper.   FRIDAY, MAY 17, 1935   One Penny

£120,000 FOR A LONDON HOSPITAL

Big International Research Centre

NEW WAR ON 'NERVES'

A GREAT impetus to the study of nervous diseases—a study which the stress of modern life makes daily more important—will be given by the gift to a London hospital of £120,000 by the Rockefeller Foundation.

Trustees of the Foundation have promised to contribute £60,000 towards the cost of the building and equipment of the proposed institute for the teaching and study of neurology at the National Hospital for Nervous Diseases, Queen-square, Bloomsbury.

They are to make a further contribution of £60,000 towards the endowment of the teaching and research activities that will have their centre in the new building.

An eminent nerve specialist told the *Daily Mirror* last night that the gift will prove of enormous benefit to the study of nervous ailments.

World Centre

"Modern life is daily becoming more and more strenuous and trying," he said, "and that has brought in its train a steady increase in the number of victims of nervous diseases.

"With the foundation of the proposed institute, which will come into being so much earlier because of this gift, those diseases can be studied very much more effectively.

"Any medical man, whatever his nationality, turns to the National Hospital to learn the subject of neurology. Throughout the world it is recognised as the leading institution for such work and students of every nationality come there to study the complex problems of neurology.

"To that extent the hospital is an international institution, and that, no doubt, explains this contribution from the Rockefeller Foundation.

"The work carried on there has been greatly hampered by lack of funds and the inadequacy of the accommodation.

"When the new institute has been added to the hospital, it will be possible to take more students and to conduct a more intensive campaign against this great problem of nervous diseases."

The sum required for the whole scheme is nearly a quarter of a million pounds, of which the trustees' gift represents half.

Five Drown in Dock Plunge

FAMILY TRAPPED AS CAR SINKS

FECAMP, Thursday.

FIVE people were drowned this evening when a family party in a car plunged into the Berigny Dock here.

The victims were M. Hubert Gentil, his two daughters aged twelve and ten, his mother aged eighty, and his aunt aged eighty-five.

His wife, Mme. Gentil, who was also in the car, was the only member of the party to escape with her life.—Reuter.

THE FLEET'S IN! COME AND PAY IT A VISIT

Chilly breezes and a choppy passage failed to check the first invasion of jolly crowds determined to see something of their Navy during the Home Fleet's Jubilee visit to Southend. Here are a few of them beside the mighty 16 in. guns of H.M.S. Nelson. Above: Jack holding up a little visitor to show her the helmet of a diving suit.

Girl with Red Beret Killed by Train Fall

A GIRL with a red beret was killed last night when she fell from a Southern Railway electric train on the Three Bridges (Sussex) side of Balcombe tunnel. She had dark bobbed hair and was wearing a belted overcoat. Nothing was found which would establish identification immediately.

She is believed to be Dorothy Hincock, aged twenty, of Bermondsey, who had spent her last two nights in a Bermondsey Salvation Army hostel.

She was unemployed.

In her coat pocket were a ticket available between Hayward's Heath and London, twopence, and a paper bearing the name of a London hostel.

Trains in both directions were delayed through the tragedy.

EARL'S HEIR WEDS U.S. RADIO STAR

VISCOUNT MOORE, son and heir of the Earl of Drogheda, yesterday married Miss Joan E. Carr, American radio star, in the chapel of the Municipal Building, New York, says Reuter.

The engagement was announced three weeks ago.

£10,000 RICHER AT 105

MR. Matthias Ferguson, of Moher Lavey, County Cavan, Ireland, who is 105, has received notification of a legacy of £10,000 left him by a daughter, who has died in America.

ORCHIDS IN BLAZE

Valuable orchids, belonging to Mr. F. J. Hanbury, of Brockhurst, East Grinstead, packed ready for dispatch to Chelsea Flower Show, were saved by the East Grinstead brigade last night from a fire in a potting shed.

LAWRENCE: "FAINT HOPE"

Second Boy Given Secrecy Warning

FROM OUR OWN CORRESPONDENT

BOVINGTON CAMP, Friday Morning.

NINETY hours after his motor-cycle collided with a pedal-cycle, Aircraftman Shaw, better known as Lawrence of Arabia, was still unconscious this morning, but was maintaining his strength.

After visiting the hospital last night Mr. Shaw's brother, Mr. A. W. Lawrence, said to me:—

"It is a case of touch and go, and I am afraid the chances of my brother's recovery are very slender."

The official bulletin stated:—

"His strength has been maintained during the day, and there is still a faint hope of his ultimate recovery."

"There is nothing we can do except to wait and hope," said Mr. Lawrence.

It was revealed yesterday that when Aircraftman Shaw's motor-cycle collided with a cycle ridden by a butcher's boy named Hargreaves, another boy, also riding a pedal cycle, was near.

This boy, Frank Fletcher, aged fourteen, of Bovington Camp, was uninjured, and was able to give an account of the accident to the military police, but he was warned not to speak of it to anyone else.

OUR BETTERS IN AFRICA

"Many There Are More Courteous Than We Are"

AMONG the Africans, I have met many people who can match us in all the finer qualities, who are, many of them, more intellectual than we are, who are certainly more courteous than almost all of us, and who are, many of them, far more deeply religious."

This impression of his recent world tour was told to a meeting of the London Missionary Society, at Queen's Hall, last night, by Dr. F. W. Norwood, of the City Temple.

"I wonder why it should ever be supposed," he said, "that the mere colour of a man's skin confers some great privilege upon him."

THE DAILY MIRROR, Tuesday, May 21, 1935.

Broadcasting - Page 22

Daily Mirror

THE DAILY PICTURE NEWSPAPER WITH THE LARGEST NET SALE

THE OTHER MAN'S JOB—PICTURE, Page 17

No. 9,820   Registered at the G.P.O. as a Newspaper.   TUESDAY, MAY 21, 1935   One Penny

BOBSLEIGH'S DERBY SENSATION

Leg Trouble—Second Favourite To Be Examined To-day

JOCKEY CLUB FIRE

EXCITEMENT gave way to sensation at Newmarket yesterday when, with the fire at the Jockey Club Rooms still blazing, there came the news that:—

Lord Derby's Bobsleigh, one of the favourites for the Derby, had been found to be amiss.

The discovery was made when, after Bobsleigh had finished work on the heath, it was noticed that he was a bit "short" in the near hind leg.

A veterinary surgeon is to examine the colt to-day. Last night Mr. Colledge Leader, the Stanley House trainer, said that he was of the opinion that all will be well with Bobsleigh in a few days.

Bobsleigh.

TURF TRAGEDY IF—
By BOUVERIE

A Turf tragedy will be a very real and the only description to apply to Bobsleigh's mishap should it prove more serious than it is regarded at the moment.

During the winter Lord Derby's colt stood out as the only one with an apparent chance against the Aga Khan's brilliant collection—Bahram, Theft and Hairan.

Two of the trio have since been tried and found wanting, judged on the Derby standard, and events this year have left Epsom a question of Bahram or Bobsleigh?

Great hopes have always been held that Lord Derby would celebrate his seventieth year by leading in the Jubilee Derby winner.

Price Further Shortened

They flagged somewhat when Bobsleigh was well beaten by Bahram in the Two Thousand Guineas, only to be revived with double strength when the colt made a brilliant comeback at the expense of Hairan in the Newmarket Stakes last week.

Such, indeed, was the impression made by Bobsleigh's victory that from 5 to 1 his price for the Derby was immediately cut by half.

Since then it has been further shortened, and the indications were that he would have been favourite on the day had all gone well.

The racing world will wait anxiously for a favourable report from the veterinary surgeon to-day, for a mishap, however slight, can have serious consequences with the great race only a fortnight away.

BLAZING CEILING FALLS ON WORKMEN

Three hours elapsed before the work of four brigades got the upper hand of the fire at the Jockey Club.

The new building, adjoining the old, was completed only about a month ago. It is believed that the outbreak started in the old buildings. Flames found a way through a hole near a window, setting alight the interior of the card room.

Workmen tried to put out the flames, but had to run for safety when the ceiling collapsed on them.

A fireman was knocked unconscious by falling brickwork, and another man was badly cut by falling slates and timber.

So rapidly did the flames spread that the billiards room was soon a mass of flames. Voluntary workers, wearing improvised smoke-masks of wet handkerchiefs, worked valiantly in saving valuable paintings, books and furniture, but many of the paintings were burned, and others were ruined by the heat and water.

The fire could be seen for miles around, dense smoke making a screen across the High-street, which became congested with sightseers.

'LAWRENCE'S NAME WILL LIVE'—THE KING

LAWRENCE of Arabia's brother, Mr. A. W. Lawrence, received this message from the King yesterday:—

"The King has heard with sincere regret of the death of your brother, and deeply sympathises with you and your family in this sad loss.

"Your brother's name will live in history, and the King gratefully recognises his distinguished services to his country, and feels that it is tragic that the end should have come in this manner to a life still so full of promise."

Plans for Lawrence's funeral are in page 5.

THE KING AS HOST TO 150 DIPLOMATS

AMBASSADORS and Ministers from nearly every country in the world were the guests of the King and Queen last night at a State dinner party at Buckingham Palace.

Seated at a long horse-shoe table, the 150 guests, wearing full dress uniforms heavily laced with gold, made an impressive picture against the white and gold background of the dining room.

At the centre of the table sat the King, resplendent in the full dress scarlet and gold uniform of Colonel-in-Chief of the Irish Guards. At his side was the Queen, a lovely figure in a gown of opalescent paillettes, embroidered in diamanté, which shimmered and glistened in the light.

THE KOH-I-NOOR

The Queen wore diamonds in her corsage, the great Koh-i-noor among them, and a tiara of magnificent diamonds in her hair.

The Prince of Wales, the Duke and Duchess of York, the Duke of Gloucester, the Princess Royal and Lord Harewood, Princess Alice and the Earl of Athlone were present.

Courses were served on gold plate by footmen in resplendent State livery of scarlet and gold, with knee breeches and powdered hair.

Magnificent pieces of gold from the King's famous collection of plate were displayed around the table.

No toasts were drunk.

Explosion Rocks Aerodrome

ONE DEAD AND FIVE HURT IN TWO ACCIDENTS

ONE man was killed and five injured in two explosions at Portsmouth yesterday.

The municipal airport was shaken last night when a twenty-gallon petrol tank burst in the hangar of Airspeed, Ltd.

The tank was shattered. Four men working in the hangar were flung in all directions and burned about the head and arms.

They are Andrew Drummond, twenty-six, of Widley-grove, Portsmouth; William Pike, twenty-six, Esskward-road, Portsmouth; John Dunn, twenty-seven, of Ludlow-road, Woolsdan, Southampton, and George Lister, twenty-eight, of Copnor-road, Portsmouth.

All are in Portsmouth Royal Hospital.

The other explosion occurred as an acetylene cylinder, thought to be empty, was being taken into a boiler house at the Portsmouth Dockyard.

Edward Ford, a labourer, was killed. Another labourer, named Burton, was injured.

NEW "YARD" CHIEF

ON the recommendation of Lord Trenchard, the Metropolitan Police Commissioner, the Home Secretary has approved the promotion of Colonel the Hon. Maurice Drummond, Assistant Commissioner, to the status of Deputy Commissioner.

TRYING IT ON.—An ingenious device outside a shop in Shaftesbury-avenue, W., by means of which women shoppers can, in effect, try on dresses in the street. It consists of a cabinet containing a frock and by means of an optical illusion the onlooker sees herself apparently wearing the frock.

"FLYING TENOR" FOR LONDON AGAIN

Covent Garden Deputy Who Has Become a Star

COVENT Garden's "flying tenor" is to fly back to England because London opera-goers want to hear him again.

He is Torsten Ralf, who at a moment's notice dashed by 'plane to London from Frankfort to sing Lohengrin when Max Hirzel was unable to take the part owing to a cold.

So great a success did he make that an extra performance of "Lohengrin" has been arranged so that he may sing the part again in response to requests that have been arriving at Covent Garden ever since the one night that he appeared there.

The performance is to take place on May 30, and Mme. Rethberg will take the part of Elsa.

But for Herr Hirzel's indisposition, Herr Ralf would never have sung at Covent Garden at all. He came as a deputy and has become a star.

Herr Ralf is a German-trained Swedish singer. He is thirty-four.

THE DAILY MIRROR, Thursday, May 23, 1935.

Broadcasting - Page 20

Daily Mirror

THE DAILY PICTURE NEWSPAPER WITH THE LARGEST NET SALE

GUILDHALL "FAMILY PARTY" —Page 3

No. 9,822 Registered at the G.P.O. as a Newspaper. THURSDAY, MAY 23, 1935 One Penny

AIR FORCE TO BE TREBLED

NONE BUT THE BRAVE

The Black Prince (Edward III) kneeling to receive a jewel token from the Fair Maid of Kent (Joan Countess of Kent, whom he married)—a scene at yesterday's rehearsal of The Pageant of England to be held at Langley Park, Slough, Bucks, from May 28 to June 11.

Conductor Dies at Royal Concert

PRINCESS INGRID AMONG THE AUDIENCE

WHILE conducting a concert before Princess Ingrid of Sweden and the Crown Prince Frederic of Denmark at Stockholm yesterday, M. Lizell collapsed, dying shortly afterwards.

M. Lizell was one of Prince Frederic's oldest friends.

The concert was part of the festivities arranged in connection with the marriage, to-morrow, of Princess Ingrid to Prince Frederic, states Reuter.

AUDIENCE SPELLBOUND

Fifty royal personages, part of an audience of 4,000, saw M. Lizell fall towards the close of the second item in the programme.

The Crown Prince of Sweden summoned the Court physician, who was only in time to confirm M. Lizell's death.

LAWRENCE—BY HIS MOTHER

"He Was Honourable, Always Self-Sacrificing"

HANKOW, Wednesday.

LAWRENCE of Arabia's final epitaph was uttered by his shy, grey-haired, bespectacled mother when she arrived here from the interior.

She said: "My son was always self-sacrificing. I am sure he met his death in avoiding hurting another. He was a good, upright, honourable man, elevated by God for a great purpose which I think he accomplished.

"He came out of the war with clean hands. He despised people who made money out of the war."

Mrs. Lawrence is hurrying back to England. Dr. Lawrence, Aircraftman Shaw's brother, is ill with dysentery.—Reuter

1,500 'Planes, 2,500 More Pilots, 20,000 More Men

FOR HOME DEFENCE

"Britain's home air force is to be nearly trebled. If this is insufficient, we shall increase it, whatever the cost."— LORD LONDONDERRY, Minister for Air.

"Everything necessary for our air defence is to be put in hand immediately."—MR. BALDWIN.

THESE two vital statements were made yesterday in the defence debates in Parliament, evidence of Britain's determination to attain security in the air.

Sir Philip Sassoon, Under-Secretary for Air, stated in the Commons that the R.A.F. expected to obtain 5,000 pilots from the light aeroplane clubs.

Lord Londonderry, in the Lords, said that by March 31, 1937, the home strength of the Air Force, excluding the fleet air arm and overseas units, would be 1,500 first-line machines. This compares with an actual first-line figure of 580 at present, excluding the fleet air arm, and with a total of 840 which we should have reached by the same date under the programme of expansion announced last July.

2,500 more pilots and 20,000 more other ranks will be required. This year 1,200 to 1,300 new pilots are to be put into training and hundreds of officers and men who were due for discharge would be retained.

"We shall require a good deal more than the number of machines mentioned in this year's air estimates from the aircraft industry," said Lord Londonderry. Assurances of the industry's full co-operation had been already received.

Lord Weir, Director-General of Aircraft Production and later Minister for Air during the War, is to assist the Secretary for Air in an advisory capacity on questions of policy in supply production and industry.

More Training Schools

Five new Royal Air Force training schools would be added to the five already in existence. The new programme means seventy-one new squadrons for home defence in present and next financial years, instead of twenty-two under the present programme.

In addition to eighteen new stations under the present programme, thirty-one more new stations of different sorts would be required under the new programme.

The cost would be substantial, and a supplementary estimate would be presented during the present session.

Germany's capacity to multiply the output of aircraft factories in a short space of time was a matter of the gravest concern.

"In a country under a dictatorship," said Lord Londonderry, "the organisation of industry, the mobilisation of all the various manufacturing activities connected with the output of aircraft and aero engines and the munitions of war from the air, is a matter of comparative simplicity.

"The people of these islands, on the other
(Continued on back page)

Lord Weir.

TRIBUTE TO LORD ROTHERMERE

Referring to Viscount Rothermere's efforts to secure a stronger Air Force, Lord Londonderry said:—

"I gladly recognise the spirit of patriotism which has prompted the noble viscount. I ask him to assist the Government and myself by impressing upon our people the vital importance of the capacity of the industry for a vastly increased output."

Great waves breaking over the chutes and diving boards of Cliftonville (Kent) bathing pool yesterday, when many cross-Channel passengers thought longingly of that Channel tunnel.

Miss Northumbria, Miss Lily Weiss, of Leeds, winner of a Venus competition for which 60,000 entries were received.

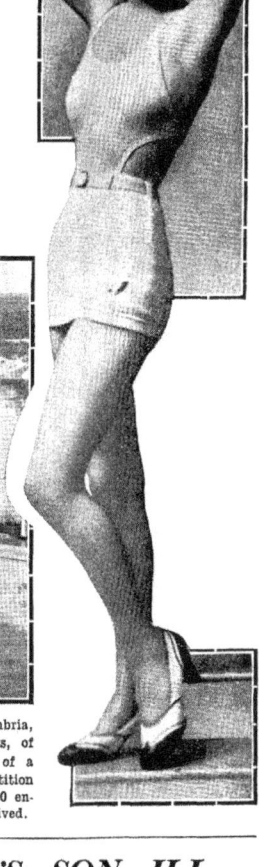

MR. LANSBURY'S SON ILL

Father's Dash to Bedside from House of Commons

MR. GEORGE LANSBURY, the Leader of the Opposition, who was to have closed the defence debate in the House of Commons last night, was called away at an early hour to the bedside of his son, Mr. Edgar Lansbury.

Mr. Edgar Lansbury, who has been ill at his Mill Hill home since the beginning of the year, was slightly worse. Last night he was stated to be very seriously ill.

Mr. George Lansbury said: "My son Edgar is a little worse. He is very seriously ill.

"I have been to see him every day, but I received a message while I was in the House of Commons to-day asking me to go to him."

Mr. Ramsay MacDonald did not attend the debate. He will arrive in London early this morning by train from Edinburgh.

Daily Mirror

THE DAILY PICTURE NEWSPAPER WITH THE LARGEST NET SALE

Broadcasting - Page 20

ROYAL VISIT ARRESTS —Page 2

No. 9,827. Registered at the G.P.O as a Newspaper. WEDNESDAY, MAY 29, 1935. One Penny

Amusements: Page 18

NORMANDIE'S RECORD BID TO-DAY

U.S.-Bound with 2,000 Passengers

£11,000,000 SHIP IS OUT FOR "RIBAND"

FROM OUR SPECIAL CORRESPONDENT
The Comte de Segonzac
LE HAVRE, Tuesday.

AT five o'clock to-morrow sirens will sound over Le Havre. The liner Normandie, France's £11,000,000 challenge to the world, will glide from harbour on a maiden Atlantic voyage that all France expects to make history.

Those siren shrieks will drown the clamour that political and financial unrest has this week sounded in Frenchmen's ears. To-morrow, for France, is Normandie's Day.

For on this floating Grand Hotel France has staked all. In return she hopes to win the Blue Riband of the Atlantic.

At present this is held by the Italian liner Rex with a speed of 29.2 knots and a time of 4 days 13 hours 58 minutes. In trials, 160,000 h.p. engines have driven the Normandie at nearly 32 knots.

So the world's largest liner sets out with a wonderful chance of becoming the world's fastest liner.

Boy's Message for U.S.

On board will be 2,000 passengers, 1,000 crew and staff, and probably 500 workmen still completing the interior.

Among the passengers will be Mme. Lebrun, wife of the French President and "godmother" of the liner, and a young boy, Roger Echigut, chosen out of 20,000 to carry a message from the boys of Paris to boys in America. He will be received by President Roosevelt.

All night and every night during the voyage there will be galas.

All day people will be exploring the miles of "streets" stretching the 1,000-ft. length of the Normandie. And these are some of the things they will find:—

- Winter gardens with exotic birds;
- Dining room 100 yards long;
- Luxury kennels for pets hidden in a dummy " funnel;
- Clinics; a cinema;
- A cellar stocked with old wines;
- A children's playground

Passengers, when New York is reached, will not have seen more than half the ship. Her size staggers the imagination. It so staggered the imagination of one passenger yesterday that he called up the purser and asked him for a cabin not more than ten minutes from the sea.

It is more than likely that the Normandie will hold the Blue Riband for a year.

By next May Britain's Queen Mary, with turbines expected to develop 200,000 h.p. will be ready to challenge.

FRANTIC QUEST FOR RANSOM

TACOMA (Washington), Tuesday.

AS the minutes creep on towards the zero hour set by the kidnappers, the parents of the nine-year-old George Weyerhauser, who was kidnapped last Friday, are frantically trying to raise the £40,000 demanded.

The ultimatum expires at lunch time to-morrow.

They are reported to have made contact with the kidnappers but the police are disregarding the plea not to interfere.—Reuter.

LIKE A VAST PROMENADE DECK

The imposingly-spacious bridge of the Normandie, looking as vast as the promenade deck of any ordinary liner.

TWO U.S. STARS ARE HERE

Grace Moore Tells Her Film Secrets

Mrs. Helen Wills Moody.

SANG BEFORE MIRROR FOR 4 MONTHS

They are here, and all London longs to see them:—

GRACE MOORE, the American opera star, who reveals her film secrets in the interview printed below, and

HELEN WILLS MOODY, lawn tennis star, who is to play at Wimbledon (see page 2).

BY A SPECIAL REPRESENTATIVE

THE most beautiful soprano in the world, who for four months practised singing in front of a mirror to make sure that she didn't make ugly faces, arrived in London last night to sing at Covent Garden.

She is Grace Moore, the star of the film "One Night of Love," who is to make her debut at Covent Garden in "La Boheme" on June 6. The King and Queen are going to Covent Garden on June 12 to hear her sing.

All seats for her three appearances at Covent Garden are sold. While she was making the journey from Paris to London yesterday queues besieged the box office at the Royal Opera House.

By mid-day 6,000 seats had been sold, and by the time Grace Moore reached London there was not a seat to be had.

Smiling, thrilled with the thought of appearing at Covent Garden, Grace Moore is more of a film star than an opera singer.

In a broad American accent, she told me in her suite at Claridges some of the secrets of her film, "One Night of Love."

"Being an opera singer is like taking a vacation compared with making a film," she said.

"When I went to Hollywood I found it was very hard work being a film star.

"For four months I practised singing in front of a mirror. I had to forget everything I had learned. I had to practise and practise until I could sing a high note without making an ugly face.

Miss Grace Moore on her arrival at Victoria.

"Now, since I have made this film, my whole life is changed. When I sang in opera I sang for six months in the year and had six months holiday.

"I didn't have to worry what I looked like or where I went.

"Now, whenever I go out, people are watching me. I am a film star and they expect me to look like I do on the screen. I worry about my eyelashes—whether I ought to have nice curling ones like they saw in the film.

"I have to look smart and beautiful all the time. My husband has practically given up his career on the films to help me with mine.

"Of course I am very thrilled to sing at Covent Garden. And to sing before the King and Queen is the biggest thrill of all," added Miss Moore.

I asked Miss Moore how she looked after her figure.

"I do exercises," she said, "and I ride and swim and play tennis, but most of all special exercises," and then she dashed off to make a news reel little more than an hour after she landed in England.

She must be the hardest working opera singer in the world.

MR. LANSBURY'S SON DEAD

Father's 27-Hour Vigil

MR Edgar Lansbury, son of Mr. George Lansbury, the Leader of the Opposition, died late last night at his home at Mill Hill, Middlesex, at the age of forty-eight.

For twenty-seven hours his father had kept unbroken vigil at his bedside.

Mr. Edgar Lansbury had been ill since the beginning of the year, and last Wednesday his condition became so grave that Mr. George Lansbury was called to his bedside from the House of Commons, where he was to have closed the defence debate.

A friend said, "It was a tragic vigil for Mr. Lansbury. He was very deeply attached to his son and he feels his loss intensely."

Mr. Edgar Lansbury, as author of "George Lansbury, My Father," published last year, was fined £20 at Bow-street for contravention of the Official Secrets Act. He had inadvertently quoted passages from official documents without realising their confidential nature.

In January, 1930, his wife, Moyna McGill, the actress, gave birth to twin boys.

WORLD MESSAGES TO QUINTUPLETS

THE Dionne quintuplets at Callander (Ontario) celebrated their first birthday yesterday by gaining an ounce in their aggregate weight, which now totals 84lb. 6½oz.

Messages of congratulation from all parts of the world inundated the hospital where the quintuplets live, says Reuter.

It is estimated that 15,000,000 Americans and Canadians heard the quintuplets on the wireless last night.

The microphone picked up splashings in the bath and a terrific squeal from Yvonne. All five were introduced to their unseen listeners. Each in turn contributed a happy gurgle except Emilie, who cried bitterly.

THE DAILY MIRROR, Thursday, May 30, 1935.

Broadcasting - Page 22

Daily Mirror
THE DAILY PICTURE NEWSPAPER WITH THE LARGEST NET SALE

SAILING OF THE NORMANDIE —Page 3

No. 9,828 Registered at the G.P.O. as a Newspaper.   THURSDAY, MAY 30, 1935   One Penny

Amusements: Page 10

SEA-AND-AIR MOTORING ERA
'Flying Car' Dream

YOUNG GERMAN DRIVES ACROSS THE CHANNEL

THE prospect of a new motoring era, when cars will speed on water and through the air as well as along the road, was opened up last night.

Speaking in London, Senor de la Cierva, inventor of the autogiro, visualised a "flying motor-car," which would revolutionise our present ideas of the term "Flying Squad."

A young German inventor landed at Dover last night after a six-and-a-half-hour Channel crossing in a motor-car fitted with paddles on the rear wheels.

He is Herr Jakob Baudig. From his home in Coblenz he had travelled in his amphibian to Calais by road. Yesterday morning he put off from Calais accompanied by a French trawler.

For the first few hours the weather was fine with a light northerly wind, but later rough seas held him up and the tide carried him out of his course.

When he landed on Dover beach he was cheered by hundreds of people—the first man to motor from Germany to England without boarding a ship.

Weighs One Ton

An hour and a half was spent at the entrance to Dover Harbour putting the amphibian "through its paces" for the benefit of sightseers and news-reel cameramen.

This is the specification of his invention:—
Length: 14ft.
Weight: One ton.
Land speed: 20 m.p.h.
Water speed: 5 m.p.h.
Engine enclosed in water-tight compartment.

—AND NOW THE AUTOGIROCAR

It was in a lecture at King's College, London, last night that Senor de la Cierva visualised a vehicle capable of flying like an autogiro and of running on the roads like a car.

He declared that contrary to general belief the autogiro was potentially capable of very high speeds, competing with the aeroplane.

He emphasised the autogiro's value for police, ambulance and survey work.

LONDON HAS BEST DRESSED WOMEN

"WALKING down London streets one is likely to see more well-dressed women of every class than in any other capital of the world," said Captain A. Cunningham-Reid, M.P. for Marylebone, at the Wholesale Fashion Trades Association dinner in London last night.

Six Shot Dead in Mine Riots

EUROPEANS ARM TO DEFEND HOMES

EUROPEANS are arming themselves for protection in Northern Rhodesia, where serious rioting has broken out among 9,000 native miners.

Six natives have been shot dead in a clash with police at Luanshya, where the Riot Act has been read.

An entire regiment says Reuter, has been entrained for the copper belt, and last night a contingent of European and native members of the British South African Police from Bulawayo and district were hurriedly mobilised for service.

Additional men will join the train at other points on the journey north.

HOSES CARRIED THROUGH HOMES

NEARLY 100 people had to leave their homes in South Tenter-street, Stepney, this morning while firemen fought a blaze at an adjoining works.

Firemen carried hoses through houses to reach the flames.

For more than an hour many people, called hurriedly from their beds, stood about in their nightclothes.

Many children, wrapped in blankets, slept in their mothers' arms.

Herr Jakob Baudig in mid-Channel with his land-water motor-car following in the wake of his convoying trawler. On page 3 he is seen arriving at Dover.

THE QUEEN DROPS IN FOR A CHAT

With 100 Proud Hospital Patients

THE Queen paid a surprise visit to the British Home and Hospital for Incurables, Streatham Common, yesterday.

The first intimation the authorities had of the visit was when her chauffeur opened the main doors and announced to a startled page boy: "The Queen would like to look over the home."

Her Majesty was shown through the wards and over the nursing quarters. She chatted with over a hundred patients.

The oldest patient, Miss Mary Rose, had a long talk with the Queen.

In an interview afterwards Miss Rose said, "I remember the Queen coming here and talking to me thirty years ago when she was Princess of Wales."

(Picture on back page.)

ONE DEAD, FOUR HURT IN SHIP EXPLOSION

ONE deck-hand was killed and four others were injured by an explosion on board the British steamer Drakepool, bound for Italy from West Hartlepool.

The Drakepool is a sister ship to the Millpool, which sank in the North Atlantic with the loss of all hands last winter.

The dead man was W. N. Balchin, of Beaumont-street, London, W., and the injured were S. G. Gladwin, of Alma-street, West Hartlepool, G. E. Porter, of Trindan-street, R. Jackson, of Princess-street, Hartlepools, and T. Laws, of Blandford-street, Hartlepools.

"BIG THREE" FOR B.B.C.

Sweeping Changes at Broadcasting House

HIGH B.B.C. officials in the various Regions have been notified of an entire reorganisation by the Board of Governors at Broadcasting House.

Three new executive posts have been created in place of the present post of Controller of Programmes.

Colonel A. Dawnay is at present Controller of Programmes, but he is due to retire in the autumn and it is then, the *Daily Mirror* is informed, that Sir John Reith's new triumvirate will come into power. The three posts are:—

Director of all Regional Broadcasting.—Mr. Charles Siepmann, formerly Director of Talks; he will act as liaison officer at Broadcasting House between Regional directors.

Controller of all Talks in all Programmes—Empire and Home.—Major Gladstone Murray, who will retain his present office of Director of Information and Personal Relations.

He will be assisted by Mr. Cecil Graves, the Director-General of Empire and Foreign Service.

Director of Television.—Mr. Roger Eckersley, present Director of Entertainments.

Appointment Welcomed

The chief effect of this reorganisation will be felt at the Regional stations which have been controlled by directors directly responsible to Sir John Reith.

Mr. Siepmann's appointment is regarded as an excellent idea by Mr. Percy Edgar, Midland Regional director and chairman of the Regional directors.

"I feel that such an appointment can only be of great help," he told the "Daily Mirror" last night.

"It means that now we have a representative at the head office."

THE DAILY MIRROR, Friday, May 31, 1935

Daily Mirror

THE DAILY PICTURE NEWSPAPER WITH THE LARGEST NET SALE

Broadcasting - Page 22

FRENCH PREMIER COLLAPSES —Page 3

No. 9,829 Registered at the G.P.O as a Newspaper. FRIDAY, MAY 31, 1935 One Penny

Amusements: Pages 26 and 27

BRITAIN LOOKS TO 1960
World Air-Mail Service Daily

PRINCESS'S BABY

'PRESS-THE-BUTTON' CARS ON OUR ROADS

BRITAIN is looking to the future. The next twenty-five years will be as rich in progress and achievement as have been the years of King George's reign. Men are everywhere visualising the brave new world that lies before them.

With the Channel crossed by car and an expert's prophecy of an autogiro to run on roads, the prospect of a sea-and-air motoring era has this week been opened up. Yesterday, the Postmaster-General, speaking at Swansea, said that in 1960 we should have telephones in every home, air mails daily from most parts of the world, and events presented to us by television.

During the next three years the Post Office will be spending £34,000,000 mainly on telephone development. That figure is one small item in the bill of progress.

What else does 1960 hold in store for us? Signalling systems on roads, cars driven by touching switches, films in schools, Hollywood extinct. Those were some of the forecasts given to the *Daily Mirror* last night.

HER HUSBAND'S JOKE.—Mrs. Roosevelt, wife of the American President, laughs as she listens beside Mr. Josephus Daniels, to the presidential speech to Congress on the Soldiers' Bonus Bill.

Princess Otto von Bismarck, whose husband is Counsellor of the German Embassy in London, with their baby son, Count Karl Alexander, after his christening yesterday at the German Church, Montpelier-place.

HOLLYWOOD DOOMED?

"WHAT is your dream of 1960?" the *Daily Mirror* last night asked leading figures in industries and art. And these were their answers:—

MOTORING
Still Restrictions

SIR HERBERT AUSTIN:—England will be intersected with great arterial roads, reserved for high-speed traffic.

No doubt these roads will be governed in the same way as railway lines are to-day—probably with a similar system of signalling and level crossings.

Our present roads will in many cases become more or less obsolete or only used by farmers and slow traffic.

Except for the steering cars in those days will, I think, be controlled simply by pressing various buttons, as is done in elevators at the present time.

No doubt the increase of speed will bring with it many dangers, and I think that in 1960 there will still be some form of restriction in congested or dangerous areas—even the arterial roads.

One must realise that even now the average speed of a fast car equals the average speed of many railway trains.

FILMS
Talkies as an Art

MR. HERBERT WILCOX:—We shall have coloured and stereoscopic films.

There will be a central dissemination of films from some organisation similar to the B.B.C., and films will be televised on different wave-lengths into the home.

I think that would be a good thing for the film industry, as it would popularise actors as wireless has done.

I think Hollywood in 1960 will be derelict. It has served a useful purpose, but in the years to come talking pictures will grow as an art.

Hollywood is 3,000 miles away from the nearest intellectual centre, which is New York.

Films will be universally adopted as a medium for education in schools. This would make teaching so much more effective, particularly in the case of geography.

SHIPPING
Comfort Before Speed

MR. FRANK CHARLTON (Director of Cunard-White Star Line and financial expert):—People will travel abroad in comfort. The tendency now is to build with a view to the comfort of passengers as well as speed.

I do not think that 1960 will see any bigger vessel than the Queen Mary, and it is almost
(Continued on back page)

Execution 'Divine Law'

CORONER'S REBUKE TO MRS. VAN DER ELST

"Mrs. Van der Elst's demonstration was a protest against the divinely instituted moral law. She would be wiser if she devoted her energy to saving souls."

SO said the Salford coroner, Mr. R. Stuart Rodger, yesterday, during the inquest on John Harris Bridge, the twenty-five-year-old Salford murderer.

He was referring to the scenes which occurred outside Strangeways Prison, Manchester, yesterday as the execution was taking place.

Last night Mr. Stuart Rodger told the *Daily Mirror* that he believed that the moral laws which were given to Moses, as opposed to the ceremonial laws, were intended for all persons and all times.

But he did not develop his argument. He said he had been very ill for eight weeks.

FELL 800ft. TO DEATH
Parachutist Killed Before Crowd

WATCHED by hundreds of people, Ivor Price, twenty-seven, a parachute jumper attached to Sir Alan Cobham's air display, fell 800ft. to his death while making a parachute jump at Woodford (Cheshire) Aerodrome last night.

Price's jump was the last event of the evening, in which he and Miss Naomi Heron-Maxwell did a double leap from two 'planes.

Price jumped off a few seconds before Miss Heron-Maxwell. His parachute did not open and he could be seen turning over and over as he hurtled to the ground. Women in the crowd fainted.

Miss Heron-Maxwell landed safely.

SET AFIRE BY LORRY

Playing a hose on a railway coach which caught fire on Dover Admiralty Pier yesterday from a blazing Army lorry. The wreck of the lorry is seen lying across the rails. It was loaded with 6in. blank shells and blazed up after being in collision with a locomotive.

Girl Golf Star in a Scene

THIRTY caddies nearly ruined the final of the British women's golf championship at Newcastle, Co. Down yesterday.

The caddies were annoyed because Miss Pam Barton, the eighteen-year-old London girl—who, after a gallant fight, was beaten in the final by Miss Wanda Morgan by three and two —changed her caddie just before going out.

George Murphy had been carrying Miss Barton's clubs all the week, but yesterday she was dissatisfied with him and dispensed with his services. Another lad carried the clubs.

Other caddies thereupon followed the match in the first round, applauding loudly every winning stroke by Miss Morgan.

On completion of the first round Miss Barton spoke to officials of the Ladies' Golf Union. Murphy was then paid the fee of six shillings to which he would have been entitled had he carried Miss Barton's clubs.

Before the second round began the caddies were addressed by Mrs. J. B Walker, the Irish international golfer, who asked them to be "good sports." There was no further demonstration.

Miss Barton told a reporter that she was not worried by the "barracking."

THE DAILY MIRROR, Tuesday, June 4, 1935.

Daily Mirror

Broadcasting - Page 20

THE DAILY PICTURE NEWSPAPER WITH THE LARGEST NET SALE

No. 9,832 Registered at the G.P.O as a Newspaper   TUESDAY, JUNE 4, 1935   One Penny

MORE BRITISH 'QUAKE VICTIMS —Page 3

Amusements: Page 8

ALL RECORDS FOR NORMANDIE
Final Dash Wins Her Blue Riband

TIME CUT BY 1¾ HOURS

Wild Greetings

France's super liner, the Normandie, has won the Blue Riband of the Atlantic. She made the crossing—3,192 miles from Southampton to the entrance of New York Harbour—in 4 days, 11 hours, 42 minutes.

MORE than 100,000 roared their congratulations as the Normandie docked yesterday afternoon after the maiden voyage that has won for her this speed record of the sea.

Her run (states Reuter) compares with 4 days 13 hours 27 minutes set up by the German liner Bremen, and the record of 4 days 13 hours 58 minutes set up by the Italian liner Rex for the longer run from Gibraltar to New York.

So great was the concourse of people in the vicinity of the pier when the Normandie docked that all traffic was brought to a standstill.

A thousand longshoremen swarmed on to the pier to search for the 250 available jobs of handling the luggage. The inspector, unable to cope with the yelling crowd, flung out among them the 250 brass working badges, and the excited men scrambled madly for them.

As the giant Normandie slowly made her way to the huge new 4,000,000 dollar pier of the French Line, which is still far from completed, she passed America's mightiest merchantman, the Leviathan, now forlorn in dock, with her paint peeling off.

Two Mishaps

Two fireboats playing jets of water like fountains accompanied the Normandie to the dock, while an aeroplane, equipped with gigantic amplifiers, cruised overhead and broadcast the Marseillaise.

A couple of minor mishaps accompanied the docking.

The steel hawser holding her fender to the pierhead snapped, and one man narrowly escaped being drowned. Ten piles of the pier, too, were smashed and floated away.

The Normandie made the crossing at an average speed of 29.68 knots, and made another day record from Sunday to Monday with an average of 31.55 knots. She can now claim all passenger vessel records for the longest day's run, the highest speed and the shortest crossing.

What the Queen Mary thinks page 2.

Steaming past the skyscrapers—the Normandie's triumphant arrival at New York yesterday, after winning the Blue Riband of the Atlantic for France on her record-breaking maiden voyage.

Operation on The Princess Royal

AN operation is to be performed on the Princess Royal, who is suffering from exophthalmic goitre.

The Princess is in a London nursing home, into which she went from her home in Green-street, Mayfair, on Sunday night.

The following bulletin was issued last night:—

"The Princess Royal has for some time been suffering from exophthalmic goitre.

"Although the health of her Royal Highness has improved under medical treatment, complete cure is not being effected thereby. It has therefore been decided to treat the thyroid gland by operation."

The bulletin is signed by Dr. L. F. R. Knuthsen, Sir Thomas Dunhill and Lord Dawson of Penn.

THE SYMPTOMS

Exophthalmic goitre's symptoms are an enlarged thyroid gland, rapid action of the heart and palpitation, tremor and extreme nervousness.

Women are more frequently affected than men.

With the Earl of Harewood the Princess lunched on Sunday with the King and Queen at Buckingham Palace.

In April the Princess Royal, on the advice of her doctors, cancelled a number of her public engagements.

At the end of last year she was ordered to rest as she experienced a slight recurrence of the nervous strain from which she had previously suffered.

LIGHTNING KILLED HIM IN SHELTER

LIGHTNING killed one man and injured three others during a thunderstorm at Leconfield, near Beverley, East Yorks, last night.

The dead man was John Henry Drew. With his companions he was sheltering under a canvas cover over a mound of potatoes when the mound was struck by lightning.

Countess Haugwitz Reventlow, formerly Princess Alexis Mdivani (Barbara Hutton, the Woolworth heiress), and her Danish husband at the St. Lazare Station on their arrival in Paris yesterday.

OWNER'S 80–1 DERBY TIP

Hoping for Best with Pry II

"I think I shall win both the Derby, with Pry II, and the Oaks with Papyrette."

MR. R. H. W. W. Simms was in this optimistic mood yesterday when he attended the Derby lunch at the Press Club, London.

Pry II stands at 80-1 in the betting.

But Mr. Frank Butters, who trains for the Aga Khan, would not commit himself beyond this:—

"All my horses are well. According to the bookmakers and the form book, I am in for a bumper Derby. I am hoping for the best."

Some of the sayings by other owners of Derby horses were:—

Lord Derby: Fairhaven will run jolly well
Lord Astor: Field Trial is quite well.

Miss Nuthall Not for Wimbledon

"CANNOT HOLD RACKET" SAYS MOTHER

"DAILY MIRROR" SPECIAL NEWS
BY OUR TENNIS CORRESPONDENT

MISS Betty Nuthall will not play at Wimbledon this year for the first time since she was fourteen years old.

Miss Nuthall is suffering from a shoulder injury which has not responded to treatment.

This was discovered by her mother, who noticed after her return from America, last year, that she held a teacup in a peculiar way.

It was hoped that in a week or two she would be quite fit again, but last night Mrs. Nuthall told me that her daughter would not enter for Wimbledon.

"She feels no pain," Mrs. Nuthall told me, "but she cannot hold a racket."

Duchess of Kent at Charity Ball

THE Duke and Duchess of Kent were among the dancers at the Derby Ball at Grosvenor House last night, organised by Lady Milbanke, in aid of the Rosemary Ednam Ward at the Royal Northern Hospital.

The Duchess wore a dress of white crêpe with a cape of dark blue silk net. She had a small tiara of diamonds.

Prince and Princess Nicholas of Greece, the Duchess's parents, were with the royal party.

Lady Hulton put up for auction a blank canvas by Mr. Lynwood Palmer, but bids came slowly, and eventually Lady Milbanke announced that Lady Hulton had offered 300gns. for the canvas.

"Here is a blank canvas to be painted by the most famous animal painter of our time with the picture of the horse the buyer cares to name," said Lady Hulton. "I myself am going to pay 300gns. for it. I am ashamed of you all."

"I was so disappointed that a better effort could not be made as it was in aid of charity," Lady Hulton told the Daily Mirror later.

"In every other way the ball has been such a huge success that one feels hurt that a better effort was not made on this point to help a good cause."

THE DAILY MIRROR, Wednesday June 5, 1935.

Daily Mirror

Broadcasting - Page 20

THE DAILY PICTURE NEWSPAPER WITH THE LARGEST NET SALE

MUMMY IN CELLAR MYSTERY —Page 3

No. 9,833 — Registered at the G.P.O. as a Newspaper. — WEDNESDAY, JUNE 5, 1935 — One Penny

Amusements : Page 24

ONE, TWO, THREE FOR AGA KHAN?

New Derby Record Likely in Great Race To-day

THE KING TO ATTEND IF WEATHER IS FAIR

The King, who, it is understood, has thrown off all the effects of his chill, hopes, if weather conditions permit, to go to Epsom for the Derby to-day with the Queen.

By BOUVERIE

WHATEVER the result of the Derby to-day, 1935 will go down in racing history as the Aga Khan's year. Never in living memory has an owner had such a chance of providing first, second and third in the greatest race in the world. It has been possible before; to-day it is highly probable.

Bahram, unbeaten and only once extended, was an odds-on chance until the final call-over last night, when support for Hairan caused him to go out to 5 to 4 against. That was the only reason. There is nothing wrong with the favourite, but his price was too short for the small backers who turned to Hairan to give them a more attractive bet.

Theft, although third in the betting, probably deserves second place because he has only twice been beaten. On each occasion Bahram was his conqueror.

Weak Opposition

Hairan has also been beaten twice. The first time was at Doncaster last season, when the firm ground was against him. This year he was beaten by the ill-fated Bobsleigh in the Newmarket Stakes, but even then he finished eight lengths in front of the next best.

When they line up to-day the records of the big three will read :—

BAHRAM 1 1 1 1 1 1
THEFT 1 2 1 1 1 1 2
HAIRAN 1 1 3 1 2

There are fourteen other runners in to-day's race. Between them they have not won as many races as Bahram and Theft have shared, and seven of them are still waiting for their first victory.

(Continued on back page)

THE RUNNERS AND JOCKEYS

(Race to be run at Epsom, 3 o'clock 1½ miles, 5 yards)

001 **FIELD TRIAL** (Lord Astor) .... R. Dick
  Colours: Light blue, pink sash and cap.
200 **ROBIN GOODFELLOW** (Sir Abe Bailey) .... T. Weston
  Colours: Black and gold hoops, gold cap.
003 **PEACEFUL WALTER** (Mr. A. E. Berry) .... J. Marshall
  Colours: Black, pink hooped sleeves, pink cap.
01 **FAIRHAVEN** (Lord Derby) .... R. Perryman
  Colours: Black, white cap.
112 **FIRST SON** (Mrs. C. Evans) .... R. A. Jones
  Colours: Mauve, cerise hoop on body and sleeves, cerise cap.
10 **SCREAMER** (Lord Glanely) .... A. Wragg
  Colours: Black, red, white and blue belt and cap.
00 **PLYMOUTH SOUND** (Lord Astor) .... J. Brennan
  Colours: Light blue, pink sash and cap.
322 **ASSIGNATION** (Mrs Corlette Glorney) .... S. Donoghue
  Colours: Old gold, green sash, quartered cap.
123 **SEA BEQUEST** (Mr. C. W. Gordon) .... E. Smith
  Colours: Cherry, cornflower blue sash and cap.
12 **THEFT** (H.H. Aga Khan) .... H. Wragg
  Colours: Green and chocolate hoops, chocolate cap.
1 **BAHRAM** (H.H. Aga Khan) .... F. Fox
  Colours: Green and chocolate hoops, chocolate cap.
2 **HAIRAN** (H.H. Aga Khan) .... G. Richards
  Colours: Green and chocolate hoops, chocolate cap.
0 **FAIRBAIRN** (Lt.-Col. Giles Loder) .... C. Smirke
  Colours: Yellow, dark blue sleeves, black cap.
414 **PRY II** (Mr. H. W. W. Simms) .... M. Beary
  Colours: Pink, black sleeves, hooped cap.
044 **BARBERRY** (Mr. E. T. Thornton-Smith) .... S. Smith
  Colours: Lilac, scarlet belt, gold cap.
00 **JAPETUS** (Sir Abe Bailey) .... F. Lane
  Colours: Black and gold hoops, gold cap.
000 **ST. BOTOLPH** (Mr. F. W. Dennis) .... H. Beasley
  Colours: Blue and white check, red sleeves, red cap.

The Aga Khan's Bahram, hot favourite for to-day's Derby.

THE ODDS LAST NIGHT

5-4 BAHRAM (t and o)
11-2 HAIRAN (t and o)
10-1 THEFT (t and o)
100-7 FIELD TRIAL (t and o)
100-6 SEA BEQUEST (t and o)
100-6 FIRST SON (o, 20 t)
28-1 FAIRHAVEN (t and o)
33-1 ASSIGNATION (t and o)
33-1 FAIRBAIRN (t and o)
50-1 SCREAMER (t and o)
60-1 ROBIN GOODFELLOW (t and o)
66-1 PRY II (t and o)
80-1 PLYMOUTH SOUND (t and o)
100-1 JAPETUS (t and o)
150-1 PEACEFUL WALTER (t and o)
200-1 BARBERRY (t and o)
200-1 ST. BOTOLPH (t and o)

French Cabinet Resigns

BOUISSON REFUSES TO TRY AGAIN

Paris, Tuesday.

THE new French Government formed by M. Fernand Bouisson on Saturday was defeated in the Chamber of Deputies last night and has resigned.

A vote of confidence was taken on the question of giving the Cabinet full dictatorial powers to deal with the financial situation. The voting was 264 to 262 against the Government.

When the announcement of the defeat was made Ministers left the Chamber to draw up their letter of resignation. Many Deputies shouted "Dissolution! Dissolution!"

So great was the tumult that the sitting was suspended.

The news spread rapidly through the city, where it created an immense sensation. Riots in the streets were feared by the authorities, but the crowds were kept on the move and all was peaceful at midnight.

The whole district surrounding the Elysée was thick with strong detachments of police. Companies of mobile guards with carbines slung over their shoulders were posted in the streets.

On M. Laval's advice, President Lebrun urged M. Bouisson to try to form a new Cabinet, but he declined.

(Messages from Reuter, Exchange and Central News)

GOLF'S MY GAME!

I'D NEVER MAKE A JOCKEY ANYWAY!

The Aga Khan, owner of the three most favoured runners in the Derby, is an enthusiastic golfer, and at Roehampton yesterday morning seems without a care about the race

THE DAILY MIRROR, Thursday, June 6, 1935

Daily Mirror

Broadcasting - Page 22

THE DAILY PICTURE NEWSPAPER WITH THE LARGEST NET SALE

THE 'YARD'S' NEW CHIEF —PAGE 3

No. 9,834 Registered at the G.P.O. as a Newspaper.   THURSDAY, JUNE 6, 1935   One Penny

Amusements : Page 28

THE QUEEN AT THE DERBY

"Try these, mother.... Can you see all right now?" says the Duke of Kent, offering the Queen his own glasses.

BOUVERIE BEFORE—

Aga Khan the King's Guest After Jubilee Win

BOUVERIE'S 50-1 OUTSIDER SECOND

1. Bahram (H.H. Aga Khan) .... F. Fox
2. Robin Goodfellow (Sir Abe Bailey) .... T. Weston
3. Field Trial (Lord Astor) .... R. Dick
4. Theft (H.H. Aga Khan) .... H. Wragg

Betting: 5-4, 50-1, 9-1, 100-8.

AFTER his victory in the Jubilee Derby—watched by the King and Queen and their four sons—the Aga Khan was the King's guest at dinner at Buckingham Palace last night.

With fifty-seven other members of the Jockey Club, he sat at a long table in one of the white and gold dining-rooms on the first floor of the Palace.

There were no women guests, and after dinner the King proposed the health of the winning owner.

The Queen, who usually dines out with friends on Derby night, this year decided to stay at home. She dined alone at the Palace.

In the West End green and chocolate, the Aga Khan's racing colours, figured in decorative schemes. Overseas visitors to London gave parties and helped to make it the biggest Derby night for some years.

At Newmarket Bahram was given just a little extra feed.

The King's Cigarette

In the royal party at Epsom were Prince and Princess Nicholas of Greece and Lord Harewood. The Duchess of Kent celebrated her first visit to the Derby by picking the winner.

She had a ten-shilling note on Bahram and one on Theft, which was unplaced.

A delightful family party scene in the royal box was witnessed just before the race.

The King seemed in high spirits. He brought out a silver cigarette case and smoked a cigarette. Then, noticing that the rain had stopped, he picked up two heavy cushioned chairs and carried them down to the front of the box, refusing all offers of help.

The race itself was run in bright weather. All the morning it had rained, sometimes so heavily that few people remained on the course, but the weather cleared up just in time.

A Derby tip ignored, by David Walker— page 2. Pictures on pages 16 and 17.

—AND **AFTER!**

BOUVERIE, whom you see here pondering over the possibilities of the race, gave three horses out of the first four in the Derby.

He knew there was nothing to beat Bahram. But he also knew everyone was looking for an outsider at 50 to 1 that would beat the bookmaker.

Bouverie found him in **Robin Goodfellow.**

His only mistake was in missing the third horse! His selection, Theft, finishing fourth at 100 to 8, robbed him of a triple triumph.

The Aga Khan got the winner of the Derby—but Bouverie got the first two, and there he is on the right marked X, duly celebrating the event.

SHOT WITH GIRL BESIDE HIM

Mystery of Dead Soldier in Wood

FROM OUR OWN CORRESPONDENT
ALTON (Hants), Thursday morning.

BELIEVED to have been lying unconscious in a wood for thirty hours, a seventeen-year-old girl was found near Bordon Camp late last night by the body of a young soldier.

The discovery was made at a lonely spot known as Rhode Hill, between the villages of Selborne and Blackmoor.

Constable's Watch

The soldier, Corporal Harry Parker, twenty, of the 1st Oxfordshire and Bucks Light Infantry, had been shot through the head.

The girl, Ruby Cole, aged seventeen, a domestic servant, of Bordon, has head injuries.

She was rushed to Alton Hospital, where her condition is critical. A police constable is waiting by her bedside.

The couple were reported missing on Tuesday.

Medical examination has shown that the soldier had been dead more than twenty-four hours.

Letters Left

Near his body a discharged Army pistol and a bottle were found.

Corporal Parker's home is at Bradford, and several letters were found in his clothing addressed to people living there. Another letter was addressed to his commanding officer.

ENGLISH HOME FOR BARBARA HUTTON?

COPENHAGEN, Wednesday.

COUNT Haugwitz and his bride, formerly Miss Barbara Hutton, heiress to the Woolworth millions, who are coming to London in a fortnight, state that they may make England their permanent home.—Reuter.

THE DAILY MIRROR, Tuesday, June 11, 1935.

Broadcasting - Page 20

Daily Mirror
THE DAILY PICTURE NEWSPAPER WITH THE LARGEST NET SALE

NEW CHANCE FOR YOUTH —Page 2

No. 9,838 Registered at the G.P.O. as a Newspaper.   TUESDAY, JUNE 11, 1935   One Penny

Amusements: Page 22

WHERE 44 R.A.F. MEN DIED

The utter devastation of the Royal Air Force station at Quetta, India, by the earthquake that took toll of 50,000 lives and inflicted immense material damage. Here forty-four British airmen, including one officer, were killed outright, while others received injuries to which they succumbed later. Left: With nose and mouth covered by a medical respirator owing to the risk of contracting disease from the contaminated air.

BOY HOUDINI MAKES HIS NINTH BREAK TO FREEDOM

His Weekly Escape from Detention | Police Say It Is "Black Magic"

FROM OUR OWN CORRESPONDENT
STOCKPORT, Monday.

THE fourteen-year-old boy Houdini has done it again. For the ninth time in as many weeks he has escaped from a Home Office correction school, and the authorities are very annoyed.

The boy, whose home is in Dudley, disappeared to-day from the school at Offerton, near Stockport.

It was his fourth escape from that school, and he had been brought back only on Sunday night after escaping last week.

A Stockport police official said to me last night:—

"I am not surprised. The lad's brought black magic with him from the Black Country. He's a nuisance and will have to be properly suppressed.

"These getaways, with their consequent police searches and rail fares, are now becoming expensive."

Here is the remarkable story of his escape last Wednesday:—

Clad only in his nightshirt he slid down a drain-pipe. Then he picked up some old socks, and a woman's overcoat. From the dressing-room of Stockport Football Club he took a pair of football shorts, and clad in this strange garb he travelled by train to Dudley.

The Handicap Failed

Several times he was seen in Dudley. Once, he said, he darted into an empty house and ran to the third story with the police hot on his heels.

He eluded them by hanging from the window-sill outside the house. When the police had gone he pulled himself back into the room.

He spent Thursday evening in a cinema, getting in by an emergency exit. Police, meanwhile, watched his home and he was recaptured at 8 a.m. the following day.

Exciting, but not the most exciting of this "elusive Pimpernel's" many adventures.

After one escape his captors took his bootlaces and braces from him. They thought that would be a handicap.

But it wasn't enough. He got away and went home by train—first class.

Once his passion for reading accounts of his exploits nearly ended in his capture. He went too near to a police station to buy a paper.

Another time he spent a night in a graveyard.

Drove Him Off with Umbrella
AGED WOMAN SAVES DAUGHTER

HER aged mother went to the rescue of Miss May Withers, thirty-one, when she was attacked by a man between Aldershot and Ewshot last night.

Miss Withers and her mother were walking on the common near their home, Warren Cottage, Ewshot. Suddenly a man jumped from some bushes and struck Miss Withers on the head.

As she fell unconscious the man, it is alleged, tried to grab her, but Mrs. Withers struck him several blows on the face with her umbrella, causing blood to flow.

Alarmed by her cries for help, the man ran away in the direction of Aldershot.

Police are searching the district for the man. He is described as tall, dressed in civilian clothes with no hat; his hair is brushed back from his forehead.

Not far from this spot only a few weeks ago a Mrs. Warren and her daughter, both of London, were attacked by a man in military uniform.

ADMIRAL'S WIFE HURT

LADY Fullerton, wife of Vice-Admiral Sir Eric Fullerton, and daughter of the late Lord Fisher, was injured in a motor accident on the Royston-Cambridge road yesterday afternoon.

She was on her way to Cambridge when the car mounted a bank, crashed into a telegraph pole and finished up in the hedge.

CINEMA ORGANIST TURNS RECITER
Kept Audience Entertained When Lights Went Out

CINEMA organist turned reciter when an electric supply failure lasting an hour and twenty minutes cut off film shows in the Orpington district last night.

At one of the cinemas the show stopped and the organ could not work. The organist then went on to the stage and entertained the audience until the electricity was restored.

The districts affected included Petts Wood, St. Pauls Cray and St. Mary Cray, Kent.

POLICE CALLED TO HOLIDAY CROWD

SOUTHEND police were called out early to-day to disperse 300 holiday-makers who had missed the last train from the L.N.E.R. station.

The stranded crowd, including about fifty children, demanded a special train. This the station authorities refused.

The police conducted the people to the sea front. They waited under the pier and in the shelters until the first train to London.

PAGAN BRIDES' VOWS AT BONFIRE
Forest Rites as Men Leap Through Flames

PAGAN marriages before a flaming bonfire and a weird fire dance in the heart of a forest near Berlin were features of lurid Whitsun ceremonial carried out yesterday by followers of the Pagan German Faith movement.

The two bridal couples, says Reuter, sat on a bench in front of the bonfire in a forest clearing. On their heads the brides wore floral garlands.

After an address by the local pagan leader, the couples stood up and gave their word to "keep their bodies pure, to love the country, and to serve the State."

Little children gave the couples rings, which were exchanged.

When darkness fell ten young men bearing torches listened to an invocation pronounced by the pagan leader. Then one man recited an oath and leapt over the flames, others following. It was the pagan fire dance.

They Said Yesterday

"A MILLION babies in Britain go without a doctor's care." What is to be done? A headmistress explains her scheme on Page SEVEN.

"Modern youth won't think or read." A challenge that demands to be taken up. Why not a youth crusade as an answer? See Page TWO.

"Britain and the Empire are leading the world out of the depression." All the way from Ontario comes this good news—into Page FIVE.

"He safeguarded your lives when he could." Lady Haig was the speaker. Ex-Servicemen supported her defence of her husband. See Page SEVEN.

"No Popery." Just that phrase shouted at a Premier. It started a demonstration. Where? Answer in Page SIX.

THE DAILY MIRROR, Monday, June 17, 1935

Daily Mirror

Broadcasting - Page 20

THE DAILY PICTURE NEWSPAPER WITH THE LARGEST NET SALE

No. 9,843 — Registered at the G.P.O. as a Newspaper.   MONDAY, JUNE 17, 1935   One Penny

TWO RAIL CRASHES IN 12 HOURS —Page 3

Amusements: Pages 8 and 16

LIGHTNING DESTROYS CHURCH

5-Hour Fire on Anniversary

STORMS' HAVOC IN THE SOUTH

A sunny June afternoon. The sun shining... Suddenly the sky darkens. An angry gust of wind. Rain and hailstones fall in a solid white sheet. Vivid lightning wreaks widespread havoc. ... Then the sun returns.

SUCH were the freak storms that swept Britain yesterday. In the south fruit crops were damaged, buildings wrecked, gardens and streets flooded.

At Bromley (Kent), Holy Trinity Presbyterian Church, set on fire by lightning, was almost completely destroyed. Last night, after firemen had been at work five hours, only the steeple, four walls and the organ were left.

Yesterday was the fortieth anniversary of the church's building and a thanksgiving service was to have been held at night. Women members of the congregation watched in tears their £20,000 church reduced almost to a ruin.

The church was struck twenty minutes before scores of children were to have assembled for the afternoon service.

An eye-witness told the *Daily Mirror* that a column of blue fire extended from the clouds to the stone cross on the western end of the church. Soon the timbered roof was blazing.

After the fire the cross was blackened but intact. A stained glass window below depicting the Ascension was also undamaged.

Fireman C. Wood, of Bromley, fell from the 45ft. high roof and suffered from concussion. Fireman F. Gosden was struck by falling timber and his back was injured.

Hero of the fire was the Rev. W. Musselwhite, vicar of St. John's Church, who lives close by. He was the first to enter the church and turn on the hoses before the Bromley and Beckenham Fire Brigades arrived.

He was drenched as he later helped to drag the hoses to the church. He left the scene after some hours to conduct the evening service at his own church, which he placed at the disposal of the Rev. F. W. Armstrong, minister of the Presbyterian Church.

* * *

CROYDON had one of the worst storms for many years. Rain and hail flooded the main London road at Norbury to a depth of nearly two feet.

Lightning shattered the chimney of a flat of Lower Addiscombe-road, Croydon. Eighty-one-year-old Mrs. Williams was sitting in her invalid chair by the fire. She was smothered in soot and had to be treated for shock.

At almost the same time a house in Woodside Court-road, about fifty yards away, occupied by Mr. and Mrs. F. A. Sussenbach, was also struck. The drawing-room curtains caught fire, dropped on to a settee and set it alight.

Air Liner Carries On

An air liner bound for Paris left Croydon Aerodrome. Lightning played round it. The pilot carried on. His plane was soon lost to sight in the screen of hail.

Two houses in Dunheved-road, West Croydon, were also struck. The roof, tiles and gutter of one were blown off and inside walls of the rooms on the second floor badly damaged.

At the other end and chimney were damaged and a hole burned in the ceiling of the second floor. The fire-grate was blown from its position into the middle of the room.

At BEXLEY HEATH seventy-seven-year-old Mr. and Mrs. Henry Birch, of Walkers Cottages, were sitting in a room when the roof was split and a bedroom ceiling collapsed. Their daughter had left the bedroom only a few minutes before. Sparrows' nests in the roof beam caught fire.

(Continued on back page)

The blazing church at Bromley, Kent. A picture of the burned interior is on the back page.

FIRE PANIC AT WEDDING

Bride Trapped by Flames

MAD RUSH

NEW YORK, Sunday.

A MAD stampede of 250 guests at a wedding in a public hall here to-day resulted in one being killed and forty injured.

Flames suddenly enveloped the canopy under which the bride, Miss Pearl Sokolower, was sitting, waiting for the ceremony to begin.

Like wildfire they ran round the hall, consuming scores of flags with which it was decorated. So great was the panic that many people leaped from the windows.

The bride herself was badly burned and has been taken to hospital.—Reuter.

MUSIC FOR 8,000 BY THE KING'S ORDER

HUNDREDS of persons in Sandringham Park yesterday saw the King walk to church and noted his Majesty's rested and cheerful appearance.

Later the King visited his stud farm at Wolferton.

Although the King's recent slight illness has prevented him from joining the Queen at Windsor, it was by his command that the bands of the Royal Horse Guards and Grenadier Guards played for 8,000 people who visited the town yesterday.

Empress of Britain—Rescue Race Through Fog

CREW TAKEN OFF BLAZING STEAMER

THREATENED by a fire raging in the forward bulkheads the crew of the 5,000-ton British steamer Kafiristan was saved by the Empress of Britain after she had raced to the rescue during a dense fog in the Gulf of St. Lawrence yesterday.

The Empress of Britain, C.P.R. crack liner, bound from Southampton for Quebec, took on board all the men in safety.

A salvage steamer has left Quebec for the scene.

An earlier report stated that the Kafiristan had collided with the Empress of Britain, and was endeavouring to make for the nearest port.

The Kafiristan, owned by the Hindustan Steam Shipping Co., of Newcastle-on-Tyne, was carrying a cargo of coal.

Her crew of about thirty-three are mainly Newcastle and Sunderland men.

The captain of the Kafiristan is Captain Busby, of Newcastle-on-Tyne.

Three Versions

Colonel Sir George McLaren Brown, European manager of the Canadian Pacific Railway, in an interview with a *Daily Mirror* representative last night, said that he had received three versions of the incident from various sources.

The first was from Quebec, which reported that the Empress of Britain had been in collision with the Kafiristan and was standing by; the second was a radio message which confirmed the collision; the third, the official version, stated that the Empress of Britain had taken off the crew of the Kafiristan following the fire.

BLIND GIRLS WIN RACE

FOUR blind girls comprised the boat crew which won the half mile race at the Women's Amateur Rowing Association regatta at Hammersmith.

They were members of the Sports Club for the Blind.

The girl who coxed them belonged to a rival club and sacrificed her chances in the race which followed in order to help them.

LORD CARSON HAS A GOOD DAY

"LORD Carson has had a good day," was the bulletin issued last night at his home in the Isle of Thanet.

Although not yet out of danger, Lord Carson continues to maintain the improvement shown during the last two days.

Daily Mirror

THE DAILY PICTURE NEWSPAPER WITH THE LARGEST NET SALE

Broadcasting - Page 22

BRITISH TRADE SPURT —Page 2

Amusements: Page 24

No. 9,844 Registered at the G.P.O. as a Newspaper. TUESDAY, JUNE 18, 1935 One Penny

15,000,000 WOMEN WARNED OF THREAT TO RIGHTS

AFRICA AND BACK IN A DAY

Captain W. E. Percival, the aircraft designer, climbing out of his light aeroplane at Croydon yesterday evening after flying to Africa and back on the same day. Leaving Gravesend at 1.30 a.m., he breakfasted at Oran. He finished the return journey before 6.30 p.m., in time for dinner. See story on page 3.

"We Must Fight" Says Suffragette of 91

BY A SPECIAL REPRESENTATIVE

"*There is a widespread attack being made on women's equality. Unless we are prepared to defend our freedom we shall lose what we have won.*"

A FRAIL, white-haired woman of ninety-one uttered this warning to the 15,000,000 women voters of Britain yesterday.

She is Mrs. Charlotte Despard, sister of the late Earl of Ypres. As a pioneer suffragette she went to prison several times. To-day, thirty years after, she is still champion of her sex.

Despite her age she has just arrived in London from her Irish home to address a series of meetings.

Mrs. Despard reproaches the women of Britain with being neglectful of the rights won by the last generation.

Woman may still fight against man's dictatorship. But not against fashion's.—See P. 3.

The Task Ahead

"Girls to-day are too apt to think that now they have the vote, everything has been won and they need not trouble themselves any further," she says.

"But a lot remains to be won. Women still have not got equal pay for equal work, and they still lose their jobs if they dare marry.

"In Germany and Italy we can watch women losing the rights they had. They are being again told to regard themselves as inferior creatures.

"The old argument that 'a woman's place is the home' is being used to take away women's freedom.

"It is no use Englishwomen saying: 'That cannot happen in our country.'

"It can, and I believe it will unless we are ready to fight to keep our rights just as hard as we fought to win them."

Whirlwind Tour

Mrs. Despard will begin her 91st birthday lectures in London on Thursday. A whirlwind tour of the suburbs will follow.

She will be speaking on behalf of the Women's Freedom League—the organisation she once led, in the pre-war militant days, "not to buy anything that is not absolutely necessary" as a means of obtaining votes for women.

For London remembers Mrs. Despard mainly as the tall, straight-as-a-lance figure leading defiant processions, speaking from the plinth of the Nelson Monument.

But it has something else to remember her by. Despard House, in Currie-street, Nine Elms, a child welfare centre, was her gift to Battersea Council.

MRS. CHARLOTTE DESPARD. "*Women—guard your freedom.*"

67 GAMES—AND HAD TO RETIRE

In Fight to Reach Wimbledon

A YOUNG man who works in an office and only plays tennis at week-ends, wanted to play at Wimbledon. He tried to qualify.

After battling away for over three hours at the Roehampton Club yesterday he was compelled to retire in a state approaching physical collapse.

But one of the longest tennis matches on record goes down in the official annals—S. H. Hawkins beat D. B. Jarvis 5—7, 4—5, 6—4, 12—10, 7—6, retired.

HUSBAND ACCUSED OF HER MURDER

Mecca Visit for Bride

HER LIFE'S AMBITION

ONE of the most romantic journeys made by a bride is planned by a twenty-four-year-old London girl who is to be married next Tuesday.

She intends to make a visit to Mecca and Petra in the course of following in the footsteps of a famous ancestor, John Lewis Burckhardt.

The girl is Miss Gabrielle Burckhardt, who is to marry Dr. W. McElroy, of Belfast.

For years it has been Miss Burckhardt's ambition to copy the romantic exploits, over a century ago, of John Lewis Burckhardt, the Swiss traveller and Orientalist and brother of her great-great-grandfather.

The girl's mother, Mrs. Ethel Lewis Burckhardt, of Lancaster Gate, said last night that Miss Burckhardt hopes to leave England before Christmas.

"Several years ago, when she told Lawrence of Arabia of her intentions, he wished her every success, at the same time laughing at the ambition of a mere child.

"It may be necessary for my daughter to wear a disguise at times, but the journey is not dangerous if the party is well equipped."

Britain on Top

IN trade and in sport Britain was feeling on top of the world yesterday.

For trade returns showed the May exports as the best for four years. The figures are on .... Page 2

British machines swept the board in the Manx Junior T.T. race. Not one foreign machine finished .... Page 7

And in the Test match at Nottingham the England team forced the South Africans to follow on. The play is described on .... Page 30

The younger generation didn't lag behind. British boys, returning from a tour in the United States, were said to have made a great impression by their good behaviour. What they think of America is on .... Page 10

There'll be plenty to carry on the tradition, for Britain is producing more boy babies than girls .... Page 6

THE KING OUT FOR CANTER

On Jock, His Favourite White Pony

HOLIDAYMAKERS at Sandringham had a pleasant surprise yesterday when they saw the King cantering along the road on his favourite white pony.

The King, who looked greatly improved in health, was not at first recognised.

His favourite mount, known to everyone on the estate as "Jock," has been specially brought to Sandringham since the King became well enough to ride.

As the King much prefers an hour in the saddle to motoring, it is probable that Jock and his royal master will be seen together frequently in the next few days.

JANET GAYNOR HURT

WHILE chasing a colt during a scene from "Way Down East," which is being filmed at Santa Cruz, Janet Gaynor, the film actress, tripped and fell and fainted. She is now confined to her bed with slight concussion and internal injuries.—Reuter.

BIGGER GERMAN NAVY FEAR IN FRANCE

PARIS, Monday.

FRANCE is believed to have returned a chilly reply to the British Government's communication regarding the Anglo-German Naval conversations. The reply will be officially presented in London to-morrow by the French Ambassador.

It appears that the French Government neither refuses to adhere to the agreement in preparation in London nor assents to the understanding on which it is based, and the Note is understood to argue that the increase of the German fleet to thirty-five per cent. of the British Navy would create a grave problem for Germany's Continental neighbours.—Reuter.

Mrs. Barbara Valerie Wynn, aged twenty, whose husband, Harry Wynn, aged twenty-two, of Robin's Nest, Towyn Way, Towyn, near Abergele (Denbighshire), was remanded yesterday, charged with her murder. It was stated that Wynn surrendered to the police at Rhyl. Later his wife was found dead with throat wounds at Robin's Nest. The couple were married at Easter.

THE DAILY MIRROR, Wednesday, June 19, 1935.

Daily Mirror

Broadcasting - Page 20

380 CONVICTS IN PIT MUTINY —Page 3

THE DAILY PICTURE • NEWSPAPER WITH THE LARGEST NET SALE

No. 9,845 Registered at the G.P.O as a Newspaper. WEDNESDAY, JUNE 19, 1935 One Penny

Amusements: Page 8

GERMANY'S NEW U-BOAT POWER

Can Build as Many as British Empire

FRANCE SEES A DANGER

Germany, given by Britain the right in certain circumstances to have a submarine tonnage equal to that of the whole of the British Empire. France, seeing danger in the concession, declaring that she may have to build up her naval strength as a protection.

THAT is the situation this morning following the publication of the White Paper which revealed the texts of the Notes exchanged between Britain and Germany on the agreement reached in the recent naval talks.

France is angry. She considers that Britain is condoning German naval re-armament.

It is understood she reserves to herself complete liberty of action and adheres to her general disarmament policy that all questions relating to arms, land, sea or air, should be considered together.

Task for Mr. Eden

Mr. Eden, Minister for League Affairs, will go to Paris on Friday, and this, his first mission since he was given Cabinet rank, will need all his tact.

He will try to persuade the French Government to the British view of the situation—that the only real policy is to seek to keep Germany's rearmament within bounds by freely negotiated agreements.

This is the position between Britain and Germany following the agreement.

It is now definitely established that the future state of the German Navy in relation to the aggregate naval strength of the members of the British Empire is to be in the proportion of 35 to 100.

This is to be a permanent relationship, and Germany has agreed to adhere to the ratio in all circumstances, unless there is an agreement between the two Governments.

This means that if Germany considers herself threatened by a speed-up or great increase in another Power's naval programme, and Great Britain does not consider herself so threatened, the German Government promises to consult us before increasing her navy.

In the event of Great Britain refusing to recognise Germany's need to the increase, the 35 per cent. ratio will remain binding on Germany.

But in the matter of submarines, Germany, while not exceeding the ratio of 35 to 100 in respect of total tonnage, is to have the right to possess a submarine tonnage equal to that of the British Empire.

The German Government, however, undertakes that Germany's submarine tonnage shall

(Continued on Back Page)

HITLER CAN BUILD MANY LIKE THIS NOW

BRITONS EVER SHALL BE SLAVES

DREAMS of freedom—Mr. G. B. Shaw shattered them in a broadcast talk last night.

"For at least twelve hours of your day," he said, "Nature orders you to do certain things and will kill you if you don't. This leaves you twelve hours. Here again Nature will kill you unless you earn your living or get others to earn it for you."

"If you live in a civilised country your freedom is restricted by laws enforced by the police. If you don't obey those laws the courts will imprison you, and if you go too far, kill you.

"Your landlord may refuse to let you live on an estate if you go to chapel instead of to church, or if you vote for anybody who is his enemy

As for the employer, "He may dictate the cut, colour and condition of your clothing, as well as your hours of work. He may turn you into the street."

"Let us stop singing 'Rule Britannia' until we make it true," was Mr. Shaw's advice.

"Keep smiling" was his motto, and keep smiling he did, despite Ascot's showers. He also contributed, in his own original way, to the great parade of fashion. Further Ascot pictures are on pages 14 and 15.

Ascot's Six Fashion Tips— and a Pair of Goloshes

By CECILIE LESLIE

ASCOT, Tuesday.

ASCOT, the world's most fashionable race meeting, was turned into a display of mackintoshes, muddy shoes and dripping umbrellas on its opening day.

Its best fashion tip was in the Duchess of Kent's hat. The brim, a foot wide, was white inside and black outside. The crown was white like the lining, and hardly visible from one angle, where the brim turned up in an almost rectangular sweep.

The Duchess wore a dress of black taffeta with a jabot of scarlet chiffon at her neck.

Here are five more Ascot fashion tips seen in the dresses:—

1. **Tailored lace** is this year favoured. These dresses are tight fitting and have no frills whatever. One or two had a short coat, the majority not even having this to relieve the tailored lines.

2. **All manner of suits.** Printed crepes of exotic floral patterns were used for coats and skirts. The blouses were made of the predominant colour in the pattern. Some suits also in beige flannel, rose-coloured linen, tweed and taffeta.

3. **Long dresses,** very simply cut, one or two reverting to the 1914 hobble-skirt and swathed hips. Very few dresses made in the traditional Ascot fabrics of voile and organdie.

STRIKING CONTRASTS...

... *As provided by the royal hats at Ascot:—*

The Queen's turquoise-coloured toque, the Duchess of York's pink-beige bonnet and the Duchess of Kent's enormous cartwheel hat of black and white.

4. **Colours.**—This year women wore startling shades like vermilion, or white, black or powder-grey.

5. **Hats.**—Either very big or very small. An unusual Ascot vogue was the felt hat, usually only straw. One or two women brought an alternative hat with them, and many ensembles were completely changed after the rain had ceased, and the women exchanged their dark hats for the more summery ones.

Unexpected sight: Pair of goloshes worn by a famous London hostess, Mrs. Claude Leigh.

THE DAILY MIRROR, Saturday, June 22, 1935.

Broadcasting—Page 23

Daily Mirror

THE DAILY PICTURE NEWSPAPER WITH THE LARGEST NET SALE

NEW MOVE TO CHANGE EUROPE —Page 3

No. 9,848 — Registered at the G.P.O as a Newspaper. — SATURDAY, JUNE 22, 1935 — One Penny

Amusements : Page 4

ARMED ULSTER FACES CRISIS

MISS BRITAIN

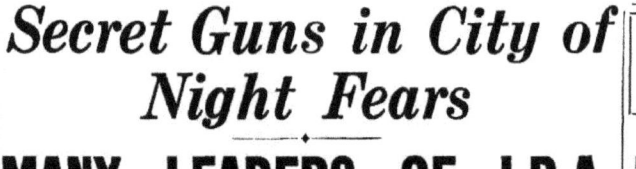

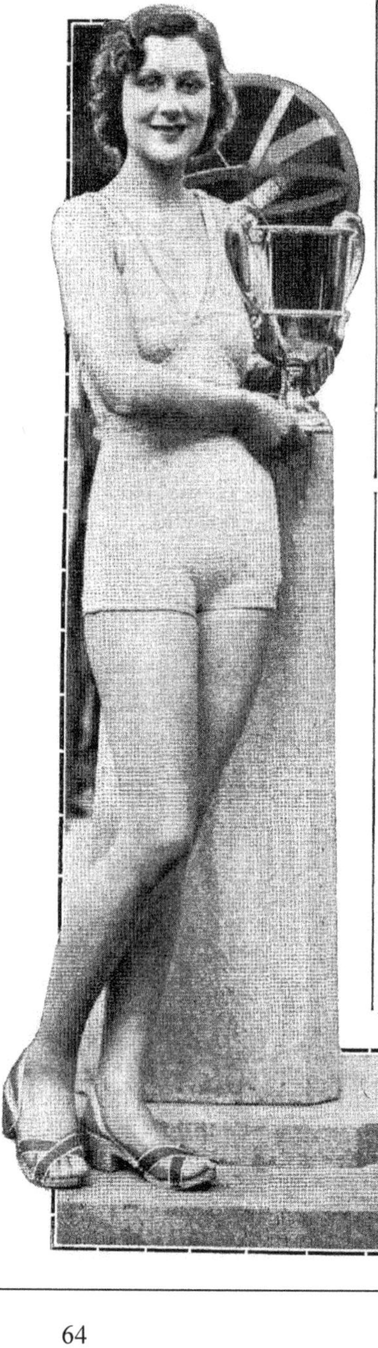

Secret Guns in City of Night Fears

MANY LEADERS OF I.R.A. CROSS THE BORDER

From STUART E. YOUNG
"DAILY MIRROR" SPECIAL CORRESPONDENT

BELFAST, Friday.

THIS great industrial city—part of Great Britain, and less than twelve hours' journey from London—is an armed camp of secret forces—a city where many carry death in their pockets.

For Ulster is on the brink of a crisis as grave as any since the establishment of the Northern Ireland Government.

The next two days will show whether the measures taken by the Northern Government will be sufficient to check the spread of the disorders which have made the Belfast dock district a place of terror at night for weeks past.

Sunday is a fateful day, for, unless Sir Dawson Bates, the Minister for Home Affairs, refuses permission, thousands of Orangemen will march to various churches in the city for their annual service.

It is expected that the processions will be held, but the routes will be carefully arranged to avoid passing through Catholic districts.

A hopeful sign is that last night for the first time in many weeks there were no outbreaks of violence.

Political observers believe that if the Government continue to show a firm determination to check any rioting from whatever side, the tension will ease of itself.

Armed Cars Out

Policemen are at every street corner and armoured cars and steel-grated lorries drive through the streets, crammed with members of the Royal Ulster Constabulary.

Members of Parliament, Ministers, lawyers and social workers to whom I have talked in the past two days agree that there are more arms secretly held in the city than at any time before, and the presence of the illegal Irish Republican Army in the Six Counties is acknowledged by all.

Estimates of its strength vary from 5,000 to 20,000. The army is alleged to be drilled and directed by leaders from the Free State.

I have been assured that in the last few weeks many I.R.A. leaders have crossed the border secretly, and are in the North ready for any emergency.

A coup by the I.R.A. is not suggested, but Catholics complain that they have been subjected to repeated attacks by Protestants, and that they can no longer hold on without retaliation.

Trouble Comes Easily

And Protestant organisers reply that the recent outbreaks have in the first instance been due to Catholics. With unemployment rife, the spread of Catholics from Southern Ireland is a grave source of friction.

But sectarian feeling in Ulster at all times runs so high that a scene in one street turns into a district-wide fight in a flash.

I have been solemnly assured that accordion bands, in which parties of youths parade the streets playing provocative rallying songs and gather a large procession, have caused much recent trouble.

KEEPERS OF THE KING'S PEACE
A member of the Royal Ulster Constabulary beside an armoured car.

DEATH FALL FROM BRIDGE

Hundreds See Man Crash 80 ft.

UNKNOWN

HUNDREDS of people saw a man fall from Highgate Archway, N., to the roadway below—a distance of 80ft.—late last night.

He died soon after admission to St. Mary's Hospital, Highgate Hill.

Early this morning his identity had not been established. He is middle-aged.

Before he fell the man was seen to alight from a car.

BEAUTY QUEEN

Miss Muriel Oxford, of Eltham (London), Miss Home Counties, adjudged the most beautiful girl in the Miss Great Britain beauty competition held in London. See back page.

SHIPWRECKED— BABY SLEPT ON

Mrs. Broz, wife of Dr. Broz, of Yugoslavia, with her six-month-old son on arrival at Paddington yesterday. The ship in which they were travelling—the Danzig oil tanker, D. L. Harper—stranded on rocks west of the Lizard. The passengers were taken off by the Lizard lifeboat and throughout the adventure the baby slept peacefully in his mother's arms.

Lifeboat Search for Two Men

EMPTY BOAT BEACHED AT MIDNIGHT

FROM OUR SPECIAL CORRESPONDENT
RAMSGATE, Saturday Morning.

RAMSGATE lifeboat was out searching in the darkness early to-day following the discovery of an empty 16ft. rowing boat drifting off the North Foreland.

The boat, containing clothing, including the jackets of two men, a woman's music case, and a large amount of money, was beached at Broadstairs just before midnight. It was towed ashore by a motor-boat.

It had been hired at Margate four hours previously by two young men, one believed to be a chauffeur in Margate.

Two hours after the men left Margate coastguards sighted the boat three miles to the east. A strong current was sweeping it away.

It is believed that the men left the boat for a swim and lost their bearings as the boat was swept away from them.

When the lifeboat put out the fog had lifted.

Other sea dramas on page 3.

THE DUCHESS OF KENT

THE following official statement was issued from 3, Belgrave-square, S.W., yesterday:—

"The Duchess of Kent has cancelled her forthcoming engagements, and she is not undertaking any further functions this summer."

THE DAILY MIRROR, Monday, June 24, 1935.

Daily Mirror
THE DAILY PICTURE NEWSPAPER WITH THE LARGEST NET SALE

Broadcasting—Page 22

STRIKE THREAT ON THE QUEEN MARY —Page 2

No. 9,849. Registered at the G.P.O. as a Newspaper. MONDAY, JUNE 24, 1935 One Penny

Amusements: Pages 18 and 20.

BRITAIN LEADING THE WORLD

24 Nations' Bid for Our Sports "Crowns"

WE HEAD PROSPERITY DRIVE

BRITAIN LEADS THE WORLD TO-DAY.
IN SPORT it is on top of the world at the beginning of the greatest week in the sporting calendar.

At Wimbledon begins the two-week Battle of the twenty-five nations; twenty-four nations challenging Britain's hold on the tennis "crowns"—the men's and women's singles titles.

IN TRADE Britain is playing a leading part in getting the world back to prosperity. It is sending 117 experts to a conference on reviving world trade. (See page 3.)

And in the strength of Britain and her Empire lies an example to the world. Germany believes in that strength. Hitler's Envoy, Herr von Ribbentrop, said so yesterday. (See the back page.)

This is the programme for the week's festival of sport:—

Lawn Tennis.—Wimbledon championships.
Golf.—The Open championship at Muirfield (all the week).
Boxing.— Jack Petersen, British heavyweight champion, v. Walter Neusel, of Germany, on Tuesday at Wembley. Seaman Watson, former British feather-weight champion, v. Freddie Miller (America), holder of the world's title, on Thursday at Liverpool.
Athletics.—Britain v. Finland, on Saturday at Glasgow.
Cricket.—England v. South Africa. Second Test, at Lord's, begins on Saturday

In addition to these great international contests, there is racing at Folkestone, Newcastle, Newbury, Havdock Park, Sandown Park and Ayr.

Outstanding events are the Northumberland Plate at Newcastle on Wednesday and the Summer Cup at Newbury on Thursday.

Jock McAvoy, British middle-weight cham-

AT WIMBLEDON TO-DAY
Order of play, beginning at 2 p.m.:—
CENTRE COURT
F. J. Perry (Great Britain) v. M. Rainville (Canada) V. B. McGrath (Australia) v. W. L. Allison (U.S.A.), H. Henkel (Germany) v. J. Borotra (France), J. H. Crawford (Australia) v. J. Brugnon (France)
COURT 1
S. B. Wood (U.S.A.) v. E. Itoh (Japan). E. R. Avory (Great Britain) v. H. W. Austin (Great Britain), F. H. D. Wilde (Great Britain) v. D. Budge (U.S.A.), I. G. Collins (Great Britain) v. C. Boussus (France).

pion, defends his title at Manchester to-night against Al Burke.

Britain holds, through Henry Cotton, the golf Open, won by an Englishman last year for the first time since 1923.

His challengers come from five continents. They include Lawson Little, the American holder of our amateur title, the American professionals, Kirkwood, Macdonald Smith and Picard, and Syd Brews, the South African, who was runner-up to Cotton last year.

The prospects are discussed by F. Stacey Lintott on page 31.

H. E. Lainson Wood, our tennis correspondent, sums up the Wimbledon prospects on page 28

TWO PAIRS OF TROUSERS

HE'S 100, BUT—
WELL, SEE PAGE 17

ENGLAND'S NEW MAN FOR SECOND TEST

The England team to meet South Africa in the second Test match at Lord's, on Saturday, will, it was announced last night, be selected from :—

R. E. S. Wyatt (captain) (Warwickshire), N. S. Mitchell-Innes (Oxford University), Sutcliffe (Yorkshire), Leyland (Yorkshire), Verity (Yorkshire), Hammond (Gloucestershire), Ames (Kent), Nichols (Essex), Clark (Northamptonshire), Mitchell (T. B.) (Derbyshire), Langridge (James) (Sussex), and Farrimond (Lancashire).

Farrimond, a newcomer to Test cricket in England, will keep wicket.

WHAT'S THE BIG IDEA?

Participants in one of those quaint old English ceremonies—tutti men stuff or floral dance? It looks like it, but the fact is the sea looked so inviting that bridesmaids, complete with bouquets, and groomsmen, complete with silk hats, all went paddling after the wedding of Miss Fallis Gatfield and Mr. Claude Pearse at Morecambe, Lancs.

50 Police Stand Guard Over Mr. Anthony Eden

THEY WILL RING OUR EMBASSY IN ROME DURING HIS VISIT

FIFTY picked Italian policemen were guarding Mr. Anthony Eden in the British Embassy in Rome last night. They will remain on duty so long as the Minister without Portfolio remains in the Italian capital.

Mr. Eden reached Rome from Paris yesterday evening, and his first talk with Signor Mussolini takes place to-day at the Palazzo Venezia.

Signor Mussolini was not at the station to greet the visitor, who was welcomed on his behalf by M. Suvich, Under-Secretary of State for Foreign Affairs, and Baron Aloisi, Italy's delegate to the League of Nations. The British Ambassador (Sir Eric Drummond) was also on the platform to greet his countryman.

A small crowd had gathered at the station to see Mr. Eden's arrival, and when they caught sight of him some of them exclaimed, " How young he is." (Mr. Eden is thirty-eight.)

There was a pleasing informality about the station greeting. Mr. Eden and Signor Suvich wore ordinary lounge suits. There were no soldiers, and only a slightly augmented force of police.

LORD CARSON

"Lord Carson has passed a quiet week-end and is getting on steadily," his doctor reported yesterday.

It is understood that it will be a day or so before he is able to leave his sick-room.

Church Protest Walk-Out

CHURCHWARDENS and parishioners walked out from St. Luke's Church, Leicester, yesterday morning and held a service of their own.

It was a protest against services being taken by anyone but the vicar, Dr. S. Shannon, who is in prison for not attending Leicester Bankruptcy Court for his public examination.

A diocesan lay reader, Mr. E. H. Wright, sent by the Rural Dean to take the services, was faced with an empty church, and after exchanging friendly greetings with the churchwardens and parishioners, who numbered about twenty, he went away

Mr. W. Collington, peoples' warden, who conducted a protest service, took as his text the words: "Therefore he that delivereth me unto you hath the greater sin."

THE DAILY MIRROR, Wednesday, June 26, 1935.

Broadcasting - Page 20

Daily Mirror

THE DAILY PICTURE NEWSPAPER WITH THE LARGEST NET SALE

GERMANY'S SUBMARINE PLEDGE
—Page 3

No. 9,851 Registered at the G.P.O. as a Newspaper. WEDNESDAY, JUNE 26, 1935 One Penny

Amusements: Page 18

TWENTY STORMS RING LONDON

Four Railway Lines Blocked : Six Deaths : Towns in Darkness

HAVOC'S SPREAD THROUGH NIGHT

TWENTY STORMS RINGED LONDON YESTERDAY. THROUGH THE NIGHT THEY WERE SPREADING NORTHWARDS.

Behind them, across a 200-mile stretch of country, was left a trail of havoc.

Four railway lines were blocked. Landslides barred Southern Railway tracks a quarter of a mile from Dartford Station and near the entrance to Merstham Tunnel (Surrey).

The G.W.R. Box Tunnel was flooded to a depth of 11ft., the Bath-Chippenham service dislocated, and Corsham Station platforms were 3ft. under water.

The L.M.S. line between Towcester and Banbury was washed away for some considerable distance. All traffic was suspended.

Train on Fire

An electric train containing about fifty people narrowly escaped disaster when twenty feet of the wall of railway cutting opposite Kingstown mail boat pier, Dublin, collapsed under the weight of flood-water, and the train ran into the debris.

Although there was flood-water on the line, the train caught fire and was badly damaged.

There was alarm when the mishap occurred, but men passengers restored order among the women and children, who were carried over the flooded line some two hundred yards to Kingstown Station.

The driver of the train was apparently unaware of the danger until within about fifty yards of the breach in the wall, and then a vivid flash of lightning revealed the mass of debris in front.

By Candlelight

At the height of the storm towns were plunged in darkness.

Ashby-de-la-Zouche (Leics) was completely paralysed by an electricity failure.

At Ashby Cottage Hospital an emergency case had to be examined by candle-light.

Emergency men dispatched in lorries to discover where the damage lay had to cover between twenty and thirty miles.

Towcester, too, was plunged into darkness. Three people were killed by lightning and three more deaths from heat were reported.

Following the hottest June night in London for sixty-four years the temperature dropped 10deg. early yesterday afternoon, but conditions became uncomfortably oppressive.

"A cooler current, coming up across the warm surface current was responsible for the storms yesterday," an Air Ministry official told the *Daily Mirror* last night.

"Weather in the south of England will be cooler, but close. There is little risk of further storms."

400 Fogbound

Four hundred holidaymakers in the pleasure-cruising liner Killarney and over 100 passengers in the Lerwick to Aberdeen tourist flagship, St. Magnus, were fogbound at sea in the Orkney Islands area last night.

The air mail from Inverness to Kirkwall was cancelled.

Details of the storm—Page 2

MAN'S VIGIL IN WRECKED VILLAGE

FROM OUR SPECIAL CORRESPONDENT

CORSHAM, Tuesday Night.

A LONELY signalman to-night keeps vigil at the G.W.R. station here over a wrecked village.

Tons of mud, washed down from neighbouring hills by the storm, has swept all before it. Streets and pavements are covered to a depth of 2in.

A gang of platelayers are standing by, as it is feared that several yards of railway track have been washed away.

Water, 8ft. deep in the station, laps into the stationmaster's office and on to the roadway.

The station is still isolated, though the water is gradually subsiding.

At Laycock, a small village further down the line, a road bridge was washed away by the torrential rain.

The signalman on duty is Mr. Grey. Near his cabin, which is surrounded by a high mud bank, a terrific cascade of water is still pouring.

He told me that Signalman J. Kent, who was on duty when the storm broke, had just got a train away. *Ten minutes later the flood raged past. Ten minutes that meant safety for the train's seventy passengers.*

AMAZING FLOOD SCENES

Marooned motorist eyeing the rising waters after these had stalled two cars under the railway bridge at Worcester Park, Surrey. Left: Parents in Malden carrying their children home from school. At Cheam, the children, once home, went out paddling in the street, as will be seen on centre pages. Other flood pictures also on pages 14, 15 and 28.

STONER REPRIEVED: TO SERVE A LIFE SENTENCE

"IN THE CASE OF GEORGE PERCY STONER, CONVICTED OF MURDER AND SENTENCED TO DEATH, THE HOME SECRETARY HAS RECOMMENDED A REPRIEVE WITH A VIEW TO THE COMMUTATION OF THE CAPITAL SENTENCE TO ONE OF PENAL SERVITUDE FOR LIFE."

THIS Home Office announcement last night brings to an end one of the most amazing "human triangle" dramas of recent years.

Stoner, the eighteen-year-old chauffeur, was found guilty at the Old Bailey on May 31 of the murder of his employer, Mr. Francis Mawson Rattenbury, sixty-seven, a retired architect, at the Villa Madeira, Bournemouth. He was recommended to mercy.

The dead man's thirty-eight-year-old widow, Mrs. Alma Rattenbury (Lozanne, the song-writer), who was tried for murder with Stoner, and found not guilty, committed suicide.

Days of Dread

When Stoner's mother heard of her son's reprieve, she said: "At last the disappointment and anxiety which we have experienced are over, but my relief and joy at this news are clouded by the thought that I shall not see my boy at home for so many years."

"We felt sure that they would not carry out the extreme sentence," said Mrs. Stoner, "but there was always that awful dread of hearing nothing."

The news spread quickly in Bournemouth and very soon people were flocking to the Stoners' bungalow to offer congratulations.

TRAWLER SINKS IN FOG —CREW RESCUED

AFTER a collision yesterday in dense fog with the Grimsby trawler Croxby in the North Sea, twenty-five miles from Aberdeen, the trawler Ebor Belle, registered at Grimsby and owned in Aberdeen, sank while being towed to port.

Her crew of nine were rescued by the Croxby.

Neusel Batters Petersen to Defeat

CROWD OF 70,000

SEVENTY thousand people, most of them drenched by a sudden downpour of rain, saw Walter Neusel, of Germany, force Jack Petersen, British heavy-weight champion, to retire at the end of the tenth round of their fight last night.

They saw an exhibition of heavy hitting rarely equalled in recent boxing history.

Once again it was Petersen's eye that played him false. A gash received in the first round was a handicap all through.

Neusel's left eye was closed in the ninth round, and at the premature ending both men had given and taken punishment until each was in a state of collapse.

Shortly before the contest a rain storm spoiled hundreds of women's evening dresses, and the dress shirts of the men were reduced to sodden miseries.

Full story of the fight—Page 26.

THE DAILY MIRROR, Monday, July 1, 1935.

Daily Mirror

Broadcasting - Page 20

THE DAILY PICTURE NEWSPAPER WITH THE LARGEST NET SALE

NATION-WIDE HUNT FOR GRIERSON
—Page 3

No. 9,855   Registered at the G.P.O. as a Newspaper.   MONDAY, JULY 1, 1935   One Penny

Amusements : Pages 16 and 18

THRILLING BROOKLANDS RESCUE
SPORTSMAN'S CHOICE

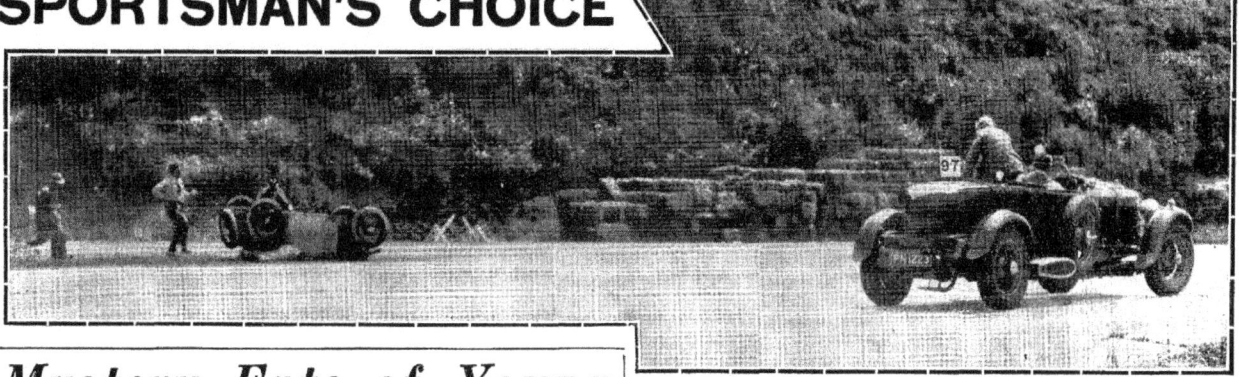

Mystery Fate of Young Couple on Cliff—Did Both Fall to Death?

GIRL IN SEA—NO TRACE OF MAN

FROM OUR OWN CORRESPONDENT

FLAMBOROUGH, Monday morning.

A MAN and girl are believed to have been killed by falling into the sea from the 400ft. Bempton Cliff, near Flamborough, yesterday.

Police searching until darkness fell last night failed to solve the riddle of the fate of the young couple. So far neither of the bodies has been recovered.

The couple were seen climbing a dangerous path on the cliff. Then, soon afterwards the body of a girl was seen floating in the sea.

This mystery faces the police: Was the body that of the girl seen on the cliff? Did her man companion fall with her to death?

Dennis Dooks, of Bempton, was the first to reveal that there had been a tragedy. He was walking along the cliffs when, about 200 yards out at sea, he saw through field glasses the body of the girl.

He described her as having ginger or auburn hair, a green dress and green shoes.

He left some people at the top of the cliff and notified the police, but on his return with the police the people had disappeared.

Later Mr. T. Croft, of Jameson - villas, Hull, reported that he had seen a couple climbing the cliffs in one of the most dangerous parts. The body of the girl floating in the sea answers to his description of the girl climbing the cliffs.

Bempton Cliff

A girl also reported that she had seen two bodies in the sea. At once the police began to search the cliffs and the sea, with Dooks signalling directions to them from the cliff top, and a Flamborough town councillor, Mr. George Mainprize, who was in a police boat, stripped, dived overboard and swam ashore to search the rocks at the base of the cliffs.

But of neither the girl nor the man could any trace be found.

Young Rescuer's Ambition

"I SHOULD like to get a life-saving certificate, but I don't know how," said Thomas Evans, eighteen, of Silver-street, Deal, while the holiday crowd was still cheering him for saving a girl from the sea.

Doesn't know how! And that was his fourth rescue in twelve months.

Many sea and river tragedies were reported yesterday.

Ten-year-old twin brothers were drowned in the Forth and Clyde Canal, Glasgow, within 200 yards of their home.

One of the boys, James MacMillan, of Whitelaw-street, got into difficulties while swimming. His cries for help were heard by his brother Francis, who immediately dived to his assistance.

James disappeared, and before help could reach him Francis, too had sunk.

Two hours after he had left his hotel at Westgate-on-Sea to go for a bathe, the body of Arthur William Chappelle, forty-eight, a cosmetic manufacturer, of Welbeck Laboratories, Blandford-street, London, W.1, was seen floating at St. Mildred's Bay and was brought ashore by a boatman.

An aeroplane joined in a search last night for the body of George Campbell, fourteen, of Leigh-road, Leigh-on-Sea, who was drowned in the Ray Creek at Leigh.

While the Berkshire British Legion thanksgiving service was being held in the St. George's Chapel, Windsor Castle, a message was sent in to Mr. J. Cole, a member of the Wallingford Branch. His son had been drowned in a bathing accident.

WRAPT IN MYSTERY

Arriving in London last night to compete for the title Miss Europe 1935 in the beauty contest at Torquay, Miss Tunis kept up the custom of her country by hiding her face behind a veil. So we must wait until she faces the judges this week to see her features.

POLA NEGRI TO WED BRITISH M.P.

NICE, Sunday.

POLA Negri, the Polish film star, formerly Princess Serge Mdivani, revealed to-day that she is to be married to an English Member of Parliament in six months.

She did not wish his name to be known at the moment.

"I have known my fiance for the past five years," she said, "and the marriage was decided on six months ago."—Reuter.

Mr. G. Baker, of Hove, is a sportsman. He was within sight of the finishing point —and a special award—while competing in the Junior Car Club's high-speed trial at Brooklands, when he saw Mr. A. C. Goodman's car overturn after hitting a sandbank, and the driver and passenger pinned underneath. He pulled up a moment before flames burst from the upset car, and, heedless of the danger from other cars, he and his mechanic (seen leaping out) dashed across the track and put the flames out with a fire extinguisher. With the help of officials, who are seen running up, they rolled the overturned car clear of its occupants, who were practically unhurt. Then Mr. Baker returned to his own car and finished the race.

Two Trapped Under Tigers

CAGE CRASHES ON BOYS

CHILDREN ran screaming to their homes, while mothers hastily locked the doors when two tigers were roaring with fury as their travelling cage fell from a lorry and trapped two boys yesterday.

Attendants from a circus were unloading cages containing wild animals at the back of the Queen's Palace of Variety, High-street, Poplar, E., when suddenly a rope holding the tigers' cage snapped.

The cage crashed, and Victor Lundale, aged six, of Grosvenor-buildings, Manisty-street, Poplar, was trapped underneath.

Another boy, Patrick Sheehan, aged eight, also of Grosvenor-buildings, had his foot pinned by the cage.

"There was a terrific din," a woman living in Grosvenor-buildings told the *Daily Mirror*.

"The tigers were roaring and hurling themselves at the bars, while children ran up the street screaming Attendants had to lift the cage to release the two trapped boys."

Lundale and Sheehan were taken to Poplar Hospital, where Lundale was detained in a critical condition.

It was impossible for the tigers to escape.

To add to the confusion in the street other wild animals, including lions and polar bears, heard the roaring of the tigers and soon the street resounded to the combined growling and roaring.

People became frightened Within a few minutes the street was clear of pedestrians.

THE DAILY MIRROR, Tuesday July 2, 1935

Broadcasting—Page 20

Daily Mirror

THE DAILY PICTURE NEWSPAPER WITH THE LARGEST NET SALE

ANOTHER LONDON BUS STRIKE
—Page 3, Col. 3

No. 9,856 Registered at the G.P.O as a Newspaper. TUESDAY, JULY 2, 1935 One Penny

Amusements: Page 21

BROTHERS' 27 DAYS IN THE AIR

Ocean 'Phone Talk to "Daily Mirror" After Landing

This was the home of the Key brothers for twenty-seven days.

"IT WAS FINE AND DANDY"

BY TRANSATLANTIC TELEPHONE

"Yes, sir... I'll say we've beaten the record.... We've had anxious moments.... Now we're fine and dandy."

IT was thirty-one-year-old Al Keys, back to earth after nearly a month in the air, speaking to the *Daily Mirror* from Meridian (Mississipi) early to-day.

With his brother, twenty-four-year-old Fred, he had just landed at the airport after breaking all air endurance records in their home-made 'plane, Ole Mississipi.

Their total time in the air was 27 days 5 hours 33 minutes.

Through all that time they had seen nothing but their monotonous fifty-mile triangular course; heard nothing but the drone of their engine.

Faced Storms

"I'm rather deaf," Al told me. "Otherwise we are both none the worse.

"But I must say it's been a tough proposition, and we've had some anxious moments. At one time we were encircled by a terrific thunderstorm.

"Another time we were lashed by a hailstorm. Almost the only sort of bad weather we didn't have was snow.

"Then it was a close call when we had a short circuit and a fire started. We had to work like steam with extinguishers to get that little bother settled.

"I may say to you British folk that my brother and I are very proud of our crazy machine.

"You can tell your womenfolk too that our wives did their bit by cooking and preparing for us some fine meals, which were brought up by a refuelling 'plane. But, gee, it's good to be able to eat a meal in comfort again, and have the youngsters around."

Al has a son aged five. Fred has a daughter aged four.

Anxious Wait

Mrs. Al laughed with delight when I spoke to her.

"It's been an anxious wait," she said, "there is no denying, but it's good to be able to give him a hug again.

"My sister-in-law and I have just been hanging round that aerodrome, cooking meals and talking to make the time go faster."

Asked whether she would permit her husband to leave her for so long again, she replied, with another chuckle, "I suppose that's up to him." Then she rushed away to cook another meal.

When the brothers Keys took off on their record-breaking flight they were unknown, the laughing stock of experts. They landed to fame and riches. America's fuel and aviation concerns were there to greet them with contracts.

The present flight started at 12.32 p.m. on June 4. Days passed.

An aviation company offered the flyers £120 a day for every day they remained up after beating the record.

Last Thursday they completed 23 days 2 hours 41 minutes 30 seconds in the air, beating the official record by an hour.

They went on and beat the unofficial record of 648 hours

SPORTS SHOCKS
At Lord's and Wimbledon

SUTCLIFFE, of Yorkshire and Ames, of Kent, may not play in the third day of the Test match against the South Africans at Lord's to-day.

Both pulled leg muscles during play yesterday.

This is a sad blow for England, who are fighting with their backs to the wall.

South Africa are 238 runs ahead with four second innings wickets to fall.

England with two of her best bats absent, will be in a bad way.

* * *

BUNNY Austin was beaten by Donald Budge (America) after a terrific match which lasted more than two hours.

When it was over Austin was so exhausted that after he had run to the net to congratulate his opponent, he lay flat by the Umpire's chair.

The most relieved person was Mrs. Austin. She was all smiles. "I am so thankful it is over," she said.

"It is all so bad for him, and I do wish he would give it up. Thank goodness he is beaten; now we can have some peace."

* * *

MRS. Helen Wills Moody got a fright on Court One. She lost her first set 3—6 to Mlle. Cepkova, the eighteen-year-old Czechoslovakian. And in the second set she was three down, but rallied to win 6—4. She took the last set 6—2.

The Queen at Wimbledon, page 2 Yesterday's results page 27.

MUST NOT HEAR OF FRIEND'S DEATH

BOBBY Abel, the famous England and Surrey cricketer, is dangerously ill at his home in Handforth-road, Kennington. He is seventy-seven.

His daughter and sons are trying to keep from him the news of the death yesterday of his great friend, Billy Brockwell, with whom he used to open the batting for Surrey.

"My father is practically blind now," said Mr. Alfred C. Abel last night. "His sight has been steadily failing him ever since he ceased playing in 1904. If only he could see the Oval again I know that it would be an enormous comfort to him in his illness.

"Every night I go to see him, for it was my mother's last wish before she died that I should look after him."

DEATH FOR LOYALTY.—Mrs. Gertrude Bongers, of St. John's Wood, N.W., who with her husband was found gassed to death in a car on the Yorkshire Moors near Hawes. A letter read at the inquest stated she accepted death out of loyalty to her husband. See page 3.

M.P.s Resent Britain's 'Surrender to Mussolini'

By A LOBBY CORRESPONDENT

M.P.s were attacking the Government last night. It would not have needed much manoeuvring to produce a condition of crisis.

And the reason was Britain's part in the Italo-Abyssinian dispute as revealed earlier in the day by Mr. Anthony Eden—particularly the offer of a strip of British territory to Abyssinia to avert a conflict.

"Contrary to tradition and unwarrantable surrender to Mussolini," was the prevailing Conservative view of the situation.

Questions were already pouring in last night, and it is clear that a demand for a debate at an early date will have to be conceded by the Government.

One question challenges the Government's right to make the offer to the Abyssinians at all.

Constitutionalists maintain that Somaliland is a protectorate, held by Britain under a treaty, and that the Government had no authority to propose to hand over any strip of territory.

Yesterday's debate in the Commons.—Page 7.

TWO DROWN IN THAMES DRAMAS

TWO rescue dramas, in which a man and a child were drowned, were enacted on the Thames last night.

A barge capsized at Charlton Bank, Greenwich, throwing four men into the water.

Charles Sealey, aged fifty, of Lucas-street, Upton Park, was drowned. The three other men were dragged to safety.

When nine-year-old Freda Schnerovitz, of Brunswick-street, Stepney, fell into the Thames at Tower Bridge Police-Constable R. Heard, of Port of London Authority officer, dived repeatedly, fully dressed, to her aid.

He only gave up when exhausted. The child is believed to have been swept away by the current.

Daily Mirror

THE DAILY PICTURE NEWSPAPER WITH THE LARGEST NET SALE

Broadcasting - Page 20

"DAILY MIRROR" JUBILEE EIGHT —Page 5

Amusements: Page 18

No. 9,857 Registered at the G.P.O. as a Newspaper. WEDNESDAY, JULY 3, 1935 One Penny

NIGHT ATTACK ON THREE GIRLS

NEW CANDIDATE FOR COLLARS

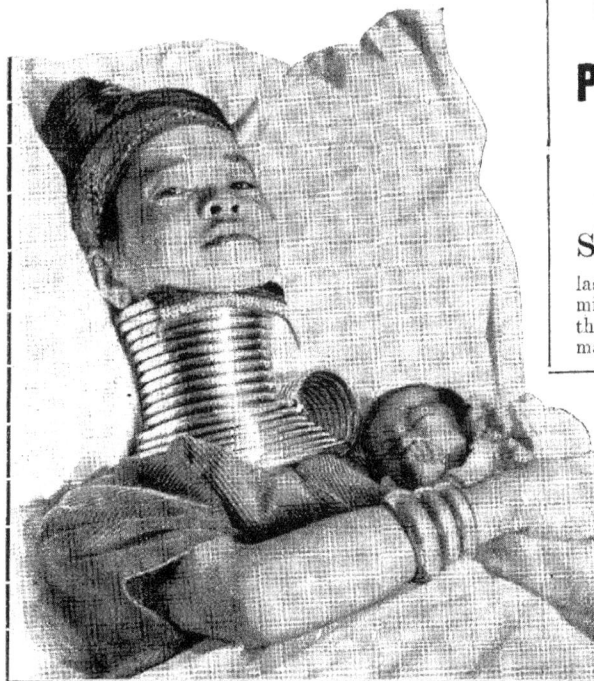

Bloodhounds in Manhunt Over Common

POLICE STOP CARS: BUSES SEARCHED

FROM OUR SPECIAL CORRESPONDENT

FARNHAM (Surrey), Wed. morning.

SEVENTY policemen, many in cars and on motor-cycles, were called out last night to join in a great hunt over miles of lonely woodland and common in the Frensham and Churt districts for a man who had attacked three girls

Bloodhounds were used. Hundreds of motorists were stopped and questioned. Buses were pulled up and searched.

Some of the police who joined the hunt were playing cricket against the village team at Churt when a breathless constable ran on to the ground to give the alarm. Without waiting to change the men were rushed away in tenders.

Struck on the Head

One of the girls, who was alone on the Common, was hit on the head by her assailant and seriously injured.

She is Miss Ainslie, daughter of Mr. Walter Ainslie, a neighbour of Mr. David Lloyd George at Churt.

Soon afterwards, not very far away, two other girls, who were walking together, were attacked. It is believed that the same man is responsible for the two attacks.

At the Farnham Infirmary, where these two girls were taken, the matron told me that she was bound to secrecy, and was not to divulge any information.

Nor were the names of the girls revealed. They are both aged about twenty, and are believed to be visitors to the district.

Hiding in Bushes

They were on Frensham Common, a stone's throw from the main road and within sight of many large houses, when a man dashed upon them from behind some bushes.

They were knocked to the ground and, it is understood, struck on the head with a sandbag.

When one of the girls recovered sufficiently she ran to the road crying, "Help, help," and

(Continued on back page)

Admiral Sir William W. Fisher.

Admiral's Fall Into Harbour

FROM OUR OWN CORRESPONDENT

PORTSMOUTH, Tuesday.

ADMIRAL Sir William Fisher, Commander-in-Chief of the Mediterranean Fleet, fell from his barge into Portsmouth Harbour to-day—and the matter was officially dismissed as "of a very minor character and of no importance."

For the Admiral suffered no ill-effects from his unexpected ducking. Naval ratings grasped him and he was dragged to safety.

It all happened when Sir William was about to land from his barge at the Gosport pontoon. The boat failed to go astern, and was carried broadside on by the tide under the prow of the pontoon.

The companion steps were carried away by the collision and the Admiral, who was dressed in civilian clothes, toppled over into the water.

Ducking and rescue were all over in less than a minute. Then the Admiral returned to his temporary flagship—H.M.S. Resolution

11 IN MISSING 'PLANE

Moscow, Tuesday.

A PASSENGER 'plane with eleven people on board is reported missing east of Khabarovsk, on the Manchurian-East Siberian frontier.—Reuter.

MEN ANGERED BY BUS STRIKE SETTLEMENT

"Rights Surrendered"

SETTLEMENT of London's bus strike was announced at 1.30 this morning, but there were scenes of disorder when the terms were revealed to the men at Nunhead—the garage where the strike started.

Cries of "You have surrendered the men's interests," drowned the words of Mr. Collison, the branch delegate, when he attempted to explain the terms.

When he endeavoured to persuade the men to accept the decision and return to work, dozens cried "We won't."

Transport and General Workers' Union delegates had decided unanimously to call off the strike following the meeting between their representatives and the Transport Board at the Board's offices.

To take part in yesterday's negotiations, Mr. Harold Clay, national secretary of the Passenger Section of the union, flew with three other officials from the Isle of Man.

At the same time meetings of busmen were being held at the Old Kent-road, Catford, Barking, Seven Kings and Bromley depots.

Yesterday's strike began at Nunhead. The strike spread rapidly to ten other depots.

GIRAFFE-NECKED WOMAN'S BABY

Mu Proa, one of the giraffe-necked women from Burma now touring Britain, with her baby daughter, who was born in a Carlisle nursing home the day after the circus had left for Edinburgh. The baby does not take after mother in length of neck yet. The first of the series of rings put on Paduang girls will not be placed round her neck for two years, and by that time both mother and child will probably be back in sunny Paduang.

140 Feared Dead in Ship Crash

TOKIO, Wednesday.

IT is feared that 140 people were drowned to-day when the steamer Senzan Maru (1,144 tons) crashed into the Midori Maru (1,725 tons) amidships.

The Senzan Maru's bows penetrated the engine room of the other vessel, which sank in three minutes.

The Midori Maru carried 168 passengers and a crew of eighty-five.

The collision occurred near Shodo Island in foggy weather.—Reuter.

The Midori Maru passengers, says the Exchange, were returning from a pleasure excursion

Three Men Shot in Procession

ARMED CARS PATROL STREETS

CROWDS watching an Orange procession in a Belfast street last night saw a man drop to his knees and fire a number of shots at the marching men.

Three men were hit. Their injuries are serious, but not dangerous.

Another man standing at the door of a house some distance away had his arm grazed by a bullet.

The procession, headed by a band, was marching to an Orange hall to obtain a banner for the 12th of July celebrations and the shooting took place at the junction of North Queen-street and Clifton-street.

The district, which is part of the dockland area, is in a state of tension and extra police have been drafted in.

For the first time since the withdrawal of the ban on processions in the York-street area the police patrolled the streets last night in armoured cars. A search for arms was carried out

Further disturbances took place after the shooting, the windows of a public house were smashed and in the same district police had to make another baton charge.

Earlier in the day there was some stone throwing by rival religious groups in the Brown-street area and many windows were smashed.

Crowds in this district were dispersed by baton charges on Monday night

Daily Mirror

THE DAILY PICTURE NEWSPAPER WITH THE LARGEST NET SALE

Broadcasting - Page 20

FOREIGN OFFICE STOP SALE —Page 2

Amusements : Page 8

No. 9,858 Registered at the G.P.O. as a Newspaper. THURSDAY, JULY 4, 1935. One Penny

"EVIL SPIRITS" PERIL WARNING
Bishop Attacks Seance Methods

HIS FRIENDS BELIEVERS

A BISHOP warned people last night against the peril of getting into touch with evil spirits by means of Spiritualism.

The Bishop was Dr. Winnington Ingram, Bishop of London.
The warning came in an attack on spiritualism in which, he admitted, some of his best friends believed.

The attack brought a swift reply from Lady Conan Doyle. Spirits, so far from being evil, she said, would help to make the Church a living thing.

But a psychologist agreed with the Bishop. To the Bishop's warning against the spiritual menace, he added a warning against the menace to health.

"Very Dangerous"

In the current issue of his diocesan leaflet, Dr. Winnington Ingram says that spiritualism has again "raised its head" in the diocese and it cannot be ignored.

"Most willingly would I avoid saying anything," he writes, "as some of my best friends believe in it and also one or two of my leading clergy, to say nothing of men like Sir Oliver Lodge, whom the world honours and respects.

"I feel that this attempt to communicate through mediums with those in the other world is all wrong, is very dangerous, is dishonouring to the dead, and is a waste of time for the living.

"Even those who practise it admit its dangers and further admit that you may get into contact with most unpleasant spirits who can do you nothing but harm.

"I believe that the mediums, consciously or unconsciously, read the thoughts of those who come to them, and that this is the explanation of the revelations which appear to come from the other world, and which deceive many."

Attack "Monstrous"

Lady Conan Doyle described the Bishop's attack as "monstrous statements."

"I would say to him that Spiritualism is the greatest support of what the clergy are teaching in the churches at the present time," she told the *Daily Mirror*.

"If the Church kept in touch with the spirits it would be a living thing, and the world would not be in such a materialistic state.

"There are people who have been driven to the depths of despair, but who have found comfort and inspiration in the teachings of Spiritualism."

Professor F. A. P. Aveling, the eminent psychologist, of King's College, supported the Bishop's statement.

"Nothing that I personally have investigated in connection with Spiritualism will stand up to criticism," he said. "The Bishop is right. I do know that Spiritualism is a very dangerous thing to tinker with."

CLERGY "ILLOGICAL"

LORD Molesworth told the *Daily Mirror* last night that it seemed utterly illogical to him that the clergy should set up Christ as an example to follow in His life, and then stop short at his death and resurrection.

"He came to conquer death," added Lord Molesworth, "and to show us that though the material body was cast aside, the spirit lives and could come back to life to love and console those who were left."

Tynesiders out in small craft to bid a last good-bye to the Mauretania.

Mauretania's Last Radio to 'Daily Mirror'

After making twenty-eight years' Atlantic history for Britain during a great and glorious career, the Mauretania sent her last radio message last night to the "Daily Mirror."

Stopping off the mouth of the Tyne to give a last salute to her birthplace, the gallant old lady went on to her grave—Rosyth, where she is to be broken up.

By Radio from DAVID WALKER
(Our Special Correspondent Aboard)

IN THE FIRTH OF FORTH,
Wednesday Night.

HERE we are in the Firth at last. The Mauretania's last journey is nearly over.

After this message has been sent the small wireless cabin on the top deck will be dismantled and the batteries removed. The Mauretania has received and sent her last message.

Already most of the passengers have left. Some time after midnight the gallant old lady will steal silently up the Forth to Rosyth.

At 5 a.m. the last words will be written in her log, and her story of more than 2,000,000 miles of travel will come to an end.

At ten this morning on her journey to the grave the Mauretania stopped for a short while opposite the place of her birth.

It was from the Tyne that she came triumphantly to answer Germany's North Atlantic challenge nearly thirty years ago.

She was surrounded by small craft bringing hundreds of people to say "farewell." As she got under way again, sirens and hooters from all the vessels around her sounded together.

In brilliant sunshine aeroplanes zoomed round her like flies, and as we gradually left smaller boats behind we could just hear the sound of hundreds of voices singing "Auld Lang Syne."

DESTROYER SEARCH IN 'PLANE-IN-SEA MYSTERY
Midnight Find of Oil on Water

AIRCRAFT, a destroyer and a lifeboat searching at midnight for a 'plane which had come down in the sea three miles north-west of the Needles found only a patch of oil on the water.

This morning the fate of the 'plane's two occupants—and the identity of one of them—remained a mystery.

The machine, a Westland-Wessex three-engined 'plane, was owned by Cobham Air Routes. It was piloted by Flying-Officer Ogden, aged thirty, of Bognor, and its one passenger had chartered the 'plane to carry him from Guernsey to Bournemouth.

Sir Alan Cobham said to the *Daily Mirror* this morning:—"I cannot understand how this can have happened. The pilot was in constant wireless communication throughout the trip with Portsmouth Aerodrome.

"About five minutes before he was due to land at Bournemouth, the pilot stated that he had developed engine trouble. But the machine could have flown perfectly easily on two engines.

"Two minutes later all wireless communication ceased."

The S O S picked up at Portsmouth was passed on to the lifeboat station at Yarmouth.

Two aeroplanes from Portsmouth and an R.A.F. flying boat circled over the Solent and Needles, while the Yarmouth lifeboat cruised for four hours over a wide area, but all that could be seen was the patch of oil.

The destroyer Rowena continued the search through the night with searchlights.

GLORIA'S MOTHER LOSES AGAIN

New York, Wednesday.

JUDGE Carew's decision awarding the custody of Gloria Vanderbilt to Mrs. Gertrude Whitney, was upheld to-day by the Appellate Division of New York's Supreme Court.—Reuter.

"Want a black cat for luck? I'm jolly nearly all black and worth a dozen cats." Miss Britain with a newly-found friend yesterday, when competitors for the title of Miss Europe at Torquay (Devon) visited picturesque Cockington Forge.

Daily Mirror

THE DAILY PICTURE NEWSPAPER WITH THE LARGEST NET SALE

Broadcasting - Page 22

DIVORCED WIVES ARE AMBITIOUS! —Page 3

No. 9,860 Registered at the G.P.O as a Newspaper. SATURDAY, JULY 6, 1935 One Penny

Amusements: Page 8.

BRITISH GUNS FOR IRELAND

And Britons Are Shot Down

GREAT WAVE OF SMUGGLING

Gunmen lying in wait at Sheridan's Cross, near the Ulster-Irish Free State border, yesterday fired on four policemen, gravely wounding one of them below the heart. The gunmen escaped.

The wounded man was just going on customs duty at the border when the party were ambushed.

There was a rustle behind a hedge, a momentary glimpse of two men, a cry of warning. . . . Then shots rang out.

Below a *Daily Mirror* special correspondent reveals how the gunmen get the weapons with which they shoot down servants of the British Empire.

'On Top of Arsenal'

BY A SPECIAL CORRESPONDENT

WHEN an I.R.A. gunman takes aim at a policeman, the chances are ten to one that his bullet will be fired from a British revolver. The same odds apply in the Free State. It is an ironic touch that the men who hate the British Empire attack its servants with British weapons.

Not since the civil war has gun-running between England and Ireland been so active.

An official told me that the weapons found on arrested men are almost invariably of British manufacture.

"Before the war they were mostly German," he said, "but to-day 90 per cent. of smuggled weapons are British. This is no reflection on the maker, who can hardly be expected to know where the revolvers he sells are destined to be used."

Thousands Armed

"There is an impression here that most of these revolvers are exported to the Continent and there sold to the smugglers.

"Nobody knows how many weapons there are in the country, but there is no doubt we are living on top of an arsenal. Every member of the I.R.A. is armed, and that body boasts of 20,000 men in its ranks.

"Ireland, North and South, is riddled with secret societies. Ostensibly they are formed to protect some interest.

"When they get too notorious they change their names, but the trouble-makers in their ranks carry on just the same.

"And nearly all the members of these societies are armed, which means thousands more weapons.

"Some of the rifles in the possession of revolutionaries date from the Loyalist preparations of 1914. They are rusty and only just able to fire, but the injury inflicted by a bullet from a rusty weapon is all the worse."

LONDON TO PARIS IN 52 MINUTES

FROM London to Paris in fifty-two minutes! This new air record was set up yesterday by Captain Hubert Broad, piloting a De Havilland Comet machine.

The previous record for the journey was fifty-nine minutes.

Eyes Right! With kilts and arms swinging in perfect rhythm, the 2nd Battalion Seaforth Highlanders march past the Prince of Wales, their Colonel-in-Chief, who presented new Colours to them at Dover yesterday.

Headless Body of Man Found in Lonely Field

C.I.D. WORKING ON MURDER THEORY

THE headless body of a man with, it is stated, the mark of a knife in the chest, was found yesterday in an isolated field near Westerham Hill, Kent. Later the head was found nearby.

The man had apparently been dead about six months, and the detectives investigating the mystery are working on three theories to account for his death:—

That he cut his throat,
That he was poisoned, and
That he was murdered.

A rent book was found on the body, but owing to long exposure to the weather the name had become obliterated. There is nothing else to give a clue to the man's identity.

The discovery was made by Mr. Henry John Selby, of Westerham Hill, Kent, while he was walking in the fields.

The body has not been identified.

16 AIR GIANTS FOR RUSSIA

Moscow, Friday.

Sixteen of the world's largest land 'planes similar to the lost Maxim Gorky will be constructed immediately, according to a decision of the Council of Commissars, in memory of the catastrophe of May 18, when forty-nine lives were lost.

This squadron of huge 'planes will be built by voluntary subscriptions.

The Maxim Gorky, the world's biggest aeroplane, was intended for propaganda. Its features included a loud speaker capable of being heard distinctly on the earth from a height of nearly a mile, photographic and cinema laboratories with long-range cameras, a newspaper printing works with a rotary machine weighing 500lb. and capable of turning out a small newspaper.—Central News.

ROYAL WEATHER FOR ROYAL REVIEW

Perfect sunshine may favour the King's Review of the Royal Air Force to-day at Mildenhall and Duxford.

There is a risk of occasional showers, but generally the weather forecast is "bright, with good visibility."

The Prince of Wales is flying from Fort Belvedere to Newmarket, where he will join the King on his journey by road to the aerodromes.

First-comers to Mildenhall last night were regarded with a fine spectacle—the floodlighting of the 'planes by powerful searchlights. Many motorists spent the night in the open.

All about the Review and how to get there on page 12.

NON-STOP EXPRESS WHISTLE

WHEN the Merseyside express was speeding north about forty miles from Euston last night the engine whistle jammed, resulting in an incessant shriek.

People living near the railway line at Leighton Buzzard and elsewhere rushed in alarm to the stations.

The whistle was silenced by the engine crew.

The Prince of Wales decorating Recruit Payton, best recruit of the Royal Marine Depot with the King's Badge during his visit to Deal yesterday.

BRITON AGAIN AFTER 8 YEARS

Woman Wins Her Fight

AFTER an eight-years' fight to regain her British nationality, a woman has been granted a naturalisation certificate. She is Mrs. Winifred Lewellin de Jan—Miss Winifred James, the author.

"It does not mean a glow in the heart," said Mrs. de Jan last night, "because I have always been British, however much they tried to make me be a traitress to my country."

Mrs. de Jan married an American citizen in 1913, but the marriage was dissolved in Panama.

HUSBAND - FINDING IS EASY IF—

"MEN think that for women marriage is an achievement, but there is nothing easier than marriage if women have a low standard in husbands."

That is what Lady Simon, wife of the Home Secretary, told her audience at Wycombe Abbey Girls' School speech day yesterday.

THE DAILY MIRROR, Tuesday, July 16, 1935.

Daily Mirror

Broadcasting - Page 20

THE DAILY PICTURE NEWSPAPER WITH THE LARGEST NET SALE

BEVERLEY NICHOLS WRITES ON PAGE 10

No. 9,868 Registered at the G.P.O. as a Newspaper.   TUESDAY, JULY 16, 1935   One Penny

Amusements: Page 22

1,000 MILES AT 145 m.p.h.

BRITISH CAR ROARING TO NEW RECORDS

FROM OUR SPECIAL CORRESPONDENT
BONNEVILLE SALT FLATS,
Utah, Monday.

ONE THOUSAND MILES AT AN AVERAGE SPEED OF 144.93 MILES AN HOUR.

THIS is one of the amazing records set up for Britain to-day by the all-British car in which John Cobb and his co-drivers, T. E. Rose-Richards and C. J. P. Dodson, are attacking the 24-hour record at Bonneville Salt Flats, Utah.

Cobb took the wheel for the first spell. Round the ten-mile circuit marked on the bed of a dried-up salt lake he roared through record after record now held by the American driver, A. J. Jenkins.

For the first 100 miles Cobb averaged 144.9 m.p.h. Reaching the 300-mile mark he had pushed the average to 147.2. At 500 miles it was 147.6—well ahead of Jenkins's 132.6 m.p.h.

In the first three hours Cobb averaged 147.6 m.p.h., as compared with the 132.9 m.p.h. attained by the American driver.

Rose-Richards Takes Over

After 591 miles a stop was made for refuelling, and Rose-Richards took over the wheel.

While he was in charge the amazing figures for the 1,000 miles were set up. Then, at 1,210 miles came Dodson's turn.

At this point—after eight hours' driving—the average had dropped to 143.3 m.p.h., due to the effect of the terrific heat on the drivers.

It is 117 degrees in the shade; a breathless, scorching heat that makes the slightest action a torment. And we are only watching!

It is something of a miracle that the drivers have kept going at all in such conditions. They are wearing smoked glasses to prevent sun-blindness.

The sun did in fact prove too much for Dodson. During a halt he was overcome by heat and exertion and had to be medically attended. Cobb took his place in the car.

I was talking to Cobb soon after he made way for Rose-Richards.

He told me how delighted he was with the way his Napier-Railton—the lap record holder at Brooklands—was running.

An official broke into our talk. "If it keeps going as it is at present it's a sure thing all records will be broken," he said.

Last Thursday Cobb set up five new records at the Salt Flats, when he exceeded the previous fastest speeds for fifty kilometres, fifty miles, 100 kilometres, 100 miles and 200 kilometres.

Cars carrying the members of the British Legion who have gone to Berlin to establish friendship with German ex-Service men, passing through dense crowds, who gave the Nazi salute, on their arrival at the Friedrichstrasse Station. See story on Page 3.

Our Sailor King Joins His Fleet

BY A SPECIAL CORRESPONDENT
PORTSMOUTH, Tuesday morning.

KING George the Fifth, the Sailor King, joined his Fleet last night.

As he stepped on board the royal yacht, Victoria and Albert, to survey the mighty fleet of 157 ships which were lying at anchor off Spithead he was wearing the blue and gold uniform of an Admiral of the Fleet.

The King arrived at Cosham railway station with his three sailor sons, Admiral the Prince of Wales, Rear-Admiral the Duke of York, and Commander the Duke of Kent.

The moment he alighted from the train word was flashed to the dockyard, and immediately a signal was run up at the main signal tower.

At once every ship of the Fleet, and every other vessel in the waters, down to the humblest tug and ferry, "dressed over all." A wave of fluttering flags swept down the lines of grey warships.

The King made a six-mile drive through the city on his way to the Victoria and Albert yacht, moored at the southern jetty in the Dockyard.

When the royal car drew up at the foot of the scarlet gangway a distant naval saluting battery began to fire a royal salute of twenty-one guns.

Last night the King began the Naval Jubilee celebrations by entertaining admirals and senior officers of the shore establishments to dinner in the Victoria and Albert.

Ashore it was carnival night in Portsmouth and Southsea. Until long after midnight the streets and sea-front were crowded with visitors, and thousands made their way to the piers to look out over the water where the lights from the ships made Spithead look like the skyline of a great city.

On the beach midnight bathing parties were in full swing, and on Southsea Common there were scores of midnight picnics.

Time table for the review on page 24. Pictures on back page.

Listen for the Guns

THE roar of the Fleet's guns during the exercises to-morrow morning will, it is expected, be heard over a large area.

People who notice the sounds at great distances are invited to tell the Superintendent, Kew Observatory, stating the times as nearly as possible.

MUSSOLINI IS GOING TO AFRICA

ROME, Monday.

MUSSOLINI is expected to pay a visit to Eritrea, East Africa, within the next few weeks.

He will review the troops and make a number of encouraging speeches before the campaign, which, it is expected, will be launched, simultaneously, next November.

Fifty-five thousand more men were mobilised by Italy yesterday for service in East Africa;

More men also were called to service with the Air Force; and

Ten more submarines were ordered to be launched.

Italy's new mobilisation brings the total of her troops called up since the Italo-Abyssinian tension became acute to 275,000 men.

Mussolini, it is reported, is intent on wiping out in blood the memory of the Italian defeat at Adowa, and may even force a battle on the same ground.—Reuter.

Princess Rassari Heshla Tamanya, a cousin of Haile Selassie, the Emperor of Abyssinia, stated in New York yesterday that the Emperor has been preparing for war with Italy for the past six years.

"Munitions have been stored in mountain caches, troops have been trained by foreign officers, tunnels and dugouts have been dug for protection against aerial attack," added the Princess.

C. J. P. Dodson, John Cobb (centre), and (right) T. Rose-Richards.

THE DAILY MIRROR, Thursday, July 18, 1935.

Daily Mirror

Broadcasting - Page 20

THE DAILY PICTURE NEWSPAPER WITH THE LARGEST NET SALE

No. 9,870 Registered at the G.P.O as a Newspaper. THURSDAY, JULY 18, 1935 One Penny

JANE —Page 9

Amusements: Page 24

EVERY-CHURCH-A-CINEMA PLAN

Archbishop as Head of New Film Board

BY A SPECIAL CORRESPONDENT

EVERY church with its own cinema—that is the vision many churchmen are now striving to fulfil.

It was revealed last night that the Church has its own Film Board—the Cinema Christian Council—with the Archbishop of Canterbury as president.

The council, formed as a result of a recent meeting at Lambeth Palace, will [encourage] the use of films in religion.

It is felt that there is a growing demand for religious films, suitable for use in churches and mission halls.

The council will co-operate with film producers, distributors and exhibitors to further its aims.

The council also aims at:—

Bringing together in conference representatives of all organisations interested in raising the moral and æsthetic standard of the cinema with a view to united action to secure the production and exhibition of wholesome entertainment films.

Developing practical use of films among clergy, ministers, teachers and social workers for religious and instructional purposes.

A member of the new council told the *Daily Mirror* last night that the new body would try to provide church people with films for exhibition in church halls.

ABYSSINIA—LEAGUE COUNCIL TO MEET

League of Nations' Council is to meet on a date between July 25 and August 2 to deal with the Abyssinian dispute, says *Central News*.

Heroic Wife's Rescue Bid

HELD UP DROWNING DOCTOR FOR 15 MINUTES

HEROIC attempts at rescue were made by the wife of Dr. Grainger Bisset, of Glasgow, when the doctor was drowned in a boating accident in the Firth of Clyde at Isle of Arran last night.

Mrs. Bisset, her three young sons, and a companion, were rescued in dramatic circumstances by two boatmen.

Dr. Bisset had taken his family and his sons' companion, Albert Mollison, also of Glasgow, to Holy Island, three miles from Lamlash, Arran, in a small boat.

They had a picnic on the island and were returning when a heavy sea developed and the boat capsized.

Mrs. Bisset, who is a strong swimmer, made a gallant attempt to save her husband.

She kept him afloat for fifteen minutes, but ultimately he was dragged underneath by the strong current. Dr. Bisset was the only non-swimmer in the party.

Mr. Whitney Straight with his bride, Lady Daphne Finch-Hatton, after their wedding. Right: Bridesmaids in fish-net caps and flower-trimmed frocks.

BID TO BEAT AMY'S CAPETOWN RECORD

1,000 Miles More—Half a Day Less

IN the 'plane in which he broke the Australia-England solo record, Mr. H. L. Brook, the thirty-five-year-old Harrogate airman, left Lympne, Kent, at 12.38 a.m. to-day on an attempt to fly to Capetown in four days.

The record—4 days, 6 hours, 54 minutes—is held by Mrs. Amy Mollison.

A score of people saw him take off. Heavy clouds obscured the moon and there was a slight northerly wind.

The weather was reported to be heavy over the coast of France.

His Flannel Suit

Brook wore a brown leather coat, flannels and suede shoes. He carried his luggage in a small leather handbag.

His plans are: Cairo (2,500 miles) by the end of the first day; Juba, second day; Broken Hill or Bulawayo, third day; Capetown, fourth day.

To succeed he will have to be in the air nearly all the time, with only brief snatches of sleep.

Discussing the flight, Mr. Brook said that he realised he was faced with a much bigger undertaking than the winning of the Australia to England record.

"I have got to do 1,000 miles more than Mrs. Mollison, who used the west coast route," he said.

"I do not think it is possible to do it, but I am going to have a jolly good try."

WIFE ATTACKED NEAR HER HOME

"Flying Squad" Search

MOBILE police were rushed to the Cheam district of Surrey last night when a report that his wife had been knocked down and attacked by a man near her home was made to the police by Mr. F. W. Bissett, of Shirley-avenue, Cheam.

Mrs. Bissett described the man as being of medium height. He was wearing a sports coat.

The attack took place at a lonely spot. The man sprang upon Mrs. Bissett from behind and struck her on the head.

Sutton police took charge of investigations, and at midnight officers were still searching.

Chain-Mail Headdress of Millionaire's Bride

BY A WOMAN CORRESPONDENT

ST. Margaret's, Westminster, was packed with guests yesterday for the wedding of Lady Daphne Finch-Hatton, daughter of the Earl and Countess of Winchilsea, and Mr. Whitney Straight, the young American millionaire racing motorist.

Gleaming plated silver lamé with a triple pointed train made Lady Daphne Finch-Hatton's gown. Instead of a wreath she wore a Crusaders' headdress of silver chain-mail studded with orange blossom buds.

Fourteen bridesmaids in blue organdie muslin wore little fish-net caps with flower posies on one side.

THE DAILY MIRROR, Monday, July 22, 1935.

Daily Mirror

Broadcasting - Page 21

THE DAILY PICTURE NEWSPAPER WITH THE LARGEST NET SALE

GOVERNMENT'S ANSWER TO NEW DEAL —Page 5

No. 9,873 Registered at the G.P.O. as a Newspaper. MONDAY, JULY 22, 1935 One Penny

Amusements: Pages 16 and 22

GREEK THRONE DRAMA IN HOTEL

Three Men—And the Future of a Nation

TALKS SECRECY

By A SPECIAL CORRESPONDENT

BEHIND the locked doors of a room in a London hotel yesterday an ex-king listened while a man from his own country told him his chances of once again becoming a ruler.

In that quiet room were ex-King George of Greece, his brother, Prince Paul, and M. Kotzias, the powerful Mayor of Athens. For six hours they were in secret conference.

Six hours. And at the end of their talk the ex-King knew just how the people of his rumour-ridden country are reacting to the stories of an early restoration of the monarchy.

He learned, too, the latest moves in the intricate game of politics now being played in Greece, and details of the autumn plebiscite which will settle his fate for the immediate future.

During the conference all callers at the hotel were carefully questioned, and anyone who was not a guest or the friend of guests staying in the hotel was refused admission.

ROYALISTS' FAITH

But the very secrecy of the discussions has added to the feeling of uncertainty in Greece.

Was the Mayor the bearer of good tidings for the King?

Were the Monarchists planning a coup d'etat to place the ex-King on his throne?

This (states a Reuter message) the Royalists deny.

They declare that they are willing to await the result of the fateful plebiscite, confident that a landslide in their favour will sweep the country.

And M. Kotzias has stated that he has no authority from his country to make any definite proposals to the ex-King.

"At present in Greece there is an increasing enthusiasm for the monarchist cause. When I return to Athens I shall make an official statement to the people concerning my meeting with the ex-King."

How to change the bedding of a spinal case who must not be lifted? Here is a surgeon's solution of the problem, seen at University College Hospital, London. Bedding is placed on top of the patient. Both sets of bedding with the patient "sandwiched" between are clamped in and swivelled round until the old bedding can be lifted off at the top. New bedding is substituted and one more turn restores the patient to his original position with bedding changed.

Elephant Lured Up the Alps

PANTING and stopping; starting ... panting ... and stopping again, the elephant and Hannibal II—Mr. Richard Halliburton, American writer and adventurer—reached the Hospice of St. Bernard, in the Great St. Bernard Pass, yesterday in their attempt to cross the Alps from France to Italy like Hannibal I.

Five hundred spectators followed them the last steep mile and a half to the summit.

The ascent, says Reuter, had not been easy for the elephant, unaccustomed to the rarefied air of the Alps, and towards the end he was induced to proceed by bribes of pieces of sugar.

Two Tragic Children

A FIVE-DAY-OLD baby ... its father killed in an air disaster before learning of its birth ... its mother kept in ignorance of her husband's death for twenty-four hours.—See Page 2.

A five-year-old child on board a liner, England-bound ... its mother lost overboard despite gallant rescue attempts.—See Page 5.

Midnight Fight to Save Trapped Cave Explorer

STONES HAIL ROUND RESCUERS

FAR underground in a disused lead mine in Middleton Dale, Derbyshire, a dramatic fight was still going on early to-day to save the life of a man trapped while "pot-holing."

Thousands gathered anxiously awaiting the result. Among them was the man's father, who had dashed over from Rotherham.

Bernard Watson, twenty-six, of Litton House, Bawtry-road, Rotherham, secretary of the Rotherham Cave and Cavern Exploring Club, was exploring caves with four other friends when they found the old lead mine with a shaft running down an incline for 150 yards, and then dropping down a vertical shaft about 15ft.

Watson got down the shaft. Without warning the side caved in and buried him up to the armpits.

His friends struggled in vain to release him. They lowered a bucket, but as fast as he filled this more stones fell.

Miners' Rescue Team

The North Midland Coal Owners' Rescue Team were called from Chesterfield. Onlookers assisted in sawing wood to prop the sides of the shaft, but a fall of roof impeded progress.

Stimulants were given to the imprisoned man, and though in pain he bore up extremely well.

Time after time there were further falls of stone, but in the flickering candle-light the rescuers increased their efforts, and at midnight two rescue workers had got into the shaft with Watson.

There were still hours of work before them, for after Watson had been released he had to be lowered down the 100ft. cliff side which leads to the road.

HUNT FOR GOLD

EXPECTING to come back "fantastically wealthy," a company of English people—one a woman—are leaving Southampton in a few days' time to hunt for gold round the Great Lakes, Northern Ontario.

The leader is Mr. Denis Dollard. His companions include Mrs. John Lambton, airwoman, and Mr. A. F. A. Coyne, geologist.

Mr. Coyne told the *Daily Mirror* last night that while in Canada a Mrs. Emily Ellis told him how her father struck gold in 1882.

He believes that the gold may be that which Radisson, the French voyager, discovered in 1662.

TEST SURPRISE

CRICKETERS will rub their eyes to-day—at the twelve names from which the team to meet the South Africans in the fourth Test match at Manchester next Saturday will be selected.

The selectors have recalled these Boys of the Old Brigade—Maurice Tate, the Sussex bowler, and Duckworth, the Lancs wicketkeeper.

Five years have passed since either of them appeared in a Test team—in 1929 against the South Africans. Tate, it is true, went to Australia in 1932-33—after an outcry against his original omission—but he never played.

Another change from the Leeds match is the inclusion of Leyland—his lumbago is better. Clay, who was present at Leeds but did not play, is picked, and so is Robins, who played in the first Test.

Five Yorkshiremen are in the list—yes, Sutcliffe is not one of them.

Names on page 26.

Maurice Tate

Daily Mirror

THE DAILY PICTURE NEWSPAPER WITH THE LARGEST NET SALE

Broadcasting - Page 20

200 'PHONE TALKS ON ONE WIRE —Page 3

No. 9,876 Registered at the G.P.O as a Newspaper. THURSDAY, JULY 25, 1935. One Penny

Amusements: Page 22

IKON CARRIED AT A WEDDING

Count Orloff-Davidoff and his bride, the Hon. Elizabeth Scott-Ellis, with the little son of Princess Nikita of Russia carrying the holy ikon that was kissed by the bride and bridegroom during the ceremony.

Women Mob Bride Who Walked on Gold

A MOB of hundreds of women and girls mobbed the Hon. Elizabeth Scott-Ellis, daughter of Lord Howard de Walden, one of Britain's richest men, and Lady Howard de Walden, when she was married at the Russian Church, Buckingham Palace-road, W., yesterday, to Count Orloff-Davidoff.

As she arrived at the church the bride started up from her seat with a cry as the car seemed to mow through crowds of half-fainting women.

Before she left Seaford House, her home in Belgrave-square, the bride had had slipped into her shoes by her little page pieces of gold, upon which, according to Russian custom, she had to walk to the church.

Three hundred people only, relations and intimate friends, were allowed to witness the wedding yesterday of Miss Dorothy Chamberlain, daughter of Mr. and Mrs. Neville Chamberlain, and Mr Stephen Lloyd at Chelsea Old Church.

Children from the slum areas of Westminster, where the bride works with an organisation that arranges for their summer holidays, were among the privileged guests.

BRITONS IN SECRET AIR FORCE

To Aid Abyssinia in Case of War

WARNING BY THE "BLACK DRAGONS"

WHILE WAR PLANS to aid Abyssinia by a foreign air force, formed and maintained by wealthy secret backers with the aid of British, American and French airmen, were being made yesterday—

"ORDERS" to the Japanese Government to take measures to prevent the war were issued by the all-powerful Japanese Society of the Black Dragons.

TWELVE Aviators—four British and the remainder Americans and French—are already enrolled in the secret air force for Abyssinia. They will leave the French Riviera towards the end of August for Abyssinia (says the Central News).

They will be headed by a Chicago aviator, and will be provided with planes of Dutch and German manufacture.

The leader, in an interview last night, said:—

"Arrangements have been completed for the formation of a foreign air force and the 'planes will be ready for us when we arrive in Abyssinia.

"We are now having the necessary injections to ward off tropical maladies."

It is understood that the enterprise has wealthy private backers behind it.

Order to Japan

THE famous "Black Dragon" society of Japan has called upon the Japanese Government, says a Reuter Tokio message, to take "adequate measures" to settle the Italo-Abyssinian conflict.

It was the Black Dragons who were responsible for Japan's declaration of war against Russia in 1904; and

For Japan's withdrawal from the League of Nations.

When a little old Japanese of eighty lifts his finger and points to a certain person, that person, be he prince or coolie, priest or politician, quakes with fear.

"Do This"—It Is Done

The little old man is Toyana Mitsuru, head of the dreaded centuries-old Association of the Black Dragon.

No other man in Japan wields such power as The Big Tree, as he is known. He has but to say "Do this" to a Government and it is done.

And when he points not one of his followers will fail to inflict the penalty he indicates, be it disgrace, ruin, or even death.

The Big Tree belongs to no political party.

Not only in Japan does he hold sway. In China, with its teeming millions, are to be found myriads of devoted followers of The Big Tree.

Yet, with all this power at his finger tips, the little old man lives humbly and quietly

Horse Vanishing

THE horse is rapidly disappearing from the streets of London

Between 1924 and 1933, stated Mr. Hore-Belisha, Minister of Transport, in the Commons yesterday, horse-drawn vehicles declined from 210,276 to 81,075, a reduction of 61.4 per cent.

ALL SENT GREETINGS TO THE KING

FROM every corner of Great Britain and Northern Ireland, from the Channel Islands and the Isle of Man, Jubilee greetings were sent to the King.

The Home Office acknowledged these good wishes last night—in twenty columns of a supplement of the *London Gazette*.

Organisations of every kind—religious, political, sporting, industrial, professional, municipal bodies from the great boroughs to the smallest hamlet and numbers of private individuals are included.

WHOLE REGIMENT GETS "C.B."

SIMLA, Wednesday.

THE 1st Battalion of the King's Liverpool Regiment, stationed at Jubbulpore, has been confined to barracks pending investigation into an alleged fight between men of the regiment and villagers.

It is stated that thirteen villagers were injured in the encounter and that one man died.

According to Army headquarters in Simla, a woman of Karodi Village was frightened by a soldier. It is alleged that she feared she would be molested and gave an alarm.

The villagers turned out and attacked the soldier. The man was rescued and is now in hospital.

The next night, it is said, a party from the regiment raided a village, mistaking it for Karodi, and attacked the villagers.—Exchange.

YOUTH HATH CHARMS

"Great snakes!" You may well say so. This little boy, one of a number of schoolchildren who were treated to a visit to the London Zoo, has seemingly discovered that in spite of his youth he is a snake charmer. Curled round him is an African python, seven feet long.

DEATH-BED TIP OF A TRAINER

It Won by a Short Head

MR. John Carr, the sixty-four-year-old northern racehorse trainer was dying, and knew it.

Almost at his last hour, on Tuesday night, he sent for his old friend, Mr. J. Hamer, the Lancashire brewer, who had been his chief patron, and for whom he had prepared Boy Friend for the Church House Handicap at Liverpool the next day.

Mr. Hamer hurried to the bedside of his trainer, and friend.

There, Mr Carr said to him:

"Boy Friend has a very good chance. Whatever happens to me he is to run in that race—and win."

Yesterday morning Mr. Carr died of pneumonia Yesterday afternoon the Church House Handicap was run.

A few minutes past three o'clock this message came over the sporting tape in the *Daily Mirror* office:—

3.0—Liverpool: 1, Boy Friend; 2, Conway; 3, Tuapse. Won by short head;

And Mr. Hamer told the *Daily Mirror* later:

"It was out of respect to Mr. Carr's wishes that I ran the horse."

THE DAILY MIRROR, Friday, July 26, 1935.

Daily Mirror

THE DAILY PICTURE NEWSPAPER WITH THE LARGEST NET SALE

Broadcasting - Page 20

WATER IN R.A.F. 'PLANES' PETROL TANKS
—Page 5

No. 9,877. Registered at the G.P.O as a Newspaper.   FRIDAY, JULY 26, 1935   One Penny

Amusements: Page 22

CHORUS GIRL REPLIES TO BISHOPS

"Semi-Nudity" War Just Silly

BUT IT HAS BEGUN

BY A SPECIAL CORRESPONDENT

FIRST shots were fired last night in the battle over "semi-nudity" on the English stage.

The Bishop of London (Dr. Winnington Ingram) is leading the army of protesters, the Public Morality Council; the Bishop of Kingston is his aide.

At the quarterly meeting of the governing council of the Public Morality Council yesterday the principle was confirmed that dress on the stage should cover the front of the body from above the breast to below the hips.

Before the echoes of the opening salvoes of the meeting had died away, a chorus girl had stood forth boldly to take up the challenge.

She is Miss Marie Tompson, who is in the chorus of the musical comedy "Love Laughs," at the Hippodrome, and this is what she told the *Daily Mirror*:—

"I think the Bishops' rule about stage dresses is simply stupid, and I should like to meet them and tell them so.

"However, the representatives of the Morality Council should have a very happy time going round looking for infringements! I hope they won't be too shocked.

"It has always seemed a curious thing to me that the clergy should concern themselves so much about the dress of chorus girls. I am sure I don't understand why.

"I think it is simply silly making all this fuss about what girls should wear on the stage," she added. "Why can't they leave us alone?"

Yesterday, at the meeting in London, the Public Morality Council had planned its campaign.

Reconnoitring parties—representative of the Council—will visit all theatrical shows. If they find infringements of the standards set by the Council, reports will go to the Lord Chamberlain.

Allies? The Council hopes to win them from the camps of the theatrical profession itself.

"We are not prepared to tolerate any longer any exhibition of semi-nudity on the stage in emotional surroundings," said the Bishop of London.

And this answering volley came from Mr. Godfrey Tearle, president of British Equity:—

"What is this Council? Is it a body competent to make rules? I have a great respect for the Bishop of London.

(Continue on back page)

O.K.?

THIS HAPPENS ON OUR ROADS EVERY DAY

Although the Ministry of Transport announces that last week road accidents caused four deaths fewer than the week before, the above scene remains all too common. Motor-cyclist receiving first-aid after he and his machine had been in collision with a car near Bursledon, on the road between Portsmouth and Southampton, yesterday. His motor-cycle lies a twisted mass of metal and one of his shoes has come off in his fall.

VICAR DIRECTS FIREFIGHTERS

Church Threatened by Works Blaze

THE son and daughter of the Rev. Herbert Salmon, vicar of St. James's Church, Shoreditch, warned families and helped them to leave their homes early this morning when fire broke out at the Metropolitan Plywood Company's factory in Scrutton-street.

Part of the blazing factory was only a few feet from the church and vicarage, and the vicar's son, Mr. H. Salmon, who is nineteen, was awakened by smoke pouring into his bedroom.

He aroused his mother and father and sixteen-year-old sister, and they all had to leave owing to the great heat.

Mr. Salmon then ran in his pyjamas to give the alarm, while his sister went round warning different families whose homes were threatened.

As soon as the firemen arrived a district call was sent out, and 100 firemen with eighteen engines attended.

Hoses were dragged through the churchyard, and firemen stood with their backs to the church wall with their helmets reversed owing to the terrific heat, and stopped the fire from reaching the church.

The vicar, with his wife, also helped in calling out occupants of nearby houses. He gave a hand at dragging the hoses through the churchyard, and pointed out to the firemen the best places from which to tackle the blaze and prevent the flames from reaching his church.

Devotion

DAUGHTER'S VOW 24 YEARS AGO

TWENTY-FOUR years ago, Louise Emma Miskin, a nurse, was engaged to be married.

Then her fiancé died. Broken-hearted, she tried to forget her sorrow in service. She dedicated her life to her aged parents.

Eight years later her task became more exacting. From then onwards, for sixteen years, night and day, she never left their side.

"A wonderful record of service," said the coroner, Mr. Owen Stuchbery, at the Maidenhead inquest, yesterday, on Louise Emma Miskin's ninety-four-year-old mother, who died after falling in her bedroom. Accidental death was the verdict.

"Ideally Happy"

But her mother's death, though it ended seventy-one years of happy married life, has not ended Miss Miskin's task. Years of service have whitened her hair, but they have hardened neither her pleasant features nor her heart.

"I only hope," she told the *Daily Mirror* last night, "my father, who is ninety-three, will be spared to me for some years yet.

"My home life has been ideally happy, and I have enjoyed every minute looking after them."

An old friend of the family said: "One of the happiest moments of Miss Miskin's life was when she handed to her parents a letter from the King on their sixty-ninth wedding anniversary."

Mr. Miskin is a retired storekeeper. Their home is in Belmont-crescent, Maidenhead.

ELSIE JANIS HURT

MISS Elsie Janis, the American actress, is slowly recovering at East View, New Jersey, from serious injuries received in a collision between her car and a motor lorry. Her collarbone was fractured and her head was badly cut. The lorry driver, says Reuter, has been taken into custody.

Baroness Christa von Bodenhausen

German Baroness to Wed Briton—Three Weeks' Romance

ONLY three weeks after the couple first met, notice was given yesterday at Caxton Hall Register Office, London, of a marriage between Hugo Bulkeley Brassey, son of Captain Robert Brassey, of Davies-street, W., and the Baroness Christa von Bodenhausen, a kinswoman of the Queen.

"The marriage will take place on Saturday morning," the Baroness told the *Daily Mirror* yesterday, "and in the afternoon we shall go off to Biarritz on our honeymoon.

"After that we sail for Australia, but I hope I am not saying goodbye to England for good.

"I met Mr. Brassey only three weeks ago."

THE DAILY MIRROR, Thursday, August 1, 1935.

Daily Mirror

Broadcasting - Page 20

THE DAILY PICTURE NEWSPAPER WITH THE LARGEST NET SALE

No. 9,882 — Registered at the G.P.O as a Newspaper. — THURSDAY, AUGUST 1, 1935 — One Penny

BEVERLEY NICHOLS WRITES ON — Page 10

Amusements : Page 22

200 PEOPLE FLEE FROM FLAMES

DOVER BOAT TRAIN ON FIRE

Harbour police, seamen and luggage porters attacking a fire in coaches of an empty Continental express on a siding of the Admiralty Pier at Dover yesterday. Two of the coaches were destroyed and two others damaged. The harbour tug, Lady Brassey, assisted the fire brigade with her powerful pumps to overcome the blaze.

2 a.m. Blaze Menaces Many Homes

FLOOD PERIL

NEARLY 200 people raced from their homes early this morning when a blaze at a big London cabinet works threatened many houses.

Intense heat from the giant flames burst water pipes in the works, and to prevent flooding the district's water supply had to be cut off.

The fire wrecked the works of J. Bloom and Son, Bracklyn-street, New North-road, Hoxton, and a huge crowd of people, some of whom were in their night clothes, saw 100 firemen battle with the flames.

Hail of Wreckage

Hoses had to be dragged through some of the nearby houses.

As the firemen worked blazing debris crashed all around them.

Then the roof of the works fell with a deafening roar.

At 2.30 this morning all danger to nearby houses was past.

When it was discovered that water was gushing from pipes at the works, people in the district were warned to fill pails so that they would have supplies sufficient to last them until after breakfast.

Then the whole of the district's water supply was cut off.

Trains Held Up

Trains were temporarily held up near Clapham Junction Goods Station early to-day when fire broke out at a timber yard in Culvert-road, Battersea.

Four Southern Railway coaches were damaged by fire in a siding yesterday at the Admiralty Pier, Dover.

When fire broke out at a silk works at Stowmarket yesterday the brigade's chief anxiety was to keep the flames from reaching the explosives works nearby of Nobel Finishers, Ltd.

The silk works had recently been acquired by Nobels, who intended to rehouse their Slough works there. It took several hours to subdue the flames.

"MAD FROLIC" AT GRETNA GREEN

Girl Freed from a 5 a.m. "Marriage"

WARNING that "people who go to Gretna Green should realise that they are playing with fire and may burn their fingers" was given by Lord Pitman in the Edinburgh Court of Session yesterday.

He described a visit paid to the famous smithy by a young couple the month after they had met at a dance as "just a mad frolic which was not intended by either of them to constitute a marriage."

In the circumstances of the case, as related to him, he granted a decree to prevent the man from saying he was the girl's husband.

Marie Bindman, of Montague-street, Edinburgh, brought a successful action against William Fieldman, of Hospital-street, Glasgow, by which she asked the Court to order that Fieldman must stop saying that she was her husband.

Never Lived Together

Lord Pitman, in giving his decision, said the couple met at a ballroom on a number of occasions, and it was on the way home from a dance that Fieldman proposed marriage. The couple immediately took a taxi to Gretna Green and went through a marriage ceremony there at 5 a.m.

On their return the girl went to her aunt's house. Nothing was said of the escapade by either of them at the time, and they never lived together as husband and wife.

Miss Bindman's case was that she never looked upon the ceremony as being a ceremony of marriage and that the Jewish religion did not recognise any such ceremony as constituting marriage.

Twelve Men in 7-Hour Fight to Save Pony in 15-ft. Deep Well

FROM OUR OWN CORRESPONDENT

ALTON (Hants), Wednesday.

FROM eleven o'clock this morning until six o'clock this evening twelve men laboured frantically to rescue a pony, Tommy, from a circular well fifteen feet deep and sixteen feet across, which was three parts full of water.

The entrance to the well, built of bricks, is only two feet in diameter at this point, and how the pony, which is twelve hands, fell through is a mystery. Its owner thinks it must have gone in backwards.

When I saw the pony, not many hours after its rescue, it was contentedly munching a feed in the stable.

Emptying the Well

Mr. Albert B Lambert, of Hawthorne-lane, Four Marks, near Alton, told me a graphic story of the rescue:—

"I was building a fence around a haystack when my wife shouted to me that the pony was missing," he said. "At last I found him swimming in the well.

"For hours men who came to my assistance lifted out the water with buckets, but that being slow, we borrowed a pump and started pumping out the water.

"We got thousands of gallons of water out and then I went down the well on a ladder. The men brought cartloads of hay and threw it down. It had the effect of soaking up the water and lifting the pony up a little.

"We then erected a derrick and eventually got him out—although once he fell back."

55 PERISH IN SUBMARINE

FIFTY-FIVE men, most of them cadets of naval schools, perished when disaster struck a Soviet submarine during exercises in the Gulf of Finland.

The submarine—the B3—was taking part in a complicated manoeuvre with the Baltic Battle Fleet. It was lying just below the surface when a naval motor-boat cut into it and tore a hole in its side.

With appalling suddenness the submarine sank, carrying every one of the men aboard her to death.

At once, with other vessels of the fleet standing round, salvage work was begun, but early to-day the B3 had not been raised.

Meanwhile the Soviet Government has taken action to recompense the relatives of the fifty-five victims.

A decree has been issued giving the families 10,000 roubles each and a grant of personal pensions to individuals, states Reuter.

FRANCE FINDS BRITISH BEST

BRITISH "models" are inspiring France. Often it's the other way round.

Paris now has a police college like that at Hendon. It was opened yesterday. All newly-promoted inspectors will be given a three-months' intensive course.

And France's colonial broadcasting system and programmes are soon to be reorganised on British lines, for the Minister of Posts and Telegraphs found "British Best" after studying several nations' systems.

STRANGE PARTNERS these two notices side by side in the window of a boarding house at Porthcawl, Glamorgan. The explanation is that fleas are scarce nowadays, and the proprietor of a flea circus has to advertise.

THE DAILY MIRROR, Monday, August 5, 1935

Daily Mirror

Broadcasting - Page 20

THE DAILY PICTURE NEWSPAPER WITH THE LARGEST NET SALE

MARY SAYS 'THERE'S NO ROMANCE' —Page 2

No. 9,885 Registered at the G.P.O. as a Newspaper. MONDAY, AUGUST 5, 1935 One Penny

Amusements: Pages 6 and 14

CHOSE DEATH TO SAVE CHILDREN

Removing the wreckage of the aeroplane from the Morden-Edgware railway line. Another picture on the back page.

R.A.F. Pilot Dives to Doom on Live Rail

FOUR MEN WERE KILLED WHEN TWO 'PLANES CRASHED IN FLAMES YESTERDAY. VICTIMS OF THE FIRST TRAGEDY WERE A R.A.F. PILOT AND HIS OBSERVER. THE MEN WHO LOST THEIR LIVES IN THE SECOND CRASH WERE A FLYING INSTRUCTOR AND HIS PUPIL.

By a Special Correspondent

His 'plane was crashing.... Below him was the electric railway.... On one side was a field in which scores of children were playing... on the other a row of houses..

THIS was the choice which faced the R.A.F. pilot, yesterday, soon after he had taken off with six other 'planes, from Hendon (Middlesex) Aerodrome.

He chose the railway. The machine hit a bridge, fell on the lines, touching the electric rail, and burst into flames.

The pilot, Flying-Officer Robert Louis Nimmo, whose home is at Chalfont St. Giles, Bucks, and his observer, Aircraftman S. J. Marbutt, of the Auxiliary Air Force, were trapped and burned to death. People who raced to the scene saw Flying-Officer Nimmo in the midst of the flames "appealing with his eyes" for help that no one could give him.

The signal-box at Colindale, 200 yards away, was set on fire as the fuses blew out. Fire also broke out at Burnt Oak Station when the switchboard fused.

The current was cut off, and all trains between Golders Green and Edgware were held up for hours

The seven 'planes had taken off to fly to Tangmere (Sussex) for the annual camp.

The 'plane fell right across the Edgware extension of the Piccadilly line.

Dying Pilot's Agony

People from the houses who ran up the embankment to render what assistance they could were powerless. By the time they reached the wrecked 'plane it was a mass of flames, and it was impossible for them to get near it.

Some of them saw the death agony of the pilot as he mutely appealed with his eyes for help.

The fire was eventually put out by a R.A.F. fire tender, which rushed to the scene from Hendon Aerodrome.

A minute before the 'plane crashed a train travelling to the City had passed over the spot. When the crash occurred another train was standing at Burnt Oak Station.

The first man to reach the blazing wreckage was Mr. A. L. Hasler, of Arundel-square, Barnsbury, who was visiting friends in Booth-road.

"It would have been suicide to touch the machine," he said. "Sparks were flying from the rails and flames were leaping about 30ft. into the air. The heat was terrific.

"I could see the pilot, and I am sure he was not dead—he seemed to be appealing to me with his eyes, but within a few seconds
(Continued on back page)

ROMANCE.—Viscount de Balbi and his bride, Miss Ethel Shaw, daughter of a Yorkshire miner, after their wedding at New Edlington. See page 3.

Briton's Ransom Money at Bandits' Lair

PEKIN, Sunday.

THE release of Mr. Gareth Jones, the British journalist held to ransom by bandits near Kuyuan, is expected almost immediately, as the ransom money has reached Paochang.

The money was sent by car from Kalgan with a protective escort of cavalry, and those accompanying it have made contact with the bandits.

Mr. Jones should be free by to-morrow afternoon at the latest. The amount of the ransom money is not revealed.—Reuter.

THOUSANDS MADE BEACH THEIR BED

TWELVE thousand people sleeping out beneath the stars, the beach, boats, bandstand and shelters packed with them —that was Southend last night.

It was the most amazing night known in all the resort's history.

The esplanades were thronged. Well-dressed women and girls lay sleeping on deck chairs in the band enclosure Those unable to sleep spent the hours "smoking in bed."

Many girls undressed, piling their clothes under their deck chairs.

And the Corporation decided to keep the town lights on throughout the night.

Go-As-You-Please

But Southend was only one of the bright spots in this greatest go-to-the-seaside holiday that Britain has known since The Depression set in.

Lured by the certainty of fine, warm weather, scores of thousands of people, in determined mood to spend every possible moment by the sea, set off yesterday morning all prepared to sleep on the beaches, ready to begin to-day at cock-crow.

When dusk set in last night, they "staked-out" their bed claims with ground sheets and blankets.

Some of the resorts, with a keen anticipation, had prepared for their sleepers.

Record Crowds

At Brighton, the favourite bed-pitches were under the piers!

Every resort reported record crowds yesterday.

First prize must go to the family at Brighton who sat down to their beach midday meal of roast joint, complete with vegetables.

Night scene pictures and holiday tragedies —page 2.

THE DAILY MIRROR, Tuesday, August 6, 1935.

Daily Mirror

Broadcasting - Page 22

THE DAILY PICTURE NEWSPAPER WITH THE LARGEST NET SALE

No. 9,886 — Registered at the G.P.O as a Newspaper. TUESDAY, AUGUST 6, 1935 — One Penny

SIX LOVERS PARTED BY DEATH
—Page 3

Amusements: Page 8

In the Air
On the Road

HOLIDAY SPEED—AND SLOW DOWN

India Dash 42 Hours, Brighton Crawl 5½

WITH DESERT SAND

CAR JAM AT MIDNIGHT

AS late last night Bank Holiday traffic was crawling back to London along the Brighton road at ten miles an hour, a man was completing the last lap of an air dash that had brought him from India in forty-two hours.

Just compare the two. Brighton to London, fifty-six miles, in five and a half hours. Karachi to London, 4,900 miles, took only eight times as long.

The magic carpet which brought Mr. W. W. K. Page, a barrister, who practises in Calcutta, back to England for his annual holiday, was an ordinary air liner—a Douglas K.L.M.—just speeding up because it was held up for a day by a monsoon.

And Not Tired

Mr. Page said last night that owing to this hold-up the air liner left Calcutta on Saturday morning instead of on Friday.

"On Saturday night we arrived in Karachi," he said, "and left there again on Sunday morning at five o'clock. That night we came down at Heliopolis at 7.15.

"And to-day we took off from Heliopolis at 4 a.m. We landed at Amsterdam, where I changed into another 'plane, and here I am in London at 11 p.m. I should have been here two hours earlier but for a delay in Amsterdam.

"Tired? Not a bit of it. The journey was not in the least fatiguing. It seems almost incredible that only yesterday I was in India."

Now for Britain's big Bank Holiday crawl.

At midnight last night there was a slowly moving traffic queue stretching from Brighton to London.

It was estimated that more than 4,000 cars an hour passed through Crawley during the evening.

On the Portsmouth road the figures were the heaviest ever recorded by the A.A., 5,000 cars an hour passing the crossroads at Esher.

Here the traffic assumed terrific proportions as belated cars returned from the Navy Week display at Portsmouth, from Sandown Park races and from Brooklands.

An official of the A.A. paid the women drivers a compliment last night: "The standard of driving as compared with previous years was much higher!"

BOY DROWNED

THREE men dived, fully clothed, into the River Thames, at Limehouse, last night, to the aid of two boys who were in danger of being swept away by the tide.

One of the boys, Thomas Loomes, aged twelve, of Elsa-street, Stepney, was taken from the river in an unconscious condition and died within a few minutes. The other boy, Eric Homer, also of Elsa-street, was little the worse for his experience.

Rotten Row, in Hyde Park, where the flower of London fashion rides and also walks, was a desert yesterday, and in this desert poor children, whose parents cannot take them to the seaside, were making sand castles.

LYNCH TERROR IS RULING U.S. AGAIN

BY A SPECIAL CORRESPONDENT

LYNCH law is ruling again in the Southern States of America. In seven days three men have gone to terrible deaths at the hands of wrath-frenzied white mobs; another, a negro accused of stabbing a woman, is being hunted to his doom by 100 members of the Vigilantes.

And even while the terror reigns, the lynchers are being supported by some of the nation's prominent men.

Ex-Governor Rolph, of California, who stated after a recent case, "It is the best lesson California has ever given this country," has found a supporter in Public Prosecutor James Davies, who said yesterday that he deplored the dilatory methods of the State.

Another who believes that lynching is "excusable in some cases," is ex-Judge John L. Pattison.

By transatlantic 'phone he said to me last night:—

"When the feeling of the populace is aroused it is, I think, dangerous to check the mob, and it is advisable to let them run their fury out. Otherwise many more lives would be involved."

The latest case of lynch law, revealed yesterday, has all the horror of those which preceded it. The body of the victim, a negro named Bates, was found by the police dangling from a bridge near Pittsboro, Missouri.

This man had been hunted down with hounds after a white girl had declared that one night while she was in bed a negro had climbed up to her window and demanded to be let in.

400 Cavalry Horses "C.B."

FOUR hundred horses were confined to barracks at Hounslow, Middlesex, yesterday for having influenza.

They belong to the 7th Hussars stationed at Hounslow Cavalry Barracks.

The outbreak is so serious that entries at Hounslow Heath Bank Holiday Horse Show, organised by the West London Squadron of the Imperial Legion, were only forty-four.

Influenza among animals is not regarded as very dangerous.

But 400 horses at Hounslow are wondering why nobody has ever invented a horse-sized pocket handkerchief.

PILOT BLINDED BY OIL SAVES FIVE

THOUGH temporarily blinded by oil from a burst pipe, which had stopped the engine of his 'plane, the pilot talked calmly to his five passengers—two of them children—as he made a forced landing.

The 'plane struck a bank as it landed in a field at Northwood, Ramsgate.

Although the undercarriage and wing-tip were damaged, the passengers, all holiday-makers taking a joy "flip" from Ramsgate Airport yesterday, escaped with a shaking.

The pilot of the 'plane, Flight-Lieutenant C. E. Eckersley-Maslin, in an interview last night, said:

"When the oil pipe burst, the front windows of the 'plane were sprayed with oil. I got an eyeful of it. I succeeded in getting one of the windows of the cockpit open and piloted the machine back by hanging half out of the window."

Did Airman Faint 33,000 ft. Up?

PARIS, Monday.

WHEN France's only stratosphere 'plane crashed in flames near Bonnieres this afternoon, the pilot, M. Cogno, was burned to death.

It is believed that he was overcome, and fainted, while at a height of 33,000ft.

For more than three years the Farman brothers, who are half English, and were among the earliest pioneers of aviation, have been working to perfect this machine, which has only just been completed.—Reuter.

Daily Mirror

THE DAILY PICTURE NEWSPAPER WITH THE LARGEST NET SALE

Broadcasting—Page 21

BRITISH SOLDIERS OF FORTUNE FOR ABYSSINIA —Page 2

No. 9,890. Registered at the G.P.O as a Newspaper. SATURDAY, AUGUST 10, 1935. One Penny

Amusements: Page 18

DISCOVERED QUIET—AND WERE AFRAID

Family Who Knew Only City Life

BY A SPECIAL CORRESPONDENT

Calves with trees growing out of their heads, pigeons with trousers on, pears that were not pears at all.

THESE are some of the marvels about which a Bermondsey woman has been telling her neighbours after her first visit to the country.

For over forty years she had lived a drab life in Bermondsey, her longest excursion a trip to Greenwich and Southend.

Until Jubilee Week she had never been nearer the West End than Guy's Hospital. Hyde Park is only a name to her, it means no more than Timbuctoo.

And then, like some unbelievable dream, she was whisked down to the country for a fortnight with two of her children. Now she keeps pinching herself to make sure that it was all real.

Guests of Village

Last night, in her spotless little flat, she told me of some of the things—to her unbelievable things—which so amazed her during her unforgettable fortnight, when she was the guest of the rector's wife, Mrs. Hoyle, and the villagers looked after the mother and her two children. Their kindness has made an incredible change in the health of her eight-year-old daughter and her six-year-old son, who had been desperately ill with pneumonia.

"That stillness— it is almost frightening!" was how the mother summed-up the country to me.

"All my life I had lived in the noise of Bermondsey, and it made me feel funny to be in the midst of that absolute peace. It was a day or two before I could get used to it and realise that there was nothing to be afraid of!

"We have never had such a glorious time in our lives, and we were treated like the royal family. We had the run of a lovely home, we were even waited on by servants.

"I saw some green figs growing there for the first time in my life, and I was so astonished (*Continued on back page*)

AFTER THE COLLISION

An exclusive picture showing Harry Pannell, who, with the Dragon's skipper, Captain A. E. Jupe, had a narrow escape when the seaplane struck the yacht, standing amid the tangled rigging of the damaged craft. Inset is a portrait of Captain Jupe.

TWO GAMBLERS LOSE TO DEATH

"This fatal curse of gambling —on horses, dogs or anything else—brings human misery and distress."—A Coroner, yesterday.

WILLIAM F. Stiling, Glengarry-road, Dulwich, went to Sandown Races on August Monday—came home —committed suicide.

His brother at the inquest yesterday said: "He had gambled since he was ten . . . gambled on anything." A policeman stated that in the house was a mass of unpaid bills . . . and five orphaned children.— Suicide verdict

* * *

A GREYHOUND on which a Belfast man had bet sixpence failed to win. In temper the gambler put his fist through a pane in the bookmaker's window . . . severed an artery in the wrist . . . died in a few minutes.—Verdict Accidental death

---

Comedian Wanted Dog to Bite Him— and It Did

A man wanted a dog to bite him at Ealing yesterday.
A dog was found.
The dog bit the man.
The man was taken to hospital.

MR. Harry Tate, the comedian, working on a new production at an Ealing film studio, had to be chased and bitten (slightly) in the seat of his trousers.

A whippet which looked as if it could bite intelligently (and lightly) was produced.
Harry dashed across the scene according to instructions.
The whippet followed.
Harry fell, also according to instructions.
The whippet jumped and bit—not in the seat of Harry's trousers, but in the calf of his leg.
Harry was taken to hospital, where he had the wound cauterised and six stitches inserted.

AIRBOAT HITS YACHT

Skipper Caught in Rigging

A flying-boat racing along Southampton Water to take off. . . .
A six-metre yacht sweeping across its path. . . .
A crash—and the yacht's mast and rigging fell . . . the flying-boat alighted. . . .

THIS remarkable collision took place off Calshot yesterday.

The yacht was struck by one wing of the flying-boat—a R.A.F. machine—whose pilot, by skilful handling, brought it down a short distance away. Afterwards it taxied back to the air station.

Mr. A. Jupe, of Sepia Cottage, Warsash, Hants, the skipper of the yacht the Dragon, owned by Mr. H. F. Edwards, of London, who is staying at Seaview), was badly bruised on his neck and shoulders by the falling mast and rigging.

His cabin boy, Harry Pannell, fifteen, of Osborne-road, Warsash, was below at the time and was unhurt.

Sails in the Water

Captain D. H. MacMillan, hydrographical surveyor to the Southampton Harbour Board, who raced to the scene of the accident in a survey launch from a quarter of a mile away, told the *Daily Mirror*:

"I heard the 'plane taking off, and on turning round saw it had struck the mast of the yacht. The mast was hanging over the side, with the sails and rigging in the water.

"When I arrived I found the man and the boy somewhat dazed. I rendered first aid, and a R.A.F. speed boat, which had raced out from the air station, towed the yacht back."

Struck 20 ft. Up

Mr. Jupe, who has been skipper of the Dragon for the past two seasons, gave a graphic description of the crash.

"I was at the tiller, and making for Hamble Yacht Repairing Yard, when the accident happened," he said. "The craft had previously run foul of a naval whaler before the start of the races at Cowes, and we were going in for repairs.

"The flying boat came up from astern. Suddenly it left the water and was about twenty feet above my head when it struck the yacht.

"It is a marvel that I am still alive. I was carried several yards along the deck, and smothered in sailing equipment."

Westward won the race for the J class, finishing a mile ahead of Endeavour.

Actress, Injured in Car Crash, Plays on—

THOUGH she was injured in a motor accident while on her way to a theatre at Nice, Mlle. Regina Camier, the famous French actress, insisted on playing her part.

The car in which she was travelling overturned in a ditch cut during road excavations. It is stated, says Reuter, that no warning light had been left by the workmen.

Mlle. Camier was pinned beneath the car for some time, and was badly bruised. She continued her journey to the theatre on foot.

"PAGANISM" OF 1935

"IN the country the Christian Church is confronted with a paganism which is becoming more definite and self-conscious."

So said the Dean of St. Paul's, the Very Rev W. R. Matthews, addressing the world convention of Churches of Christ at Leicester, yesterday.

He declared that the Christian Church was passing through a crisis of almost unparalleled severity.

Twenty years hence the civilised world would be either very much more Christian or very much less so.

"The signs of the times are not encouraging," he said. "In more places than one the battle seems to have turned definitely against the Church.

"One of the chief obstacles to the presentation of the case for Christianity to-day is that Christians appear to the outsider to be hopelessly divided among themselves, and even spending more energy in controverting one another than in converting the world."

Daily Mirror

THE DAILY PICTURE NEWSPAPER WITH THE LARGEST NET SALE

Broadcasting - Page 20

VILLAGE SHOOTING DISCLOSURES —Page 2

No. 9,892 Registered at the G.P.O as a Newspaper. TUESDAY, AUGUST 13, 1935. One Penny

Amusements: Page 22

GALLI-CURCI, 3,500 MILES AWAY, SINGS FOR US

Her Voice as Beautiful as Ever After Operation

GALLI-CURCI, in a Chicago hospital bed 3,500 miles away, was singing last night—specially for the *Daily Mirror*. Sweet and beautiful as ever, the notes came over the transatlantic telephone.

The voice that has thrilled millions had come unharmed through the delicate operation for goitre which the prima donna had undergone.

After she had sung for me (writes a *Daily Mirror* special representative) Galli-Curci laughed, and her laugh took in a whole octave and several notes above.

Mme. Galli-Curci.

Must Be Careful

"I really mustn't sing much," she said, "it is dangerous for me just after the operation. I am getting on splendidly, marvellously, but I must be careful for the present."

Surgeon Evans, who has been looking after her since the operation, chipped in: "We are entirely satisfied with the result of the operation, and you can take it from me, there need be no fear for Madam's voice," he said. "You have heard, and you can tell that it is going to be all right."

Then Galli-Curci came on the line—laughing again that most musical laugh I have ever heard—full and mellow.

"I Am Not Afraid"

"No, I can't sing any more to you just now," she said, "but I'm not the slightest bit afraid—my voice will be all right."

Galli-Curci was operated on on Saturday, occasionally singing a few notes so that the surgeons could study the effect on her voice. Dr. Arnold Kegel, who was in charge, met the singer in India last March. He went to America with her and has had her case under constant observation ever since.

Robot Army Goes Over the Top

OUR robot army went "over the top" yesterday, and struck the first blow in most elaborate manœuvres in England for many years.

The "battle" was opened by the 6th Infantry Brigade, the only unit in the British Army that is entirely mechanised. Not a single horse took part; even the officers were unmounted.

While the 6th Brigade was demonstrating its mobility in one part of the battle area the 1st Tank Brigade was operating in another spot.

From north, south, east and west troops are converging on a vast area covering parts of Sussex, Hampshire, and Wiltshire.

About 50,000 officers and men are involved as well as several cavalry regiments, over 200 tanks, masses of artillery and many armoured cars.

Territorials will figure prominently in the operations.

TWO BEAUS TO HER STRING!

George and Percy, the London Zoo's King penguins, couldn't decide which of them should have the honour of taking the girl friend out for a walk, so they both came along.

THE BLUSHING BRIDE AT NUDIST WEDDING

300 Guests—And Fishermen Gatecrashed

WITH the Mayor "properly dressed in his robes of office"—he had a piece of ribbon round his waist—the blushing bride wearing a scanty lace handkerchief, and the bridegroom in bathing slips, a wedding was performed yesterday at the Ile du Levant nudist colony, off the Toulon coast.

In brilliant sunshine the 300 guests assembled, dressed like the bride and groom. And fishermen came "gatecrashing" from neighbouring islands.

The bridegroom (states the British United Press) was twenty-six-year-old Leon Lair, of Franco-British parentage, his bride, pretty twenty-two-year-old Rene Galland, who made one concession to the occasion, for she carried a bunch of flowers.

They Met in Paris

After the marriage everybody adjourned for a vegetarian wedding lunch.

Then the bride and groom set out for their honeymoon in a dinghy to spend a fortnight on an uninhabited island.

The couple met a few months ago at a social function in Paris. They were both dressed on that occasion.

SMUTS'S WARNING

"IF the League should fail at the critical moment it will shake the whole system of civilisation to its foundations," said General Smuts, interviewed by Reuter's Durban correspondent yesterday.

He was referring to the Abyssinian dispute, and added: "It is possible that Great Britain may be able to keep out of this as far as Europe is concerned. But a great conflict in Africa on the borders of British territory must have serious repercussions on British territories in Africa, as well as on the Sudan and Egypt."

FOR CHEER OF FEALTY

An officer giving the signal for a cheer of allegiance to the Emperor (on dais) when the latter held a review of Abyssinian troops on the outskirts of his capital, Addis Ababa.

NOW THERE IS ANOTHER "HAPPY CHAP"

The "How He Proposed" series in the "Daily Mirror" has added yet another name to the list of "happy chaps"—and happy girls!

NURSE L. Lakin, of Royal-road, Sutton Coldfield, nr. Birmingham, tells us about it in a letter she heads: "Three cheers for the 'Daily Mirror.'" Here is her letter:—

"Thanks to your paper I am now the happiest girl in the world—and this is why:

"For the last year I have been on friendly terms with a young man—one of the best but very quiet and shy. He has never given me a sign whether he cared for me other than as a friend... until this morning, when his letter to me contains this:

"'Dearest, I have been eagerly scanning the proposals each day in the 'Daily Mirror,' and I notice that many shy chaps have plucked up courage to put the question.

"'Please will you marry me, dear, and make me one of those happy chaps?'

"I have just telegraphed one word—'YES'—and now I am eagerly awaiting my 'off duty.'"

THE DAILY MIRROR, Wed., August 14, 1935.

Daily Mirror

THE DAILY PICTURE NEWSPAPER WITH THE LARGEST NET SALE

Broadcasting - Page 20

WOMEN OF BIG IDEAS —Page 3

No. 9,893. Registered at the G.P.O. as a Newspaper. WEDNESDAY, AUGUST 14, 1935 One Penny

Amusements: Page 16

800 PERISH IN DAM HORROR

2-Mile Wall of Water Sweeps Homes Away

Their homes overwhelmed by a terrific wall of water two miles wide, 800 people, most of them women and children, are believed to have been drowned in the village of Ovada, Italy, and the district around by the bursting of a dam.

An area of countryside 25 miles by 16 miles has been laid waste.

FROM OUR SPECIAL CORRESPONDENT

GENOA, Wednesday Morning.

I HAVE spent a night of terror in the stricken area around Ovada, learning from the people who have suffered, who are now homeless, the full horror of the disaster.

They have told me how, when the water poured down upon them, nothing could stand against its force. Like a scythe it swept through houses, cut down railway bridges, tore up roads.

Many people were trapped before they could escape to the higher land, many others were caught by the death water as they tried to run before it.

Once caught, there was no escape from the grip of the water. It bore them along on its wildly-seething surface, bore them along to death.

Trapped in Cellars

In the poorer sections of Ovada the fatalities were terrible. Here, like rats, people were drowned in their basement homes. Others were crushed under the crashing masonry.

Hundreds of people crowded on to the roofs of the houses while the waters swirled beneath them, but in many cases they were eventually engulfed.

In places that had escaped the full force of the racing water and where houses still stood there were pitiful scenes, exhausted women clinging to their babies, others searching frantically amid the wreckage for children they had lost and hoped against hope to find alive.

Troops camping near the town were rushed to give aid. There was little that they do. Rescue efforts by firemen were also in vain so great was the volume of water.

It was almost impossible to get help to the stricken towns from outside, the roads had gone, and the railways. Telephone and telegraphic communications had been completely disrupted.

When I left the authorities were doing their best to erect dams and throw pontoons across to the isolated groups of people, but it is impossible to curb the waters.

The dam which burst was that at Lake Ortecella, in the Province of Alessandria, and Ovada is about twenty-five miles from Genoa. The primary cause of the disaster was a terrific storm which was felt over a wide area of Northern Italy.

STORM WRECK

Wreck on the beach of Herne Bay of the pleasure cruiser Pathfinder, which, on her way to Calais, was unable to live up to her name, for, in the midst of engine trouble, a midnight gale blew up and drove her ashore. The five persons on board landed safely.

Driving a Motor-Cycle at Two-Years-Old

WITH JILL, AGED 3, IN SIDE-CAR!

Meet the world's youngest motor-cyclist—Leonard Malcolm Vale-Onslow, aged two years. Leonard's father is Mr. L. L. H. Vale-Onslow, of Livery-street, Birmingham, a well-known grass track rider.

Leonard wanted a machine when he saw father riding about on one. He cried till—

Father constructed a 1½-h.p. cycle, 4ft. in length and capable of a speed of 40 m.p.h. Then father thought again—and throttled the engine down to 15 m.p.h. maximum!

And on this, two-year-old Leonard, complete with crash helmet, rides round a nice flat field on a farm as fast as they will let him—gear changing, turning and braking like an expert.

Leonard did not content himself merely with riding; he wanted to know all about the machine, and is now able to name every part and describe its function.

The machine has been improved since he became proficient.

Attached to it now is a neat little sidecar. Cousin Jill, aged three, is the inveterate passenger.

Baby Vale-Onslow's grandfather was a constructional engineer and his own father, who is only thirty, started in the motor-cycle line when he was ten. **Picture on page 3.**

SHE MAY BE BLIND AND DUMB

Baroness Maud Thyssen, who was injured in Prince Alexis Mdivani's car when he was killed, is expected, according to a Reuter message from Barcelona, to lose the sight of her left as well as her right eye. It is also feared she may never be able to speak again.

"Chars" Good Turn to Their Church

Many of the parishioners of All Saints' Church, South Wimbledon, are charwomen.

And because it is holiday-time they have little to do—so they are doing their church a good turn.

They have banded together, turned the vicar out of his church and set to work cleaning it.

The vicar (the Rev. Hammond Torrance) is carrying on as best he can in the Mission Hall.

WIVES' VIGIL BESIDE 2 SHOT MEN

Two wives kept vigil in hospital last night beside their husbands, who were seriously wounded in a shooting mystery.

DOCTORS were still making a desperate fight to save the lives of the two men early this morning.

A man was detained by the police in connection with the affair.

The injured couple are:

Robert Barnett, aged thirty, of Charman-road, Redhill (Surrey), who is suffering from shot wounds in the throat and side, and

Leslie George Knight, aged twenty-six, of Ourhome, Madeira-walk, Redhill, who has eye, ribs, and thigh injuries.

They are the sons of partners in a Redhill building concern, and were working in the firm's yard in Pengates-road, Redhill, when they were shot.

An ambulance was rushed to the yard and the injured men were taken to Redhill Hospital.

An examination revealed that Knight was in danger of losing the sight of one eye, and he was quickly transferred to Moorfields Eye Hospital, City-road, London.

While Mrs. Barnett kept an anxious vigil at Redhill, Mrs. Knight and her mother accompanied Knight in the ambulance to London.

So that she could remain near her husband, Mrs. Barnett booked a bed in Redhill Hospital.

Mr. Barnett's mother died only last week. Mrs. Knight left the eye hospital late last night and returned home.

Driver Dies at Wheel of Crowded Bus— Girl Killed

WHEN the driver died at the wheel of a crowded bus at Bristol last night the vehicle killed a girl cyclist and injured her friend.

The bus driver was Charles Ivor Evans, of Gloucester-street, Clifton. The dead girl, Valda Sparks, aged sixteen, of Pearl-street, Bedminster, was crushed against a wall. Her friend, Joyce Morton, also of Pearl-street, escaped with slight cuts.

A youngster resorts to browbeating when cajolery has failed to get his friend to accompany him into the sea at a Kentish resort.

THE DAILY MIRROR, Wednesday, August 21, 1935.

Daily Mirror
Broadcasting - Page 20

THE DAILY PICTURE • NEWSPAPER WITH THE LARGEST NET SALE

No. 9,899 Registered at the G.P.O as a Newspaper. WEDNESDAY, AUGUST 21, 1935 One Penny

ANOTHER BIG LINER TO BE SOLD —Page 8

Amusements: Page 16

LEAPT TO DEATH
WHILE WIFE LAY DYING
Sandhurst Man's Fight Against Poverty

TRAGEDY has ended the romance of an ex-public schoolboy—believed to be a Sandhurst man—who married against the wishes of his family, fought his way through poverty, dealing in lamp-shades at a costermonger's stall in Caledonian Market to make ends meet.

The man, Mr. Roland Lee Booker, aged forty-five, of Bramshill-gardens, Dartmouth Park-hill, Kentish Town, an artist specialising in lamp-shade work, was found dead in an area at the back of his house, having apparently fallen 25ft. from a third-story window.

His wife was found unconscious in the basement of the house suffering from head injuries from which she died later in Highgate Hospital.

The tragedy was discovered by Mr. Charles Alfred Nutting, of Winscombe-street, Islington, whose garden adjoins the back of Mr. Lee Booker's home.

Attacked with Chopper

He heard a scream, followed by a thud, and dashing into his garden, climbed an adjoining wall, and found Mr. Booker lying dead in the area.

Police were called, and when they broke into the house they discovered Mrs. Flora Lee Booker, aged forty-five, dying in the basement. She had apparently been attacked with a chopper, her husband then plunging to his death from a window.

There was some money near her, and two attaché cases. When the cases were opened they were found to contain the lamp-shades which Mr. Lee Booker had designed to make a living.

His Trips to Market

A neighbour said to the Daily Mirror yesterday: "The Bookers were extremely attached. I have heard that they had married against the wishes of Mr. Lee Booker's family.

"Mr. Lee Booker served as an officer during the war and had spent some time in America. He suffered severe head wounds and had a silver plate in his head.

"After the war Mr. Booker had to make a living to support his wife. He was a clever artist, so he set about designing lamp-shades which he took himself to Caledonian Market."

Went to Sandhurst

Another neighbour told the Daily Mirror: "When Mr. Lee Booker first came to this district about ten years ago he appeared to be prosperous, but as the years went by he became poorer and poorer.

"In the end he and his wife were reduced to scavenging around dustbins and calling on houses with a barrow and collecting rags and bones, which they sold for what few pence they could get.

"At their stall in Caledonian Market, which his wife helped to manage, they sold second-hand clothing of all kinds, in addition to the lamp-shades.

"Mr. Booker went to Sandhurst, where he received the latter part of his education and military training."

Jack Van, aged nineteen, at Reading yesterday beside the aeroplane in which he was about to go up for a trial flight.

Atlantic Flight at Nineteen
HE WANTS TO GO HOME THAT WAY

WITHIN a few days a nineteen-year-old airman will start off on a journey by which he hopes to achieve the ambition of his life—to be the first Canadian to fly the Atlantic.

Everything is in readiness; he is now waiting only for favourable weather before he leaves Baldonnel, Ireland, on a non-stop solo flight to Quebec.

The adventurer, Mr. Jack Van, is a laconic young man. Only on the subject of aviation does he show anything like enthusiasm—and then he hides it behind a matter-of-factness.

Flying Since Fifteen

"I don't really care about anything except flying," he told the Daily Mirror yesterday, "and I've been the same since I was quite a kid.

"Experience? Well, I've been flying since I was fifteen.

"My aim is to do this east-to-west journey in fifteen hours and land at Quebec, my home town.

"I am used to long flights—but not so long as this one! The biggest I have done was ten hours non-stop, in Canada."

Mr. Van's 'plane is a Hawk Major, with Gypsy engine. He has been in England for eighteen months, flying, studying English aviation methods, testing—and hoping.

He hopes to start his adventure some time during the week-end. "I just want to fly home," he said simply.

Mr. Van's father is a Quebec lumber merchant.

PUT ME IN CHILDREN'S WARD?—SEZ YOU!

FROM OUR OWN CORRESPONDENT
BOLTON, Tuesday.

FOURTEEN-YEAR-OLD Brian Speak, of Belmont, near here, was admitted to Bolton Infirmary yesterday for an operation to reset his leg, which had previously been broken.

Brian was put in the children's ward but he thought he should have been put in the men's.

He registered his protest by getting up when the nurse's back was turned and escaping from the hospital in another boy's clothes.

As soon as his departure was discovered nurses searched the hospital, police scoured the moorland roads near his home, and his father began a three-hour search on his motor-cycle.

When the hunt was at its height Brian entered his home unnoticed and startled his mother, in the middle of a conversation with his sister, with a filial "Sez you!"

He returned to the hospital this morning—but not to the children's ward.

Brian Speak, of Belmont, Bolton.

DOGS HAVE THEIR DAY

Every dog has his day—especially to-day, for he looms large in the news.

On page three the story is told of an ex-J.P. who is going to prison voluntarily to punish himself for striking and hurting a dog.

How dogs were the cause of a charge of manslaughter and two inquests is revealed on page five.

On the back page is the story of the dog that was brought back to life after being dead forty-five minutes.

ABANDONED

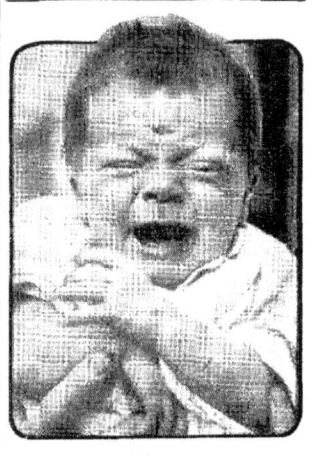

Aged about two weeks, this baby boy was found abandoned on the steps outside the Regal Cinema, Marble Arch.

THE DAILY MIRROR, Friday, August 23, 1935

Daily Mirror

Broadcasting - Page 20

THE DAILY PICTURE NEWSPAPER WITH THE LARGEST NET SALE

SCIENTISTS' WAR ON ROAD DEATHS —Page 2

No. 9,901 Registered at the G.P.O as a Newspaper. FRIDAY, AUGUST 23, 1935 One Penny

Amusements: Page 22

SKELETON CABINET ON GUARD IN LONDON

Britain to Keep All League Pledges

BY OUR DIPLOMATIC CORRESPONDENT

A SKELETON Cabinet is standing by to deal immediately with any emergency which may arise out of the Italo-Abyssinian dispute

This is the chief outcome of yesterday's all-day meeting of the full Cabinet.

At that meeting it was decided to:—

Re-affirm the decision to adhere to all the obligations under our treaties and under the Covenant of the League.

Continue the ban on the export of arms to both Italy and Abyssinia.

I understand on the latter point that unless the Italian Government adopts a more reasonable attitude, a committee of the Cabinet and Sir Samuel Hoare have been given authority to grant limited licences for the export of munitions.

The door is still left open for negotiations for peace between Britain and France on the one hand and Italy on the other.

The atmosphere in official circles may be described as one of restrained optimism.

Italy May Change Her View

It is believed that the general view held by the majority of the Cabinet is that if Britain and France work together in close unity they may, without having to resort to the imposition of sanctions, force the Italian Government to adopt a more pacific point of view.

One thing is certain. Even if the League should decide to impose sanctions (and this can only be done after an act of aggression has been committed) Britain will not assume responsibility for being alone in endeavouring to enforce them.

It is of some significance that the Cabinet will not meet again before the meeting of the League Council on September 4 which is to consider the threat of war. Most of the Ministers, other than those forming the skeleton Cabinet, are returning to their interrupted holidays.

R.A.F. Chief's Visit

It is expected that Mr. Ramsay MacDonald will preside to-day over a meeting of the Committee of Imperial Defence.

Some significance was attached yesterday to the fact that while the Cabinet was in session, Air Chief Marshal Sir Edward Elling-

(Continued on back page)

WHAT SANCTIONS MEAN

Should any member of the League resort to war in disregard of its covenants . . . it shall be deemed to have committed an act of war against all other members of the League, which hereby undertakes immediately to subject it to the severance of all trade or financial relations. . . .

It shall be the duty of the Council in such case to recommend to the several Governments concerned what effective military, naval or air force the members of the League shall severally contribute to the armed forces to be used to protect the Covenants of the League.

CHANNEL VICTOR

Mr. Haydn Taylor (nearer camera), the Cleethorpes, Lincs, dentist, who left Cape Gris-Nez, France, at 1.35 a.m. yesterday, swimming the last few yards to the beach at Dover, where he landed at 4.25 p.m., having swum the Channel in 14h. 48m. Left: Mr. Taylor chaired after coming ashore. He finished remarkably fresh.

Mrs. Roland Lee-Booker, of Bramshill-gardens, Dartmouth Park-hill, Kentish Town. Dread of another war is believed to have led to a brainstorm which caused her husband, a wounded ex-officer, to attack her and to leap to death from a third floor window as she lay dying.

ENOUGH DYNAMITE TO DESTROY WHOLE TOWN

SINGAPORE, Thursday.

TWO Japanese were charged to-day with the illegal possession of 200 sticks of dynamite and 100 detonators and fuses—sufficient to blow the whole of Singapore sky-high.

The charge followed a raid by police on a house.—Exchange

"Never Again!" Says the Man Who Swam Channel

DENTIST WINS "UNCANNY" BATTLE

MR. Haydn Taylor, a Cleethorpes (Lincs) dentist, swam the Channel from Cape Gris-Nez to Dover yesterday in 14h. 48m.

The twentieth person to achieve the feat and the first this year.

Then he told the "Daily Mirror": "I wouldn't do it again for anything.

"It was terribly gruelling, particularly towards the end. I made a good start, though in half an hour I ran into choppy seas, and it remained choppy more or less.

"At 4.30 a.m. I found myself in a patch of water with a nasty swell. I was glad when dawn broke and the uncanny feeling of the darkness was over.

"At 5.35 I could see the lights of Dover, and three hours later the cliffs were clearly visible."

When Mr. Taylor was four miles off Dover at 10.30 a.m. he could make very little headway.

It was not until nearly 1 p.m. that he again made good progress.

A Doctor Fails

The current was carrying him westward, and at one time it looked as if he might be carried on to Folkestone. But he made a gallant fight across the tide, and eventually landed on the rocks at the foot of Abbott's Cliff.

His time was fourteen minutes' slower than that of Frau Emma Faber, the Austrian woman who swam the Channel in August last year; and fifteen minutes slower than that of the London swimmer, Mr. E. H. Temme, in 1927. The record time is 11h. 5m. by Georges Michel, a Paris baker.

Mr. Taylor's swim began as a race against Dr. Brewster, of Southwark, London—who gave up after three-and-a-half miles.

---

2 WOMEN TRAPPED IN ELECTRIC WASHING MACHINE

MRS. Emily Johnson, aged seventy-three, of Lower Broughton, Salford, was putting her washing through an electric wringer at her home last night when her hand was caught in it.

Her daughter, Mrs. Minnie Lawrence, aged forty-three, ran to her aid, but in her efforts her hand was also caught.

The two women had to carry the wringer upstairs into a neighbour's house before they were released—with the help of a spanner.

FOUND DEAD AFTER 3-MONTHS HUNT

A BODY believed to be that of Mr. Stanley Moore, a Sunderland bank clerk on a climbing holiday in the Isle of Skye, who has been missing since May 10, was found last night.

It was twelve miles from the spot where the body of his fiancée, Miss Barbara Nicholson, was discovered. For three months search for Moore had failed.

THE DAILY MIRROR, Saturday, August 24, 1935.

Daily Mirror

Broadcasting - Page 18

RAMON NOVARRO TALKS ABOUT MARRIAGE
—Page 6

THE DAILY PICTURE NEWSPAPER WITH THE LARGEST NET SALE

No. 9,902 Registered at the G.P.O as a Newspaper.   SATURDAY, AUGUST 24, 1935   One Penny

Amusements: Page 16

MUSSOLINI EXPLAINS HIS AIMS

"Nothing Will Stop Italy"

"Italy will pursue her aims—with Geneva, without Geneva, or against Geneva.

"A nation on the march, as is the Italian nation to-day, cannot be stopped by the static conception of the life of peoples."

WITH eyes flashing and in tones deliberate and emphatic, Mussolini made these declarations in an interview in Rome yesterday.

Deeply bronzed, a picture of perfect health, he threw back his head and laughed when complimented on his cheerfulness in the face of the international situation.

"In my spirit at this moment lies my strength," he said. "I have just been swimming like a fish."

For an hour Mussolini frankly discussed Italy's aims and her justification for her action in Abyssinia.

Charge Against Abyssinia

"For forty years Ethiopia has been hostile towards Italy," he said. "She has attacked our soldiers, killed our officials and civilians, and has been preparing an army to attack us.

"These operations of ours differ in no way from the military operations which other Colonial Powers have conducted in Asia and Africa."

When asked his opinion of the contention in some quarters that the Covenant had modified the Convention of 1888, which assured free passage of the Suez Canal in times of war as well as peace, Mussolini replied:—

"The Covenant is part of the Versailles Treaty, which, under Article 282, reconfirmed the full force of the 1888 Convention.

"Britain, in the protocols of 1891 and 1894 recognised that almost the whole of the territory of Ethiopia is included in the sphere of Italian influence. These protocols are still in force."

[British United Press copyright in all countries.]

Harley-street specialist for Italy's troops—Page 7.

ALL CHRISTENDOM CALLED TO PRAYER

THE Executive Committee of the Universal Christian Council has sent the following telegram to the Pope, the League of Nations and the heads of the Governments of Great Britain, France, Italy, Abyssinia and the United States of America:—

"The Executive Committee of the Universal Christian Council, composed of representatives of many Churches meeting at Montreux, profoundly moved by the seriousness of the present crisis, with the grave danger of war between two Christian nations, appeals to the whole of Christendom to unite in prayer and in declaring that such a war, undertaken without recourse to arbitration or other means of peaceful settlement, is an intolerable wrong to mankind and a sin against the law of Christ."

THE PRINCE OF WALES STARTS NEW SPORT

The Prince of Wales has bought a new craft—and started a new sport. The craft is seen above in the water at Cannes, where the Prince noticed it while on holiday. It is called a "pedallo," and is fitted with two floats and bicycle pedals. It is propelled from inside the lightly-constructed cabin shown on the right with the Prince beside it. A pedallo seats two people and floats in a few inches of water.

M.P. to Wed Daughter of Mr. Winston Churchill

PROBABLY IN SECRET, SHE SAYS

THE engagement was announced last night of Mr. Duncan Sandys, Conservative M.P. for the Norwood Division of Lambeth, and Mrs. J. M. Bailey, formerly Miss Diana Churchill, eldest daughter of Mr. Winston Churchill.

"The wedding will take place shortly, perhaps within two or three weeks," Mrs. Bailey told the Daily Mirror.

"It will be very, very quiet. We do not know yet when and where it will take place.

"As a matter of fact, it will quite probably be a secret ceremony."

Mr Sandys also refused to disclose the wedding plans.

"It will take place in a church somewhere in London," he said to a Daily Mirror representative.

"Miss Churchill and I met only a short time ago after the Norwood election. I know that she followed my campaign with interest."

Mr. Sandys is twenty-seven, and Mrs. Bailey is twenty-five.

Screen Test "for Fun"

Mr. and Mrs. John Milner Bailey were married in December, 1932, and Mrs. Bailey was granted a decree nisi last February. Mr. Bailey is the son of Sir Abe Bailey, the South African millionaire, by his first marriage.

Mrs. Bailey, who has auburn hair, is one of three sisters and has inherited much of her father's versatility. She has travelled with Mr. Churchill, and has helped him in his election campaigns.

She has taken a keen interest in V.A.D. work, and once went on duty with the hop-pickers in Kent.

In 1932, when in the United States, she underwent a screen test—but "only for fun."

Mr. Sandys won Norwood in the by-election last March.

Son of Captain George Sandys, former Conservative M.P. for the Wells Division of Somerset, Mr. Sandys was educated at Eton and Oxford. Entering the Diplomatic Service in 1930, he served at the British Embassy in Berlin until 1933.

Mr. Sandys and Mrs. Bailey at the London restaurant where they dined last night.

BIG GERMAN LOAN

BERLIN, Friday.

THE Reichsbank to-day announced a German internal loan for 1,000,000,000 marks (£83,300,000 at present rates).

The loan is to be used for the re-employment and public works programme.—British United Press.

HIS 'DREAM WOMAN' WAS EIGHT MONTHS OLD

THIS is the story of a balloon and of a young Irishman whose dreams of romance were shattered.

Elaine Dodd, of Bilston, Staffs., sent up the winning balloon in a local floral fete competition.

It was returned from Strabane, Co. Tyrone, by a youth who asked that the fair winner should write to him, enclosing her photograph.

He added that he was nineteen and on the look-out for a wife.

Elaine Dodd is eight months old.

MOTHER'S LONDON-BRIGHTON WALK

AT eight o'clock last night a grey-haired woman arrived at Brighton Aquarium. She had completed a walk from London (fifty-six miles) in 13h. 30m.

The woman, Mme. Herbelin, a native of France, is fifty and has three children. She is a teacher of languages.

After her long walk—for the most part in the rain—she seemed quite fresh.

THE DAILY MIRROR, Wednesday, August 28, 1935.

Daily Mirror

Broadcasting - Page 20

THE DAILY PICTURE ♦ NEWSPAPER WITH THE LARGEST NET SALE

RECKLESS YOUTH
—See Page Two

No. 9,905 — Registered at the G.P.O. as a Newspaper. — WEDNESDAY, AUGUST 28, 1935 — One Penny

Amusements : Page 18

CLIFF RACE TO SAVE LOVERS

Hauled 120 Feet to Safety When Tide Trapped Them

Coastguards risking their lives by descending a 120ft. cliff to save marooned holidaymakers whose lives were menaced by the tide.... A stationmaster rescuing three drowning boys.... An all-day search for a woman who had been swept out to sea on an air cushion.

THESE are some of the dramatic incidents that occurred round Britain's coasts yesterday—dramas which have added more names to the list of civilian heroes.

Newquay (Cornwall) coastguards received an urgent phone call last night that three holidaymakers had been cut off by the tide near Lusty Glaze.

Mr. W. H. Strong, chief of the local coastguards, and another coastguard, Mr. A. H. Parr, rushed to the scene by car with life saving equipment.

With a life-line they descended the cliff face and rescued:—

Miss Lydia Simpkins, aged twenty, of Burns-road, Alperton, Wembley;
Mr. Standford George Brentnall, of Worston-road, Burnham-on-Sea, and
Mr. Alfred Fieldman, of Summerville-avenue, Moston, Manchester.

Miss Simpkins and Mr. Brentnall are sweethearts and are to be officially engaged on Miss Simpkins's twenty-first birthday.

Here is Mr. Strong's own graphic story of the rescue:—

"Within three minutes of hearing by telephone that some visitors were cut off by the
(Continued on back page)

Miss Lydia Simpkins, of Burns-road, Alperton, and (right) Mr. S. G. Brentnall, of Burnham, Somerset.

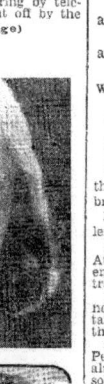

SOAP-BOX DERBY

Watched by 60,000 People

Such things can happen only in one place—America. What would the countless English boys who run through our streets with their soap-box racers, say if 60,000 people turned up to watch a Soap-Box Derby? Yet this is what happened, as the picture shows, at Akron, Ohio, where competitors shot down a sloping 1,181ft. course at breakneck speed.

Blazing Car on Buffers of London Express

WITH a blazing car on its buffers, the 4.15 p.m. Inverness to London express train tore along the track for a quarter of a mile last night.

Crashing into the car, which was empty, at a level crossing at Dalnaspidal, in the Highlands, the engine left the line.

Fortunately, none of the coaches jumped the metals. The passengers were much alarmed, but no one was injured.

The car involved belonged to Mr. James Douglas, employee of Balfour Beatty and Co., contractors at the Grampian electricity scheme at Dalnaspidal.

Mr. Douglas opened the gates outwards to drive across the metals, but when his car was half-way across the engine stalled.

Then he saw the express roaring towards him, and just had time to jump clear.

He stood at the side of the track and watched the express strike the car with a terrific crash.

The car immediately burst into flames, and the train, with a screeching and screaming of brakes, began to pull up.

Hardly had it passed Douglas when the engine left the metals.

A breakdown gang was sent from Blair Atholl, and shortly after nine o'clock the engine was placed back on the railway and the train resumed the journey.

The 4.35 p.m., a second express from Inverness to Euston, had been held up a short distance up the line, and it also passed through the single line which was being operated.

After the two London trains had reached Perth it was decided that they should be run almost non-stop in order to try to make up some of the lost time.

DURSTON'S OPERATION

JACK Durston, the England and Middlesex cricketer, was taken yesterday from his home in Princes-gardens, North Acton, to the West London Hospital suffering from appendicitis.

An operation was performed, and early this morning he was stated to be progressing favourably.

ANTI-GOD BRITONS

Christians Here in "Big Minority"

Not more than twenty per cent. of the people of Britain are Christians.

THAT was the estimate given yesterday by Dr. W. R. Matthews, Dean of St. Paul's.

He was speaking during a discussion on marriage vows at the conference of the Modern Churchmen's Union at Cambridge.

Dr. D. J. M. Creed, Ely Professor of Divinity at Cambridge, spoke of "the propaganda which aims at undermining the permanence of the marriage tie."

This propaganda, he said, does not reflect the general mind of the community.

"If responsible public opinion becomes anti-Christian or if pressure is put by the Government on the Church to acquiesce in measures which are plainly opposed to Christianity, then, of course, the separation of Church and State would have to be demanded by the Church," declared the Rev. J. F. Clayton, Reader of the Temple.

NEW BOOK—PRICE £100,000!

NEW YORK, Tuesday.

"LAWRENCE of Arabia's" last manuscript, "The Mint," has been acquired by a New York publishing firm, and the first ten copies will be issued at the price of £100,000 each.

No sales are expected at this prohibitive price, which has been fixed to protect copyright pending publication, to be made as soon as possible.

The manuscript runs to 69,569 words, and it is stated that Mr. Nelson Doubleday, the head of a big publishing firm, acquired it during a recent visit to England.

According to the firm's announcement, the book cannot be published in England at least until certain living persons mentioned in it have died.

The manuscript is understood to discuss Lawrence's attitude towards the British Government resulting from the Cabinet's refusal to honour promises which he alleges were made to the Arabs.

The work is written under the pseudonym of "A.C. Ross"—"A.C." meaning "Aircraftman."—British United Press.

£50,000,000 OF SWEETS YEARLY

OVER £50,000,000 of chocolate and confectionery are produced in Britain every year;

And more Welsh people eat sweets than any other section of the population. The percentage in Wales is 97.5; elsewhere 90.

These facts were given at a Press view of the annual exhibition of the industry at Olympia, yesterday, when it was stated that:

Sweets were first made in this country hundreds of years ago and one firm exhibiting is over 200 years old;

Well over 100,000 people are in the regular employ of the industry;

Sales of milk chocolate are growing at a tremendous rate.

Thanks to the Jubilee celebrations, and many open air attractions of the season, the chocolate trade has enjoyed a phenomenally busy summer.

THE DAILY MIRROR, Monday, September 2, 1935.

Broadcasting - Page 20

Daily Mirror

THE DAILY PICTURE NEWSPAPER WITH THE LARGEST NET SALE

BOY STRIPPED AND TARRED
—Page 3

No. 9,909 Registered at the G.P.O. as a Newspaper. MONDAY, SEPTEMBER 2, 1935 One Penny

Amusements: Pages 14 and 17

ARCHBISHOP JUSTIFIES WAR

Lady Alice Scott driving to Crathie Church from Balmoral yesterday morning, seated beside the Duke of Gloucester and opposite the King and Queen.

Sanctions as 'the Duty of Christians'

IF THEY ARE NECESSARY

If the use of armed forces were necessary for the effectiveness of the League Covenant, we ought to be prepared to use them.

THIS statement was made by the Archbishop of York, Dr. William Temple, in a broadcast last night on "The Christian's Duty." It was really a broadcast on the Italo-Abyssinian crisis.

The Archishop added:—

"For the League to employ force against an aggressive member is no more 'war' in the proper sense of the word than a baton charge by the police against a mob engaged in destruction is a riot on the part of the police.

"There is nothing unchristian in it. It is the only way of carrying out the Christian duty of using law with its sanctions for the securing of justice.

"If it becomes necessary to uphold law by force, however, it is important that there should be enough force available. To use force and then be worsted will wound fatally the cause of justice.

Britain's Part

"What must not be left in any doubt," the Archbishop went on, "is our purpose to operate the machinery of the League if our neighbours will join us in doing so. We have pledged our word."

Dr. Temple declared that if our neighbours could not see their way to join in any effective action, Britain must recognise that she was not bound to do so by herself. It would be wrong to do so.

"Suppose the League decides on the application of sanctions; suppose Italy resists by force; then, most reluctantly, we should be committed to fighting Italy.

"But that would not mean that Great Britain and France and the rest were, as separate and allied nations, at war with Italy; it would mean that they were lending their force to uphold a decision made by the community of nations.

"The trouble is that we have, as yet, no vivid sense of that community of nations. If a great body of Christians could not only see with their minds that it is a scandal to the Christian name that Christians should fight, but should be actually scandalised in their own feelings at such a prospect, that alone would go far to prevent war.

"If all the nations who are members of the League were ready to support the decisions of the League there would be no fighting."

Dr. Temple.

BRITISH JOCKEYS TRIUMPH

BRITISH jockeys rode the first three horses in the Ostend Grand Prix yesterday.

Steve Donoghue won the race on M. Leon Volterra's Admiral Drake, Charles Elliott rode M. Marcel Boussac's filly Corrida, which was second, and Gordon Richards was on the Aga Khan's Theft, which was third. There was only a length and a half between first and third.

Story on page 21.

Campbell Will Test Bluebird To-day

Special Interview by Transatlantic 'Phone

SIR Malcolm Campbell is getting a hustle on in his latest attempt to break his own record.

On Friday he arrived in Utah, where he hopes to drive Bluebird at 300 m.p.h. over the salt beds of the desert. Yesterday he told the *Daily Mirror* over the transatlantic telephone that he is making a trial run to-day.

Then, if all goes well, he means to go for the record on Thursday or Friday.

"I can't tell what will happen yet," Sir Malcolm said. "To-morrow's run will show how the wheels are going to grip the salt beds.

"I shall try Bluebird at about 240 m.p.h., and after that shall be able to tell what chances I have of doing 300.

"If everything is all right I shall have a go at the record on Thursday or Friday.

"Donald, my boy, who came out here with me, is thoroughly enjoying himself.

"Would you ring my wife? Tell her we are both feeling fine and give her my love."

SHOWER OF WHITE HEATHER FOR DUKE AND HIS FIANCEE

By KATHLEEN LITTLE

BALLATER (near Balmoral), Sunday.

WHEN will the Duke of Gloucester present his fiancée, Lady Alice Montagu Douglas-Scott, with the engagement ring? Everyone wants to know.

When Lady Alice arrived at Balmoral yesterday she waved a ringless hand to the crowd.

At Crathie church this morning she did not remove the glove from her left hand, but on the third finger there was no mark of a ring.

The Duke leaves the Castle to-night to return to his military duties at Catterick. Will he give her the ring before he goes, or will she not receive it until they meet again?

These are just two of the host of questions—which so far remain unanswered—concerning the quietest royal engagement anyone remembers.

When will the wedding take place?

Although the Duke had not seen his fiancée since before the announcement of their engagement, he was not waiting for her when she arrived at Balmoral

She was met by the Queen, who kissed her affectionately. Not until five minutes later did the King and the Duke arrive.

A crowd of people waited nearly two hours to see Lady Alice arrive.

Their babies slung in their tartan shawls, young Scottish mothers dashed in front of the car with lucky white heather.

Two hours before the service began at Crathie Church this morning, visitors had formed a queue in the hope of being able to attend the service

Lorry Hooter Sounded Town's Reveille Too Early

IN the small hours of yesterday Alton (Hants) stirred in its sleep.

Through closed windows came—

Kra-a-a-a-a-a—

"The fire siren," said the inhabitants, and turned over. But on went the siren.

They stuffed pillows into their ears, pulled the clothes over their heads. Still the noise went on.

Alton had had enough. Hundreds of heads popped out of hundreds of windows and demanded of one another what was wrong.

* * *

In Ackenden-road, a party of revellers coming home from a dance heard the noise.

They went to the caretaker of a garage; and when he popped *his* head out of the window said:—

"Stop the electric horn on your lorry in the garage. It's raising the town!"

Alton turned over, and nothing stirred

THE DAILY MIRROR, Tuesday, September 3, 1935.

Broadcasting - Page 20

Daily Mirror

THE DAILY PICTURE NEWSPAPER WITH THE LARGEST NET SALE

No. 9,910 Registered at the G.P.O. as a Newspaper. TUESDAY, SEPTEMBER 3, 1935 One Penny

DUKE OF GLOUCESTER'S PYJAMA DASH TO FIRE—Page 5

Amusements : Page 18

ITALIAN ATTACK LAUNCHED?

2,500 Troops Reported in Abyssinia— Natives in Flight

PARIS FACES A CRISIS

About 1,000 Italian troops, with 1,500 native soldiers, were reported last night to have crossed the border into Abyssinia.

THE point at which they are said to have crossed is west of Assab in the Danakil country.

The Danakils, says the message (from Reuter's correspondent at Diredawa), are fleeing and abandoning their homes.

It adds that great defensive preparations are going on at Diredawa, including preparations for the arrival of several thousand Imperial guards to defend the railway.

No confirmation of the report could be obtained up to a late hour last night; from Rome came a denial of any troop movements.

The spot at which the troops are reported to have crossed is north of French Somaliland.

French Cabinet Crisis

Crisis over the Abyssinia dispute may wreck the French Cabinet.

At a momentous interview in Paris yesterday between M. Laval, the French Premier, and M. Herriot, President of the French Radical Party (both members of the French delegation to the League Council), it is understood authoritatively that M. Herriot issued an ultimatum to

LEAGUE'S DAY OF FATE

How the fourteen nations sitting on the Council of the League, which meets to-morrow, view the crisis—page 5.

the French Premier, says our diplomatic correspondent.

He has told him in uncompromising terms that unless he adheres to the League Covenant in relation to the dispute, he (M. Herriot) will state his individual point of view supporting sanctions, whatever the Premier may state.

For some time past there have been grave suspicions regarding the French Premier's sincerity in relation to League policy.

Ever since M. Laval's interview with Signor Mussolini a year ago, rumour has been busy suggesting that the French Premier concluded a secret agreement with the Duce, giving him a free hand in Abyssinia in the event of hostilities.

If M. Laval, fearing to endanger Franco-Italian friendship, opposes the League principles the inevitable challenge from M. Herriot cannot fail to bring down the Laval Government.

Looming largely over the situation is still the Abyssinian oil deal.

The British Minister at Addis Ababa has informed the Foreign Office that there is no British participation in the deal.

Abyssinia is said to be receiving an immediate payment of £200,000, with which she is purchasing arms and munitions.

Mr. Anthony Eden is on his way to Geneva for the Council meeting to-morrow. Before leaving Paris he had a long conference with M. Laval.

All-Ways Aeroplane

IT CAN FLY STRAIGHT UP AND BACKWARDS!

BY A SPECIAL CORRESPONDENT

AN aeroplane which can rise vertically from the ground, has no propellers, can fly backwards or forwards, land on a patch of ground no bigger than a tennis court, and remain stationary in the air for any length of time is being built in a workshop within a mile of Piccadilly-circus.

It is the invention of Mr. N. Pemberton Billing, war-time M.P., inventor, journalist and theatrical manager.

He has been working on the plans for this 'plane for two years, and it will be ready for a trial flight in four months time.

No wood or canvas is being used in its construction. Everything in the aeroplane is made of either steel or duralumin.

Six rotating wings with fins on the end of each replaces the propeller. One set moves in clock-wise and the other in an anti-clockwise direction.

If the engine fails in mid-air, the aeroplane can descend to the ground as if by parachute.

ROYAL MOURNERS

Gustaf Adolf, Crown Prince of Sweden, and his daughter, Princess Ingrid, wife of the Crown Prince of Denmark, arriving at Brussels for to-day's funeral. With them is the Crown Princess of Sweden.

15 DIE IN BLAZING 'PLANE

Hit Power Cable and Fell Like Meteor

FIFTEEN people on their way to attend California's Labour celebrations were killed yesterday when the air liner in which they were travelling crashed in flames at Los Angeles (says Exchange).

The aeroplane was flying out of the fog-bound airport to Saugus to pick up more passengers to attend the celebrations when the machine lost altitude.

It struck overhead power cables, burst into flames and fell like a blazing meteor on to a building, which caught fire and was wrecked.

Another message from America, this time from San Francisco, reveals that nine people had miraculous escapes from death in Puget Sound yesterday when the palatial steam yacht Nacomas was blown up by an internal explosion.

FOUND BY S O S

The sender of a swab, which proved positive for diphtheria, to the Royal Institute of Public Health, Queen-street, W.C., on Saturday, was traced last night as the result of a broadcast S O S on Sunday to doctors in the London area.

The person affected has been sent to hospital.

IN CIVILISED 1935

A FOX-CUB, its jaws lashed together with whipcord, has been found dead near a well-known hunt covert at Nantwich, Cheshire.

Unable to eat or drink, it had slowly starved to a terrible death. The outrage has caused great anger in the Cheshire Hunt country.

THE DAILY MIRROR, Wednesday, September 4, 1935.

Broadcasting - Page 20

Daily Mirror

THE DAILY PICTURE NEWSPAPER WITH THE LARGEST NET SALE

ABYSSINIA: ARMIES MASSING — Page 3

No. 9,911 Registered at the G.P.O. as a Newspaper. WEDNESDAY, SEPTEMBER 4, 1935 One Penny

Amusements : Page 18

ABYSSINIAN MIDNIGHT SENSATION

The famous car Bluebird travelling at speed.

301 m.p.h. RECORD— CAMPBELL DID NOT KNOW

Life's Ambition Realised After Officials' Error

AFTER FIRST BELIEVING THAT HE HAD FAILED, SIR MALCOLM CAMPBELL YESTERDAY ACHIEVED HIS LIFE'S AMBITION BY SMASHING THE WORLD'S LAND SPEED RECORD WITH AN AVERAGE OF 301.337 MILES AN HOUR. THIS FEAT WAS PERFORMED IN HIS CAR BLUEBIRD AT BONNEVILLE SALT FLATS, UTAH.

Speed!

Bluebird's terrific speed of 304.311 m.p.h. on the first run almost equalled the United States aeroplane speed record of 304.98 m.p.h.—Reuter.
And Sir Malcolm Campbell is fifty.

FOR hours after he had made his amazing dash, Sir Malcolm believed that he had failed.

It was first announced that although he had reached a speed of 304.311 m.p.h. in one direction his average for the double run was 299.875 m.p.h.

Although he had smashed his own world record, he was dissatisfied because he had set his heart on achieving an average of 300 m.p.h.

He had practically made plans to make another attempt later in the week.

Then, at three o'clock this morning, came the sensational announcement that the official Contest Board of the American Automobile Association had corrected the mean average speed made by Sir Malcolm to 301.337 m.p.h. in both directions over the measured mile.

The Board explained that the original figure of 299.874 m.p.h. was due to a miscalculation of his time.

Sir Malcolm subsequently announced that he would leave immediately for New York, sailing for London next Monday.

Twice yesterday he was within an ace of disaster, says Reuter. A tyre went flat when he was travelling at 280 m.p.h., and at the end of his first run, and it was only the superb handling of the giant motor by Sir Malcolm that prevented him from turning over.

Secondly, he was nearly blinded by the steam of the car and the salt which rushed through the air vents in the radiator.

Drove Almost Blind

"I might not have been here to talk to you," he said directly after his first run.
"At one time I was driving almost blind because of the salt and steam of the car."
Actually Sir Malcolm established four new world records.
He became the first man in the world ever to have travelled at over 300 miles an hour on land;
He covered a measured mile at 304.311 miles an hour, the fastest speed ever covered over any measured distance;
The average speed for the measured mile was 301.337 m.p.h.,

WINNING SMILES

Farnborough's Carnival Queen nursing one who is equally the town's pride—Mary Hampshire, the champion baby in the "Open to All England" class of the baby show which was held at Farnborough

Sir Malcolm Campbell—the latest portrait.

In his anxiety to get to his father to congratulate him, young Donald Campbell leapt out of the touring car in which he watched the race before it had stopped, tumbled and skinned his hands.

Lady Campbell spoke to Sir Malcolm over the transatlantic telephone last night.

Viscount Wakefield of Hythe last night sent the following cablegram to Sir Malcolm Campbell:—

"My warmest and heartiest congratulations on your magnificent achievement. You have nobly upheld the high reputation of British engineering and earned the admiration of motorists and sportsmen of all nations.

"May I now appeal to you to rest content on your laurels?—Wakefield of Hythe."

A Queen's Funeral

HOW Belgium said farewell to her Queen is told in words on page 2 and in pictures on pages 14 and 15.

U.S. Firm Drops Oil Deal After Peace Plea

BY OUR DIPLOMATIC CORRESPONDENT

ON the eve of Geneva's fateful discussion on the Abyssinian-Italian dispute it was revealed at midnight that the oil concession to the African Development and Exploitation Corporation—negotiated by the Englishman, Mr. F. W. Rickett—is to be cancelled.

The announcement was made by the State Department at Washington after members of the Board of the Standard-Vacuum Oil Company had informed the Department that their corporation owned the concession and were prepared to terminate their part in it.

They had been told by Mr. Cordell Hull, Secretary of State, that the granting of such a concession at this time was a serious obstacle to the maintenance of peace (states Reuter).

Earlier in the day, however, another American, Mr. Leo Y. Chertok, a New York broker, claimed to have "got ahead" of Mr. Rickett in securing oil and mineral concessions in Abyssinia.

Early to-day he declared that the latest development would not affect his group.

At Geneva to-day statesmen have the fate of nations in their hands—the fate of nations and the lives of their peoples.

And by its handling of a situation that has become so delicate, the League must stand as the saviour of peace—or be condemned.

Britain and France, especially, have a big part to play.

So far the two Powers have not reached an agreement on sanctions, and they will present separate statements to the League Council on the Three-Power Conference with Italy.

This is because they want to avoid any appearance of an Anglo-French united front against Italy, which might have the effect of antagonising her at the outset.

Yesterday was a day of preparation, of statesmen visiting statesmen, of vital meetings, fateful talks.

Mr. Anthony Eden was in conference with the French Premier, M. Laval, for more than thirty-five minutes, and then visited M. Avenol, Secretary-General of the League.

Later he was conferring with Mr. Stanley Bruce, the Australian delegate and Senor de Madariaga, the Spanish delegate.

Then he motored through a thunderstorm to Aix-les-Bains to dine with Mr. Stanley Baldwin.

The Italian delegates arrived in Geneva with eight large and carefully roped and sealed wooden cases.

In these cases was the entire information which Baron Aloisi, the chief Italian delegate, will lay before the League Council in support of his country's case.

Meanwhile prominent Ethiopians are putting forward tentative suggestions that there should be a British mandate over Abyssinia

FOR WORLD PEACE

EVERY seat in Westminster Abbey was occupied half-an-hour before the beginning of last night's service of prayer for the peace of the world, and many people stood throughout the service.

Prayer was offered for Divine guidance for the Council of the League

THE DAILY MIRROR, Wednesday, September 11, 1935.

Daily Mirror

THE DAILY PICTURE NEWSPAPER WITH THE LARGEST NET SALE

Broadcasting—Page 20

BARONET BUYS LINER FOR £100,000

No. 9,917 Registered at the G.P.O. as a Newspaper. WEDNESDAY, SEPTEMBER 11, 1935 One Penny

Amusements: Page 18

ARMED GUARD FOR AN INVENTOR

PEER OF 82 TO WED TO-DAY

SISTER-IN-LAW IS HIS BRIDE

BY A SPECIAL CORRESPONDENT

AN eighty-two-year-old peer is to be married in a London register office to-day to a widow aged eighty-one. His white-haired bride will be supported on crutches.

The bridegroom is Lord Monteagle, of Brandon, who, himself, walks with difficulty, owing to failing eyesight.

The bride is Mrs. Julia Emma Isobella Spring Rice, Lord Monteagle's sister-in-law. His first wife died in 1922.

Lord Monteagle, who wears a pointed grey beard and dark glasses, is a trim figure despite his years.

"Yes, I am going to be married," he told the *Daily Mirror* yesterday. "It will be in London, but I won't say anything more about it than that."

Mrs. Spring Rice, the bride, recently had a fall resulting in an injured thigh.

Mrs. Julia Spring Rice photographed yesterday. She walks with crutches at present following a recent fall which injured a thigh. Left: Lord Monteagle of Brandon.

Stranded Holidaymakers Hauled 80ft. Up Cliff

A PARTY of holidaymakers, including a honeymoon couple and a schoolgirl, were hauled to safety by a rope after they had become stranded 80ft. down the face of the cliffs at Trebarwith, near Tintagel, yesterday.

The stranded people were Mr. and Mrs. C. Curtis, from London, staying at Trevalga, Boscastle; Mr George Thompson, Mr. Green, Miss J. Hopwood and Mrs. Stanley Jones, from Manchester, on holiday at Trebarwith; and Mr. and Mrs. J. Lunt and their two daughters, who reside at Cringle Wood, Raglan-road, Sale, Manchester, holidaying at a farm at Bossinney, Tintagel.

The party found themselves suddenly cut off and were unable to climb the cliff.

Some friends gave the alarm and they were hauled to the top by a lifebuoy rope, the rescuers having a difficult task on the slippery slope.

The holidaymakers had to leave mackintoshes and bags behind and were cut and bruised as they were pulled up.

BUS STRIKE TO END?

BY 456 votes to 447, a majority of only nine, the West Wales and Swansea bus and tramway men who have been on strike for nearly a month decided last night to return to work providing suitable arrangements can be made with the employers.

Keeping Secret of "Electricity from a Powder"

FROM OUR SPECIAL CORRESPONDENT

MAIDSTONE, Tuesday.

IN the lighted room of a riverside house here to-night a man crouched over a table connecting electrical wires, fitting electrical plugs, and preparing quantities of a strange white powder.

In the same room sat an armed detective keeping guard; beside him lay an Alsatian wolfhound.

The man is Mr. Ernest Gooch, a Maidstone builder. He claims to have invented a way of making electrical energy which will revolutionise the electrical world as it exists to-day.

Almost for Nothing

His invention, he says, will make electricity so cheap that a whole house can be lighted for a month for 4d. His own house is lit by this means, and at that cost.

He is preserving the strictest secrecy about his invention until to-morrow, when he has to give a demonstration of it to Mr. E. Hoadley, the Maidstone Borough Electricity Engineer.

Mr. Hoadley said to me to-night: "I heard of Mr. Gooch last Friday when he came into my office to borrow a volt-meter.

"In the course of conversation with him, he mentioned a remarkable discovery of his.

"I questioned him and he was very reticent, but he told me that

by means of his invention it would be possible to light 100 lamps and drive a 1 h.p. engine for a month at a cost of 4d. I gathered that he manufactured his energy by means of a white powder which he refuses to describe, a jar and some metal plates

Mr. Gooch's Fears

Mr. Gooch said that if I would go round to his house at three o'clock to-morrow (Wednesday) he would arrange a convincing demonstration for me. I am going round to see his demonstration with my mind absolutely open.

"His discoveries may revolutionise all laws of electricity as we know them to-day. On the other hand they may not."

Mr. Gooch refused to see me. He spoke to me through a window of the first story room in which he was working. He said that he would have to be working all night preparing his demonstration and could not spare a moment.

"I don't want anybody to know about my discovery until I am ready," he said. "So it is no use your trying to see me. The fact of the matter is that I am afraid of people finding out my secret before I am ready to divulge it."

Mr. Gooch was at one time employed in a motor garage, but recently he started a business of his own as a builder and repairer of motor-cycles.

The mysterious white powder which forms the key point of his electrical experiments costs about a penny an ounce. That is all that is known about it.

LADY BERTHA RESIGNS

CHANGES in the Queen's household were announced in last night's *London Gazette*.

The Hon. Jean Hamilton Bruce, a maid of honour to Her Majesty, has been appointed Woman of the Bedchamber in place of Lady Bertha Mabel Dawkins, resigned.

Lady Bertha Dawkins, who has been Woman of the Bedchamber since 1907, becomes an extra Woman of the Bedchamber. She is the daughter of the first Earl of Latham.

The Hon. Jean Hamilton Bruce is a sister of Lord Balfour of Burleigh.

Daily Mirror

THE DAILY PICTURE NEWSPAPER WITH THE LARGEST NET SALE

Broadcasting - Page 20

LAVAL WARNS MUSSOLINI
—Page 3

THE DAILY MIRROR, Saturday, September 14, 1935.

No. 9,920. Registered at the G.P.O. as a Newspaper. SATURDAY, SEPTEMBER 14, 1935 One Penny

Amusements : Page 6

Smugglers in Car with the Royal Arms

BY A SPECIAL CORRESPONDENT

WHEN a magnificent 40-h.p. limousine bearing the arms and insignia of the King of the Belgians crossed the Franco-Belgian frontier yesterday, it was stopped by Customs officials, who arrested the bogus liveried chauffeurs as tobacco smugglers.

For some time now, militia at the Customs House on the lonely frontier road near Tourcoing, Belgium, have been saluting the royal car as it flashed on its way through the night.

Behind its screened windows, they supposed that royalty was travelling on its way, and the limousine had been given free passage to either side of the frontier.

Did not the royal car carry the arms of the Belgian Royal House on its brightly polished panels ?

Suspicion was at last roused by the too-frequent trips which the car made across the border.

Inquiries revealed that the limousine had passed out of Belgian royal hands some months after the death of the late King Albert.

Early yesterday, when the lights of the bogus royal car were seen approaching the Customs House, four officials lay in wait with their own fast car.

The chase began. It was continued on foot when the "royal chauffeurs" took to their heels after a tyre-burst.

Their arrest followed, and many hundreds of pounds of foreign tobacco were discovered in the abandoned limousine with the royal arms.

MERCY ERRAND AT 80

At eighty years of age Mrs. Elizabeth Pritchard, of Gaerwen, Anglesey, is going alone to Chicago.

She started on an errand of mercy yesterday. She is to comfort a brother who has been bereaved and, if she can, persuade him to return to Anglesey.

DICTATOR PROMISES BETTER HUSBANDS

NUREMBERG, Friday.

TWENTY thousand Nazi women in neat white blouses and black skirts cheered Herr Hitler to-night when he told them that "motherhood is the highest nobility that woman can attain."

They cheered when he declared that the Nazi ideas about women differed from those of the other parties whose system entailed the selling of thousands of girls to "White Slave traders."

And they cheered when he said the Nazi system was giving them braver and decent husbands—"training real men for the women, decent, brave and honourable."

(From Reuter and British United Press.)

Mr. Rickett's frank smile on arrival at Croydon Airport yesterday.

LADY ALICE'S WEEK-END

FROM OUR SPECIAL CORRESPONDENT

SELKIRK, Friday.

LADY Alice Montagu-Douglas-Scott, the Duke of Gloucester's fiancée, who arrived in Selkirk from London at six o'clock this morning, is leaving to-morrow to stay with friends in Yorkshire near Catterick Camp, so as to be able to spend the week-end with the Duke.

She is expected to return to Selkirk on Monday.

She had a busy day to-day dealing with her correspondence.

MR. RICKETT REVEALS ALL

Debunks Mystery Man of Abyssinia

By A SPECIAL REPRESENTATIVE

WITH disarming frankness Mr. F. W. Rickett, "mystery man of Abyssinia," laid bare the secrets of his famous oil concession when he arrived in London yesterday.

Smiling, confident, humorous, the English financier who was the centre of the world's attention for days and who caused consternation in half a dozen Foreign Offices, set about proving that he was not so mysterious as credited to be as soon as he stepped from the air liner in which he had travelled from Rotterdam.

"Going to Stick to It"

"First of all," he told me, "I have never travelled on this deal under any name than my own. I never called myself Goldstein. If I wanted an alias it would probably have been something like Dr. Smith.

"With regard to the Abyssinian deal, my concession is valid, and I am going to stick to it lock, stock and barrel.

"I shall not pay a visit to the Foreign Office. I have not been approached by them on the subject, and if they wanted to see me they would send for me.

"The oil concession was undertaken long before there was any trouble in Abyssinia. I flaunted no Governments, and I am not interested in politics. There was no intrigue about it.

"I have done all this as a business man, and the concession is entirely mine.

"I am an Englishman of the deepest dye. I have the finest concession the world has seen for some time, and I am happy and proud to have pulled it off. I wish I could have done it in London."

Mr. Rickett replied "No" when asked if he was going to offer the concession to any other American or British interests.

"I hope the concession will be developed almost at once," he added.

Rome's reaction to M. Laval's speech, page three.

Lost Necklace: Lost Dog

SOMEWHERE in the maze of streets between Paddington Station and Connaught-square, W., lies a £1,000 pearl necklace. . . . Somewhere in the same neighbourhood is roaming a pedigree fox-terrier, worth £100.

Both have been lost by Miss Davinia Rothschild, and she would rather have the dog found than the necklace.

Miss Rothschild went to report to the police the disappearance of the dog, Peggy. On the way the necklace was lost.

"The necklace was a birthday present," she told the *Daily Mirror*. "I have only had it a week. It is of graduated pearls with a double-eagle clasp of diamonds.

"But I am more worried over the loss of the dog.

"You see, I was taking care of her for my brother, who is in Vienna. Goodness knows what he will say when he hears it has been lost."

Miss Davinia Rothschild.

FRED PERRY MARRIED FIRST PICTURE

HIS FILM STAR BRIDE

Fred Perry, British and world lawn tennis champion, with his film star bride, Helen Vinson, after their marriage at Harrison, New York State, on Thursday night. They managed to avoid being married on Friday, the thirteenth, by exactly five minutes. Mr. and Mrs. Perry will be in England in January. See page 4.

THE DAILY MIRROR, Monday, September 16, 1935.

Broadcasting - Page 20

Daily Mirror

THE DAILY PICTURE NEWSPAPER WITH THE LARGEST NET SALE

"HANGED MAN" HOAX ON POLICE
—Page 2

No 9,921 Registered at the G.P.O as a Newspaper. MONDAY, SEPTEMBER 16, 1935 One Penny

Amusements : Pages 16 and 18

NEW 'PURGE' IN GERMANY
Drastic Jew Laws

NATIONAL FLAG IS NOW THE SWASTIKA

Ban on Mixed Marriages

While drastic laws dealing with German Jews were being passed by the Reichstag last night, the country was buzzing with rumours that another "purge" was to take place in the next few hours.

THIS followed a mysterious interruption of the broadcast of Herr Hitler's speech from Nuremberg, where the German Parliament was in session.

Before the Chancellor had begun to speak the wireless was suddenly switched off, and all attempts in Berlin to discover the reason met with failure.

In some quarters it was believed that wholesale arrests of former Communist officials were about to take place.

One rumour which quickly spread was that a drastic purge of "unsatisfactory" elements in Germany had been planned.

Mixed Marriages Ban

The law regulating the Jewish question in Germany, which was passed unanimously by the Reichstag, lays down:

No marriages are to be allowed between Jews and German.

Such marriages will be null and void even if contracted abroad; only the Public Prosecutor, however, can file claims for such annulment.

No Jew may employ a German maidservant under the age of forty-five.

No Jew may hoist or fly a German Reich or national flag He may, however, fly the Jewish flag.

Illegal intercourse between Jews and Germans is forbidden.

Imprisonment, with or without hard labour is the penalty for offences against this law.

Another law regulates German citizenship making a distinction between "State subjects" and "Reich citizens."

It provides that everyone protected by the Reich is a "State subject," but only a select group may become "Reich citizens," and only "Reich citizens" will have full personal rights

In order to become a "Reich citizen," a German must prove that he is of German blood

A third law declares that the Swastika is the national flag and also a trade flag.

Hitler's speech to the Reichstag was the shortest in his career as Chancellor

He warned the signatories of the guarantee of the autonomy of Memel (Britain, France, Italy and Japan) to take action " before things take a turn which will be regretted everywhere."

The State he added, was making an attempt in the new legislation to adjust the Jewish problem once and for all.

If it were not successful then sterner measures would be adopted—Reuter, Central News and B U P

WAVES 30 MILES FROM THE SEA

Driven on by floods in the Humber, eagre or tidal wave yesterday, which had travelled thirty miles up the River Trent to Gainsborough. Ten thousand people from all over the Midlands gathered to see it. It was the biggest for years. The flood which it produced spread the river at Owston, near Gainsborough, as far as adjacent houses.

River Dyke Bursts and Wrecks Thirty Homes

TOWN FEARS NEW DISASTER

FROM OUR OWN CORRESPONDENT
BARTON-ON-HUMBER (Lincs)
Sunday Night.

FLOOD WATERS OF THE HUMBER BURSTING THROUGH A 4FT. THICK DYKE BROUGHT DESTRUCTION TO MORE THAN THIRTY HOMES HERE TO-DAY.

To-night the district lived in fear of havoc even more widespread, when high tide returned, but zero hour passed without a new disaster.

The 20ft. gap in the dyke through which the water swept with a roar this morning, driving families from their breakfast tables into upstairs rooms has been filled in with bags of cement, sand and planks

Doors of the cottages had been locked and battened up with clay and boards to a height of 4ft

All the families in the area had left their homes—by order.

If the repairs to the dyke, feverishly made by gangs of men, will hold through to-morrow all immediate danger will have been passed.

It was the roar of water that first warned householders this morning of the approaching flood.

In a few moments lower rooms were four feet deep in water. Then the torrent subsided Rescue and salvage work began at once. The chairman of the urban council, one of the first arrivals, immediately opened a relief fund

A harvest thanksgiving service at the Salvation Army hall was interrupted to appeal for volunteers. The service was abandoned and Salvationists were rushed in cars to the stricken area

The men's lobby of an adjoining chemical works was converted into a canteen and a shelter for the homeless families. Women in tears surveyed the wreckage of their homes.

There were pathetic scenes as householders, ill working men, carried the remains of their belongings outside to higher ground

Eye-Witness's Story

Mrs. Beverley told a graphic story.

" I was standing by the pump in the yard when I saw water dripping through the great wall.

" Then I heard a crash, saw part of the wall collapse, and ran for my life. I had hardly set foot indoors when a terrific volume of water flooded the kitchen I gathered up my two children and ran upstairs.

Other parts of the dyke, in all about 100 yards long and 12ft. high have been badly cracked

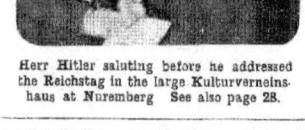

Herr Hitler saluting before he addressed the Reichstag in the large Kulturvereinshaus at Nuremberg See also page 28.

DISTRESSED BARONESS AT GRAVE OF PRINCE MDIVANI

BARCELONA, Sunday

BARONESS Von Thyssen showed signs of great distress to-day when she visited the grave of Prince Alexis Mdivani, in whose car she was travelling when he was killed in a crash near here in July.

Photographs of the Baroness's jewels, valued at £40,000 which are alleged to have been missing since the accident were to-day circulated to the police.

It was reported just over a week ago that the Spanish police had given up their attempt to solve the mystery of the jewels' disappearance Reuter

Baroness Maud von Thyssen

Daily Mirror

THE DAILY PICTURE NEWSPAPER WITH THE LARGEST NET SALE

Broadcasting - Page 20

CHANCE SAVES SEVEN — Page 3

No. 9,923. Registered at the G.P.O. as a Newspaper. WEDNESDAY, SEPTEMBER 18, 1935 One Penny

Amusements: Page 16

THREAT TO STOP NATION'S MILK

THIS SIGHT WAS BANNED

Kuda Bux having his feet examined after one of his walks. Above: Walking barefoot over the 25ft. stretch of red-hot charcoal.

VIOLET MELNOTTE DEAD

MISS Violet Melnotte, the West End theatre owner, died late last night at a London hotel after a long illness. She was eighty-two.

In July last year notice was given that Miss Melnotte was to marry Mr. Archibald Patrick Moore, her young manager at the Duke of York's Theatre. She gave his age as thirty-one. Later it was announced that the marriage would not take place.

Fifty-nine years ago she made her first appearance on the London stage. Then in 1892 she built the Duke of York's Theatre with her husband, Frank Wyatt. It was called the Trafalgar Square Theatre, but by permission of the King, then Duke of York, the name was changed.

Noel Coward has every reason to remember that she produced at the Duke of York's his first full-length play, "Easy Virtue."

Secret Fire-Walking in a Back Garden

HOSE TURNED ON TWO WATCHERS

BY A SPECIAL CORRESPONDENT

FANTASTIC precautions were taken yesterday to keep secret a demonstration of Eastern mysticism in a suburban back garden.

In an unsuccessful effort to conceal the happenings from a photographer and myself:—
A hose was turned on us;
The select audience was asked to step between us and the demonstration, one of fire-walking;
An umbrella was raised in the bright sunshine to impair our view, and
Screens were hurriedly erected

As a last resort, a boy vainly tried to deflect the sun's rays into our eyes by means of a mirror. But his aim was uncertain and from behind a curtain of trees we could see perfectly.

Promenade of Fire

I was able to watch this super-mystery through the courtesy of people whose house overlooks the garden in Woodmansterne-road, Carshalton, Surrey, where the demonstration was given by Kuda Bux, a Kashmiri.

In a further effort to prevent us from watching the exhibition, police called at the house to ask our hostess whether she objected to our presence!

The scene of this secrecy-shrouded show was a raised lawn.

In it had been dug a pit, 25ft. long and 6ft. wide, divided half-way along its length by a strip of turf.

Into this trench had been heaped seven tons of oak logs, which had been fired early in the day.

Shortly before the demonstration half a ton of charcoal was poured from sacks on top of the burning logs, to hold the heat, and at last Kuda Bux's promenade was prepared.

Smoke drifted from the handle as the rake was held over the fire, and a cotton pad tied on a stick was scorched immediately it touched the glowing embers.

The Inspection

Then up went the umbrella, up went the screens and the audience huddled together to obstruct our view.

But I saw the barefoot Kuda Bux walk deliberately to the edge of the trench. Without hesitation he stepped off the grass on to the charcoal, red-hot and, in parts, even white-hot. Unhurriedly he paced his fiery path.

It seemed as though his only difficulty was to walk evenly along the rough footing. Certainly he showed no apparent concern at the temperature.

When he had walked as far as the dividing strip of turf, he stepped off on to the lawn, and solemnly balanced himself on one leg while the medical men peered at the foot of the other.

Intently they examined those surprising soles to try to probe the secret of this young man's abilities.

144 m.p.h. FOR 12 HOURS

CAPTAIN G. E. T. Eyston, roaring round the Bonneville salt flats, is believed to have set up a new twelve-hour record of 144.12 m.p.h. in his attempt to establish new figures for the twenty-four hours, says Reuter.

The previous record was held by Jenkins at 129.74 m.p.h.

"I am delighted with the performance," said Captain Eyston.

Price 'War' May End Supply on October 1

Britain's milk supply may be cut off on October 1.

LONDONERS will have to be their own milkmen if a dispute between the Milk Board and distributors becomes open warfare.

The trouble is over a halfpenny a gallon, which the Milk Board say the distributors must pay the farmers without raising the price to the consumer. The Board hold that the farmer is not getting a fair share of the price paid by the public.

The Central Milk Distributors Committee has instructed the trade not to sign the new contract (a virtual refusal to distribute milk after October 1).

The Milk Board's reply is: "The Board are making arrangements to deal with the situation and to see that the consuming public are supplied with milk on and after October 1."

Plans to Distribute

How London and the country will be supplied with milk if the distributors "strike" on October 1—the beginning of the new contract year—was explained to the *Daily Mirror* last night by Mr. T. Baxter, chairman of the Milk Board.

London will be divided up into 500 centres to which milk will be delivered in bulk by the Board.

To these centres people will have to go to get their supplies.

Large provincial cities, such as Birmingham and Manchester, will have similar arrangements, while smaller cities and towns would be supplied by producer-retailers of milk, who are not affected by the dispute.

"I do not think it will come to anything in the nature of a strike," he said. "If the distributors appeal to the Minister of Agriculture the case will go before a committee of investigation."

FOUGHT ATTACKER

Mrs. H. T. Dunn, who fought off a man who attacked her on the road near Liss (Hants) and then sought refuge in a cottage, where she collapsed. The police are searching for the man. See page 2.

THE DAILY MIRROR, Saturday, September 21, 1935.

Broadcasting - Page 20

Daily Mirror
THE DAILY PICTURE NEWSPAPER WITH THE LARGEST NET SALE

DUCE'S "NO" TO BRITAIN AND FRANCE
—Page 3

No. 9,926 Registered at the G.P.O. as a Newspaper. SATURDAY, SEPTEMBER 21, 1935 One Penny

Amusements: Page 16

ROYAL WEDDING DATE

DYING MINER'S FAREWELL NOTE

Abbey Ceremony for Duke on November 6

IT was officially announced from Balmoral Castle last night that the wedding of the Duke of Gloucester and Lady Alice Montagu-Douglas-Scott will take place at Westminster Abbey on Wednesday, November 6.

This date is slightly earlier than had been generally anticipated.

Preparations for the ceremony will be pressed forward at once by the Lord Chamberlain and the other high Court officials.

When the King returns to Buckingham Palace next Saturday a Privy Council will be summoned so that he may give his formal consent, under the Great Seal of England, to the marriage.

Westminster Abbey authorities have been informed of the date, and preliminary outlines of the ceremonial are already under discussion.

The ceremony, it is expected, will follow closely that for the wedding of the Duke and Duchess of Kent at the Abbey last year, but no details have yet been decided.

Primate to Officiate

It is not yet settled who will conduct the service, but it is probable that the Archbishop of Canterbury and the Dean of Westminster will be among the officiating clergy.

The wedding date was decided, it is understood, after consultation between the Duke and his fiancée and the King and Queen.

It is in, or near, Camberley that the newly married couple may have their first home.

Duke of Gloucester.

Lady Alice Montagu-Douglas-Scott, the royal bride-elect.

'INDECENT' BOOKS IN LIBRARY

Official Replies to Attack

"*Absolutely indecent and unsuitable, especially for young girls.*"

THIS criticism of two books obtainable at Wood Green Public Library, was made by a member at a meeting of the local ratepayers' association.

The borough librarian at Wood Green told the "Daily Mirror" last night that the two books complained of are recognised as of outstanding literary merit.

"The complaint," he said, "is the only one we have received concerning these or any other books in the library for the last two years.

"We take every care to eliminate books of an undesirable type, and each new book is read by members of a panel appointed for that purpose."

Mystery of Big Earthquake Shock

IN Britain, Japan, Australia, and in France yesterday, seismographs recorded earthquake shocks.

All reports agreed that the shocks were even more severe than those recorded during the New Zealand disaster in 1931.

The epicentre was placed at somewhere in New Guinea.

But the only actual news of any 'quake received in London was a six-seconds shock at Bona, in Algeria, which destroyed two houses and cracked several others.

CHALKED NOTE TO WIFE IN DEATH PIT

A TREASURED stone lies in the home of one of the victims of the North Gawber Colliery disaster. It bears his farewell to his wife.

An official touring the underground area, where the full force of the explosion was felt, noticed a large piece of stone in the wall on which was clearly chalked:—

"Farewell, Fanny, old pet * * * *"

The writing was found to be that of Albert Ibberson, of Allendale-terrace, Mapplewell. As he lay in the pit terribly burned and in great agony, realising that he was dying, he scrawled his pathetic last message to his wife, Mrs. Fanny Ibberson.

The stone was removed and taken to the dead man's home.

Ibberson, who was fifty-three, was married only four years ago. His widow is left with a baby.

Says He Was "Executed" as a Spy

CAPETOWN, Friday.

A MAN who claims to be an "executed" spy is causing a good deal of controversy in South Africa.

The man, living at Bloemfontein, says he is Commandant Gideon Scheepers, a notorious Boer spy, who was said to have been executed by the British at Graaf Reinet.

According to his story he was led out at dawn to be executed, but a friendly sergeant distributed blank cartridges, and allowed him to escape after he had simulated death.

It is known that Scheepers's "grave" was opened by a Commission of Inquiry after the Boer War, and that it was found to be empty.

However, Wilfred Harrison, formerly of the Coldstream Guards, now swears that he saw Scheepers shot through the heart, saw the doctor certify him to be dead, and then assisted at the burial.

Harrison explains that the reason the body of Scheepers was not found when the grave was opened was that the searchers did not dig deep enough.

On the other hand, many of those who have examined the man's story are inclined to believe that it may be true.—British United Press.

150 NAZIS ARRESTED

ANOTHER "Inquisition" has been launched against Nazis in Vienna.

Police last night made a secret raid on an office in the Hernals suburb and arrested 150 Nazis (says Reuter).

A list containing many names was found by detectives.

It is expected that other police swoops are imminent.

THE DAILY MIRROR, Saturday, September 28, 1935.

Daily Mirror

THE DAILY PICTURE NEWSPAPER WITH THE LARGEST NET SALE

Broadcasting - Page 20

QUIET CORNER - - Page 14
DOCTOR'S DIARY - Page 17
EUSTACE - - - - - Page 6
ARGUEBIT - - - - Page 7
THE STARS SAY - Page 16
FREE PATTERN - - Page 22

No. 9,932 Registered at the G.P.O. as a Newspaper. SATURDAY, SEPTEMBER 28, 1935 One Penny

Amusements: Page 16

BUT HE WAS SOON ALL SMILES AGAIN

Alexander Thynne's distress puzzled his fellow page, Douglas Scott, during yesterday's rehearsal for Tuesday's wedding of Mr. P. A. C. Bridgewater and the Hon. Vanda Vivian at St. Paul's, Knightsbridge. Below: Luckily, Lord Vivian was there, and soon had the little bridal attendants all laughing.

112 m.p.h. RECORD BY STREAMLINE TRAIN

On Eve of 'Silver Jubilee' Service | The Driver Says, "Not All Out"

BY A SPECIAL CORRESPONDENT
On board the Silver Jubilee, Friday.

RACING level with an aeroplane, the new L.N.E.R. streamline express Silver Jubilee, on its trial run from King's Cross, has just set up a British rail speed record of 112 m.p.h.

That was at Three Counties, on the Bedfordshire, Cambridgeshire and Herts borders. Now, as I write this, we are racing on through a blurred countryside at about 100 m.p.h.

Towns, trees, farms, fields flash by. Excited crowds are gathered on platforms and at crossings, but from the wide, double-glass windows of the restaurant car, we see them only as a mist of faces.

We put our hands out of the window and they were nearly blown from us.

One passenger tried to shake a pipe out of the window—he got his hand back, but not his pipe.

Regular Service

Drawn by its enormously powerful engine, The Silver Link, this latest and grandest addition to British railways is hurtling along like some imaginative ideal of Jules Verne.

We were due to cover the twenty-seven miles from Hitchin to Huntingdon at an average speed of 80.8 miles an hour. We had to slow up.

I learn that this is due to the fact that though we left King's Cross at 2.25, we have caught up the 1.40! We are ten minutes early already.

An official tells me that we have covered the twenty-seven miles at an average speed of 104.9 miles an hour—shattering all world records for the distance.

"Not All Out"

On Monday this train—built in honour of the King's Jubilee, and streamlined throughout —will start a regular service between King's Cross and Newcastle, leaving Newcastle each morning at 10, and King's Cross each evening at 5.30, doing the 268-mile journey in exactly four hours.

With 112 m.p.h. the Silver Jubilee missed world record—held by Germany—by only 8 m.p.h.

The feat has been a triumph for imperturbable Driver A. Taylor, of King's Cross, who piloted it, and for Fireman J. Sluty.

And this is what Driver Taylor, tall and middle-age, says of his engine:

"We could easily have gone faster if we had wanted to—we were not all out by any means."

Fast Run on L.M.S.

The London, Midland and Scottish locomotive Silver Jubilee also carried out an exceptionally fast run yesterday from Coventry to London.

Hauling a special train of ten coaches, weighing 345 tons, this engine covered the 94 miles from Coventry to Euston in eighty-six minutes start-to-stop, at an average speed of 65.6 m.p.h.

SIR JAMES JEANS IN 'WHIRLWIND COURTSHIP'

VIENNA, Friday.

FRAULEIN Susi Hock, the charming brown-eyed twenty - four - year - old Viennese beauty who, it was announced to-day, is to become the bride of the famous British scientist, Sir James Jeans, spoke to-night of her "whirlwind courtship."

It was while on a concert tour in England in June—she is an organist known in Vienna and abroad—that she met Sir James Jeans.

"It all happened at whirlwind speed," she declared, smiling happily.

"We fell in love almost instantly. I had, however, to leave England in July, but after almost three months' separation Sir James suddenly turned up in Vienna a week ago.

"He proposed to me and I accepted.

"I am so happy, and we are going to be married very soon.—Reuter.

Picture on the back page.

Card-Playing Law Muddle

"PURE SKILL" IS WHAT COUNTS | BUT CLUBS NOT WORRIED

IF you play a quiet game of cards for money—a game not of pure skill—in your club then you are breaking the law.

That was the ruling at London Sessions yesterday by the Judge, Sir Herbert Wilberforce. He held that any game of cards "that is not a game of pure skill" is illegal if played for money on premises used mainly for card playing.

When a Daily Mirror representative spoke to officials of the big clubs last night they did not seem at all alarmed.

They were, however, indignant over any suggestion that bridge was a game of chance.

Colonel J. H. M. Beasley, chairman of Crockford's Club told the Daily Mirror: "It is not the first time some judgment such as this has been given. But clubs like this are licensed to play certain games.

"You cannot play faro or baccarat, of course, and until ten years ago poker was not classed as a game of skill, and we were not allowed to play it here. Then there was a test case, and it was decided that poker was a game of skill, so we could play it at the club.

"Bridge is definitely a game of skill—duplicate matches have proved that. As regards chance in a deal—that can be greatly exaggerated.

"In a recent match of 150 rubbers one more ace only was dealt to one pair of partners than to the other in six hundred hands—that was 1,223 aces to 1,222.

"On the law of averages, dealing works out all right."

U.S. INVITES THE WORLD TO TALK

WASHINGTON, Friday.

THE U.S. State Department has issued an invitation from President Roosevelt to the nations of the world to take part in a third "World Power Conference," to be held at Washington from September 7-12 next year.—Reuter.

The last World Power Conference was at Stockholm in 1933, when problems of the power supply of heavy industries and land and sea transport were discussed.

THE DAILY MIRROR, Monday, September 30, 1935.

Daily Mirror

THE DAILY PICTURE NEWSPAPER WITH THE LARGEST NET SALE

Broadcasting - Page 21

GARBO FILM SERIAL - Page 18
BELINDA - - - - - - Page 22
QUIET CORNER - - - Page 15
DOCTOR'S DIARY - - Page 17
EUSTACE - - - - - - Page 6
THE STARS SAY - - - Page 5

No. 9,933 Registered at the G.P.O as a Newspaper. MONDAY, SEPTEMBER 30, 1935 One Penny

Amusements: Pages 16 and 23

TWO WOMEN PROPHESIED THEIR DEATHS

Dramas of Novel and Play Come True

RACING AGAINST FATE

TWO women—both named Winifred—who in novel and play had foretold their own deaths, died during the week-end.

WINIFRED HOLTBY, first-rank English novelist, knew that death could not long be delayed, yet she dedicated the last few speeding months of life to producing some of her most brilliant and telling work.

She had two books to finish. A few days ago she penned the closing words, but one is left without a title. For yesterday Winifred Holtby died in a London nursing home.

WINIFRED HOWE, twenty-three-year-old London playwright, one-time typist, fell to her death from a sixth floor department in New York. Eight months ago her play "Summer's Lease" was produced in London.

It told of a typist who wrote a play, became famous. But in the end it showed a girl heartbroken, "with nothing to live for."

From beginning to end it was the life drama of its young author, Winifred Howe.

Her Friends Amazed

Miss Holtby was taken dangerously ill three years ago, and since then she had never been in good health.

With a grim determination that amazed her friends she wrote the world-famous "Mandoa, Mandoa!" and a few days before her last illness forced her to lay down her pen, finished a book dealing with a county councillor.

"She was a brilliant writer and journalist, and the world of literature is very much the poorer for her death," Lady Rhondda, one of her greatest friends, told the *Daily Mirror* last night. "I have never met anyone who could express herself in her novels so well."

Few of Miss Holtby's friends knew that she was so ill, although they suspected it.

"She did an extraordinary amount of work in the last two years," another friend told the

(Continued on back page)

Miss Winifred Howe, who fell out of window to her death in New York.

Miss Winifred Holtby, who has died after winning a race with death to finish a novel.

LED NAZIS— IN "HEIL"

Once Germans' War Prisoner

COLOGNE, Sunday.

LEADER of the British war prisoners now touring Germany, Captain McCabe, called for a heil for Hitler at a gathering here to-day of 4,000 war prisoners.

Telegrams were sent to the King, the Prince of Wales and Hitler.

The verdict of the British party on their reception at Muenster last night was, "they will hardly believe us at home when we tell them about it."

A march-past, in which the military took part, took place on the Dome-square this afternoon, where Captain McCabe took the salute standing between Herr Oberlindober, head of the Disabled Soldiers' Association, and the general commanding Cologne.—Reuter.

Noel Coward's New Role—Godfather

Noel Coward and John Gielgud will be godfathers when the five-weeks-old son of Emlyn Williams, the actor, is christened at Chelsea Old Church on Thursday.

Among the guests will be the entire cast of "Night Must Fall," the successful play written by Emlyn Williams, in which he is himself appearing.

Another Torso Mystery

POLICE RADIO SHIP FOR HELP

FROM OUR OWN CORRESPONDENT
LIVERPOOL, Sunday.

Discovery of the torso of a man, minus arms and legs, on the bank of the Mersey, has provided Liverpool C.I.D. with an identification problem.

The body was left on the bank by the receding tide.

An examination of clothing still on the body revealed laundry marks which proved that the garments had belonged to a married man at present at sea.

Urgent messages were sent to the vessel asking the man if he had given away any clothing before he sailed, and the police are now awaiting a reply.

THEY PROPHESIED

THREE years ago, after recovering from a serious illness, Winifred Holtby wrote a short story in which a man was given three years to live.

Her friends knew then that in the story all the emotions she gave to the man were the emotions she felt herself—her love for the fields, the hills, that she soon would be leaving.

* * *

WINIFRED Howe's play, "Summer's Lease" dealt with real life ... It told how a typist wanted to become a playwright; how she became successful and fell in love ... how romance ended in tragedy for her

Real life ... the life and death of Winifred Howe.

BRIDEGROOM IN BANDAGES

And the Cause Was His Wedding Suit

WITH his head in bandages a bridegroom defied hospital doctors and went to St. John's Church, Bromley-road, Bromley, Kent, for his marriage during the week-end.

And the cause of the bandages was his wedding suit.

Harold Mason, twenty-six-year-old van driver, of Napier-street, Bromley, was cycling home in haste with the wedding suit he had just collected from his tailor, when the string of the parcel broke. Paper and suit became entangled in the bicycle wheels and Harold Mason turned a double somersault.

Meanwhile at church people waited. At last a telephone message from Bromley Hospital explained the delay.

The best man went off by car. Back came the bridegroom—*without his wedding suit.*

Despite his injuries the service went on.

Wapping Fire Serial

Escape from Rubber Fumes

"May go on burning for another week," is an expert's opinion on the fire at Colonial Wharf, Wapping. There is now little fear that it will spread, but there is still a danger of walls collapsing owing to the steady stream of water that has been pouring on the building for days.

The smell of burning rubber is still a source of irritation over a considerable area around, and many families have taken temporary accommodation elsewhere.

Another instalment to-morrow.

THE DAILY MIRROR, Tuesday, October 1, 1935.

Daily Mirror

THE DAILY PICTURE NEWSPAPER WITH THE LARGEST NET SALE

Broadcasting - Page 22

EUSTACE - - - - - - Page 10
QUIET CORNER - - - - Page 16
THE STARS SAY - - - Page 18
DOCTOR'S DIARY - - - Page 19
BELINDA - - - - - - Page 26
GARBO FILM SERIAL - Page 27

No. 9,934   Registered at the G.P.O as a Newspaper.   TUESDAY, OCTOBER 1, 1935   One Penny

Amusements: Page 18

8 ROYAL BRIDESMAIDS CHOSEN

Lower left: Miss Claire Phipps, who is fourteen. Left to right: Miss Ann Hawkins, aged seven; Lady Mary Cambridge, who is eleven; Lady Angela Scott, Lady Alice's younger sister; Miss Moyra Eileen Scott, aged sixteen; and Lady Elizabeth Scott, who is thirteen.

Princesses Among 7 Children

SEVEN of the eight bridesmaids who will attend Lady Alice Montagu-Douglas-Scott at her wedding to the Duke of Gloucester in Westminster Abbey on November 6 will be under the age of seventeen.

The bridesmaids, it was announced last night, will be:—

Princess Elizabeth
Princess Margaret Rose
Lady Mary Cambridge
Lady Elizabeth Scott
Lady Angela Scott
Miss Moyra Eileen Scott
Miss Ann Hawkins and
Miss Claire Phipps.

Golden headdresses will complete the all-British dresses of these bridesmaids. Their frocks are being made to harmonise with the Abbey tone colours.

Their designer, Mr. Norman Hartnell, in order to produce the effect he wants has been allowed to view various materials in the Abbey both in daylight and artificial light.

Both the designs for the bridesmaids' dresses and for that of the bride were approved by the Queen before she left Balmoral.

The bridal gown will be of satin; for the honeymoon exclusive Scottish tweeds are being made.

Ambition Fulfilled

The order for the dresses fulfils the life-long ambition of a young Cambridge student.

When Norman Hartnell, at the age of twenty-one, came down from Cambridge and told his friends he would take up dress designing as his profession he was laughed at.

Yet within a few years Norman Hartnell was able to open the most luxurious dress salon in London.

It was there on Saturday that slim, good-looking Lady Alice talked for an hour to Norman Hartnell and told him what she wanted.

Four hundred girls employed in the showrooms were on tip-toe with excitement when news spread that the Duke of Gloucester's bride-to-be was in the salon.

"I hope I'll be chosen to sew her dress," is the wish of everyone of those 400 girls.

Secretary Appointed

Miss Sibil Pimblett, daughter of Dr. W. H. Pimblett and Mrs. A. M. Pimblett, of Preston, has been appointed secretary to Lady Alice to help her in the pre-wedding rush of correspondence.

Miss Pimblett, who graduated at Oxford, was secretary for five years to Viscountess Falmouth. Last year she acted as Mayoress of Preston, when her mother was mayor.

WHO'S WHO OF THE BRIDESMAIDS

Princess Elizabeth and Princess Margaret Rose, daughters of the Duke and Duchess of York.
Lady Angela Scott: Lady Alice's youngest sister.
Miss Moyra Eileen Scott: Aged sixteen, daughter of Lord Francis George Scott, and a niece of Lady Alice.
Lady Mary Cambridge: Aged eleven, daughter of the Marquis of Cambridge, who is a nephew of the Queen.
Miss Ann Hawkins: Aged seven, a niece of Lady Alice, and daughter of Lady Margaret Hawkins, who married Commander Geoffrey Alan Brooke Hawkins. Lady Margaret is the Duke of Buccleuch's eldest daughter.
Miss Claire Phipps: Aged fourteen, a cousin of Miss Ann Hawkins. Her mother is Lady Sybil Phipps, sister of Lady Margaret.
Lady Elizabeth Scott: Aged thirteen, a niece of Lady Alice, and daughter of the Earl of Dalkeith.

Princess Elizabeth and Princess Margaret Rose, the two daughters of the Duke and Duchess of York. The elder is nine, the younger five. Left: Lady Alice, wearing the new shaped beret when she went shopping in London yesterday.

JOE LOUIS AT CHURCH—AND THE PEOPLE SAID "AMEN"

DETROIT, Monday.

JOE Louis and his bride and about 2,000 other people went to church in the Calvary Baptist Chapel. Five thousand others stood outside.

Joe and Mrs. Joe stood near the pulpit. He had his arm round his bride. They were presented with a bouquet on which was a ribbon bearing the words, in golden letters, "Welcome home." The congregation showed its approval of the boxer by whistling and stamping.

But the great moment came when Pastor James Martin shook the boxer by the hand and shouted, "You're doing more to help our race than anybody since Lincoln."

"Amen to that, brother," roared the congregation.

"He don't smoke," went on the preacher.

"Amen," replied the crowd.

"He don't pour red-hot liquor down his throat," was the next call of the pastor.

"No, sir, amen to that," said the congregation.

The preacher: "He fights clean and he shall stand before Kings."

The crowd: "Amen to all that." B.U.P.

NO 'YES' FROM JOAN

"I CAN'T get Miss Crawford to say 'Yes.' I've proposed so many times I can't remember the number."

In these words Franchot Tone, film actor, told of his failure to persuade Joan Crawford to marry him, when he returned to New York yesterday from California.—B.U.P.

THE DAILY MIRROR, Thursday, October 3, 1935.

Daily Mirror

THE DAILY PICTURE NEWSPAPER WITH THE LARGEST NET SALE

Broadcasting - Page 22

EUSTACE .... Page 10
QUIET CORNER .... Page 16
THE STARS SAY .... Page 18
DOCTOR'S DIARY ... Page 19
BELINDA .... Page 26
GARBO FILM SERIAL - Page 21

No. 9,936 Registered at the G.P.O. as a Newspaper. THURSDAY, OCTOBER 3, 1935 One Penny

Amusements: Page 18

ABYSSINIA FIGHT
Many Dead in Clash with Invaders

50,000 ITALIANS OVER BORDER—EMPEROR WIRES LEAGUE

FIGHTING broke out yesterday in Abyssinia, when Italian and Abyssinian troops clashed in the northernmost part of the country, just over the Eritrea border, which is undemarcated.

Fifty thousand Italian troops, divided into three columns, crossed the border. They were equipped with fifty aeroplanes, tanks and machine-guns.

The "Daily Mirror" correspondent telegraphs that they were met by a Danakil war tribe and fighting took place.

Many are reported dead.

The Crown Prince of Ethiopia, with his army, is moving forward to harass the invaders.

The Crown Prince is Commander-in-Chief of the Ethiopian forces at Dessye.

His troops are the nearest Abyssinian force to the Italian advance —roughly Dessye is 160 miles away from the border.

EMPEROR'S TELEGRAM TO LEAGUE

The Emperor of Abyssinia has telegraphed the League of Nations, protesting against the Italian advance, and asking for League observers to be sent.

The Italians, says the Negus's telegram, are establishing a base in Ethiopian territory with the object of organising a big attack.

The Emperor's telegram has been circulated to all League Council members as a "matter of urgency."

CONSULS LEAVING

The Italian Legation in Addis Ababa was last evening, says Reuter, burning documents and papers in the Legation garden, and its archives have been sent to the railway station.

The Legation is preparing for a sudden departure during the weekend.

Italian Consuls are making all speed from the interior to Addis Ababa.

The Italian Consul at Adowa (scene of the Abyssinian rout of Italians years ago) disappeared yesterday from his headquarters, leaving no trace of his whereabouts. It is believed, says the B.U.P., that he has crossed the frontier into Eritrea.

Nearly 3,000 more Italian troops left Naples for Abyssinia yesterday in the steamer Umbria. The Duke of Bergamo, cousin of the King of Italy, arrived at Port Said yesterday on his way to take up his position on the General Staff in Abyssinia.

GENERAL MOBILISATION

General mobilisation is to be proclaimed in Abyssinia to-day; and chieftains have been warned to prepare to march "at a moment's notice."

The spot where the Italians have advanced is close to the frontier of French Somaliland, and the French have constructed a fence, painted red, to warn Italians of their territory.

Meanwhile, in Italy general mobilisation, long awaited, took place yesterday. At a signal 10,000,000 Italians stopped work and donned uniforms—see page 3.

King Victor Emmanuel of Italy and the Emperor of Ethiopia together in Rome. Taken about ten years ago when the Emperor, who was only crowned in 1928, was still Ras Tafari, the photograph is of special interest in view of the present situation.

MUSSOLINI'S DEFIANCE

MUSSOLINI, in a great speech to 100,000 Italians outside his office in Rome last night, coinciding with the test mobilisation of the nation, said he did not believe that Britain and France will apply sanctions against Italy.

Contrary to general expectations in Rome, he did not announce the start of hostilities.

"At Geneva they are talking sanctions," he said, according to Reuter, "but I refuse to believe that France, with her memories of the Italian dead of the Great War will agree to take part in them.

"I refuse to believe that a genuine British people will associate themselves with sanctions in defence of a barbarous nation.

"Nevertheless, we must not pretend to be ignorant of the possibility of sanctions.

"To sanctions of an economic character we shall reply with discipline and spirit.

"To measures of a military character we shall reply with military measures. To acts of war we shall reply with acts of war.

"We shall do everything possible to ensure that a colonial conflict shall not assume the range of a European conflict."

"To Your Feet, Italy!"

"We have tolerated the provocations of Abyssinia for forty years, and the time has come to put an end to them."

Mussolini closed his speech with a passionate appeal to Italians.

"Italy, Italy, Italy of Vittorio Veneto and of the Fascist revolution," he cried, "to your feet!

"Let your cries and the affirmation of your unshakable devotion reach our soldiers in East Africa and bring them comfort and assurance."

The speech was relayed all over Italy.

Immediately after the Duce concluded his speech Signor Starace, secretary of the Fascist party, called for cheers for Mussolini, and then announced that the mobilisation was over.

Wincing on his stretcher as he listened to witness, Busby Berkeley, famous Hollywood dance director, was charged at West Los Angeles with alleged manslaughter arising out of three-car smash.

Asfau Uossen Tafari, the Crown Prince of Ethiopia, who is leading a column from Dessye against the Italians, who have advanced to Mount Mussa Ali. He is nineteen years old.

Cabinet Holds Two Meetings

TWO meetings of the Cabinet were held at 10, Downing-street yesterday, and the result, states a political correspondent, is that

The British Government will remain firm in its policy towards the League.

At the second meeting the heads of all the three departments of defence were present.

They were: Lord Halifax (War Minister), Sir Philip Cunliffe-Lister (Air Minister) and Sir Bolton Eyres-Monsell, First Lord of Admiralty.

Before the first of the meetings Sir Samuel Hoare, Foreign Minister, saw the King at the Palace, and remained for some time.

Tension in Egypt.—Sir Miles Lampson, the British High Commissioner in Egypt, unexpectedly flew to Alexandria yesterday, and on arrival was immediately received by the King of Egypt.

THE DAILY MIRROR, Tuesday, October 8, 1935

Broadcasting - Page 22

Daily Mirror
THE DAILY PICTURE NEWSPAPER WITH THE LARGEST NET SALE

EUSTACE .... Page 8
QUIET CORNER .... Page 17
THE STARS SAY .... Page 18
DOCTOR'S DIARY ... Page 19
GARBO FILM SERIAL - Page 21
BELINDA .... Page 26

No. 9,940 Registered at the G.P.O. as a Newspaper. TUESDAY, OCTOBER 8, 1935 One Penny

Amusements: Page 18

BIG 13 VOTE FOR SANCTIONS

League Nations in "State of War" with Italy

GENEVA, Monday.

Thirteen nations—including Britain—by their votes at Geneva this evening automatically admitted that a "state of war" exists between themselves and Italy, according to the strictest interpretation of the Covenant. That is the general opinion here.

THESE nations are the competent members of the League Council—the votes of the two disputants were excluded —who expressed their approval of the report of the Committee of Six indicting Italy for a breach of the Covenant.

The thirteen nations who thus bound themselves to the application of financial and economic sanctions against Italy were:

BRITAIN   PORTUGAL
RUMANIA   SOVIET RUSSIA
CHILE   POLAND
ECUADOR   TURKEY
AUSTRALIA   FRANCE
ARGENTINE   SPAIN
        DENMARK

A spokesman of the League emphasised that the Council as such did not approve the report, but that each member had expressed agreement with it.

Many delegates favour restricting sanctions to a promise not to buy from Italy, thus gradually depriving her of foreign exchange and preventing her eventually being able to purchase raw materials for war.

At the private meeting of the Council in the afternoon Baron Aloisi, the Italian delegate, demanded that the public discussion on the "Big Six's" report should be postponed till tomorrow.

Mr. Eden strongly objected and eventually Baron Aloisi's request was unanimously overruled by the Council sitting in secret.

After the roll-call on the question of accepting the report Baron Aloisi declared:

"While making the fullest reservations re-
(Continued on back page)

WATCHING THEIR BOY CROWN PRINCE COME OUT OF SCHOOL

As Crown Prince Baudouin of Belgium left the Brussels school where he has resumed his gymnasium lessons, excited children from a neighbouring establishment crowded round eager to catch a glimpse of the five-year-old Heir-Apparent. This special picture is the first of Prince Baudouin since the terrible accident of last August which robbed him of his mother, Queen Astrid.

On All Fronts

IN ABYSSINIA:
Four hundred thousand warriors are marching against the invaders; Jean Alloucherie, *Daily Mirror* Special Correspondent in Addis Ababa, tells how a great double attack is being planned.
—Page Three.

* * *

IN FRANCE:
Government says "Yes" to Britain's query: "Should League Powers stand together if attack is made on one of them?"
—Page Four.

* * *

IN ENGLAND:
"Should Britain bargain with Mussolini?" people are asking. The *Daily Mirror's* exclusive interview with Il Duce, published yesterday, set them asking it. To-day famous people give their answers.
—Page Four.

The Unloaded Revolver

EARLY to-day the following statement was issued from the Ethiopian Legation in London on behalf of Liz Yosef Warqueh-Martin and Liz Benian Warqueh-Martin, sons of the Ethiopian Minister in London:—

"Many kind offers of services reach the Legation every day.

"It is our intention to reply personally to every single letter at the earliest moment, but in the meantime we are anxious to re-emphasise that, notwithstanding our very great gratitude to the writers, it is quite impossible for us to accept their generous and unselfish efforts to join the ranks of the glorious men who are offering their lives on the altar of world peace.

"We want to take this opportunity of thanking sympathisers. Our hearts go out to them. For instance, to the one who, for obvious reasons, must remain unnamed, and who, only three days ago, sent us an unloaded revolver with his apologies for not including ammunition.

"And to the hundreds of poor women who have sent us their savings, so small in some instances that they reach us in the form of postage stamps. Christianity has not failed.

PALACE AS DUKE'S LONDON HOME

BY A SPECIAL CORRESPONDENT

The Duke of Gloucester and Lady Alice Scott, after their marriage at Westminster Abbey on November 6, and their subsequent honeymoon, will probably make their home, when in London, at Buckingham Palace—at any rate, for a time.

This decision has been reached because they have been unable to find a house in the West End to meet their requirements.

I am told that when over a dozen houses in Mayfair and Belgravia had been examined without success, the Queen helped the couple in their search, and looked at several more, which she described to her son and his bride.

But with only a month to go before the wedding, the Duke decided to ask permission of the King to retain his own suite in Buckingham Palace for the use of himself and his bride as their town home.

This was readily given.

Mothers' Panic in Fire Disaster

CHICAGO, Monday Night.

AT least seven people were burnt to death when, following an explosion, flames swept the factory of the Glidden Soya Products Company here to-day.

Many others were trapped in the burning building, and four people are still missing, while thirty others were injured and taken to hospital. Immediately after the explosion a blinding sheet of flame enveloped the whole factory and devoured the walls as if they were made of paper.

An indescribable scene of confusion followed. Panic-stricken mothers raced screaming through the streets, crying out the names of their sons and daughters employed in the factory, their cries mingling with the moans of the injured.—Reuter.

Jean Alloucherie, our special correspondent in Addis Ababa, with his escort of Ethiopian soldiers. His latest dispatch is on page 3.

Daily Mirror

THE DAILY PICTURE NEWSPAPER WITH THE LARGEST NET SALE

Broadcasting - Page 22

EUSTACE . . . . Page 8
QUIET CORNER . . . . Page 17
THE STARS SAY . . . . Page 18
DOCTOR'S DIARY . . . Page 19
GARBO FILM SERIAL - Page 21
BELINDA . . . . Page 26

No. 9,941   Registered at the G.P.O. as a Newspaper.   WEDNESDAY, OCTOBER 9, 1935   One Penny

Amusements : Page 18

A BOY FOR MARINA

Prince Born at 2.5 a.m.

BOTH ARE WELL

The "Daily Mirror" has great pleasure in announcing that the Duchess of Kent gave birth to a son at her London home, 3, Belgrave-square, at 2.5 this morning.

MOTHER and child are both doing well.

Immediately afterwards news of the birth of the new Prince was conveyed by telephone to Sandringham, where the King and Queen are in residence.

The new Prince ranks seventh in succession to the Throne.

The Duchess's doctors, Mr. W. Gilliatt and Mr. A. E. Gow, were summoned to Belgrave-square late last night.

Few people among the passers-by guessed what was going on behind the drawn yellow blinds of No. 3.

Outside two closed dark limousines and a low-built sports car stood waiting.

Prince and Princess Nicolas of Greece, who came to London at the end of last week, were called to their daughter's side from the West End hotel where they are staying.

Countess Toerring, who has been staying with her sister for the past few weeks, was also in the house.

SIR J. SIMON CALLED

The Duchess of Kent only returned to her London home nine days ago, when she motored up from Chichester with the Duke of Kent.

They had been staying at Adsdean, the home of Lord Louis Mountbatten.

On Sunday the King called at No. 3 for tea.

The Duke of Gloucester and his fiancee, Lady Alice Scott, and the Princess Royal also heard the news at Sandringham, and the Prince of Wales and other members of the Royal Family were also informed.

The Duke of Kent had waited up through the small hours with his father-in-law and mother-in-law. Within a few moments of the birth of his son he was told the good news.

The Home Secretary, Sir John Simon, was called to Belgrave-square just after the doctors had arrived last night.

In accordance with the constitutional procedure, he had to be present as Home Secretary at the birth of a royal baby.

The two nurses, Nurse Louie Roberts, of Wilmslow, and Miss Ethel Smith, who came to England recently from Yugoslavia, were both in attendance.

(Continued on back page)

THE DUKE AND DUCHESS OF KENT

Daily Mirror

THE DAILY PICTURE NEWSPAPER WITH THE LARGEST NET SALE

Broadcasting - Page 22

EUSTACE — Page 10
QUIET CORNER — Page 17
DOCTOR'S DIARY — Page 19
SERIAL — Page 21
THE STARS SAY — Page 24
BELINDA — Page 26

No. 9,951 Registered at the G.P.O as a Newspaper. MONDAY, OCTOBER 21, 1935 One Penny

Amusements: Pages 18, 26 & 27

2 BRITISH SHIPS LOST IN GALE

Fears for Crew of 37—2 a.m. Radio

Mr. Henry Lothian, wireless operator of the Vardulia.

Gale in mid-Atlantic illustrating conditions described by Manchester Producer's captain in radio to the "Daily Mirror" telling of his search at last position of Vardulia early to-day. "Very improbable that crew succeeded in launching boats in the mountainous sea," ends his message.

Two British ships were lost yesterday in a gale which raged twenty-four hours. Fears for the crew of one, thirty-seven men, were intensified early to-day when the captain of one of the ships searching sent a dramatic 2 a.m. radio to the "Daily Mirror."

HE said that seven ships had been searching the Atlantic 700 miles from the coast of Ireland where the Glasgow steamer Vardulia (5,735 tons) had reported "Abandoning ship."

Then he adds:—
"We have been searching around the last position of Vardulia in a ring, each in different sections.
"At present no trace found. Search continuing.
"It is very improbable that crew succeeded in launching boats in the mountainous sea at the time."

The message came from the Manchester Producer. Among the other ships searching are the Oregon, the Newfoundland, the Blair Angus and the Danish ship Visco.

The other ship lost is the Newcastle freighter Pendennis. She was wrecked in the North Sea fifty miles off the Dutch coast. The crew of twenty-two were saved.

Hope of Rescue

"We are still hopeful that we will receive news of the rescue of the crew," said Mr. George Cooper, secretary to the Vardulia's owners, to the *Daily Mirror* last night.

"The weather has moderated and there is always the possibility that they have been picked up by a fishing trawler which is not equipped with wireless."

The master of the Vardulia is Captain Paterson. One of the crew is Wireless Operator Harry Lothian, aged thirty-three, of Great Western-road, Knightswood, Glasgow, hero of the romantic rescue of the crew of the Exeter City in January, 1931.

Married Seven Months

Lothian was married only seven months ago to Miss Mary Rooke, daughter of Mr. Cecil Bradley Rooke, a solicitor, of High-road, Whetstone.

Mrs. Lothian, who is only twenty, is going through a terrible ordeal while she waits at Whetstone for news of her husband.

Here is the story of how he saved the crew of the Exeter City.

The Exeter City was struck by a gale not many miles away from where Lothian is drifting now with his comrades.

Mountainous seas swept the captain of the Exeter City and three men overboard, and wrecked the wireless set.

Nine Hours' Toil

Lothian, in his wireless cabin, deluged with icy-cold water, toiled nine hours to repair the set.

He wrapped his clothes round the instruments to keep them dry; he rigged up an aerial. Then he sent out the S O S. The American Merchant, a liner, heard it, reached the ship and saved twenty-two.
(Continued on back page)

They Died Yesterday

The Peace Martyr

THE MAN WHO DID NOT KNOW A WAR WAS ON. Yet for years he had been Britain's Peace Martyr. You knew him as Uncle Arthur.—See the Back Page.

THE MAN WHO DEFIED THE KAISER. His name was Lord Sysonby, for twenty years Keeper of the Privy Purse.—See Page Three.

THE MAN WHO ONCE EXPLORED FURTHEST NORTH. At ninety-one he was the Grand Old Man of the North. Britain welcomed him in 1911 as America's representative at King George's coronation. See Page Two.

ITALY'S "VENGEANCE STONE."—General de Bono at the head of troops at Adowa when he unveiled a Roman monument inscribed "The dead of Adowa avenged Oct. 6 1935 XIII" (XIII is the year of the Fascist era). Carried by the Italians during their advance, the monument commemorates their comrades killed in the Adowa disaster of 1896. This picture, taken by our special correspondent with the Italian forces, was flown to Rome and telegraphed to London.

Germany Officially Quits the League To-day

FROM OUR SPECIAL CORRESPONDENT
BERLIN, Sunday.

TO-MORROW Germany officially ends her ties with the League of Nations. She has had enough of war!

Throughout the country the general feeling is that if the rest of Europe were to become involved in war, Germany would remain neutral.

Here I have seen an interesting wall map of Abyssinia and the surrounding regions. The map has been printed and issued in Italy.

One of the features is that the boundary lines between the French and English possessions and Abyssinia are clearly marked. The line is three-quarters of an inch thick.

But between Italian Somaliland and Eritrea and Abyssinia no boundaries are marked.

The map, in fact, shows the whole of Abyssinia geographically treated as part of the Italian possessions in North Africa.

THEY CALL HIM DAN!

THERE is a negro in Houston (Texas) whose full name is:
Daniel's Wisdom May I Know Stephen's Faith And Spirit Choose John's Divine Communion Seal Moses's Weakness Joshua's Zeal Win The Day and Conquer All MURPHY.

His friends call him "Dan."

THE DAILY MIRROR, Tuesday, October 22, 1935

Daily Mirror

THE DAILY PICTURE NEWSPAPER WITH THE LARGEST NET SALE

Broadcasting—Page 22

EUSTACE .... Page 10
QUIET CORNER ... Page 17
DOCTOR'S DIARY .. Page 19
SERIAL .... Page 21
THE STARS SAY ... Page 24
BELINDA .... Page 26

No. 9,952 Registered at the G.P.O. as a Newspaper. TUESDAY, OCTOBER 22, 1935 One Penny

Amusements: Page 18

COMPELLED TO HAVE DRIVING TEST FOR A LAWN ROLLER!

Even though he only drives a motor lawn-roller, Mr. Charles Hester, groundsman at Beaumont College, Old Windsor, had to have a driving test! The authorities insisted, because they discovered that he has to drive his roller fifty yards along a road to the football fields. Here are the boys watching him undergo his test. "I think I've passed," he said.

'DIVORCE RIVALS AIR PERIL'

More Danger to Nation— Says Canon

"Increase of adultery and the breaking of marriage vows are of far greater danger to our national safety than bombing from the air."

SO said Canon S. Bickersteth, Vice-Dean of Canterbury, at the Diocesan Conference yesterday. The discussion was on "The Church and Marriage."

The Bishop of Salisbury, Dr. St. Clair Donaldson, chairman of the Joint Committee of the Convocations of Canterbury and York, which has investigated the subject, said:

The Church had the right to discipline its members, and by withholding the Communion from divorcees for a time it should work towards that object. If they claimed the right to deal with their own people in this matter, they must have an understanding with the State and must have freedom.

It is one of the most serious problems of the present time. A lead from the Church was definitely overdue.

"Collusion and Perjury"

The ever-increasing rate of divorce was revolting against their consciences and commonsense.

More people were becoming determined to get rid of their partners and were evading the law by collusion and perjury—and that, forsooth, was being called "behaving like a gentleman."

The Church had to see to it that later marriages of people who re-married while their first partners were still living did not take place in churches. The marriage service must not be used for such ceremonies.

The Hon. Mrs. Hardcastle, president of the Diocesan Mothers' Union, asked whether something more than one act of misconduct proved by "one scrap of paper" could not be required

(Continued on Back Page)

Canon S. Bickersteth, Vice-Dean of Canterbury.

POISON DRAMA IN HOSPITAL

Husband Dies, Young Wife Collapses

A FEW minutes after her husband, suffering from an advanced form of tuberculosis, died suddenly from irritant poisoning in East Ham Memorial Hospital yesterday, a twenty-two-year-old wife, who had been visiting him, collapsed in a corridor of the hospital.

She was found to be suffering from a form of poisoning, and is detained in a critical condition.

The man was Michael Stern, B.Sc., twenty-six, of Osborne-road, Forest Gate, E., an analytical chemist at a paint factory, and his wife is Bertha Stern. They had been married two years.

Stern had been a patient in the hospital for several weeks. Yesterday he was given only twenty-four hours to live.

Some time after his wife had gone to visit him, as other visitors were coming into the hospital, Mrs. Stern rushed from the ward where he was lying, and collapsed in the corridor.

While Friend Waited

She was picked up by nurses. Then it was found that the man was unconscious in his bed. Doctors were called to his bedside, but he died a few minutes afterwards, and later it was discovered that death followed some form of irritant poisoning.

A neighbour of the Sterns told the *Daily Mirror* last night that from the day Stern was ordered to hospital Mrs. Stern went to live with her mother in Whitechapel.

"She slept at the house and had breakfast," the neighbour added. "The rest of the day she spent walking about the streets worrying over her husband."

Mr. Stern was educated at Queen Mary's College, Whitechapel, and lived at Stafford-road, Seaford, before moving to Forest Gate on Jubilee Day.

Mr. Michael Stern, the dead man.

Black-Outs for Parties

FROM OUR OWN CORRESPONDENT
MALTA, Monday.

AIR raid drill at Malta has given the Bright Young Things among the English population on the island a great idea.

On nights when a complete black-out was ordered, social activities at first came to a standstill.

Now they are the cheeriest evenings of all —for someone invented a "black-out party," usually a bottle party as well.

The strictly-enforced lights-out order is from nine till ten p.m.

If you are late in arriving, you may blink when the lights are switched on at ten and find yourself in the wrong party.

37 Missing Men
STILL NO TRACE
★ ★

THERE was still no trace last night of the thirty-seven men of the 5,735-ton Glasgow steamer Vardulia, lost in mid-Atlantic.

Donaldson Line, Ltd., owners of the Vardulia, stated last night that "the search for the lifeboats of the Vardulia is being continued in every possible way and we are still hopeful."

AIR THIRD DEGREE
Murderer Confesses

SANTA CRUZ (Argentine), Monday.

VERY up-to-date methods of "Third Degree" have been used by the Argentine police to obtain a confession of the murder of the two Scots, Mr. Thomas Vietch Henderson, of Jedburgh, and Mr. Donald Sutherland, of Edinburgh.

They took the suspected man, Emilio Gustavo Lajus, an hotel-keeper, for a flight in an aeroplane, and then ordered the pilot to do the most daring stunts of which he was capable.

A series of looping-the-loop, falling leaf, high-speed dives and such-like tricks demoralised Lajus's nerve and he said he would confess.

After close questioning, he revealed the details of the murders, and the police recovered 113,000 pesos (about £6,300) of the stolen money, which he had hidden.—B.U.P.

102

THE DAILY MIRROR, Wednesday, October 23, 1935

Daily Mirror

THE DAILY PICTURE NEWSPAPER WITH THE LARGEST NET SALE

Broadcasting - Page 22

EUSTACE .... Page 10
QUIET CORNER ... Page 17
DOCTOR'S DIARY .. Page 19
SERIAL .... Page 21
THE STARS SAY ... Page 24
BELINDA .... Page 26

No. 9,953 Registered at the G.P.O. as a Newspaper.   WEDNESDAY, OCTOBER 23, 1935   One Penny

Amusements : Page 28

CHILD FINDS DRUGS TO KILL 2,000

They Were Toys to His Playmates

FROM OUR SPECIAL CORRESPONDENT
Cardiff, Tuesday.

ONE THOUSAND TUBES—EACH CARRYING DEATH— WERE FOUND ON A REFUSE DUMP HERE TO-DAY

TWO men were walking along Ferry-road, Cardiff, this afternoon, when a small boy ran up to them.

Pointing to a phial in his hand, he asked:—

"If I put this in my mouth will it poison me?"

The men, W. Spear and H. W. Davies, insurance agents, living at Penarth, inquired where he had found it, and were taken to a dump nearby, where a number of children were playing with the phials.

Picking up a number the men took them to a chemist, who analysed them and said they were deadly poisons.

In each of the phials was enough poison to kill two people

Police Hunt in Dump

Going back to the dump the men collected more than 500 phials and then informed the police.

Then began a great hunt for the rest of the poisons.

Police went to the rubbish heap and found several children playing with similar phials. Others were still sorting them from the rubbish.

Detectives took possession of these and found hundreds more in the ground. Nearly 1,000 are now in the hands of the police.

Meanwhile 200 of the tubes were being tested by the police surgeon and his staff.

They were found to contain highly dangerous drugs and poisons in an active state.

"Playing with Death"

They include atrophine, sulphate and egotine, and are of French make.

"Anyone who handles them is literally playing with death," said the Deputy Chief Constable, Superintendent W. H. Harrison, to-night

In addition to the phials the police have recovered a large number of white cubes about an inch square which can easily be mistaken for sweets. These have not yet been completely analysed, but they are stated to be dangerous if eaten or in any way taken internally.

A warning to schools was issued by the police, and this evening teachers and parents brought in a large number of phials which they had taken from children.

Dump Set on Fire

The police fear that some of the children on learning that the police were searching for the phials may have thrown them away.

These may be found by someone who might not be aware of the dangerous contents

As there might still be some of the phials on the dump, the authorities ordered it to be set on fire to-night.

Atrophine is the active principle of belladonna, the juice of deadly nightshade, and though useful medicinally in small doses, it has the power of paralysing the heart and other muscles

'MERCY TRIAL' GIRL'S FAITH

BY A SPECIAL CORRESPONDENT

OUT of a side door of the Old Bailey yesterday there walked twenty - year - old Muriel Welsdon—free.

She had heard, shortly before, a jury say she was not guilty of the murder of her mother—the mother she had been told would never get well.

"No one knows," she said, "what that trial has been to me, though I knew all the time that I should be acquitted. I had faith. It is only when you are in dire trouble like I have been, when the world looks its blackest, and everyone is against you, that you realise the friends there are in this world"

"The Future"

Miss Welsdon has no plans for the future

"Something will have to be done," she told me. "My friends are rallying round me, but all I want to do now is to go away and rest forgetting the horrors of the trial

"I would, however, like to say to you so that the world can know that I thank everyone for their kindness and sympathy that has been showered upon me in my blackest hour."

Drama of her acquittal on page 2; counsel's plea and Judge's summing up are on page 9.

Miss Muriel Welsdon walking away after her acquittal at the Old Bailey.

Warship Will Carry Lord Carson Home

VISCOUNT Craigavon, Premier of Northern Ireland, in a broadcast last night, announced that the body of Lord Carson, the Ulster leader, who died yesterday, would be conveyed in one of his Majesty's ships from Liverpool to Belfast for the State funeral there.

Details of the dead leader's life on page 25.

Girl Foils Bandit

BY "FAKING" DEAFNESS

A GIRL shop assistant foiled a bandit who tried to raid a shop in Rectorygrove, Clapham, S.W., last night.

The girl, Lily Claridge, was alone in the shop, which belongs to the Bluebird Laundry Company, when a young man came in and said, "Hand over the till." The girl pretended not to hear, and asked him to repeat it.

While he was doing so she leaned under the counter, and pressed an alarm switch which connects the shop to the main building at the back.

The man immediately ran into the street. Police cars searched the district late last night, but could find no trace of the man

No Military Sanctions
—SEE PAGE 4

Daily Mirror

THE DAILY PICTURE NEWSPAPER WITH THE LARGEST NET SALE

Broadcasting - Page 20

EUSTACE .... Page 8
QUIET CORNER ... Page 14
DOCTOR'S DIARY .. Page 17
SERIAL .... Page 19
THE STARS SAY ... Page 22
BELINDA .... Page 22

No. 9,954 Registered at the G.P.O. as a Newspaper. THURSDAY, OCTOBER 24, 1935 One Penny

Amusements: Page 16

ITALY'S PEACE MOVE

THE QUEEN'S NIECE OPENS NEW FLATS

Lady May Abel Smith taking tea with Mr. and Mrs. Ferrari and their nine children in their new cottage-flat, after she performed the opening ceremony at Wyndham-road, Camberwell. These flats have been erected under a housing scheme organised by the Church Army. Lady May is daughter of the Earl of Athlone, brother of Queen Mary. (See page 5.)

THE KING AND QUEEN CALL ON ROYAL BABY

See Him for the First Time

THE King and Queen visited the Duke and Duchess of Kent yesterday afternoon and saw their infant grandson for the first time.

A small crowd was waiting in Belgrave-square when, shortly before five o'clock, the royal car drew up in front of the Duke and Duchess's house.

The King was wearing a black coat and silk hat, and the Queen was in a brown coat trimmed with fur, and toque to match.

Their Majesties were met by the Duke of Kent, who himself conducted them to the nursery, where they saw the baby Prince.

After seeing the Duchess, the King and Queen remained to tea.

Lord Trenchard's Greeting

A few hours previously the King and Queen had returned to London after a two weeks' stay at Sandringham.

They were greeted at King's Cross by Lord Trenchard. It was probably his last appearance on such an occasion as Commissioner of the Metropolitan Police, as he retires next month.

Liquid ★ ★ Fire

LIQUID fire experts were among troops who sailed yesterday from Naples for Mogadiscio, the port in Italian Somaliland, reports the B.U.P.

Abyssinia's Emperor, Haile Selassie I, is to leave Addis Ababa and join his troops in the field, thus following the custom of his predecessors who led their forces in battle against their enemies.

Abyssinian soldiers returning to Addis Ababa from the Ogaden front report that 400 Italians have been massacred in an ambush near Wal Wal.

An Italian column on the march passed three Abyssinian machine-guns camouflaged in pits which were invisible among the waste of scrub and rocks. The gunners withheld their fire until the column was directly opposite them, and then opened from both sides of the road.

Knight, Injured in Air Crash, Walks Out of Hospital

INJURED in an aeroplane crash at Great Barrow, near Chester, to-night, Sir Derwent Hall Caine walked out of the Chester Royal Infirmary though he had been told not to leave, hired a car, drove to Liverpool and addressed a political meeting.

This is his own story of his adventures:—

"I was flying from London to Liverpool alone in my Leopard Moth when I lost my bearings. I made a perfect landing in a field to get my bearings.

"I found from some farm labourers that I was at Great Barrow. I took off again and had risen about 20ft. when I crashed.

"I collapsed, and cannot remember anything more till I woke up in a private ward in Chester Royal Infirmary.

"I was covered with bruises. There were stitches in a head wound. I said that I must leave as I had a National Labour Party meeting to attend in Liverpool.

"The doctor laughed and told me not to be ridiculous—so when nobody was in the room I dressed and disappeared."

Fewer Troops in Libya

PLEASING BRITAIN

MUSSOLINI has made a peace gesture to Britain.

Sir Eric Drummond, British Ambassador in Rome, has been officially notified that the Italian Government have given orders for the withdrawal of one division of troops from Libya, an Italian colony on the western frontier of Egypt.

Information from Rome that Italy had asked for the postponement of the enforcement of sanctions in return was later denied.

It was stated that Mussolini's gesture was prompted solely by the improvement in the relations between Britain and Italy.

Official circles in London maintained a reserved attitude last night concerning the announcement.

The British response to the Italian gesture has not yet been decided, but it was pointed out that Italy still has two extra divisions in Libya.

M. Laval, the French Premier, announcing the Italian decision to the Foreign Affairs Committee of the French Chamber yesterday, said he did so with Mussolini's permission.

The French Premier stated that Mussolini indicated that he wished to make a "gesture" in response to the conciliatory efforts of France as well as to co-operate with Britain in relaxing the tension in the Mediterranean.

Paris understands that Britain will now withdraw some of her naval reinforcements in the Mediterranean.

The original intention, it is believed, was to withdraw ships totalling 75,000 tons in exchange for the withdrawal of all the Italian reinforcements in Libya.

The concentration of Italian troops in Libya was one of the reasons given by the British Government for refusing a recent suggestion by France that the reduction of British naval strength in the Mediterranean would be an aid to peace plans.

Holding Up the War?

An Italian Government spokesman last night stated that the first signs that the tension was being relaxed had emerged from the conversations between Britain, France and Italy.

The spokesman added, however, that there could be no real grounds for optimism until the machinery of sanctions had been stopped.

Concerning sanctions, it is reported that Mussolini is considering whether he should make new proposals which might have the effect of postponing the proposed trade sanctions.

Some observers in Rome believe that he is postponing the proposed southward "push" of the Italian forces in North Abyssinia pending the result of diplomatic exchanges.

Messages from Reuter and B.U.P.

Mr Baldwin's Arms Warning—page 3

NOT GUILTY...

"THE public cannot be too frequently reminded that a verdict of Not guilty means one thing and one thing only—that the jury were not satisfied that the guilt of the accused man was proved. That is a very different thing from finding that the accused man is innocent."—*Mr. Justice Talbot, in the King's Bench Division yesterday.*

Daily Mirror

THE DAILY PICTURE NEWSPAPER WITH THE LARGEST NET SALE

Broadcasting - Page 22

EUSTACE ------ Page 10
QUIET CORNER --- Page 16
DOCTOR'S DIARY -- Page 19
SERIAL ------- Page 21
BELINDA ------ Page 26
THE STARS SAY --- Page 28

No. 9,959 Registered at the G.P.O. as a Newspaper. WEDNESDAY, OCTOBER 30, 1935 One Penny

Amusements: Page 18

TWO ATTACKS ON WOMEN

One Bound and Gagged on Green

POLICE were this morning searching for two men following attacks on women late last night.

In the first case a young woman was found bound and gagged on a lonely part of Weston Green, Thames Ditton.

She was Mrs. Marjorie Stapley, aged thirty, of Lower Green-road, Thames Ditton. After treatment at a house near the spot where she was found, she was able to return home.

The spot at which Mrs. Stapley was attacked is only a few yards from the main road, which at this point is very dark. Mrs. Stapley's cries were not heard by anyone living in the neighbourhood.

She was found lying by the roadside by the wife of Mr. Albert Wright, of Wolsey-road, Esher, who went and fetched her husband from their home nearby.

Together they carried the bound woman to a house nearby and summoned the police.

Mrs. Stapley was able to give a description of her alleged assailant.

Cordon of Police

Metropolitan police officers from Molesey Station were rushed to the spot and the co-operation of the Surrey Constabulary, whose boundaries are a short distance away, was sought.

A cordon was thrown round the district and the hunt for the man began. Officers on foot, in cars, and on cycles made an intensive search of the countryside.

In the second case, a maid-companion, Miss Nellie Swingles was attacked in the house of Mr. and Mrs. F. W. D. Deverell, of Pevensey, Frome-road, Bath.

Mr. and Mrs. Deverell were away in Bath last night.

Miss Swingles was alone in the house when a man called and asked for money for a night's lodgings.

Driven Off by Dog

When she refused to help him he forced his way into the house and going upstairs began to open a number of drawers.

He heard Miss Swingles telephoning to the police, returned and attacked her, striking her several times on the head with an electric torch.

There was a struggle but a terrier dog which was in the house with Miss Swingles, turned on the man and drove him from the house.

When the police arrived Miss Swingles was semi-conscious, suffering from severe bruising of the forehead. She had to receive medical attention.

Nothing, apparently, was taken by the man, of whom Miss Swingles was able to give a fairly full description.

The police at once began a widespread search in co-operation with the Somersetshire police, adjoining whose district the house is situated.

LAST NIGHT'S ROYAL VARIETY SHOW

The audience standing for the National Anthem as the King and Queen and the Duchess of York entered the royal box for the fifteenth Royal Variety Performance in aid of the Variety Artistes' Benevolent Fund and Institution, held at the London Palladium last night.

£110,000 Bets at Stake To-day

FRONT rank candidates for to-day's Cambridgeshire were backed to win £110,000 at last night's final call-over.

There has been more betting on it than on any race within living memory.

Twenty-nine of the forty "probables" were supported. The handicap is so open that even the professional backers are puzzled. Most of them prefer Finalist, Pegasus and Law Court.

SON-IN-LAW OF SIR JAMES DUNN SHOT DEAD

Mrs. Jenkinson

MR. Anthony Jenkinson, aged thirty, son-in-law of Sir James Dunn, the Canadian financier, was found dead in his bedroom at Tite-street, Chelsea, yesterday afternoon with a wound in the head and a sporting gun by his side.

A manservant heard the sound of the shot, rushed upstairs, and found Mr. Jenkinson dying.

The servant ran across the road to the Victoria Hospital for Children, which is immediately opposite Mr. Jenkinson's house. Doctor Bramwell Jones, resident medical officer, went to the house, but on arrival found Mr. Jenkinson was dead.

In Ill-Health

Mr. Philip Dunn, brother-in-law of the dead man, said to the *Daily Mirror* last night:—

"Anthony had not been his usual cheerful self lately. He was evidently suffering from ill-health. I had asked him recently if he was in any trouble, but he had declined to answer."

No letters were left behind by the dead man. He is survived by a widow and a child.

Mrs. Jenkinson, weeping bitterly, left the house at midnight supported by her two sisters, and was driven to their West End home.

Mr. Jenkinson was a son of the late Lieutenant-Colonel George Seymour Charles Jenkinson, a relative of Sir Anthony Jenkinson, of Hawkesbury. His mother, by her second marriage, is Lady Frederick, wife of Sir Charles Edward St. John Frederick, of Lamport Grange, Northants.

Sir J. Dunn on Way to U.S.

Mr. Jenkinson was married in 1930 to Mrs. Hubert J. Duggan, the former wife of Mr. Hubert Duggan.

Before her marriage to Mr. Duggan, Mrs. Jenkinson was Miss Joan Dunn, a daughter of Sir James and Lady Gertrude Dunn.

Mr. Jenkinson, who was in the City, was a brother of Mr. Bobby Jenkinson, who married a daughter of Lady Harcourt.

Sir James Dunn, who lives in Half Moon-street, W., left on Friday for America

THE DAILY MIRROR, Thursday, October 31, 1935.

Daily Mirror
THE DAILY PICTURE NEWSPAPER WITH THE LARGEST NET SALE

Broadcasting - Page 22

THE STARS SAY --- Page 10
EUSTACE ------ Page 10
QUIET CORNER --- Page 16
DOCTOR'S DIARY -- Page 19
SERIAL ------- Page 21
BELINDA ------ Page 26

No. 9,960 Registered at the G.P.O. as a Newspaper. THURSDAY, OCTOBER 31, 1935 One Penny

Amusements: Page 24

AN OPEN-AIR ROYAL HONEYMOON

In Famous Hunting Country

BY A SPECIAL CORRESPONDENT

THE Duke of Gloucester and Lady Alice Scott are to have an open-air honeymoon.

During the period of just over three weeks which remain after the wedding at Buckingham Palace on November 6 before the Duke's leave from the 10th Royal Hussars, in which he is a major, is finished, he and his bride have planned to spend a hunting and shooting honeymoon.

Immediately after the wedding he and his bride will travel by special train to Boughton House, near Kettering, where they will spend the first fortnight of their honeymoon.

Boughton House is the traditional honeymoon house of the members of the Duke of

£200 Gift

NEARLY £200 has been subscribed by the household staffs at the Duke of Buccleuch's residences for a wedding present for Lady Alice Scott.

The money has been paid into Lady Alice's account with the request that she and the Duke of Gloucester shall choose their own present. The Duke and Lady Alice intend to buy old silver with the money.

Buccleuch's family. The late Duke, Lady Alice's father, spent his honeymoon there as well as her brother, the new Duke.

It is an immense mansion full of art treasures. The Duke of Gloucester and Lady Alice intend to spend a large part of their time hunting.

The mansion is close to the Pytchley, Woodland Pytchley and Fernie Hunts, and hunters and a horse box will be sent up there.

In addition, there are literally miles of rides in the woods in the park in which the Duke and his bride can ride every day unseen by the public.

Visit to Bride's Brother

After a fortnight at Boughton House they will go to Sandringham to stay with the King and Queen. A four-day shoot has been arranged for their visit.

On leaving Sandringham the Duke and Lady Alice plan to stay with Lady Alice's brother, the new Duke of Buccleuch, at Eildon Hall, St. Boswells, in the Lowlands of Scotland.

On December 1 the Duke's leave from his regiment, the 10th Royal Hussars, is ended, and he has already taken the Dower House at Escrick, near York, for a month.

MERLE OBERON HURT

NEW YORK, Wednesday.

MERLE Oberon, the famous English film star, arrived here on board the Berengaria this afternoon with a deep gash in her head due to an accident caused by the rough weather during the Atlantic crossing.

"I was watching the waves on the upper deck," declared Merle, "when down came the window on my head." The great liner was ten hours late in arriving here as the result of the rough trip.—Reuter.

BABY TRIED TO SHAVE!—

Then Had to Go to Hospital

BY A SPECIAL CORRESPONDENT

BLUE-EYED Tony Drewett, aged eighteen months, of Fitzroy-road, Regent's Park, watched his father shaving daily.

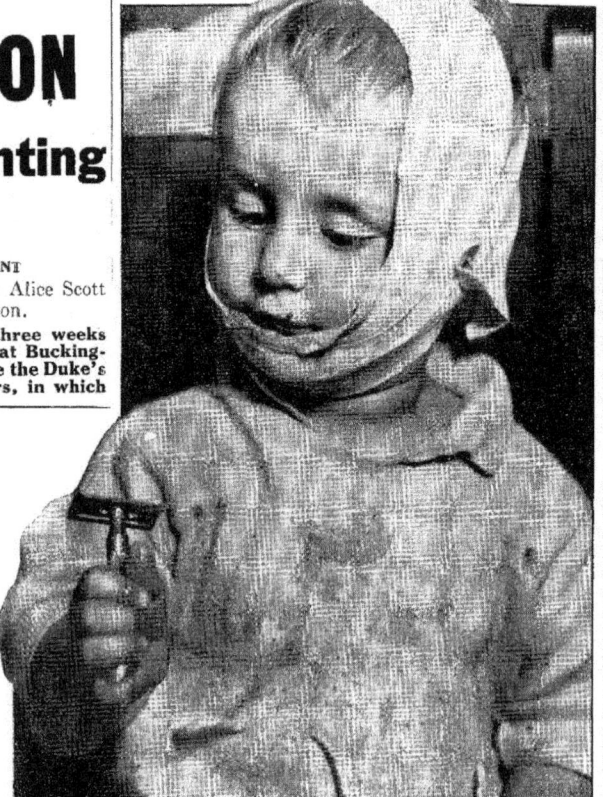

It seemed to fascinate him. His baby eyes followed the movement of the razor with delighted wonder. Tony wanted to be a he-man, too!

Daddy, a waiter, sometimes had to shave in a hurry. Yesterday he threw down his tackle on to a table and rushed out of the house.

Mother, busy with her housework did not notice young Tony clamber on to the table and explore the forbidden implements. Suddenly she saw him with his rosy face well lathered and working busily with the razor clutched in one fat fist!

Mother flew towards him. Too late! Blood was spurting, and Tony, a he-man no longer, yelled.

He was rushed to Hampstead General Hospital.

When I "interviewed" him yesterday Tony, his head almost completely swathed in bandages, had quite recovered from his accident. A he-man once more, he scorned the scars on his chin.

Forgiving Wife's "I Love Him Still"

HUSBAND WHO IS FOR TRIAL ON ABDUCTION CHARGE

A WOMAN who in court yesterday forgave her husband—who was committed for trial at Chatham accused of the abduction of a sixteen-year-old girl—talked to the *Daily Mirror* last night.

She is the wife of Edwin James Brown, of Brompton, Gillingham, Kent. He is forty-eight.

"When I went to court to-day and saw my husband," Mrs. Brown said, "I wanted to tell him I forgive him for any mistakes or misunderstandings between us in the past.

"We have been married twenty-four years, and we have had our ups and downs like every other married couple, but we have pulled together, and he has always treated me like a gentleman. I know he thinks the world of our three children.

"We have always loved one another, and if he will return to me as he has asked to be allowed to do, we can start afresh, putting the past out of our thoughts.

"He wrote to me last Tuesday, telling me he still loved me, and asking me to take him back. I love him, too."

The Browns have three children, a girl of eighteen and two boys, aged seventeen and ten respectively.

Mrs. Brown is living with her family in an apartment.

Surprised Court

In the police court the husband had asked his wife:

"In spite of all I have done, are you willing to forgive me?"

The wife's reply surprised the Court.

"Thinking it over—yes," she said.

And this despite her admission that this year she obtained a separation from him on the ground of persistent cruelty.

"You are a remarkable woman if you do," was the comment of the chairman, Mr. W. H. Thornton.

(Continued on back page)

From Man on Threshold of Eternity... To Girl He Loved

THE *Daily Mirror* is privileged to publish to-day one of the most amazing documents ever written—a last love-letter from a condemned cell, written by a man within a few hours of his execution.

We say "privileged to publish," for though the letter was written by a man convicted of, and executed for, a particularly brutal murder, it is also the letter of a man who, looking into eternity, speaks with a gallant courage and a deep, spiritual knowledge to the girl he loved.... a letter written by a man who had passed through his Gethsemane, and who, purified by the tragedy and horror of the last few weeks of his life, had put all earthly thoughts behind him, and was looking forward with serenity and peace.

Without Fear

Only a few hours separated him from the opening of the door which led to death—yet the handwriting is firm and strong—without fear; his message to his sweetheart one of love and fortitude and hope for the future.

This last letter from Alan James Grierson to Maxine Gann is given in full on page four.

ABYSSINIANS MASSING

REPORTS from the war front state that Italian airmen have discovered Abyssinian warriors massing on the Italian flanks, while Ras Kassa, with 100,000 warriors, is expected to lead a counter-attack from the Makalle area, says B.U.P.

Italy seems on the point of turning against France.

Already Italian women have started organising a national boycott against purchases of French perfumes.

Britain's peace policy—see page 2.

THE DAILY MIRROR, Friday, November 1, 1935

Daily Mirror
THE DAILY PICTURE NEWSPAPER WITH THE LARGEST NET SALE

Broadcasting - Page 22

EUSTACE — Page 10
QUIET CORNER — Page 16
DOCTOR'S DIARY — Page 19
SERIAL — Page 21
BELINDA — Page 26
THE STARS SAY — Page 28

No. 9,961 Registered at the G.P.O as a Newspaper. FRIDAY, NOVEMBER 1, 1935 One Penny

Amusements: Page 24

FRANKENSTEIN TEST IN RAVINE CRIME

Remaking Bodies from 100 Pieces

Prof. Glaister.

BY A SPECIAL REPRESENTATIVE

FRANKENSTEIN tests—in one of the most amazing experiments in the history of criminal investigation—are being carried out in the Moffat ravine murder riddle.

The mutilated bodies of the two women found there are being reconstructed from a hundred fragments in an effort to establish their identity.

Pathological experts are working under the supervision of Professor John Glaister.

Finger-print experts and detectives from Edinburgh C.I.D. have been putting in sixteen hours a day in efforts to solve the mystery.

Never before has science been called upon to play such a part in unravelling a crime riddle.

Twenty-six photographs of each of the 100 parts of the two dismembered bodies have been taken.

Professor J. C. Brash, of the Chair of Anatomy at Edinburgh University, has pursued a new line of inquiry by means of the pantograph, an instrument which is used for copying the outlines of maps, in order to discover the identity of the two heads which have been discovered.

These heads are now being compared by means of the pantograph with photographs of a number of persons who have been reported missing.

By means of the pantograph the features of the heads have been reproduced in outline, and they will be compared with the photographs of the heads of missing persons to see if there are any points of comparison.

FALSE TEETH FITTED

Professor Brash's task has been rendered enormously difficult by the fact that skin and other features have been removed from the heads.

But he is hopeful of arriving at a definite conclusion by taking measurements across certain bony structures in the heads and comparing them with measurements from the photographs of missing persons.

Dental experts under the supervision of Mr. A. C. W. Hutchinson, Dean of the Edinburgh Dental College, have made a set of false teeth which has been fitted into the jaws of the head of what is known as Body No. 2.

The false teeth have been placed in the sockets from which the original teeth had been withdrawn. It has thus been possible to produce an indication of how the mouth appeared during life.

15 FT. SCAFFOLDING

X-Ray experts have also taken photographs to assist in determining the features of the mouths of the two women.

The dismembered body of the young woman found in the ravine has been assembled, and scaffolding 15ft. high has been erected in order that it might be adequately photographed.

Medical and photographic experts are also co-operating in the examination of the human foot which was found on the side of the Glasgow-Carlisle road near Lockerbie.

The foot has been removed to the Crown laboratory in Edinburgh.

Bride To-day on Sixteenth Birthday

BY A SPECIAL CORRESPONDENT

A GIRL who is sixteen to-day will celebrate her birthday by being married at a London register office.

She is Miss Gwendoline Park, of Swan-lane, Leigh, Swindon.

The bridegroom is Mr. George Gordon Perry, a chauffeur, of Colchester-street, Pimlico, S.W. His age was given as thirty-seven in the register office notice.

Miss Perry has been helping her mother since she left school two years ago. When I saw her at home yesterday she was busy preparing for to-day's ceremony.

"I am frightfully happy and looking forward to being a married woman," she said. When told she would probably be the *youngest wife in Britain* she laughingly commented, "I suppose that is a distinction.

"I have known Mr. Perry for nearly a year," she added. "I know he is a lot older than I am, but what does that matter?"

Miss Gwendoline Park, of Swindon, to-day's sixteen-year-old bride.

ONLY SCRATCHED!

AMAZING LEVEL CROSSING ESCAPES

Scratches were the only injuries sustained by the drivers of these cars, wrecked in collision with railway trains.—Clearing away all that was left of the car driven by Mr. John Gardner, son of the licensee of the Bull Hotel, Basildon, after it had been struck by a train on the Tilbury-Pitsea line at a level-crossing near Southend. Mr. Gardner was thrown clear. When the top picture was taken Mr. Conrad P. Ropinski, a cinema operator, was still pinned somewhere in the wreckage of his car at a crossing in Cicero, Chicago. He escaped with a scratched head and chest.

NAZIS KILL 3 ITALIANS

Street Battle Follows War Argument

WARSAW, Thursday.

THREE Italians were killed and two wounded in an amazing street battle with Nazis in Danzig to-day.

An Italian living in Danzig became involved in a heated discussion with Nazis concerning Italy's action in Abyssinia.

Five other Italians from a ship just arrived in Danzig joined in and the argument developed into a fight.

Then the Nazis, it is reported, made offensive references to Mussolini.

That started it. A shot rang out. The battle was on.

The entire neighbourhood went into a panic.

Meanwhile both sides continued firing, and the battle only ended when two of the Italians, whose names are given as Carini and Vadiali, had been shot dead and a third, named Abend, had been mortally wounded.

He was rushed to hospital, but died shortly afterwards.

The Italian Ambassador in Warsaw is sending a special representative to Danzig to investigate the affair.—Central News.

The Church and Hotel Bills

THE Dean of Winchester, Dr. E. G. Selwyn, told Chester Diocesan Conference yesterday that, according to the joint report of the Canterbury and York convocations, the Church did not consider that a marriage should be dissolved unless it had irreparably broken down.

Something more than an hotel bill or mere desertion were needed to prove that a marriage had irreparably broken down.

The Church accepted the ancient principle that conscience must be followed, even if it was wrong, and if divorced persons in the Bishop's opinion remarried in good conscience he might admit them to the Sacrament.

The happiness of a marriage could not depend entirely on the affections.

A resolution affirming belief that in no circumstances could Christian men and women remarry during the lifetime of a wife or husband "without a breach of the principles by which the institution of marriage is governed according to Christ's teaching," was defeated by 98 votes to 58 at Hereford Diocesan Conference yesterday.

Daily Mirror

THE DAILY PICTURE NEWSPAPER WITH THE LARGEST NET SALE

Broadcasting - Page 20

THE STARS SAY --- Page 6
EUSTACE ------ Page 7
QUIET CORNER --- Page 15
DOCTOR'S DIARY -- Page 17
SERIAL ------- Page 19
BELINDA ------ Page 22

No. 9,963 Registered at the G.P.O as a Newspaper. MONDAY, NOVEMBER 4, 1935. One Penny

Amusements : Pages 8 and 24

A KING HEARS HIS FATE

Calm as People Vote for His Return

By A SPECIAL CORRESPONDENT

HOUR after hour through the night a telephone bell rang incessantly in a room at the top of a West End hotel.

Each time it shrilled it brought good news to a guest at the hotel—a king waiting to know the wishes of his people.

For each telephone call told of the sweeping Royalist success in the Greek poll yesterday, and each call brought the return of King George of Greece to his native land still nearer.

While his people were deciding his future, the King remained outwardly calm. But his closest companion, his personal aide-de-camp, was aware that beneath his master's composure there was a deep emotion.

Early to-day these plebiscite figures were telegraphed from Athens:—

> For Monarchy 799,151
> For Republic 12,562

The Government (according to Central News) sent a telegram to the King that the Hellenic people had voted freely and without constraint in favour of his restoration by a 95 per cent. majority.

Beyond an expression of gratitude at the results of the voting the King made no comment.

Dines with Friends

Yesterday morning, King George went for his usual walk, returning to his hotel for lunch. Last night he dined with English friends.

Hour by hour two men in the office at the hotel jubilantly noted down each fresh result that came on the telephone.

They were Major Dimitri Levidis, the King's A.D.C., who has been faithful to his Sovereign through all his troubles, and M. T. N. Petralias, a Greek official in London.

King George is expected to leave England about November 15. He will probably go from London to Paris, then to Florence, where his father, King Constantine, his mother, Sofia, and his grandmother, Queen Olga, are buried. A warship will take him from Italy to Greece.

Eternal Hatred Warning

AN extraordinary broadcast to the United States was made from Asmara last night by Count Ciano, Mussolini's son-in-law, who is leading the Italian Air Force in Eritrea.

"Sanctions, which the League in madness has voted, and is preparing to apply, will be borne with cold determination.

"But sanctions will leave their mark stamped indelibly upon those responsible for them. They will no longer be able to enjoy the citizenship of the civilised world. Against them will be directed the eternal hatred of the Italian people. Our hatred is an unforgiving hatred."—B.U.P.

Big Italian Advance—Page Three.

Briton Is Arrested as Spy

ARRESTED by Italians on the Brenner Pass, Alastair Napier, twenty-one-year-old London law student, is now in prison awaiting a possible charge of espionage.

The Italian authorities allege that Napier crossed the frontier without submitting to the regulation passport examination, and made himself suspicious by talking with Italian soldiers and by taking photographs.

If he is found guilty even of merely crossing the frontier without permission he may be sentenced to imprisonment.

Napier is a son of Mr. Louis Napier, of Fitzjohn's-avenue, Hampstead.

GOING HOME BY RAIL!

"I don't know where the others have got to, but this seems the best way home"—after the opening meet of the Berkeley Hounds at Berkeley, Glos.

"SCIENCE OF SEEING"—

AND SEEING IS BELIEVING BUT—

—this is not a Carnera among painters. It is two men at work on a stand for the "Science of Seeing" exhibition which opens at Charing Cross Underground Station to-day.

BABY FELL DOWN A WELL THIRTY FEET DEEP

But Father Saved Him in Nick of Time

FROM OUR OWN CORRESPONDENT
WELLINGBOROUGH, Sunday.

A TWO-YEAR-OLD baby boy who fell down a well 30ft. deep into 5ft. of water, at Great Doddington, near Wellingborough, Northants, was rescued to-day in the nick of time by his father.

The baby, David Collier, fell into the well, which is at the bottom of the cottage garden. When the child disappeared the father acted with great promptitude.

He slithered down into the well, cutting his elbows and hand, and miraculously avoided the child as he fell into the water beside him.

By standing on tiptoe and holding the baby aloft he was able to keep his face well above the water.

Mr. Collier's cries for help quickly attracted neighbours, and one of them, Thomas Hawkins, lowered the line with a hook attached which is used for hauling up the bucket.

Mr. Collier seized this and held on for more than ten minutes, while another neighbour, Charles Chapman, secured a long ladder.

This was lowered, and Mr. Collier, clutching the baby, clambered up and was helped out exhausted.

The child soon recovered after attention.

WARMEST NOVEMBER

THE warmest November weather ever experienced was recorded in many places in England yesterday. Temperatures of 64deg. were registered at Manchester and London.

They Put Down £200,000

ONE thousand three hundred candidates in the General Election on November 14 will to-day deposit £150 each—putting £200,000 out of circulation.

Forty candidates will know to-night that they are M.P.s. Walk-overs are twenty-seven fewer than at the last General Election. "Because the fight is keener," say the experts.

The election fight is warming up. Miss Sheila MacDonald, experienced debater, but political platform novice, is speaking for her father in the Seaham Division to-day.

SIR E. GERMAN ILL

Sudden acute indisposition prevented Sir Edward German, the eminent composer, from speaking at a dinner given in honour of Sir Landon Ronald in London last night.

He has been unwell for some time and yesterday, on the advice of a specialist, he entered a London nursing home.

THE DAILY MIRROR Thursday, November 7, 1935.

Broadcasting - Page 22

Daily Mirror
THE DAILY PICTURE ● NEWSPAPER WITH THE LARGEST NET SALE

No. 9,966 Registered at the G.P.O. as a Newspaper. THURSDAY, NOVEMBER 7, 1935 One Penny

QUIET CORNER - - - Page 9
EUSTACE - - - - - - Page 15
SERIAL - - - - - - Page 21
BELINDA - - - - - - Page 26
DAVID'S DIARY - - - Page 27
THE STARS SAY - - - Page 28

Amusements: Page 18

THE DUCHESS'S SMILE
It Was a Nation's Joy

Happily acknowledging the crowds' cheers when they drove away from Buckingham Palace, the Duke of Gloucester with his Duchess who a few hours earlier—

—had driven to the Palace as Lady Alice Montagu-Douglas-Scott.

CHILDREN'S DAY

THE DUKE'S TERRIER BARKS A WELCOME FOR THE DUCHESS

ACROSS the threshold of Boughton House last night the Duke of Gloucester led his Duchess.

A dog barked joyously. It was the Duke's Aberdeen terrier, Dougal, come, without hesitation, to greet the Duchess.

It was a welcome as spontaneous as the cheers that had rung through London's streets when the radiant bride drove to Buckingham Palace in a glass coach; or as the cheers that had filled Northamptonshire lanes when she drove with the Duke to their honeymoon home.

In her pearl-tinted wedding gown Lady Alice had won the hearts of the whole nation.

The cheers that greeted her and the Duke as they stepped on to the Buckingham Palace balcony after the stately marriage service were a nation's greeting.

It was a gracious day. And above all a children's day.

Among the bridesmaids—seven of the eight were under eighteen—were the two little Princesses—Princess Elizabeth and Princess Margaret Rose.

When, after the wedding breakfast, the Duke and Duchess left the Palace on their drive to St. Pancras Station for the honeymoon train, it was the Princesses who ran across the forecourt showering the coach with rose petals.

In the procession to the station, smiling at the crowds, was the Earl of Dalkeith, Lady Alice's schoolboy-nephew.

Their Gifts

On the platform he inspected the chromium-plated express locomotive, Silver Jubilee.

Schoolchildren—4,000 of them floodlit so that the royal couple could see them—were among those who greeted them on their drive from Kettering to Boughton House.

And, finally, as the Duke and Duchess arrived at Boughton House last night in the Great Hall were waiting two children.

They had brought with them gifts bought with children's pennies.

It was children's day.

The Story in Other Pages

The arrival at Boughton House, on page 3.

The bride leaves her home for the wedding, on page 3.

The ceremony and scenes outside the Palace; on the way to the station begins on page 4.

Pictures on pages 3, 4, 5, 16, 17, 19, 24, 25, and on the back page.

THE DAILY MIRROR, Thursday, November 14, 1935.

Daily Mirror

THE DAILY PICTURE NEWSPAPER WITH THE LARGEST NET SALE

Broadcasting - Page 20

THE STARS SAY --- Page 6
EUSTACE ------- Page 13
QUIET CORNER --- Page 14
DOCTOR'S DIARY -- Page 17
SERIAL -------- Page 19
BELINDA ------- Page 22

No. 9,972 Registered at the G.P.O. as a Newspaper. THURSDAY, NOVEMBER 14, 1935 One Penny

Amusements : Page 16

TO-DAY VOTE

BECAUSE it is your DUTY to vote.

BECAUSE your vote may be the DECISIVE vote.

BECAUSE a vote is a privilege and you must prove worthy of it.

BECAUSE failure to vote may bring disaster.

TO WOMEN VOTERS

You fought hard for the vote. USE IT.

Your vote may mean all the difference between comfort or misery in millions of homes. USE IT.

TO YOUNG VOTERS

Your vote will show whether you are fit for the full privilege of citizenship. USE YOUR VOTE.

DON'T BE VOTE-SHY because you are inexperienced. Your vote is as good as anybody's.

TO ALL VOTERS

Don't get confused. Mark your cross against the right name. If you spoil your ballot paper ask for another.

VOTE EARLY

BECAUSE you will avoid the rush hours when busy workers crowd the polling booths.

Here is a brief guide :—
For the National Government—
(1) National Conservatives
(2) Liberal Nationalists
(3) National Labour
Against the National Government
(1) Socialists
(2) Communists
(3) "Samuelite" Liberals
(4) 'Lloyd George' Liberals
(5) Cranks and Independents

No Voter Too High: Mr. Duncan Sandys, National Government candidate for Norwood, canvasses at the bedroom windows, during a final tour, by sitting on top of his loud-speaker van, which is driven by his wife, formerly Miss Diana Churchill.

SHOTS SCATTER CROWD

Man Hit in Belfast

SEVERAL revolver shots rang out during a Republican meeting in Peel-street, Belfast, last night, and Eneas Forrester, twenty-five, of Exchange-street, Belfast, fell with a bullet wound in the left shoulder.

The district in which the shooting took place is not the one in which the troubles occurred in July. It is known as the Roman Catholic area.

The meeting was being held at the corner of Peel-street and Mary-street, a few yards from Falls-road, one of the city's main thoroughfares.

Two or three hundred people were being addressed by Patrick O'Kearney, of Cork, when shots were fired from the direction of North Howard-street, about one hundred yards away.

The crowd immediately scattered for shelter, and in the rush a woman was injured.

In addition to Forrester, a fifteen-year-old girl named Josephine Connelly, of Servia-street, Belfast, received a bullet wound in the right arm and was removed to the Royal Victoria Hospital.

It is believed the shots were fired from a small car seen standing at the North Howard-street corner, and which disappeared after the shooting.

Police are searching for the gunmen.

Out with Hounds

The Duke and Duchess of Gloucester went hunting together yesterday for the first time since their marriage.

They attended the meet of the Woodland Pytchley at East Carlton Grange.

To-day's Big Vote Riddle

INDUSTRY WANTS "NATIONAL"

By A SPECIAL CORRESPONDENT

ONLY ONE PERSON IN THE WORLD KNOWS HOW YOU WILL VOTE TO-DAY—YOURSELF.

But a great many people think they have a very good idea.

By every party it is admitted, nevertheless, that this is the most perplexing election for many years.

Astute political observers throughout the country have for weeks been trying to probe the problems of the poll, and even to-day some of them have to confess themselves very much in the dark.

But trade figures published last night—details are given on page 2—spoke eloquently of the Government's record. "It is all due to the confidence engendered by the National Government," said Sir Harry McGowan, chairman of Imperial Chemical Indus-

ELECTION "BABIES"

Viscount Duncannon, Conservative candidate for Islington West, and (right) Mrs. M. Power (bareheaded), Socialist candidate for Hornsey, the two youngest candidates in to-day's General Election. Lord Duncannon is twenty-two and Mrs. Power is twenty-three. The Socialist Party's programme clearly has no appeal for the baby

Marchioness and Tutor

THE Marquis of Tavistock, son and heir of the Duke of Bedford was justified in leaving his wife.

This was the decision of Mr. Justice Bucknill in the Divorce Court yesterday, in dismissing the Marchioness of Tavistock's petition for restitution of conjugal rights.

Lord Tavistock, in his answer, alleged that his wife had formed a clandestine affection for the Rev. Cecil Squire, her children's tutor, but Mr. Justice Bucknill found that there was no evidence of any immorality, nor was there any imputation against Lady Tavistock's moral character.

"The Court," added the Judge, "has good reason for thinking that the change in her behaviour to her husband was due to her friendship with Mr. Squire.

"In the witness-box she asserted she was not prepared to cease that friendship. That being the attitude taken up by Lady Tavistock, the petition must be dismissed."

Full report—page 5.

tries. "The Government must be allowed to continue their good work."

Sir Josiah Stamp, director of Bank of England and chairman of the L.M.S. Railway, said: "This is an indication that the policy adopted by the National Government of improving the trade balance has continued to be successful. It is the duty of all to support National Government candidates."

(Continued on back page)

Up-to-Minute Election Results

SPECIAL editions of the "Daily Mirror" will to-morrow give up-to-the-minute election results.

The final Election edition will contain every result announced during the night.

THE DAILY MIRROR, Friday, November 15 1935

Daily Mirror
THE DAILY PICTURE NEWSPAPER WITH THE LARGEST NET SALE

Broadcasting - Page 20

THE STARS SAY --- Page 7
EUSTACE ------ Page 8
QUIET CORNER --- Page 14
DOCTOR'S DIARY -- Page 17
SERIAL ------- Page 19
BELINDA ------ Page 20

No. 9,973 Registered at the G.P.O as a Newspaper. FRIDAY, NOVEMBER 15, 1935 One Penny

Amusements : Page 16

SOCIALISTS ARE HELD

Government Heading for 200 Majority

SIR HERBERT SAMUEL IS DEFEATED

National Government 184
Anti-National Government 87

Number of Seats 271
This includes all results declared up to 4 a.m. to-day.

AFTER YESTERDAY'S GENERAL ELECTION RESULTS SOCIALISTS WERE SHOWING, DESPITE OPTIMISTIC FORECASTS, ONLY ABOUT FORTY GAINS.

SOCIALISTS had failed to score even half the gains on which they had reckoned, and the Government had retained seats that it had expected to lose. The prospects are that at the end of the election the Government will find itself with a majority of over 200.

The Socialists' failure was most conspicuous in London and Lancashire, where they had expected to do best.

Heartening news for the Government was the holding of the three Salford seats—generally regarded as an election "pointer."

But Socialists won back Burnley from Admiral Campbell, V.C.—vanquisher of the late Mr. Arthur Henderson in 1931. Front-rank Socialists to win back seats were : Mr. J. R. Clynes (Manchester Platting), Mr. A. V. Alexander (Sheffield Hillsborough), Mr. H. B. Lees Smith (Keighley), Mr. Herbert Morrison (S. Hackney) and Mr. F. O. Roberts (West Bromwich).

Mr. "Jimmy" Thomas In

The Liberals made a bad start. Eighteen forfeited their deposits—and then came the big blow. The three chief controllers of the Opposition Liberals' machine were defeated: Sir Herbert Samuel, the leader, Sir Walter Rea, the Chief Whip, and Mr. Harcourt Johnstone, the assistant Whip.

Lady Astor (Con., Sutton Plymouth) will sit in the new House with her son, the Hon. W. W. Astor. He captured East Fulham from Mr. Wilmot, the Socialist victor in the by-election two years ago. This will be the first time mother and son have ever sat in the Commons.

The first woman M.P. to be returned in a contest was Miss Irene Ward (Con., Wallsend), who defeated Miss Margaret Bondfield.

Mr. J. H. Thomas, Dominions Secretary, held Derby, and Mr. Lansbury and Mr. Attlee were returned. Sir Malcolm Campbell lost Deptford.

AT A GLANCE

Conservative gains ... 3	losses ... 32	Soc. gains 44	losses ... 2
Lib. Nat. gains 1	losses ... 2	Lib. gains 0	losses ... 6
Nat. Lab. gains 1	losses ... 3	Ind. gains 0	losses ... 2
Nat. gains 0	losses ... 2		
Government gains ... 5	losses ... 39	Opposition gains ... 44	losses ... 10

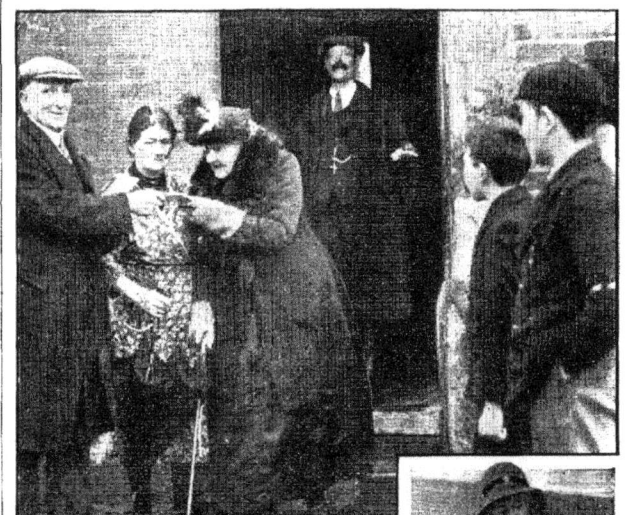

YOUTH AND AGE AT POLL

Mrs. Emma Coates, aged 105, being given her ballot paper on her arrival, unaided, at the North Curry polling station, Taunton, to vote. Right: Noella Adam, twelve-and-a-half, looking at an election notice. She voted at Croxley Green. Yet she was not the youngest voter.

87 Per Cent. Poll

AT Burnley — where Admiral Gordon Campbell, V.C. lost the seat he won from the late Mr. Arthur Henderson—87 per cent. of the electors went to the poll.

How Fight Went

THE youngest woman candidate, Mrs. M. Power, a twenty-three-year-old Socialist who opposed Captain Euan Wallace at Hornsey, was defeated by 20,174 votes.

Mr Arthur Greenwood, Minister of Health in the Labour Government, retained his seat at Wakefield with a greatly increased majority.

Mr. R. S. Hudson, Minister of Pensions, increased his majority at Southport by nearly two thousand.

(Continued on back page)

Results on Pages 5, 24 and 25

DETAILED STATE OF THE PARTIES

At the time of going to press the state of the parties was:—

NATIONAL
Conservative 167
Lib.-Nats. 14
National-Labour 3
Independent Conservative 0
National 0

ANTI-NATIONAL
Socialist 78
Liberal 8
I.L.P. 0
Independent Liberal 0
Independent 1

THE DAILY MIRROR, Saturday, November 16, 1935.

Daily Mirror

THE DAILY PICTURE ● NEWSPAPER WITH THE LARGEST NET SALE

Broadcasting - Page 22

EUSTACE .... Page 6
QUIET CORNER .... Page 16
DOCTOR'S DIARY ... Page 19
SHORT STORY ... Page 21
THE STARS SAY .... Page 22
BELINDA .... Page 26

No. 9,974 — Registered at the G.P.O. as a Newspaper. — SATURDAY, NOVEMBER 16, 1935 — One Penny

Amusements: Page 18

Smiling faces of successful Conservative candidates—Mr. G. Mitcheson, St. Pancras, S.W., Col. A. W. Goodman (side face), Islington, N., Miss Thelma Cazalet, Islington, E.

Mr. W. Craven-Ellis, who held Southampton for the Conservatives, was in good spirits, too, but Mr. Ramsay MacDonald had nothing to smile about.

GOVT.'S "MANY HAPPY RETURNS"

Confidence Vote of Nation Is Record

NATIONAL GOVERNMENT	421
OPPOSITION	179
GOVERNMENT MAJORITY	**242**

Ten results (fifteen members)—Universities, Irish and Scottish—to come

BY A SPECIAL CORRESPONDENT

IN a degree beyond the hopes of its most ardent supporters, the era of National Government celebrated its re-birth yesterday with "Many happy returns."

Never before in the Parliamentary history of this country has a Government secured such an enormous vote of confidence at the polls after four years of office.

The great Socialist attack to recapture their strongholds in the industrial areas failed in a measure that was increasingly astonishing as result after result yesterday sent the Government majority steadily mounting.

Nevertheless, though the acquisition to the strength of the National Government was consistent, the day was one of shocks and surprises.

There was a new massacre of the MacDonalds. Mr. Ramsay MacDonald, the ex-Premier, failed by 20,000 votes at Seaham Harbour against his Socialist opponent, Mr. Ernest Shinwell. Mr. Malcolm MacDonald, his son, the Colonial Secretary, was defeated in the Bassetlaw Division of Notts. In the Forest of Dean, Sir John Worthington, the ex-Premier's Parliamentary Private Secretary, was beaten.

Sir John Simon, the Home Secretary had a shock in the Spen Valley. His majority over Mr Ivor Thomas (Soc.) was only 642. In the 1931 election it was 12,956.

At Kelvingrove, the first count gave Mr Walter Elliot, the Minister of Agriculture, a majority of two over the Socialist candidate Mr H McNeil. But on a recount Mr Elliot's majority was shown to be 149.

£11,850 IN FORFEITED DEPOSITS

Failure of the women candidates was one of the great surprises of the election. Of sixty-five who took the field in contests, only nine were successful.

Sport claimed its place in the sensational results in a popular win at Swindon. W W Wakefield—"Wakers," the greatest Rugby skipper England has ever known—wrested the seat from Dr Addison.

One extraordinary feature of the election has been the number of £150 deposits forfeited by candidates who did not receive one-eighth of the votes cast in their divisions. These numbered 79, the total amount forfeited being £11,850.

One Communist will be in this Parliament. He is Will Gallacher, who won West Fife from the Conservatives by 593 votes.

Mr. E. Shinwell (Socialist) carried shoulder high after he had beaten Mr. Ramsay MacDonald (National Labour) at Seaham Harbour by a 20,498 majority.

Britain Ready for New Trade Revival

FURTHER revival of trade is certain as a result of the National Government's triumph at the polls.

Already last night feverish activity was going on behind the scenes. Important new loans will be launched at once. Municipal borrowing on a large scale is expected. And there is money in plenty to finance industry.

In the offing are important capital creations, backed by the Government for a big drive in British industry.

Every section of markets is active. It is not to be expected that the upward movement in prices will continue without a check. In fact there are points such as labour disputes, sanctions and foreign politics which may cause interruptions.

Sufficient for the moment is the knowledge that confidence in British finance and trade has been re-established.

The stock markets simply reflect views and opinions of the public. The operations of the man in the street are the major influence.

RESULTS A B C

AN A B C LIST OF YESTERDAY'S RESULTS BEGINS ON PAGE 9. THURSDAY'S START ON PAGE 26.

Gains and Losses

	Gains	Losses
Conservative ..	8	79
Lib. Nat.	2	7
Nat. Lab.	1	6
Nat.	2	2
Government	**13**	**94**
Soc.	96	3
Lib.	3	14
Ind.	3	4
Opposition	**102**	**21**

THE DAILY MIRROR, Monday, November 18, 1935.

Daily Mirror

THE DAILY PICTURE NEWSPAPER WITH THE LARGEST NET SALE

Broadcasting - Page 21

THE STARS SAY - - Page 6
EUSTACE - - - - - Page 7
DOCTOR'S DIARY - Page 8
QUIET CORNER - - Page 15
NEW SERIAL - - - - Page 18
BELINDA - - - - - - Page 22

No. 9,975 Registered at the G.P.O. as a Newspaper. MONDAY, NOVEMBER 18, 1935 One Penny

Amusements: Pages 16 and 20

FLOODS MENACE ALL BRITAIN

TRAIN WRECKED BY LANDSLIDE

Landslides Overwhelm Train

Boats Aid Marooned Families

WITH HUGE STRETCHES OF COUNTRY ALREADY UNDER WATER, BRITAIN LAST NIGHT FACED ITS WORST FLOOD PERIL FOR YEARS.

ALREADY 2.21in. of rain has fallen this month compared with 2.35in. for a normal month. The week-end deluge and gale—

- Stopped air services to and from Croydon;
- Swept away livestock from fields;
- Delayed Channel steamers;
- Disorganised road and rail traffic;
- Marooned townsfolk in upper rooms;
- Poured 30,000,000 tons of rain on Greater London in twenty-four hours.
- Brought down 1,000 tons of earth on a train travelling at sixty m.p.h.

The train was the 4.40 London-Yeovil, its sixteen vans filled with empty milk churns Roaring through a cutting between Winchfield and Hook (Hants), at sixty miles an hour early yesterday, it was overwhelmed as the banking, undermined by rains, came thundering down.

Unable to decrease speed, the engine ploughed its way into the gigantic mass of earth as far as the tender before turning over on its side. The driver, fireman and guard had remarkable escapes.

Eight of the vans were scattered all over the tracks, and as the remainder were being pulled clear another landslide occurred. All four roads to the West Country were blocked.

One hundred permanent-way men and two travelling cranes were rushed to the scene and began frenziedly to clear the track.

At midnight two of the lines had been cleared and normal services resumed.

Gardens Submerged

Rivers rose menacingly in all parts of the country.

The Thames, fed by flood waters from the River Cherwell, Mole and Wey, began to encroach on riverside meadows and submerge bungalow gardens between Staines and Walton, while a portion of the main road between Staines and Chertsey was inundated.

The rate of flow at Teddington is 5,000,000,000 gallons a day, three times the average for the past four months. When the Thames overflowed some years ago the flow was 20,000,000,000 gallons.

The Cherwell flooded many cellars, and in some instances ground floors in low-lying parts of Banbury, and motorists were held up on the Daventry road and at Broughton Castle, on the Shipston road.

Boats were rowed along many of the streets of Swanage, Dorset, including the main shop

(Continued on back page)

"A Bit of Trouble" →

"THERE was a bit of trouble on the line." This was how Guard George Coombs, of the wrecked milk train, described the crash to his wife. Mrs. Coombs noticed when her husband returned that his breakfast plate was broken. That was the explanation she got. He did not wish to alarm her.

But last night Guard Coombs told a "Daily Mirror" representative a little more about his amazing escape.

"The train started rocking violently," he said. "The next thing I knew was that the sides and flooring were being torn away in all directions, and my breakfast and belongings went with them. Then the van shot across the rails and came to rest twenty-five yards away from the track. All I could do was to hang on."

Railway line near Winchfield, Hants, after a landslide had wrecked a milk train.

The wrecked train, with breakdown gang at work

—To-day.....

WOMEN are very much in the news.
One, with a fur coat as her shroud, figures in a double tragedy told on the Back Page.

Three figure in rescue dramas that thrilled dockside crowds—as they will thrill you when you read of them on Page Four.

A hush-hush cake-maker gives away one or two secrets on Page Five—and on Page Seven buxom girls will have their pantomime hopes shattered.

* * *

PARSONS are saying something more interesting than usual.
On Page Three you will find one of them telling couples that "love making is a most delicate business"; another telling the world that it is adrift on a wave of Godlessness, and a third—a bishop at that—vowing never to gossip again.

* * *

HOUSEHOLDERS will learn just why their afternoon sleep is disturbed by the next door radio (Page Two), and on the Back Page Mr. Epstein prepares them for a shock.

THE DAILY MIRROR, Tuesday, November 19, 1935.

Daily Mirror

Broadcasting - Page 20

THE DAILY PICTURE NEWSPAPER WITH THE LARGEST NET SALE

THE STARS SAY - - Page 8
QUIET CORNER - - Page 15
DOCTOR'S DIARY - Page 17
SERIAL - - - - - - Page 19
BELINDA - - - - - Page 22
EUSTACE - - - - - Page 24

No. 9,976   Registered at the G.P.O. as a Newspaper.   TUESDAY, NOVEMBER 19, 1935   One Penny

Amusements: Page 18

SABRE CHARGE ON A MOB

Girls of 14 Lead Cairo Riots

CAIRO, Monday.

BRITISH and Egyptian mounted police charged with drawn sabres in Cairo to-day to disperse a mob of students, many of them girls between the ages of fourteen and eighteen, who tried to storm the Government hospital.

Using the flats of their sabres, the mounted police were able to drive the mob down side streets.

Demonstrators remained chanting, "Off with the British yoke. Long live Nationalism." The police report that nobody was injured in the melee.

Anti-British and Nationalist demonstrations had been resumed early in the day, when two students were wounded while trying to break through the police cordon around the Opera-square.

Death Rumour

It was in this square that the students had announced their intention of holding a "mock funeral" for their comrades killed during the past few days of Nationalist rioting.

The police forced the crowds to keep moving and diverted them into side streets, but outside the offices of an extremist newspaper several people were injured and a number arrested.

When news spread that a student wounded in last Wednesday's rioting had died in the Government hospital, 800 students tried to storm the hospital gates to seize the body for a spectacular burial.

By firing blank cartridges, however, the foot police held the mob at bay until mounted detachments arrived and charged.

In this riot girl students played a leading part. Finally the police permitted half a dozen girls to pass through the police lines to the hospital gates, where they paraded up and down shouting: " Down with Imperialism. Down with Britain."

By this evening the police appeared to have the situation well in hand.—B.U.P.

"GOOD TO SUFFER," SAYS BISHOP

DR. P. Amigo, Bishop of Southwark, speaking to a gathering of men at Lambeth last night, condemned the principle which, he said, seemed to be growing in this country to put an end to the lives of people suffering from incurable ailments.

It was contrary, he said, to the teaching of the Catholic Church, and, in his opinion, it was a very wicked suggestion.

"We have no right to take other people's lives," he said. "In my view it is good to suffer purgatory on this earth."

People did not realise the value of suffering in the world.

SHEEP IN THE FLOODS: REMARKABLE PICTURES

Eskimos—Ideal Race Says Red Emma

"The ideal world citizen!"

BY A SPECIAL REPRESENTATIVE

HIGH Priestess of the anarchists, Red Emma Goldman has a soft spot in her heart for the Eskimos. Red Emma, who has been preaching anarchism for fifty years, has returned to England after a long globe trot. She does not agree with any state of society in the world. When I asked her which people came nearest to perfection, she said:—

"The Eskimos. They have an inner discipline, but no laws, no crime, and no bloodshed. Society should rest on the co-operative relations of man with man without interference of law and authority.

"Governments exist by violence. They are costly and unnecessary, so give me the Eskimos."

Red Emma, in her capacity as the "most dangerous" woman anarchist in the world, is bitterly disappointing.

You expect a virago, bristling with bombs and daggers—but you see a genial woman.

But Emma, on the platform is still militant. "Traders in Death" will be her first lecture—at the Trades Union Club.

"I am going to talk about the munitions conspiracy," she said.

When I asked her which was the best country in the world she told me:

"England is the most free country to live in,

Husbands...

HUSBANDS are not so black as wives sometimes like to paint them.

When a Birmingham woman was granted a separation order yesterday, it was stated that

Her husband had paid her debts four times.

Had starved himself to do so.

When receiving £6 a week housekeeping, she pawned her son's and her husband's clothes.

On top of this her husband offered to forgive her. (See page 2.)

A Stockwell, S.W., licensee is so delighted at his wife's recovery from illness that he has ordered a brass band to escort her home and is making her guest of honour at a party for 500. (See back page.)

A man at Rhuddlan (North Wales), leaning on a hedge yesterday to rescue one of his sheep, which had been in the water since four in the morning. After being pulled to safety it had to be destroyed. Above: Sheep swimming through the flood waters 4ft. deep between Rhuddlan and St. Asaph. Other flood pictures on pages 14 and 15. Story, page 2.

Daily Mirror

THE DAILY PICTURE NEWSPAPER WITH THE LARGEST NET SALE

Broadcasting - Page 22

EUSTACE .... Page 8
THE STARS SAY ... Page 15
QUIET CORNER ... Page 16
DOCTOR'S DIARY .. Page 19
SERIAL .... Page 21
BELINDA .... Page 24

Amusements: Page 18

No. 9,979 Registered at the G.P.O as a Newspaper. FRIDAY, NOVEMBER 22, 1935 One Penny

GIRLS WHO INCITE SEX TALK

"To Be a Prude a Crime"

"I am prepared to defend the language at Oxford, at least so far as the men are concerned, but not so far as the women in Oxford. I think they read things into our remarks deliberately to incite us to say something suggestive to show that they are not prudes.

"To be a prude is, they think, the greatest crime a modern woman can commit."

THIS challenging comment was made last night by Mr. Peter Dwyer, the editor of the "Cherwell," one of the Oxford undergraduate magazines.

It followed a caustic onslaught on the conversation of the undergraduate which was launched in "The Granta," the Cambridge University magazine, headed "The Mouths of Sucklings."

The comment of Mr. C. Fletcher Cooke, president-elect of the Cambridge University Union Society, was:—

"I think the fact that men and women are segregated in the University has something to do with the sexual tone of conversations among undergraduates."

"The proverbial bargee," said "The Granta" article, "speaks pulpit prose in comparison with the casual conversation of modern undergraduates.

"If Lord Macaulay were to return to his alma mater in this year of jubilee," it goes on, "he would find that the success of undergraduate gatherings depended largely upon obscenity which passes for wit.

"Why is it that the undergraduates of today, so much more than their fathers, fall victims to this disease of adolescence?"

Apologising for Delicacy

"You plant in them the seeds of knowledge and you may reasonably expect to see the fairest flowers of speech. But what so often grows instead is a rank unseamed bed of blasphemy and filth.

"A raconteur wishing to divert his friends must first apologise if his story happens to be one that could appear delicate in any circle; otherwise its end is received in blank silence by an audience waiting for the expected salacious denouement.

"We can only speak for this university, but in Cambridge, at least, to be funny it is essential to be indecent.

"The excuse generally offered for this kind of conversation is that repression is harmful. But a snigger is an unsatisfactory form of safety-valve. It is neither funny nor agreeable to wallow in filth for filth's sake.

"In every conceivable field from religion to politics and back again, conventional behaviour is shocking those whose standards used to be the convention of twenty years ago; this may be the natural consequence of progress. But original sin is the least original of human topics.

"Let us for a change be thoroughly original and import a little cleanliness into our conversation."

Mr. J. N. Duckworth, the Cambridge cox, commenting on the article said:—

"It is the fashion to appear 'tough' in the University now, but I think it is passing.

"It is different at Oxford. If you came to a dinner attended by the Oxford and Cambridge crews you could tell which crew was which by the conversation, even if you didn't know beforehand."

(Continued on back page)

"IMMORAL" WILD FLOWER HUNTERS

STRONG words about "unscrupulous wild flower collectors" were uttered by the Bishop of Gloucester, Dr. Headlam in London yesterday. He said:—

"I never show a rare flower to anyone whom I know to be a collector. I am never sure whether he will go back the next day and take it for his collection.

"There are some collectors who are even worse. They not only take a specimen for themselves, but they destroy all other specimens, so that nobody else shall have them. That is the very lowest depth of immorality to which such people can go."

The Bishop told how young men from Oxford rode over to the daffodil regions of Gloucester on motor-cycles in the early morning and gathered huge masses of flowers for the market.

He had heard that a wood after it had been visited by a girls school looked "as though it had been visited by a storm of locusts."

CONVALESCENT WIFE WELCOMED HOME LIKE A FILM STAR

Silk-hatted like a bridegroom—Mr. Gradwell assisting his wife from the car on arrival back at Stockwell while the crowd cheered and the band played, and (left) carrying her over the threshold of their home.

Husband Says It with Music

AND CROWDS CHEER

BY A SPECIAL REPRESENTATIVE

WHILE hundreds of people cheered and a brass band thundered out a lively military march, Mrs. T. E. Gradwell was carried by her husband over the threshold of their home in Stockwell, S.W., last night. There were tears of joy in her eyes....

Mr. Gradwell keeps a local hotel. For hours crowds waited outside to see Mrs. Gradwell return home after recovering from a serious illness. As her car came in sight hundreds ran into the roadway.

Traffic was held up, while police officers struggled to keep the crowds from the path of the car.

Then the Clapham and Brixton Silver Band lined up in front, and to the tune of "The Exile," led a happy procession to the hotel.

There Mrs. Gradwell was the guest of honour at a cabaret and dance party given free to 500 friends.

Decorated Bar

In the bar, gaily bedecked with balloons and streamers, Mrs. Gradwell was almost too overcome by the warmth of her reception to say more than a few words.

"No bride ever had a more wonderful reception. I hardly know what to say," she said to me, smiling through her tears.

"I feel bewildered. I had no idea Nibs (her husband) had arranged all this. But it is just like him. He is only satisfied when he is making other people happy."

Mr. Gradwell took his wife to rest after she had received the congratulations of her friends.

From an upstairs room he spoke through a microphone.

During the evening money was collected to make a presentation to Mrs. Gradwell. A deputation knocked up a local jeweller, who sold them a silver soup tureen.

And so they returned in triumph. Then, too weak to walk, Mrs. Gradwell was carried into the hall, where the gift was presented to her.

Lie Test for Hauptmann

ROCHESTER (N.Y.), Thursday.

Bruno Hauptmann, convicted of the kidnapping and murder of the Lindbergh baby, is to be placed under the Lie Detector test to determine the truth of his evidence during the trial.—Reuter.

A DESCENDANT OF SHAKESPEARE

There died at New Plymouth (New Zealand) yesterday Mr. Henry Arden, who claimed to be a descendant of Shakespeare.

He was ninety years old and was born at Brighton, going out to New Zealand in 1853.—Reuter.

THE DAILY MIRROR Friday, November 29, 1935

Daily Mirror

THE DAILY PICTURE NEWSPAPER WITH THE LARGEST NET SALE

Broadcasting - Page 24

EUSTACE - - - - - - Page 8
THE STARS SAY - - - Page 10
QUIET CORNER - - - Page 18
DOCTOR'S DIARY - - Page 21
SERIAL - - - - - - - Page 23
BELINDA - - - - - - Page 28

No. 9,985 Registered at the G.P.O as a Newspaper   FRIDAY, NOVEMBER 29, 1935   One Penny

Amusements: Page 20

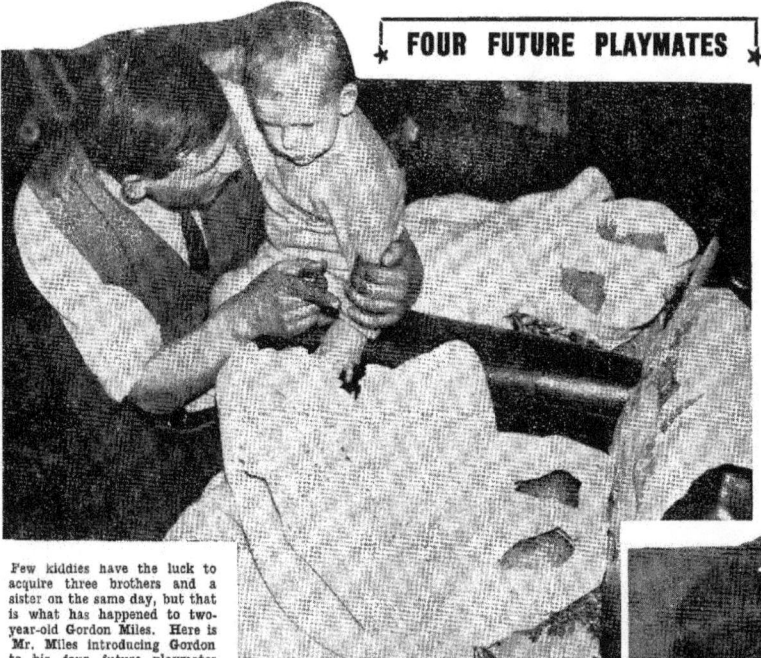

★ FOUR FUTURE PLAYMATES ★

Few kiddies have the luck to acquire three brothers and a sister on the same day, but that is what has happened to two-year-old Gordon Miles. Here is Mr. Miles introducing Gordon to his four future playmates.

Shot Wife's Lover in Hospital Bed

GIANT HUSBAND'S REVENGE

NEW ORLEANS, Thursday.

A JEALOUS husband walked into a hospital ward in New Orleans to-day, drew a revolver and shot dead a patient whom he accused of breaking up his home.

The husband is Lewis Sapp, aged forty-two, and 6ft. 7in. tall, an iron worker. His victim was Harold Bourg, aged thirty-nine, an electrician.

Sapp strode into the hospital and asked to be directed to the ward in which Bourg was recovering after an operation for appendicitis.

He walked straight across the ward to where Bourg was lying in bed, drew a revolver and snarled: "I have got you now. You broke up my home."

Then he fired five shots, while the other patients in the ward cowered in their bedsheets in terror.

Wife Faints

Four of the five bullets struck Bourg, killing him instantly.

Then Sapp threw the revolver and a package of letters on to the bed and surrendered to the police, who took him home to verify his story.

When the police car drew up at his house Sapp yelled to his wife, who had appeared at a window: "Your lover is dead I got him." Mrs. Sapp fainted.—B.U.P.

"HEAD" IS KILLED BEFORE PUPILS

Premonitions of a teacher that some tragic fate might befall his headmaster came true yesterday, when Captain George Bowerman, aged fifty-one, headmaster of the Hartshill North School, Nuneaton (Warwickshire) was killed instantly after falling from a chair.

The tragedy was seen by the teacher, Mr. S. Hill, and a number of pupils, some of whom were holding the chair for Captain Bowerman.

Mr. Hill had previously warned Captain Bowerman that he was taking a risk.

Captain Bowerman. The headmaster was engaged in erecting a platform for a church concert. He had placed a table on the stage, and on this had stood a chair.

It was while he was getting down that the back of the chair gave way.

Captain Bowerman slipped eight feet head-first to the floor and died almost instantly.

Mr. Hill told the *Daily Mirror* last night that he had often advised Captain Bowerman not to stand on chairs.

France Had a Rain of Wine

Red "wine" rained on Dinan (France) for three days this month. This is the explanation of the red rain which fell heavily and which left not the slightest sediment to account for its colour.

The rain has now been analysed by an eminent chemist, says Reuter. He states that minute fruits borne in the rain by the strong south-west winds began to ferment and thus produced a kind of "wine."

HER SISTER WHO VANISHED

Dramatic Story in Ruxton Case

FROM OUR SPECIAL CORRESPONDENT
LANCASTER, Thursday.

FROM a witness-box in which she stood for hours, a woman at Lancaster to-day told of a sister, happy and healthy one night, and next day vanished—never to be seen again.

Mrs. Jeanie Nelson, of Edinburgh, was the witness; the sister was the wife of Dr. Buck Ruxton, the Hindu doctor charged with her murder and that of a nursemaid.

Sometimes vehement, sometimes trembling and once in collapse, Mrs. Nelson described how she had waited . . . and waited for the sister who never came.

She told strange stories of the doctor's appeal to her to tell him where was the wife he is alleged to have murdered.

"My life is impossible without her," she said he wrote in a letter. "Do your best to help me keep my home together" . . .

Yet earlier he had told her, said Mrs. Nelson, that he knew his wife had "been in company in an hotel with a young boy friend

Full report of yesterday's hearing starts on page 4.

QUADS BORN IN COUNCIL HOUSE

All Doing Well

BY A SPECIAL CORRESPONDENT

IN a council house at St. Neots (Hunts), with only one doctor and a nurse in attendance, the wife of a lorry-driver yesterday gave birth to quadruplets—three boys and a girl.

And so for the second time in eight weeks in Britain a 250,000-to-1 chance came up.

There were none of the elaborate precautions which had attended the birth of other quadruplets—no rigorous guard to keep strangers away, no special apparatus to minister to the little ones.

All night the doctor and nurse had worked. The last child, one of the boys, was very weak.

Nurse Mailing told me last night:

"Dr. Harrison began to apply artificial respiration on the tiny body. After a time I relieved him.

"We took it in relays. How long we worked I have no idea. But, at last, to my great joy, I saw that we had won."

The mother of the quadruplets is Mrs. Walter Miles, of Ferrars-avenue, Eynesbury. She is thirty-three.

At midnight the quads appeared to be progressing perfectly satisfactorily.

Their father told me that there was no change in their condition.

"With babies so young as this," he said, "that is as much as one can say about them, and therefore I am quite content.

"My wife had a sleep this morning, but she has not yet got to sleep to-night. However, she is quite cheerful, and seems comfortable, and that is all that matters."

Mr. and Mrs. Miles have not yet selected names for the quads. "We are going to wait a bit before we christen them," said Mr. Miles. "Meanwhile we will just refer to them as babies 1, 2, 3 and 4.

Message to the King

"It was certainly a surprise—a big surprise, but now it is all over and I am very, very glad. I'm very, very proud of my wonderful family. My one ambition now is that we shall be able to rear them all safely.

"My wife naturally is very weak, but I am happy to say quite comfortable. The great thing now is to keep her perfectly quiet, so that she may soon be herself again and able to attend to our babies."

The weight of the children in the order in which they were born was: First, 3lb. 12½oz. (the girl); second, 3lb. 15oz.; third, 3lb. 7oz.; fourth, 2lb. 13oz.

Shortly after the children were born, a message was sent to the King's secretary informing him of the event.

After her all-night task Nurse Mailing had to rush away to attend several other cases in the village.

Last night Dr. Harrison, a keen poultry keeper, was presiding at a lecture for amateur poultry keepers in a local hotel.

The house in Ferrars-avenue, St. Neots, where the "quads" were born.

Daily Mirror

THE DAILY PICTURE NEWSPAPER WITH THE LARGEST NET SALE

Broadcasting - Page 22

DOROTHY DIX - - - Page 7
EUSTACE - - - - - - Page 10
QUIET CORNER - - Page 16
SERIAL - - - - - - - Page 21
DOCTOR'S DIARY - - Page 25
BELINDA - - - - - - Page 26

No. 9,988 Registered at the G.P.O as a Newspaper. TUESDAY, DECEMBER 3, 1935 One Penny

Amusements: Page 20

THE KING'S SISTER DIES AT 3 a.m.

Vain Fight to Save Princess Victoria

TRANSFUSION DRAMA

The "Daily Mirror" deeply regrets to announce the death of Princess Victoria, the King's sister.

SHE died at her 300-year-old home, The Coppins, near Iver (Bucks), at 3.35 a.m. to-day, at the age of sixty-seven.

The following bulletin was issued:—

"Her Royal Highness the Princess Victoria has had a peaceful death, December 3, 1935, 3.35 a.m."
"Howell Gwynne-Jones, John Weir, Dawson of Penn."

The Princess had been ill for three weeks. She became worse a week ago—only a few days after the King and Queen had visited her.

Since the start of the Princess's illness Dr. H. Gwynne-Jones, of Gerrards Cross, had been in attendance. At the week-end, alarmed by the change in the Princess's condition he called London specialists to her bedside.

It was on the advice of the latter that a blood transfusion was decided upon yesterday as a last desperate expedient to save the Princess's life. Then this bulletin was issued:—

"Her Royal Highness the Princess Victoria had acute and severe hæmorrhage from the stomach yesterday (Sunday) evening."
"Transfusion of blood was performed, but has only been of temporary benefit. The condition of her Royal Highness is critical."
"Signed, Howell Gwynne-Jones, John Weir, Dawson of Penn."

The donor for the blood transfusion is unknown.

The donor arrived at The Coppins by car and was at once ushered into the Princess's bed-chamber.

Her Hobbies

FEW stories of devotion equal that of the sacrifice of all her own inclinations made by Princess Victoria when her mother, Queen Alexandra, lay ill.

In Queen Alexandra's later years she nursed her with a kindly, never-relaxing sympathy.

Among members of the Royal Family Princess Victoria was known affectionately as Toria.

Born at Marlborough House on July 6, 1868, Princess Victoria was the fourth child and the second daughter of King Edward VII and Queen Alexandra. She was the King's only unmarried sister.

She grew up with Lady Constance, daughter
(Continued on back page)

STATE OPENING CANCELLED

THE State opening of Parliament to-day has been cancelled.

There will be no procession and the King's speech will be read by the Lord Chancellor.

£8,500,000 MORE TO PROVIDE WORK

WORKS and rolling stock replacements and improvements by the L.M. and S. Railway next year will involve an expenditure of £8,500,000.

This programme (distinct from that under the proposed Government-guaranteed loan) includes 133 locomotives, 111 locomotive boilers, 637 carriages, 9,485 wagons, 900 containers and three steamers.

Six hundred miles of permanent way will be renewed.

Woman Dies in Midnight Stabbing

A MAN AND A WOMAN WERE FOUND STABBED IN A HOUSE IN CLAPHAM AT MIDNIGHT.

The woman died within a few minutes and the man is in a critical condition in hospital.

Early to-day police were seeking to interview a man said to have been seen leaving the house.

The description and name of the man the police are seeking is stated to be known. Flying Squad cars were this morning scouring the district.

Superintendent Helby is in charge of investigations assisted by a squad of detectives and specialists, including fingerprint and photographic experts.

Neighbours who said they heard cries for help informed the police. On entering the house they found the man and the woman on the floor of a room.

Refused Baptism for Child

MR. Malcolm Macleod, an elder of the Flashader Free Presbyterian Church, Isle of Skye, has been refused baptism for his daughter, it was stated yesterday, because he is alleged to have—

Helped to gather sheep on a Saturday knowing that they were to be moved on a Sunday; and
Allowed his wife to attend a bazaar at Edinbain, Skye.

It is further stated that Mr. Nicholson, a missionary, has said that Mr. Macleod was not entitled to baptism for his child.

Mr. Macleod, who lives at Edinbain, said last night that he had "hardly slept a wink" since being asked to appear before the Kirk session to answer the suggestions made against him.

"I was very much surprised and vexed," he continued, "at the refusal of baptism, and while I do admit gathering sheep on a Saturday, I did not realise that they were to be transported on a Sunday."

Princess Victoria, the King's sister, who is lying critically ill.

Millions for Our Defences —£300,000,000 Loan

MILLIONS of pounds are to be devoted almost immediately to strengthening Britain's Navy, Army and Air Force. This was revealed last night following the issue by the National Government of two loans—one for £200,000,000 and the other for £100,000,000.

Issues of this nature were forecast some days ago when Mr. Baldwin spoke about bridging the gap in our defences.

It is not expected that the money will be entirely devoted to armaments.

In the Chancellor's election broadcast speech, and in recent utterances by the Premier and other members of the Government, it was indicated that vast schemes of reconstruction are contemplated, such as road making and the provision of factories in depressed areas.

Half the total to be issued will go to repay £150,000,000 outstanding in 2 per cent. Treasury bonds. These bonds have a market price of 101 per cent.

The degree of confidence the country has in the National Government is shown by the fact that the colossal sum asked for is to be raised in one day.

To-morrow is that day.

No financial operation of this magnitude has been attempted before on a peacetime footing.

This is the first time in our financial history that the Treasury has been able to borrow at the nominal rate of 1 per cent. in any form except Treasury bills, and to borrow by means of a public issue for as long as twenty-five years at the nominal rate of 2½ per cent.

London's New Air Defence Plan—Page 2

Margaret Evelyn Ross, fourteen, on whose death a verdict of Misadventure was returned at an inquest at Crediton, Devon, yesterday. She was found dying beneath a window at Crediton Girls' High School.

Daily Mirror

THE DAILY PICTURE NEWSPAPER WITH THE LARGEST NET SALE

Broadcasting - Page 22

DOROTHY DIX - - - Page 7
EUSTACE - - - - - - Page 15
QUIET CORNER - - - Page 17
DOCTOR'S DIARY - - Page 19
SERIAL - - - - - - - Page 21
BELINDA - - - - - - Page 26

No. 9,990 Registered at the G.P.O as a Newspaper. THURSDAY, DECEMBER 5, 1935 One Penny

Amusements : Page 8

BABY FELL FROM HER ARMS

Beryl Tomlin, fifteen-year-old nursemaid, dramatic statements by whom were read at yesterday's Cambridge inquest on the baby son of Mr. and Mrs. Terence R. B. Sanders, of Scroope-terrace, Cambridge. Mrs. Sanders gave the opinion that the girl was not to blame. Accidental death caused by the baby falling from his nurse's arms was the verdict. See story on page 4.

MAN-WITH-PAST SAVED BY GIRL

She Learned His Secret

3 LOYAL WOMEN

THREE LOYAL WOMEN—TWO OF THEM UNDER TWENTY-ONE — FIGURED IN YESTERDAY'S NEWS.

One saved a man from prison, another began to repay her dead father's "debt of honour," the third took the blame in a court case in which her brother was involved.

The first, Edith Kelly, twenty-year-old brunette, employed in a Bournemouth hotel, heard for the first time at Bournemouth Police Court yesterday that there were previous convictions against the man she loved.

Last night she spoke of the shock of what she had heard and added:—

"I felt that the past should be forgotten and have decided to stick to him. I am sure I shall be able to keep him straight."

Richard Hayward, twenty-seven, a builder's labourer, of Bournemouth, is the fiance.

Hayward was bound over after he had told the magistrates that he had arranged to marry "someone who was going to stand by him."

Miss Kelly was called before the magistrates, and the chairman, announcing the decision, said: "We want you to play the man as this woman is willing to play the woman."

"I know he will do his part," Miss Kelly said later, "and that we shall be happy, for we both love one another, and that is everything. We shall pull together and we shall soon forget the past.

"Now it is all cleared up, and he will have no secrets to keep from me. I am going to help him all I can, because I know he will deserve it.

"We have got our home together, and I am sure everything is going to be all right."

The marriage had been fixed for Saturday, but it may be postponed.

DEBT OF HONOUR

EIGHTEEN-YEAR-OLD Joan Holmes, of Tickhill (South Yorks), is determined to clear the name of her dead father by herself repaying his debts.

After his funeral the home will be sold up, and there will be just sufficient money to discharge a debt of honour.

At an inquest yesterday the jury found that the father, Ernest Holmes, aged fifty, committed suicide while of unsound mind.

The coroner said that Holmes left a note stating that his downfall was due to money troubles and horse racing.

"Joan is a very fine, level-headed girl," the Rev. J. M. Shaw, vicar of Tickhill, told the Daily Mirror last night. "She was devoted to her father, and ever since her mother's death had kept house for him.

"We are all very proud of Joan for her splendid spirit and her determination to discharge what she regards as a debt of honour."

PLEA FOR BROTHER

BEFORE Mrs Sarah Ann Lindon, thirty-two, a shop assistant, was sentenced to eighteen months' imprisonment at Birmingham Assizes yesterday, when she and her brother

(Continued on back page)

BLINDFOLD MAN DEAD ON CLIFF

Found on Ledge Hundred Feet from Top

WITH a handkerchief bound tightly over his eyes, a man's body was found on a cliff ledge at St. Margaret's Bay, Kent, yesterday.

The dead man was George Tickner Barton, forty-one, of Liverpool-street, Dover.

His body was found on a ledge 100ft. from the top of the South Foreland cliff.

The injuries were consistent with a fall from the cliff top.

Barton had a refreshment shop in Bank-street, Dover, and is stated to have been depressed lately.

Friend Tells How Stavisky Died

PARIS, Wednesday.
Strong conviction that the French financier Stavisky really did commit suicide in the villa at Chamonix where he had taken refuge, rather than fall into the hands of the French police, was expressed by M. Pigaglio, one of the last of his friends to see him alive, while giving evidence in the Stavisky case to-day.

M. Pigaglio declared that when he went to say good-bye to Stavisky for the last time he saw a revolver lying on his table beside a photograph of his wife and children.—Reuter.

The wife of Mr. Bloomberg, formerly Miss Ruby Cashel, in ballet.

Parents in Enticement Claim

A CASE believed to be the first of its kind will be heard in the High Court, probably in the early part of next term.

The plaintiff is a young man who alleges that his wife's parents enticed her away. He is claiming damages.

Mr. Maurice de Villers Bloomberg, the twenty-eight-year-old husband, is a South African author, living in London. His wife is twenty-three, and is a clever ballet dancer.

She was formerly Miss Ruby Cecilia Cashel.

Mr. Cashel   *Mr. Bloomberg.*

and she was married in London two years ago. Mr. and Mrs. Bloomberg have a son.

For some years Mrs. Bloomberg and her father have performed together in London and the provinces under the stage names of Sax and Royan.

Messrs. Gordon Blair and Co., solicitors, of Great Smith-street, Westminster, are acting for the husband. The father and mother, Mr. Leo and Mrs. Florence Cashel, of Blackpool, are represented by a London solicitor, Mr. Arthur C. Prothero, of Blackheath-road, S.E.

£15,000 JEWEL SALE SECRET

EVERY member of the staff of Christie's, the St. James's auctioneers, has been pledged to keep secret the identity of the owner of some magnificent jewellery which they are offering for sale next Monday.

Two lots, valued at £15,000 are listed in a last-minute supplement to the catalogue as being "from a private collection."

They consist of a sapphire set as a pendant, nearly as large as a penny, and a three-row necklace, composed of 63, 67 and 51 pearls, some as big as small marbles.

"This will be one of the most important jewel sales for some years," said a member of the firm to the Daily Mirror yesterday.

"Every year about this time we have a jewel sale, in good time for Christmas present buyers."

Italians Fire on Fishermen

TWO Greek fishermen were killed and fourteen wounded yesterday when an Italian destroyer fired on a fishing-boat near the Dodecanese Islands, in the belief that it was a submarine.

Secret peace moves page 3.

Daily Mirror

THE DAILY PICTURE NEWSPAPER WITH THE LARGEST NET SALE

Broadcasting - Page 24

DOROTHY DIX - - - Page 7
EUSTACE - - - - - - Page 10
QUIET CORNER - - - Page 19
DOCTOR'S DIARY - - Page 21
SERIAL - - - - - - Page 23
BELINDA - - - - - - Page 28

Amusements: Pages 30 and 31

No. 9,991   Registered at the G.P.O as a Newspaper.   FRIDAY, DECEMBER 6, 1935   One Penny

A BOUQUET FOR THE ENGINE DRIVER

Engine-drivers rarely get tips, still less flowers, but here is Driver C. Hopkins getting a bouquet at Paddington yesterday after he had brought in the Cheltenham Flyer, after its thousandth run one minute ahead of time. It had thus done the 77¼ miles from Swindon in 64 minutes.

FRIENDS

BY A SPECIAL REPRESENTATIVE

ON a street corner fourteen years ago began an acquaintance that should go down as an epic among friendships.

On this street corner in Westbourne-grove, Paddington, a newsvendor befriended an old lady who eked out a miserable existence selling guinea-pigs.

He took a small room in Westbourne-avenue, and seventy-one-year-old Emily Mary Tower and the newsvendor, forty-six-year-old Fred Nonweiler, shared it.

He earned 12s. to 15s. a week on his news stand. She had her Old Age pension. Together they weathered fourteen years of poverty and ill-health.

A few days ago the guinea-pig seller, almost blind, fell. She was taken to hospital and died at the age of eighty-five.

At the inquest at Paddington yesterday, when the coroner recorded a verdict of Accidental death, the story of supreme friendship was revealed.

"I had to do everything for her," Old Fred, now sixty, told the coroner. "I bathed her feet, as she could scarcely walk at first, but she soon walked splendidly."

Mrs. Ellen Tower, a niece of the dead woman, said that Nonweiler had nothing to gain from his kindness, and added, "I take off my hat to him."

And here's the old couple's story as Fred told it to me last night:—

"I knew when they took her away to hospital that I had lost the dearest and best pal a man could have

Starving

"I first met her on a street corner on a very cold and wet winter's day when she was broke and starving, and I was little better off. She was suffering cruelly from her feet, tramping the streets all day.

"We decided to pool the few shillings we had, and help each other. And from that day to the one when she fell we never left each other. She was a grand old lady.

"We used to sit together in the evenings, often without a fire and often without food. I would read the left-over newspapers I had, and we would discuss the news.

"Six months ago she became almost blind and could not go out again. I used to get up early in the morning, clean up the room, cook the food for the day, and then I had to go out trying to sell newspapers to keep ourselves going.

"Often she used to cry for the music she had loved in her younger days. I had been an organist and a pianist, and I loved music. It was the dream of my life to earn enough money each week to hire a piano to play for her.

"I know she used to go without food for days at a time so that I could have enough to eat when I was out in the cold. This last week has been the loneliest of my life."

As I left old Fred, tears trickled down his cheeks. He will go on selling his papers, and then return to a room now lonely after fourteen years of a friendship rarely met with in this world.

PARENTS OF QUADS TO PAY NO RENT

ST. Neots Urban Council have decided that the parents of the quadruplets shall have their house rent free for a year. Dr Harrisson stated last night that the babies had a very good day.

They had all sucked their thumbs at intervals, except Michael. They had all fed well, and their cries and little noises had been stronger.

They now take undiluted human milk. The three elder babies have seven teaspoonfuls and Michael six teaspoonfuls at two and three-quarter hour intervals.

Their pulses are strong and regular; Ann and Paul 120 beats per minute, Ernest 108 and Michael 116. Their features are becoming more defined.

The "quads" were a week old yesterday. Dr. Harrisson is astonished by the volume of sound produced by their tiny charges.

Paul, the second boy, who appears to be the brightest baby, is the leader of the quartet, waving his arms about the whole time and always succeeding in making himself heard above the combined efforts of his sister and brothers.

The babies were measured yesterday. Ernest won with 16½in., Ann and Paul were 16in., and Michael is 14½in.

Hitler Is Now George Bernard

HITLER (Hezekiah) has been renamed George Bernard Gandhi.

That is because the German Embassy protested to the Lord Chamberlain a week ago that they did not like Hezekiah Hitler as the name of a character in the play "Vicky."

Last night the Lord Chamberlain requested the manager of the Garrick Theatre to omit all references to Hitler in time for the performance.

So Hezekiah Hitler changed his name.
"I don't mind," said Mr. George Bernard Shaw last night, smiling broadly. "People will know it is not George Bernard Shaw."

LOST HIS POST, SO DIED

Mr. Edward Philip Linford, 37, of Grimston, Norfolk, who was found dead on the railway line on the evening of the day he learned that he could not be reinstated as organist at the village church. He had played there for 20 years, and recently resigned through ill-health.

Prisoners to Live Out!

IN GAOL ONLY AT WEEK-ENDS

BY A SPECIAL CORRESPONDENT

AN important experiment in the more humane treatment of prisoners is shortly to be made by the authorities at Wakefield Prison.

At present, parties of men travel daily from the prison to a place about six miles away, where they are engaged in land reclamation work.

Within a few weeks a group of hutments, electrically lighted and comfortably equipped, will be ready. In these, the work parties will sleep from Monday to Friday, returning to the prison for the week-end.

If this idea proves successful, it will be extended elsewhere on the lines of prison camps in Palestine and other British possessions.

Bright Surroundings

"The aim is to provide the men with healthy outdoor employment and keep them outside the environment of prison walls as long as possible," an official of the Prison Commission told me yesterday.

"It is much more pleasant for the men to be able to retire to bright surroundings after a hard day's work than to have to return to the prison.

"It is much more likely that they will regain their self-respect if this plan is adopted."

Warders, of course, will be in charge of the camp, but there will be the minimum of supervision.

The work of keeping the huts clean will be undertaken in rotation by the men themselves on the same lines as orderlies in the Army.

On Their Honour

The men themselves are keenly looking forward to the new regime.

Short-term offenders are lodged in Wakefield Prison, and the establishment has the reputation of being the most successful prison in England.

Occupants are placed on their honour not to try to escape from working parties. They are allowed to hang framed photographs in their cells, while they sleep on comfortable spring-mattressed beds.

POLICE RADIO CHAIN

BY A SPECIAL CORRESPONDENT

BRITAIN is to have a network of police radio stations.

Each will be inter-communicating and each will be able instantly to get in touch with motor patrols within a radius of forty miles.

This means that contact could be made in a few moments with any police motor patrol throughout the country—a most important factor in the prompt detection of crime and pursuit of criminals.

Revelation of this system of regional radio stations for police was made by Sir John Simon, the Home Secretary in the Commons yesterday.

THE DAILY MIRROR, Saturday, December 7, 1935.

Daily Mirror

THE DAILY PICTURE NEWSPAPER WITH THE LARGEST NET SALE

Broadcasting - Page 20

DOROTHY DIX - - - Page 7
EUSTACE - - - - - - Page 13
QUIET CORNER - - - Page 14
DOCTOR'S DIARY - - Page 17
SERIAL - - - - - - - Page 19
BELINDA - - - - - - Page 22

No. 9,992 Registered at the G.P.O as a Newspaper. SATURDAY, DECEMBER 7, 1935 One Penny

Amusements : Page 4

TWICE A HERO

Miss Teifi James, whose employer—

—the Rev. Emlyn Jones, of Highgate has given skin from his leg to be grafted on her. He received Carnegie certificate for saving the girl's life when her clothing caught alight.

BRITAIN EATS DANGEROUSLY

China the Best Fed Race

DOCTOR'S WARNING

Britain's national diet is dangerous.
Japan has the best-balanced dietary.
China is the best-fed nation.
The Irish type is degenerating ; and
Hawaii has lost its health.

DR. G. Arbour Stephens, one of the doctors who have just returned from the world tour of the British Medical Association, makes these assertions in an article on "A National Dietary versus an Industrial Crisis," in the current issue of the "Medical Officer."

"So much is heard these days of living on a higher plane." he writes. "What is meant by this catch phrase . . . ?

"If the height of the 'plane be reckoned in terms of physical fitness, then this nation has nothing to be proud of, especially when one thinks of its dreadful maternity rate.

"Good feeding does not depend on extravagance in food; in fact, simple, properly balanced diets can be obtained at a reasonable price, but the national palate has been disturbed.

"To restore it to a normal and healthy condition is not easy, and, in my opinion, nothing but a national crisis will bring the people back to their senses.

"As a nation it seems as if we were heading for some such crisis, and unless we can solve the problem of simple food and feeding before the crisis arrives, the outlook for this country will not be bright. Other nations are making every effort to produce their own food supplies."

Dr. Stephens declares that the internationalising of the food supplies is fraught with grave danger. A great and significant fact was that much of the cultivated soil throughout the world was becoming exhausted.

"Human beings do not suffer alone. Our animals are being fed on exhausted soils, with the result that their vitality is lowered and the germs of disease are given every chance to flourish.

"Dying" by Luxuries

"Such rubbish is talked and written about the way that Oriental nations live on rice. They no more live on rice than do Irishmen on potatoes.

"In the old days Irishmen were strong and healthy, with excellent teeth, when living in their mud cabins on potatoes; yes, but with the addition of milk, eggs, cheese, fish, bacon and chicken. To-day, since the introduction of 'luxuries' bought by selling their
(Continued on back page)

ANOTHER WAR FOR PEACE!

Reported Statement by Archbishop of York

"It may be necessary to have another great and horrible war to establish the efficacy of the League of Nations."

REUTER'S correspondent cables from New York that this statement was made by the Archbishop of York (Dr. Temple) when he arrived there yesterday.

"This generation or the next would probably have to be sacrificed," the Archbishop is reported to have stated, "because just as it took the last war to create the League so it might require another conflict to consolidate the League's position."

When the *Daily Mirror* rang up Dr. Temple at Cleveland, (N.Y.), on the transatlantic telephone last night he declined to make any further comment.

Crusade for Peace

Mr. George Lansbury, the Socialist ex-leader, in an interview last night condemned the statements attributed to the Archbishop.

"If it is true the Archbishop has made this statement and if he believes that that is possible, then it is the duty of the leaders of Christendom to begin a crusade to avoid such a catastrophe," said Mr. Lansbury.

"There is no earthly reason why the Archbishop or any of us should consider such a catastrophic end to our civilisation."

A PIGMY BESIDE HIS BIG SHIP

The Queen Mary, the world's biggest liner, made Sir Edgar Britten, her future commander, a pigmy as he stood beside her yesterday at Clydebank. Yet in a few months that gigantic bulk will be responding to his least whisper.

Saw Lorry Kill 8-Year-Old Son

'THEY WERE SUCH PALS'

FROM OUR SPECIAL CORRESPONDENT
OXFORD, Friday.

A FATHER and his eight-year-old son were inseparable pals. Each morning they set off happily together—one to work and the other to school. But this morning the father was a few minutes late having breakfast.

"I'll run on, daddy, and perhaps you'll catch me up," the child called as he kissed his mother and ran out of the house. A few minutes later the father reached the corner of the road—just in time to see his little boy crushed to death under a huge six-wheeler lorry. Without a sound the father collapsed on the pavement and was afterwards assisted home.

The boy, Roderick McDonald, was the only child of Mr. and Mrs. A. W. McDonald, of Bulan-road, Cowley, near here.

Only last Saturday the McDonalds' home rang with the sound of children's laughter, for it was Roddy's eighth birthday.

"Roddy was such a happy little chap," Mrs. McDonald, his mother, told me.

"He and his father were such pals that we changed his school recently from Headington to S. Christopher's, at Cowley, so that he could go to school the same way as his father went to work and come back with him in the dinner hour."

Roderick's father worked at a motor works. Roderick was keen on motors.

Roderick McDonald

GIRL IN FLAMES

An eight-year-old Chingford girl—Vera Atkins, of Sinclair-road,—rushed, screaming, into the street last night with her clothing alight.

Police-Constable Shiplorne, who was passing, beat out the flames.

WANTED: A FIRE

BIRMINGHAM'S new £135,000 central fire station, most up-to-date in the country, is fed up. It was opened on Monday by the Duke of Kent.

Since Monday everything has been ready . . . all the latest novelties of fire-fighting with automatic control . . . all the new devices . . . waiting . . . yet—

They can't show off all these marvels because nobody has had a fire!

Every member of the staff has been simply longing to hear the alarm bell and see the engines starting up without aid—see the door of the garage automatically opening, and instructions issuing from loudspeakers above—all done by a flick of a switch in the control room.

Up-to-date efficiency—but no work to do!

LAST BID FOR ARMISTICE

TO-DAY'S conversations in Paris between Sir Samuel Hoare, the British Foreign Secretary, and M. Laval, the French Premier (says Reuter), are regarded in the French capital as a last desperate diplomatic effort to negotiate an armistice in Abyssinia before an oil embargo is enforced.

THE DAILY MIRROR, Friday December 13, 1935

Daily Mirror
THE DAILY PICTURE NEWSPAPER WITH THE LARGEST NET SALE

Broadcasting - Page 24

DOROTHY DIX · · · Page 7
EUSTACE · · · · · · Page 8
QUIET CORNER · · · Page 14
DOCTOR'S DIARY · · Page 17
SERIAL · · · · · · Page 19
BELINDA · · · · · · Page 20

No. 9,997 Registered at the G.P.O. as a Newspaper. FRIDAY, DECEMBER 13, 1935 One Penny

Amusements : Page 6

SAVED FROM DEATH BY PRAYER

Girl Hikers' Five Days of Agony

AFTER FIVE DAYS OF EXPOSURE IN BITTERLY COLD WEATHER ON THE BLEAK MOORS OF YORKSHIRE, THREE GIRL RAMBLERS WHO DID NOT RETURN FROM A WALK ON SUNDAY WERE YESTERDAY FOUND ALIVE.

BY A SPECIAL CORRESPONDENT
GREENFIELD, Thursday.

A MIRACLE — that is how everybody here to-night regards this amazing rescue.

Their survival was a miracle of endurance. It was a miracle of prayer, too.

When at last one of the girls could speak to-night, these were the words she whispered:—

"Every night we knelt down in the grass and offered a prayer to Saint Anthony." (Patron Saint of the Lost.)

This morning not one of the moorland dwellers believed that the girls could possibly have survived the terrible weather of the past five days.

Hour after hour, the gale—sweeping an icy rain before it—had screamed across the moors.

Frost-Bite

Yet it was in one of the most exposed parts of the countryside, eight miles from the road, that the girls were found alive this afternoon by one of the little bands of searchers who were now looking only for their bodies.

They were lying exhausted. Their feet were swollen twice their normal size with frost bite, they were nearly starving.

Throughout the long five days they had walked, growing weaker and weaker, all sense of direction gone; by night they had lain down nearly frozen.

Their rescuers rushed them to the nearest police station, Upper Mill, near Saddleworth.

There they were given brandy, laid on mattresses in front of a roaring fire and covered with blankets and rugs.

For hours they were massaged.

Girl's Story

The girls are:—
Elsie Rowlands, aged twenty-one, of Clarendon-road, Crumpsall, Manchester;
Edna Connolly, aged twenty-one, of Florastreet, Broughton; and
Pauline Preston, aged twenty, of Derbystreet, Broughton.

Miss Connolly told me their story. She told how they left Greenfield with the intention of walking to Laddow Rocks and back.

"We didn't see a soul after leaving the watermen's house on Sunday afternoon till the searchers found us," she said. "We had nothing to eat save one orange which we shared on Sunday night.

"We lost our way on Sunday afternoon. Darkness came and snow started to fall. We ate the remains of our food. On Sunday night we stayed huddled together.

"On Tuesday we saw a plane flying and circling overhead.

(Continued on back page)

The three girl hikers, Pauline Preston, Elsie Rowlands and Edna Connolly, lying before a roaring fire at Uppermill Police Station after being rescued. They are being attended by a policeman's wife. Other pictures on page 14.

SHOT 3 PROFESSORS THEN KILLED HIMSELF
Ex-Lawyer Runs Amok

BY A SPECIAL CORRESPONDENT
NEW YORK, Thursday.

A MIDDLE-AGED Russian, brandishing a revolver, rushed into the Dental College at Columbia University, darted into an office, and shot a professor through the heart. He lurched into another office, wounded a second professor, dashed upstairs into a laboratory, shot dead another professor, then committed suicide.

The murderer, Vito Kussow, was a handyman in the dental department. Earlier in the day he had been discharged finally, after several previous dismissals and reinstatements, for fighting.

His victims were Professor Arthur T. Rowe, Dean of the Dental College, and Professor Paul B. Wiberg, killed; Professor William Crawford, wounded.

The gunman's shots were heard by Dr. W. C. Rappleye, Dean of the Medical School, who said to me:—

"The trouble with Kussow was that he thought he should have been higher up in the world than he was. He was a surly man, but well educated.

He was a Russian of good family and practised as a lawyer in Russia before the Revolution.

"Although he had been dismissed before for fighting he was never regarded as dangerous, and had been given fresh chances several times, chiefly at the instigation of Professor Rowe, one of his victims. Kussow had been married but was divorced."

FIREMEN FALL AS FLOOR CRASHES

FIREMEN wearing gas masks were hurled to the ground last night when the first floor of a burning building in Rivington-street, Shoreditch, collapsed.

One of the men is in the Metropolitan Hospital severely injured.

The fire occurred at the cabinet makers' works of Thomas Cox.

Fifty firemen answered a district call. Flames shot to a height of nearly fifty feet. Within a few minutes the flames spread to the adjoining premises of the Rivington Cabinetmakers' works.

One family in premises adjoining had to leave their house. After three-quarters of an hour the fire was under control.

At the same time as this fire was in progress police were preventing people from going in the main entrance to Cannon-street Station while firemen dealt with a fire on the seventh floor of the Cannon-street Hotel.

The fire was confined to one room. Using a 100 feet high water tower firemen put out the blaze in half an hour.

KILLED ON OWN HEARTH

SERGEANT-MAJOR William Hall, sixty-four years old, fought in the Boer War and the Great War.

Often he had heard the crash of firing. Not once had he been hurt.

But yesterday he died at his own fireside with the bark of an explosion sounding in his ears. At his home in Brightmore-street, Sheffield, he sat with his wife.

He bent down to light his pipe. There was an explosion in the fire.

Pieces of coal hit him violently in the chest. His wife went to his aid. But a piece of coal had pierced his lung.

OLDEST MOTORIST IN ENGLAND is the claim of Mr. John Evison, ninety, of Hemingford Grey, Hunts, a former J.P. for the county. He has just been on a car tour of North Wales.

121

Daily Mirror

THE DAILY MIRROR, Monday, December 16, 1935.

Broadcasting - Page 20

THE DAILY PICTURE NEWSPAPER WITH THE LARGEST NET SALE

DOROTHY DIX - - - Page 7
EUSTACE - - - - - - Page 15
QUIET CORNER - - - Page 16
DOCTOR'S DIARY - - Page 17
SERIAL - - - - - - - Page 19
BELINDA - - - - - - Page 22

No. 9,999 Registered at the G.P.O as a Newspaper. MONDAY, DECEMBER 16, 1935 One Penny

Amusements: Pages 20 and 21

DOWNING-ST. MYSTERY

Simon's Dash from Golf

TALK TO EDEN

BY OUR POLITICAL CORRESPONDENT

Answering an urgent telephone call while out golfing, Sir John Simon, Home Secretary, dashed back to Downing-street last night and saw Mr. Baldwin and Mr. Anthony Eden.

THEN, still clad in plus fours, weather-beaten mackintosh and trilby hat, he walked into the Foreign Office, where he ruled until Sir Samuel Hoare replaced him. He stayed an hour talking with Mr. Eden.

Mystery cloaked these anxious Ministerial talks. Mystery had cloaked the long-distance telephoning which preceded them.

The reason, I am told, why Sir John broke his week-end's golfing at Walton-on-the-Naze, Essex, was to see Mr. Anthony Eden, who had been with Mr. Baldwin earlier in the day.

It is suggested that the secret of this meeting is Sir John's knowledge—he was then Foreign Secretary—of the early stages of the Italo-Abyssinian dispute.

New Documents

Mr. Eden returns to Geneva to-morrow and will attend the League Assembly on Wednesday. It is believed that the two men discussed the whole situation, and that Sir John is preparing the Government's brief on the peace proposals.

Sir John Simon is admittedly at his best when in fighting mood. It is anticipated that during Thursday's momentous debate in the House of Commons he will speak, and that his case for the Government will be an excellent one and likely to disarm criticism.

In the early stages of the East African dispute Sir John, I am told, received a number of documents from Italy. These may be quoted in the course of the debate and may throw new light on the situation.

Meanwhile, the Government have received no reply from Rome on the peace plan. Possibly, when the League meet on Wednesday no definite information will be available. That will not make the task of the peacemakers any easier.

Secret Sessions

Mr. Baldwin, I gather, is anxious to make the issue of Thursday's debate a vote of confidence.

The question is how much can be safely said in public There is, therefore, the possibility of a secret session, of which there were only seven during the war.

Sir Samuel Hoare, who is expected to speak, is due back this afternoon.

Many people are asking why Britain's representative in Abyssinia was advised to "try to induce the Emperor on no account lightly to reject the peace plans."

Britain and France are anxious to spare Ethiopia the horrors of modern warfare. Italy's use of the deadliest poison gas is one possibility—as well as to avoid European complications.

With shoulders hunched—a dejected Sir John Simon at the door of No. 10.

Mr Anthony Eden as he left No. 10, Downing-street yesterday.

HE WAS SITTING IN A POLICEMAN'S ARMCHAIR

FATE played this scurvy little joke on a twelve-year-old Cambridge Bad Lad who had a habit of escaping from a Walthamstow Remand Home:—

The Bad Lad had just been recaptured after his fourth escape. They were taking him back to the home. The home car driver stopped for petrol in the village of Potter Street, near Harlow (Essex). And the Bad Lad made a quick dash for freedom—and got safely away. . . .

Mrs. Clements, in a quite ordinary-looking house in Potter Street, heard a knock at her door.

A boy inquired if she could put him up for the night.

"Yes," said Mrs. Clements; and put him in a nice armchair by the fire. "My husband will be in soon," she said.

And into the house came at last Mrs Clements's husband.

Police-Constable Clements !

The Bad Lad has now to make a sixth escape.

Wedding Bells for 300—One Baby

WHEN a service for young married couples was held at Blackpool last night, a hall next door was thrown open as a nursery.

But the weather was so bad that only one child was brought. This was a month-old baby, who slept peacefully while his parents were in church.

Wedding bells and the Wedding March sounded again for about 150 couples who attended the service, which was at Holy Trinity Church.

Hens as Smugglers

Berlin, Sunday.

EIGHT farmers with fields on the German-Dutch frontier at Rothenbach have been sentenced to five months' imprisonment each for teaching their hens to smuggle eggs over the frontier !

The farmers fed them on Dutch territory where corn meal and chicken food are cheaper, then drove them into German corners of their field, where nest boxes were placed.

This practice was started when the duty on Dutch eggs was last raised, and German customs officials calculate that the hens took more than 2,000,000 eggs duty free into Germany.—Reuter.

HER TOIL ENDED AT 92—IN LAKE

50 Years a Widow and Refused Pension

AFTER she had worked hard all her life, fifty years of which had been in widowhood, a ninety-two-year-old woman lost one by one her casual jobs.

Her last customer would not let her clean steps last week because of the severe weather. The customer offered her the money, and had also bought her a Christmas present, but she would not take it without doing the work.

This week-end the old woman was found dead in 2ft. of water in the lake at Alexandra Park, N.

She was Mrs. Sarah Ann Clarke, who had occupied the same room in The Grove, Crouch End, for thirty years.

Because she regarded it as charity she would never take the old age pension.

No Charity

Mr. H. W. Emm, of Clove-street, Plaistow, her only surviving relative, told the Daily Mirror last night :

"Lately her age has caused her to have fits of giddiness and one by one she lost her customers.

"When she had no work to do she would go for long walks, climbing the steepest hills in the district.

"Although so old she had a tremendous appetite. She wore four petticoats. She could neither read nor write.

"She was extremely popular in her home district and could often have had meals with other families, but she would not take them, regarding them as charity.

"She always kept the door of her room locked."

Mr. Nevill, an occupant of the house in which Mrs. Clarke lived, told the Daily Mirror last night:—

"Mrs. Clarke was remarkably active for her age.

"She was rather eccentric, and spoke little to anyone in the house."

An open umbrella was found near her body in the lake. She had apparently been in the water about twenty-four hours.

"Miss 1936" Will Be a Vamp!

MEET "Miss 1936."

Madame Helena Rubenstein, beauty specialist just back in Paris from U.S.A., has had a glimpse of the fashionable woman of next year. This is what she will look like (according to Reuter):—

"Definitely a vamp.

"Hair—red.

"Complexion—pale, bright red lips, heavily shadowed eyes.

"She will wear emeralds.

"The ingenue," says Madame, "will be rung out with the arrival of the New Year."

Mme. Helena Rubenstein

THE QUADS ARE GOING STRONG

The St. Neots quadruplets—the children of Mr. and Mrs. Walter Miles—were yesterday stated to be going on very well. They have all gained in weight since Saturday.

THE DAILY MIRROR, Tuesday, December 17, 1935

Daily Mirror
THE DAILY PICTURE NEWSPAPER WITH THE LARGEST NET SALE

Broadcasting · Page 22

10,000

No. 10,000 Registered at the G.P.O as a Newspaper.   TUESDAY, DECEMBER 17, 1935   One Penny

Amusements: Page 22

FILM STAR DEAD IN CAR
Riddle of "Pay or Die" Threat

Thelma Todd, the "Vamping Venus," who has been found dead.

THELMA Todd, famed Vamping Venus of the films, was found dead at the wheel of her car near Los Angeles yesterday.

Twice her life had been threatened. "Pay £2,000 or die," said letters she received. But she had gone on defying the blackmail gangsters.

Last night police were working on two theories: 1, That the authors of this extortion plot had carried out their threat to its terrible end; 2, That she had died from petrol fumes.

It was a maid who found Miss Todd dead, her lovely blonde head slumped over the wheel of her car, blood smeared across her mouth.

The car was standing at the rear of her roadside cafe on the Pacific Palisades to the west of Los Angeles and midway between Santa Monica and Malibu Beach.

No one in film-land had seen Miss Todd since Saturday night, when she left a gay party given by Ida Lupino, eighteen-year-old daughter of England's most famous theatrical family, at the fashionable Trocadero Cafe, popular Hollywood night haunt.

Dead Two Days

It is believed that she had been dead two days.

Last August "G-men" carried out a raid in New York following two death threats received by Miss Todd.

This was one of the grim missives Miss Todd had received:—

"Pay ten thousand dollars to Abe Lyman, New York, by March 3 and live. If not our San Francisco boys will lay you out. This is no joke."

Miss Todd, who was a school teacher, began her film career when she was elected "Miss Massachusetts" at a State beauty competition.

She was known to "fans" of the Marx Brothers as the arch blonde of "Horse Feathers" and "Monkey Business."

In 1933 she came to England to star in the film, "You Made Me Love You." It was her first visit to England.

(Messages from Central News and Exchange.)

BRIDE ENTERS CHURCH AS WOMAN DIES

FROM OUR OWN CORRESPONDENT
CLAY CROSS (Derbyshire), Monday.

AS a bride entered Clay Cross Parish Church to-day a dead woman was carried out. But the bride, Miss Hannah Spencer, of Clay Cross, did not realise that tragedy had preceded her wedding and was not told until after the ceremony that the woman — Mrs. Lillie Marriott, her former headmistress at Clay Cross Girls' School—had died.

Mrs Marriott, although she was seventy-seven, decided to attend the wedding of Miss Spencer to her nephew, Mr Alex Grassick.

Mr. George Banks, who was in the church, told me that he was in the next pew when Mrs. Marriott fell forward. With other men he carried her to a nearby surgery, but Mrs. Marriott was dead.

Mrs. Marriott taught in Clay Cross Girls School for nearly fifty years. She retired in 1927.

DUCHESS OF YORK ILL

THE Duchess of York is suffering from a slight chill and is confined to her room. Last night it was stated that her condition had not changed, but it is understood that the chill is not in any way serious.

OPEN PENKNIFE IN HIS STOMACH

A MAN who was taken suddenly ill at Bow-street Police Station was sent to Charing Cross Hospital, where he now lies critically ill, with detectives waiting at his bedside.

Doctors did not know what was the matter with him until they took an X-ray photograph. Then they saw that he has in his stomach:—
An open pocket-knife;
Three pieces of tin;
A ring, apparently containing a diamond, and an object resembling the handle of an enamelled mug.

HOME AGAIN.—Sir Samuel Hoare with a strip of plaster over his nose, in his car with Lady Maud Hoare, driving from Croydon Airport last evening on his return from Switzerland for to-day's Cabinet. See back page.

Jean Hughes, the girl who was kidnapped.

Kidnapped Child's Ordeal

FROM OUR SPECIAL CORRESPONDENT
SUTTON COLDFIELD, near Birmingham, Monday.

Kidnapped and blindfolded by strangers, a fourteen-year-old schoolgirl was taken to a house, locked up, beaten, and kept on bread and water for several days. . . .

Then to-day, without knowing how she got there, she found herself in a disused lorry. On the point of collapse, she made her way to a nearby house. Her feet and legs were black with frostbite.

THIS is the terrible story Jean Hughes, although racked with pain, has been able to tell the married couple to whom she is an adopted daughter—Mr. and Mrs. Alfred Hughes, Whitehouse Common Post Office, Sutton Coldfield.

With tears in their eyes Mr. and Mrs Hughes told me, "When she got back here her legs and feet were black and Dr Jerome, who examined her, said that the only chance of saving her feet was to take her to hospital.

"Even now it is possible that they may not be able to save her toes.

"She has described the strangers as a short and dark man and a large woman. She did not have her clothes off for the whole of the six days she was away.

"She cannot remember anything after Thursday."

Dragged in Van

The house to which she went when she dragged herself from the lorry was that of Mrs. Bown, of Woodthorne-avenue Tettenhall, near Wolverhampton.

Mr. and Mrs. Bown sent for Miss Kate Knight, missionary to Wolverhampton Police Court.

"When I saw her," Miss Knight told me, "she was hardly able to say anything about her experience because she was in such pain.

"She was put to bed, fed, and a doctor called, and later she told me that on Tuesday, a week ago, she was cycling to Shubbery School, Walmley, when a man and a woman in a motor-van stopped her, bundled her and her bicycle into the van and blindfolded her.

"When it was dark they drove the van to a cottage, took her shoes away and locked her up in a room with no window. The next day, too terrified to do anything, the man beat her when she would not sweep up the room."

THE DAILY MIRROR, Saturday, December 21, 1935

Broadcasting - Pages 14 & 15

Daily Mirror
THE DAILY PICTURE NEWSPAPER WITH THE LARGEST NET SALE

"HELP YOURSELF" RESULTS
—See Page 22

No. 10,004 Registered at the G.P.O. as a Newspaper. SATURDAY, DECEMBER 21, 1935 One Penny

Amusements: Page 14

BRITAIN'S "IF WE ARE ATTACKED...?"

Four Powers Asked

"WE ARE BACK TO SANCTIONS"

WHILE Britain last night was asking four States to define their attitude if an attack was made on a single Power, Mr. Neville Chamberlain, Chancellor of the Exchequer, declared that we were now "back to sanctions."

In a speech at Birmingham he declared:—

"We must go back to the policy of sanctions, and in due course I trust that the nations of the League will show, as I believe they will show, that they are prepared to make themselves ready to resist any attack that may be made on any one of their number."

Referring to the Italo-Abyssinian peace plan, he said:—

"We agree now we made a mistake. We did not realise at the time the shock it would cause public opinion throughout the world, which alone is quite sufficient to show that we were wrong.

"We accept the blame for it—the blame which still attaches to it.

"The proposals are dead. They will not be revived."

Then Mr. Chamberlain gave this warning:—
"Whatever the form of pressure which the League may exercise upon an aggressor in the future, the ultimate recourse, the ultimate fact
(Continued on back page)

WAR TAKES HER LAST LINK WITH HAPPY PAST

Just an old woman giving up for Mussolini's melting pot her wedding ring, only piece of gold she has, but she doesn't mind that.

* * *

It is the memories—memories of her husband, their wedding, herself as a bride, and the children.

* * *

Those stalwart sons are far away, and the daughters—all married. There isn't much left save those memories.

* * *

And now WAR has taken the last link.

25 DIE IN A SHIP EXPLOSION

RIO DE JANEIRO, Friday.

TWENTY-FIVE people are said to have been killed in a series of explosions aboard the Swedish cargo steamer Britt-Marie, according to messages from Santos, the Brazilian port.

The explosions occurred when the ship arrived at Santos from Chile.

The explosions hurled its superstructure into the sky over the dock area, and the flaming debris set warehouses alight.

The Britt-Marie sank within five minutes. It is believed that all her crew, with the exception of some who were ashore, were killed.

Dock workers and their families rushed to the scene of the disaster and began to look for the dock labourers.

They could not seek far, for the intense heat from two blazing warehouses prevented them from approaching too close.

The force of the explosions split the Britt-Marie in the centre.—B.U.P.

Lifeboat Launched by Women

While their menfolk were battling their way in fishing boats back to harbour in the teeth of a gale yesterday, women struggled waist-deep in icy water to launch the lifeboat to go to their assistance at Runswick Bay, Yorkshire.

As there were not enough men ashore to launch the lifeboat women responded to the call.

The lifeboat escorted the vessels to harbour and then, with their menfolk safely ashore, the women again waded into the sea to haul the lifeboat back.

"Fog Hold-Up—See Page 3."

POURED BOILING WATER ON HIS BABY SISTER

But May Never Know He Caused Her Death

A YEAR-OLD baby boy, who poured boiling water on his five weeks old sister, causing her death, may never know of the tragedy for which he was innocently responsible.

The Leamington coroner, at the inquest yesterday on Shirley Haycock, expressed the hope that the parents would never speak about the tragedy.

The boy, he said, was too young to be aware of what he had done. It would be a great pity that he should know of it afterwards.

The mother said she was preparing the baby's bath and left the room for a few moments.

When she returned she found the baby in a state of collapse and the little boy holding a saucepan.

A doctor said that the baby was severely scalded. He attributed the fact that no sound was heard to the shock to the girl's breathing apparatus, which prevented her from making any sound.

A verdict in accordance with the medical evidence was returned.

McAVOY WINS IN FIRST ROUND

JOCK McAvoy, British middle-weight champion, knocked out Babe Risko, world's champion, in the first round of their fight at Madison Square Garden, New York, last night.

The title was not at stake.

McAvoy floored Risko with the first punch. McAvoy again floored Risko with a right hook. This time Risko sat in the middle of the ring and was counted out.

ATTEMPTED MURDER CHARGE.—Miss Margaret Clinton Beer, nineteen, at whom Mr. Hugh Williams, assistant schoolmaster at Ash, Kent, was, when at Sandwich yesterday committed for trial on a charge of attempted murder, alleged to have shot at through a window with a humane killer.
(See story page 5.)

Daily Mirror

THE DAILY PICTURE NEWSPAPER WITH THE LARGEST NET SALE

Three Days' Radio - Pages 14 & 15

A MERRY CHRISTMAS TO ALL OUR READERS

No. 10,006 Registered at the G.P.O as a Newspaper. TUESDAY, DECEMBER 24, 1935 One Penny

Amusements: Page 16

THEIR FATHER CHRISTMAS BOXES!

PROSPERITY CHRISTMAS!

Heaviest Shopping Since the War

LUXURIES, TOO!

LED by the King and Queen, the whole nation is preparing to-day to celebrate PROSPERITY CHRISTMAS.

Not since the war has there been so much gift-buying, so much money put into the Christmas market as during the past few days.

Not since the war has there been such buying of **luxury articles**. There has actually been a rush on billiard tables!

And—this is the most significant signal of the prosperity line—

not since the war have there been such family reunions.

Railway companies report travelling receipts up by astounding figures.

Sons and daughters, unable in past Christmases to afford the cost of travelling to the old people, are this year returning in thousands. More work, more money, is the reason.

In humble homes they will gather at the fireside. Britain will be one great family, listening at three o'clock to-morrow to a voice speaking from the midst of his own family—that of the King.

But the Royal Family will be one not wholly united—for the first time for many years. The Duchess of York, with a nasty cold, has been advised not to travel to Sandringham. She and the Duke will spend Christmas rather lone'y—for the little Princesses are already with the King and Queen.

Happy England!

"Happy England," said a U.S. visitor to these shores some weeks ago to the *Daily Mirror*.

Happy England, indeed, this Christmastide. Take a glance at the news from abroad that came in last night.

GERMANY.—Her spending power reduced. Christmas recommended by the Leader as a time for careful frugality.

ITALY.—Finding millions for war. Her people enduring privations and told they must prepare for more. No Christmas festivities.

Now look at England.

"Everywhere," the Chancellor has said, "the purchasing power of the people has increased."

All industries, which are the best symptoms of the purchasing power, are expanding.

There is more money in circulation than has been known for a dozen years.

The G.P.O. report the parcels traffic a record. Four hundred thousand a day is the figure Mount Pleasant (G.P.O. headquarters) has had to deal with. Gift parcels, which alone show PROSPERITY.

And here is another sidelight on prosperity—presents to shop assistants from those regular customers who week in and week out they serve throughout the year.

Hairdressers, librarians, lingerie assistants, the hundred and one people who have their regular customers are going home each night laden with parcelled gifts—"a little present for looking after me so nicely, my dear."

"It's been years since they did it," one librarian told the *Daily Mirror*. "Once we had loads of presents at Christmas. They then fell away in the dark years. This year I have had more than thirty parcels given me, scrumptious things. They must have cost pounds and pounds."

To-day comes the last rush.

Well, indeed, can we in England to-day greet our neighbours WITH A MERRY CHRISTMAS AND A PROSPEROUS NEW YEAR.

Len Harvey playing Santa to delighted children during a children's Christmas party at his training quarters on the Barnet by-pass road. Appropriately enough, he begins training in earnest on Boxing Day for his fight with Jack Petersen at Wembley on Jan 29.

Jean Batten greeted at Southampton by the Mayor, Alderman Sanders, on arrival home with her 'plane (background) following her record flight

Wife Who Shot Her Rival Is Free

12 YEARS PAROLE

NEW YORK, Monday.

MRS. Etta Reisman, who shot and killed her husband's beautiful twenty-three-year-old secretary, Virginia Seigh, was released to-day on probation.

She was found guilty of manslaughter and came up for sentence. The Court passed a suspended sentence of from six to twelve years' imprisonment, releasing her under Court supervision.

Virginia Seigh had supplanted Mrs. Reisman in Mr. Reisman's affections and in her defence the "unwritten law" was pleaded, counsel arguing that a wronged wife was justified in taking vengeance on "the other woman."

When this plea failed, they took the line that the shooting was accidental.

A jury of eleven husbands and one bachelor wrangled for fourteen hours before giving their manslaughter verdict.

Virginia was shot outside the Reisman's home, after Mr. Reisman and the girl had confessed to Mrs. Reisman that they loved each other.—B.U.P.

Inn Wall Blown Into River

THE wall of a room was blown into the River Nene, and splintered mineral water bottles, hurled thirty yards, in a gas explosion at the Crown and Anchor Inn, Wellingborough, Northamptonshire, last night.

No one was injured.

JEAN BATTEN IS 'FLOWER OF THE AIR' TO SOUTH AMERICANS

FROM OUR OWN CORRESPONDENT

SOUTHAMPTON, Monday.

"TRY Again" Jean Batten returned to England to-day from South America with new flying records to her credit and a new name.

When she landed in South America, having been the first woman to fly the South Atlantic—nearly 2,000 miles over sea—the Brazilians lost their hearts to this slight girlish twenty-five-year-old New Zealander, and they promptly christened her Clavel del Aire, which means flower of the air.

A month ago Jean flew away from England with two evening dresses scuffed in a little bag as her only luggage.

Good-Night to 'Plane

This afternoon the Royal Mail steamer Asturias nosed her way through the fog into Southampton to bring her back again—the holder of the England-Brazil record and the South Atlantic record snatched from France.

The only increase to her luggage was a cardboard shoe box into which was recklessly thrown all her money—in cash—and some beautiful diamond and aquamarine brooches, jewellery which had been given her by admirers in America.

Her first thought on arriving in England again was for her Percival Gull aeroplane, which has spent the voyage with its wings dismantled on the deck of the Asturias.

Jean has watched over it like a child. Every night she used to go to say good-night to it before going to bed.

While giving instructions about the lifting of her 'plane to the quay, she told me something about her flight. With girlish pride she showed me four badges pinned to the lapel of her "Teddy bear" coat.

"I have been made an honorary officer of four air forces in South America," she said. "This one is Argentine; this the Brazilian Naval Air Force; this the Brazilian Army; and, this Uruguay.

"I don't think I would like to do the flight across the South Atlantic again.

THE DAILY MIRROR, Monday, December 30, 1935.

Broadcasting · Page 22

Daily Mirror

THE DAILY PICTURE NEWSPAPER WITH THE LARGEST NET SALE

DOROTHY DIX - - - Page 7
EUSTACE - - - - - - Page 13
QUIET CORNER - - - Page 14
DOCTOR'S DIARY - - Page 17
SERIAL - - - - - - - Page 19
BELINDA - - - - - - Page 23

No. 10,009 Registered at the G.P.O as a Newspaper. MONDAY, DECEMBER 30, 1935 One Penny

Amusements: Pages 20 and 21

NAZIS STARVE JEWS

Terror Revelations by Refugee Officer

Mr. James G. McDonald

"I CANNOT BE SILENT"

Systematic starving of Jews in Germany is among the revelations made in an amazing denunciation of the Nazi terror published to-day

IT comes from Mr James Grover McDonald, League of Nations High Commissioner for Jewish and Other Refugees from Germany. Mr. McDonald began his task two years ago. With his report is enclosed his resignation—because of the hopelessness of his task under its limitations.

"Convinced as I am," he says, "that a terrible human calamity is inevitable within the German frontiers unless present tendencies in the Reich are checked, I cannot remain silent."

"Impending Tragedies"

"I should be a recreant if I did not call attention to the facts, and plead that world opinion, acting through the League, should move to avert existing and impending tragedies."

Here are some of the things Mr. McDonald reports:—

"It is being made increasingly difficult for Jews and 'non-Aryans' to sustain even life.

"In many parts of the country there is a systematic attempt at starvation of the Jewish population.

"Names of Jews killed in the war may no longer be engraved on war memorials.

"So far does this hatred extend, that even the Jewish war veterans who fought and were wounded in the front line trenches have been forced from their positions in the public services."

Without Hope

"Apart from all questions of principle and of religious persecution, one portentous fact confronts the Community of States.

"More than half a million persons, against whom no charge can be made except that they are not what the National Socialists choose to regard as 'Nordic,' are being crushed.

"Tens of thousands are to-day anxiously seeking ways to flee abroad; but except for those prepared to sacrifice the whole or greater part of their savings, the official restrictions on export of capital effectively bar the road to escape.

"More than half the Jews in Germany," Mr. McDonald goes on, "have been deprived entirely of their livelihood.

"The victims of the terrorism are being driven to the point where, in utter anguish and despair, they may burst the frontiers.

"The intensified persecution in Germany

(Continued on back page)

Dying Man Near Strand Surprise

Scotland Yard inquiries into the death of Timothy Hurley, forty, of Kemble-street, Drury-lane, who was found dying in a street near the Strand on Saturday, took a new turn last night.

It was at first thought that Hurley had been attacked by gangsters.

The theory is now advanced that Hurley's death may have been due to an accident or even to natural causes.

MOTORISTS' BIG RALLY TO SEE THE KING

Thousands at Sandringham

THOUSANDS of motorists assembled at the park at Sandringham, Norfolk, yesterday to see the King and Queen, and other members of the Royal Family, attend morning service at the village church.

The King walked to church, while the Queen, accompanied by the Prince of Wales, went by car.

The King, who looked in the best of health, left Sandringham House a few minutes before the Queen and the Prince, who passed him on the way.

He was accompanied by the Duke and Duchess of Kent and the Princesses Elizabeth and Margaret Rose.

The little Princesses walked hand in hand, and attracted much attention from the crowds that had gathered to see the royal party

Mr. H. Scott.

Governor's Blood for Borstal Boy

IN a vain effort to save the life of one of their boys, the Governor and officers of the Borstal Institution, Weymouth, have given blood for transfusions. Three weeks ago the boy became seriously ill. The medical officer, Dr. Richmond, consulted with several specialists.

Blood transfusions were the only hope for saving the boy's life, said the doctors. Officers of the institution including the Governor, Mr. H. Scott, at once volunteered to give their blood.

This week-end a brother of the boy gave a pint of his blood. In spite of all these efforts the boy died yesterday.

FREE FROM WORRIES OF STATE

Sir Samuel Hoare, whose sensational resignation of the Foreign Secretaryship occurred less than a fortnight ago, watched by his wife, Lady Maud Hoare, as he practises skating at Zuoz, Switzerland. Above: Resting, with Lady Maud Hoare, after his efforts.